Responding from the Tradition

Responding from the Tradition

By Sheikh 'Ali Gomaa
Grand Mufti of Egypt

Translated by Tarek Elgawhary
and Nuri Friedlander

FONS VITAE

First published in 2011 by
Fons Vitae
49 Mockingbird Valley Drive
Louisville, KY 40207
http://www.fonsvitae.com
Email: fonsvitaeky@aol.com

Copyright Fons Vitae 2011

Library of Congress Control Number: 2011943794
ISBN 978-1891785-44-3

Printed in Canada

Contents

Contents, continued

Contents, continued

Acknowledgements

The translators would like to thank Sheikh Musa Furber and Sheikh Abdullah ibn Hamid Ali for reviewing the translation; their insight proved invaluable both in deciphering the original text, and in producing an accurate translation. Sara Swetzoff's extensive comments called our attention to many awkward and clumsy translations and brought about a much more readable version of the fatwas. Without the cooperation and assistance of Sheikh Ali Gomaa and the muftis at Dar al-Ifta al-Masriyyah this project would never have been possible. Their patient and careful explanations clarified nuances of Islamic law that we would otherwise have missed, and spending those hours with them served as a precious education. Finally, the translators would like to thank their families for their patience, encouragement, and unending support throughout this project and beyond. Any errors that remain are entirely our own.

Translators' Introduction

This book is the result both of the author's expertise and experience. His expertise derives from his extensive study and command of the Islamic legal tradition. The author's experience lies in his many years serving as mufti in both an independent and institutional capacity. Born in the Egyptian town of Bani Suwaif in 1952, Sheikh Ali Gomaa began studying the Islamic sciences at an early age. Although he did not attend a religious school as a child, by the time he graduated from high school Sheikh Ali had studied the six canonical *hadith*[1] collections as well as Maliki jurisprudence. After receiving a degree in commerce from 'Ayn Shams University, Sheikh Ali enrolled in al-Azhar University where he completed a B.A., followed by a M.A. and a PhD in the Methodologies of Islamic Jurisprudence (*usul al-fiqh*). Sheikh Ali excelled academically both at the university and in sessions with prominent scholars outside of the university setting. Among his teachers was the Moroccan *hadith* scholar and Sufi Sheikh Abdullah ibn Siddiq al-Ghumari, who considered Sheikh Ali to be one of his most accomplished students.

Sheikh Ali led an illustrious academic career at al-Azhar University where he was Professor of Juristic Methodology. In addition to teaching courses and seminars at al-Azhar, Sheikh Ali instructed numerous students outside of the university. In the mid-1990s, Sheikh Ali began giving lessons at the al-Azhar mosque. Held six days a week from the early morning until just before noon, these lessons covered topics such as *hadith* studies, *hadith* methodology, Islamic jurisprudence, juristic methodology, theology, and Sufism. The lessons were open to the public and provided religious training for students from al-Azhar as well as for students without institutional affiliations. Sheikh Ali also met with members of the public in a small office at the al-Azhar mosque where he would advise students, counsel individuals, and issue fatwas.

In 1998 Sheikh Ali began to deliver the Friday sermon at Cai-

---

1. *Hadiths* are the reports of the sayings, actions, and tacit affirmations of the Prophet Muhammad that have been preserved and collected by Muslims. The six canonical books of *hadith* are: Bukhari, Muslim, al-Tirmidhi, al-Nasa'i, Abu Dawud, and Ibn Majah.

ro's Sultan Hasan Mosque. His sermons, which focused on central Islamic concepts such as mercy and beauty, as well as issues of contemporary relevance, drew large crowds. At the end of Friday prayers Sheikh Ali would turn to the congregation and give a short lesson on Shafi'i jurisprudence that was directed towards the layperson but contained enough substance to be of interest to accomplished students of Shari'ah as well. After the lesson Sheikh Ali would answer questions posed by the congregation.

In 2003 Sheikh Ali was appointed Grand Mufti of Egypt. Since taking this position he has revolutionized the process of issuing fatwas in Egypt: Sheikh Ali transformed Dar al-Ifta from an institution that was the extension of one individual (the Grand Mufti) to a modern institution with a fatwa council and a system of checks and balances. Sheikh Ali has also added a technological aspect to the institution by developing a sophisticated website and call center through which people may request fatwas even if they are unable to come in person. During his years as Grand Mufti, Sheikh Ali has overseen the issuance of many important fatwas that strive to show Islam's ongoing relevance to people of the 21st century. The corresponding methodology is characterized by a profound respect for tradition that is balanced by the recognition of its shortcomings, and illuminated by an understanding of the specific needs of the times in which we live.

Both the official and the non-official positions that Sheikh Ali has held have helped to cultivate the unique vantage point from which he perceives and assesses the concerns of the Muslim community. The fatwas gathered in this collection are the result of his exceptional experience. Certain fatwas may seem more immediately relevant than others; however, all have been of contemporary concern to some part of the Muslim community, and all pertain to issues that have fractured the community at one point or another.

Thus, the fatwas gathered here cover a vast range of topics while sharing a traditionally grounded methodology and an expansive and contemporary vision of the world. With this collection the author intends to end debates and animosity among Muslims not by merely asserting one position's legitimacy over another's, but by showing that the richness of the Islamic tradition provides a framework within which Muslims may disagree on details while uniting on overarching values. In order to foster this unity, Sheikh Ali has issued his fatwas according to three principles. The first principle stipulates that matters may be denounced only when the entire community is in agreement; matters concerning which there is a variance of opinion should not be condemned. The second principle holds that the position of one school may not be invalidated by the position of another school. The third principle assures that a legal reasoning (*ijtihad*) is not invalidated by an alternate *ijtihad*. The adoption of these principles, Sheikh Ali hopes, will bring harmony to the Muslim community despite the natural and unavoidable differences between its members.

Lastly, it must be pointed out that some of the answers in this collection may not technically be termed "fatwas." A fatwa is issued in response to a question concerned with the legal status of a particular action. Most of the answers in this collection fall well within this category, but some do not meet the criteria: the answers to questions on historical events or those concerning the relied-upon sources of the Islamic legal schools do not qualify as fatwas. These questions have been included, however, because of their importance as issues that have fostered misconception and thus caused division within the community.

The following short essay by Sheikh Ali provides a brief outline of his methodology as stated in his own words. We include this essay in the hopes that it will aid in one's ability to interpret the fatwas from within the methodological framework of the author himself and thus deepen one's understanding of the rulings.

Tarek Elgawhary and Nuri Friedlander

The Craft of Issuing A Fatwa

By Sheikh 'Ali Gomaa
Grand Mufti of Egypt

A fatwa is the elucidation of a Shari'ah ruling concerning an occurrence in the world. Ultimately, none but God issues fatwas; others merely transmit His rulings pertaining to specific matters. The first person in Islam to carry out this role was the Prophet [s], as he was issuing fatwas by delivering the message of God. The Prophet [s] was followed by his companions, who were then succeeded by the scholars from amongst their followers (al-tabi'un). Later generations established the eight schools of jurisprudence: the four Sunni schools (the Hanafi, the Maliki, the Shafi'i, and the Hanbali), the two Shiite schools (the J'afari, and the Zaydi), the Ibadi school, and the Zahiri school.

In order to perform the duties of a mufti, one must be Muslim, sane, mature, knowledgeable, specialized, and just. One must have also attained the scholarly status of "mujtahid," which characterizes those possessing advanced ability in independent legal reasoning. There is consensus among scholars that being male is not a condition for issuing fatwas.

There is certain etiquette by which the mufti should abide and its importance is such that it may become requisite in our age. This etiquette calls on the mufti to make things easy for people by bringing them into God's religion, protecting them, and providing a means whereby they can act in accordance with a position that is acknowledged by the Shari'ah. This approach is recommended because it eases the path and thus prevents people from leaving religion entirely and falling into grave moral error. To deter people from religion would be tantamount to blocking their path to God, and the scholar must be aware of this risk. This does not mean that one may seek out license in order to dodge God's law, which is of course forbidden, but the difference between approaches is subtle to a degree that many may not understand.

The main goal of the mufti is to create a legal tool that aids in the actualization of the Islamic juristic tradition without departing from the tradition or making it a barrier to contemporary

Muslims. This technique should not be denounced; the opinion at which the mufti arrives will be one over which scholars disagree, and this is dealt with according to the following maxim: "Whoever is afflicted with something concerning which there is variance of opinion should follow those who permit the action."

The mufti should have a methodology concerning the hierarchy of evidence he employs in his rulings. When the mufti is asked about an issue, he should first consult the Quran. If he does not find evidence in the Quran, then he should turn to the Sunnah. If the Sunnah does not provide guidance on the issue, then the mufti should employ analogy in the evidence for his ruling. It is required that the rulings not breach consensus. As for disputed evidence, such as in the case of juristic preference (*istihsan*) and the law of communities that preceded us, the mufti may issue fatwas based on these sources only if his own legal reasoning (*ijtihad*) leads him to accept them as true. The protocol established by the schools of jurisprudence allows the mufti to issue fatwas following any of the *mujtahid* schools, so long as his own *ijtihad* does not lead him to believe that the truth lies elsewhere.

The expression of the fatwa should follow a particular etiquette: 1) The fatwa should be in written form; 2) Unclear phrases that carry multiple meanings should be avoided; 3) Evidence should be provided; and 4) The fatwa may not assert that it represents God's ruling with unwavering certainty.

A fatwa goes through four major stages in the mufti's mind before it is put in the form that the questioner hears or sees. These stages are: conceptualization (*al-taswir*), designation (*al-takyif*), the elucidation of the ruling (*bayan al-hukm*), and the issuing of the fatwa (*al-ifta'*).

During the stage of conceptualization (*al-taswir*), the mufti grasps the issue that has been raised by the person asking the question. A correct conceptualization must be in accordance with the reality of the inquired-upon action, and is an essential condition for issuing sound fatwas that are appropriate for the world in which we live. The burden of conceptualization rests primarily on the shoulders of the one asking the question, but the mufti should check that the inquirer is not confused by making inquiries on the four aspects of the action (time, place, people, and conditions), since the alteration of these details could effect change in the fatwa.

Designation (*al-takyif*) is the act of linking the concept under question to the appropriate categories and issues of jurisprudence.

The elucidation of the ruling (*bayan al-hukm*) involves deriving the ruling from the Quran, the Sunnah, or consensus. The ruling may also be composed through judicial analogy (*qiyas*).

The final stage generates the fatwa when the mufti applies his formulated ruling to the reality that he has perceived. At this stage the mufti must make sure that his fatwa does not go against the goals (*maqasid*) of the Shari'ah, or contravene one of its definitive texts, an agreed upon consensus, or an established legal maxim.

Fatwas differ according to their specific time, place, people, and conditions. If, for example, customs were to remain unchanged for a number of centuries, nobody would be able to change the fatwa concerning them. As for rulings that are not based on customs and local practices, as well as essential rulings based on definitive texts that embody commands and prohibitions, these fatwas do not change regardless of time, place, or people. Examples of these steadfast rulings are the obligations to pray, to fast, to pay alms (*zakat*), and to be honest and trustworthy. The permissibility of commerce and the prohibitions of fornication and consumption of alcohol also fall into this category of essential rulings.

Dar al-Ifta' al-Misriyah[2] follows a well-defined methodology in issuing fatwas. The methodology seeks to transmit the four well-known Sunni schools of jurisprudence (Hanafi, Maliki, Shafi'i, and Hanbali) while acknowledging the other schools that Muslims follow in different parts of the world (J'afari, Zaydi, Ibadi, and Zahiri) and taking them into consideration. In addition, Dar al-Ifta' often widens the scope of the evidence upon which it relies to include the schools of major *mujtahids* like al-Awza'i, al-Tabari, al-Layth ibn Sa'd, and others from among over eighty *mujtahids* throughout Muslim history. These schools' opinions are taken into account and may even be given priority of consideration according to the strength of their evidence, the need for their perspective, the purpose of the greater good, or in order to fulfill the goals of the Shari'ah.[3] This methodology reflects the values adopted by

---

2. The Egyptian institution officially responsible for issuing fatwas.

3. The preservation of life, intellect, religion, dignity, and personal property.

all scholarly societies today, in both the East and the West and throughout the Muslim world.

Dar al-Ifta' adheres to the agreements of the Islamic councils, particularly the *Majma' al-Buhuth al-Islamiyyah* (The Council of Islamic Research) under the auspices of al-Azhar, *Majma' al-Fiqh al-Islami* (The Council of Islamic Jurisprudence) under the auspices of *Munadhamah al-Mu'tamir al-Islami* (The Organization of the Islamic Conference) in Jeddah, and *Majma' al-Fiqh al-Islami* (Council of Islamic Jurisprudence) under the auspices of *al-Rabitah al-Islamiyyah* (The Muslim League) in Mecca. These agreements are of particular importance when it comes to new matters needing clarification across the Muslim world.

Dar al-Ifta' also has recourse to deriving rulings directly from the legal texts of the Quran and the Sunnah. These texts are more encompassing than all that has been mentioned above; they are more encompassing than the eight schools, the eighty *mujtahids*, and the agreements of the *fiqh* councils. Dar al-Ifta' derives legal rulings directly from their evidence in the Quran and the Sunnah when the ruling is not found in the previously mentioned sources, or when the ruling is present, but is not appropriate to the situation in question. The condition for the validity of deriving rulings directly from the texts is that the texts support the interpretation given them based on the established criteria of the scholars of juristic methodology.

The task of issuing fatwas is not so simple that anyone may boldly claim to have the requisite capabilities. The times we live in and the cultural milieu in which we find ourselves reflects the promise made by the Prophet [s] according to Samrah ibn Jundub, "This will not occur until you see great matters becoming increasingly serious and you ask yourselves, 'Did your Prophet mention something of this to you?'"[4] The state of our contemporary culture is unstable, and many of its implications have yet to be defined. Charlatans abound in the public sphere. They discuss and give advice on everything from medicinal matters to fatwas, without having the least bit of relevant knowledge and having memorized but a few verses of the short chapters of the Quran. These people have held public office; some of them want us to separate ourselves from our religion and history; some of them practice intellectual

---

4. Ibn Hibban in his *Sahih*.

terrorism. They claim it's either their way or straight to hell, but for them hell is actually paradise, and paradise is hell, for they are enemies of the truth who seek to lead people astray. The solution to all of this will require us to be patient and to affirm our commitment to freedom, while leaving the charlatans to publicly discredit themselves through their triviality and flimsy ideas. We ask God to give us forbearance and success.

General Fatwas Regarding Islam

Question 1:

What is the relationship between Islam and other religions? What are the essential elements of submission (*islam*) and faith (*iman*), and why has this religion been named 'Islam'?

Islam is the final message sent from God to humanity. It is therefore the final religion, revealed to the Messenger of God, the Prophet Muhammad [s], and intended for people of every race and geographic location. Each previous revelation was given to a certain prophet to be transmitted to a certain people. Islam differs in that it was revealed to the Messenger of God [s] for all of humankind as well as the jinn. In the Quran God says to Muhammad [s], *We have not sent you but as a mercy for all the worlds.* [21:107] He says elsewhere, *We have not sent you but to all humanity as a giver of glad-tidings and a warner, but most of humanity knows not* [34:28]. And He commands the Prophet [s], *Say: O humanity! I am the Messenger of God to you all,* [7:158]. The Messenger of God [s] confirmed this saying, "All previous prophets were sent to their peoples, but I have been sent to all of humanity."[5]

Islam is a religion of ease, and it is therefore free of hardship; God states, *And God has imposed no hardship on you in religion* [22:78]. He says also, *God wishes ease for you; He does not wish for you to have difficulties* [2:185]. God has built the outer form of the religious practice on five pillars: the two testimonies[6] of faith, the five canonical prayers, the required alms (*zakat*), the fast in Ramadan, and the pilgrimage to Mecca. Islam's creed is founded upon six tenets of belief: belief in God, the angels, the prophets, God's revealed books, the Final Day, and destiny both good and bad. A number of

---

5. Muhammad ibn Isma'il AL-BUKHARI. *Sahih Bukhari*. Dar Ibn Kathir, 1:128; Muslim ibn Hajjaj AL-NAYSABURI. *Sahih Muslim*. Dar Ihya al-Turath al-'Arabi, 1:370.

6. The two testimonies are "There is no divinity but God, and Muhammad is His messenger," similar to the *shema* prayer in Judaism; the two testimonies are what makes one enter into Islam and therefore makes its legal system incumbent. [Trans.]

doctrines branch out from the creed and are backed by the corpus of injunctions found in the Shari'ah. According to the Messenger of God [s], these doctrines number close to seventy.

These are the principles upon which both *islam* and *iman* are based, as expressed in the *hadith* of Gabriel, narrated by 'Umar ibn al-Khattab [r], who said,

> As we sat one day with the Messenger of God [s], a man with pure white clothing and jet-black hair came to us, without a trace of travel upon him though none of us knew him. He sat down before the Prophet [s] resting his knees against his, and placing his hands on his thighs and then said: "Muhammad, tell me about submission (*islam*)." The Messenger of God [s] said: "Islam is to testify there is no divinity but God and that Muhammad is the Messenger of God, to perform the prayers, pay the poor-tax, fast Ramadan, and perform the pilgrimage to the House if one finds a way." He said: "You have spoken the truth," and we were surprised that he should ask and then confirm the answer. Then he said: "Tell me about faith (*iman*)," and the Prophet answered: "It is to believe in God, His angels, His Books, His messengers, the Last Day, and in destiny—its good and bad." "You have spoken the truth." He said, "Now tell me about spiritual excellence (*ihsan*)," and the Prophet answered: "It is to worship God as if you see Him, and if you see Him not, He nevertheless sees you." "Tell me of the Hour," said the visitor, and the Prophet told him: "The one questioned knows no more about it than the questioner." "Then tell me of its portents," the visitor said, and the Prophet replied: "When the slave women shall give birth to her mistress, and you see barefoot, naked, indigent shepherds vying in constructing tall buildings." Then the visitor left. After considerable time had passed, the Prophet said to me, "Do you know, 'Umar, who was the questioner?" I replied, "God and His messenger know best." He said, "It was Gabriel, who came to you to teach you your religion."[7]

The Prophet [s] described the branches of faith when he said, "There are seventy some odd branches of faith, and shyness is a

---

7. AL-NAYSABURI, *Sahih Muslim*, 1:37.

branch of faith."[8]

The name "Islam" originates from the central tenet of submission and surrender to God Most High. Islam requires total surrender to God and Him alone, calling on one to cast away any false gods, including one's capricious desires because even indulging one's desires can be a manner of assigning partners to God. As the Quran says, *Have you seen such a one as takes for his god his own passion? Could you be a disposer of affairs for him?* [25:43]. Likewise, Islam calls on Muslims to be at peace with themselves and with the vast universe around them; as the Messenger of God [s] said, "Muslims are those who protect their brethren from their own tongues and hands."[9]

Islam is the true religion of God, for the one who chose it and designated it as such is none other than the Lord of all the worlds Himself. He states in His book, *This day I have perfected your religion for you, completed My favor upon you, and I have chosen for you Islam as your religion* [5:3]. God also says, *It is the creed of your forefather Abraham. It is He who has named you Muslims both before and in this [Revelation]; so that the Messenger may be a witness upon you, and you be witnesses upon humanity* [22:78]. That the Creator of humanity chose the name "Islam" for this religion is one of the special characteristics of this final community, which follows the final religion, and whose prophet [s] is the final prophet. The Jews, on the other hand, chose their own name based on the prayer of God's prophet, Moses [s]; as the Almighty states in Moses' own words, *"Indeed we have turned unto You."*[10] God said, *"I afflict My punishment on whom I will, but My mercy extends to all things"* [7:156]. Christians similarly chose their own designation.

This short answer should suffice to explain the relationship between Islam and previous revelations, the primary foundations of the religion, and the origin of the names "Islam" and "Muslim." May God grant mercy and peace to our Prophet, his family, and companions. And God is most high and knows best.

---

8. AL-BUKHARI, *Sahih Bukhari*, 1:12; and AL-NAYSABURI, *Sahih Muslim*, 1:63.

9. AL-BUKHARI, *Sahih Bukhari*, 1:13; and AL-NAYSABURI, *Sahih Muslim*, 1:65.

10. The Arabic here is *"hudna,"* from which it is said the name *Yahudi* (Jew), meaning one who repents, is derived. [Trans.]

Question 2:

How can one reconcile the idea that Islam is the last religion sent to humanity while it is simultaneously the same message followed by all previous prophets?

There is one theological creed that is the core of all the Prophets' teachings from Adam [s] up to the Prophet Muhammad [s]: there is no divinity except for God, and God is the Creator of all, who cares for His creation and has sent them messengers from among themselves. Therefore all of humanity is obliged to follow the teachings of the prophets sent to them throughout the ages. God has stated, *Not a messenger did We send before you except that We revealed to them that there is no god but I, so worship Me* [21:25]. God also says, *We sent not a messenger except in the language of his own people in order to make [things] clear to them* [14:4]. God informs us that the obligation to worship Him alone is the foundation of the message of all the divinely sent messengers: *Worship God! You have no other god but Him*[11] [23:32]. The Most High says, *Verily, religion with God is submission [islam]* [3:19]. Therefore the injunction to worship God alone is the foundation of the creed of Islam. Hence it holds true that Islam was the religion of all prophets with regard to their beliefs. God says, *And those who seek other than submission (islam) as a religion, it will never be accepted from them* [3:85]. God also says, *This day I have perfected your religion for you, completed My favor upon you, and I have chosen for you Islam as your religion* [5:3]. God willed Islam to be the seal of all religions in the realm of law, and for it to be the only religion in the realm of belief. In addition, Islam has a commonality with all of the previous sacred laws in its fundamentals of ritual worship and commandments and prohibitions. All of the major sins that God outlawed in previous sacred laws, such as homicide and illicit intercourse, have also been outlawed in Islam. Additional similarities abound in the fundamental rules and general acts of worship, such as prayer and alms giving. What Islam changed, however, were the particulars of prayer and the amounts of alms to be given according to the differences in peoples' means.

Thus the religion of Islam incorporates the creed of submission and its sacred law as well as the fundamentals of all previously

---

11. This is a verse that is repeated many times in the Quran as it was spoken by many prophets.

revealed sacred law. Accordingly, God addresses this community as the people for whom He has perfected religious law, upon whom He has bestowed His favor, and for whom He desires submission (Islam) as their religion. Thus the religion of Islam is the religion of this community, just as it is the religion of all the prophets and messengers.

God says, *The same religion has He established for you as that which He enjoined on Noah, and that which We have revealed to you, and that which We enjoined on Abraham, Moses, and Jesus: namely, that you should remain steadfast in religion, and be not divided therein* [42:13]. God also says, *Who turns away from the religion of Abraham except such as debase their souls with folly? Him We chose and rendered pure in this world, and he will be in the Hereafter in the ranks of the righteous. When His Lord said to him, "Submit," he said, "I submit to the Lord of the all worlds." And Abraham enjoined his sons as did Jacob, "O my sons! God has chosen religion for you, so die not except in the state of submission,"* [2:130-132]. And He said, *I am commanded to be among those who submit to God,* [10:72]. And, *Moses said, "O my people! If you have believed in God then put trust in Him, if you have indeed submitted [unto Him],"* [10:84].

God makes it clear that Abraham, Ishmael, Jacob, the Twelve Tribes, Noah, Moses, Jesus, and Solomon, as well as their followers, were all Muslims. The verses above affirm that Islam is the sole religion from the time of our master Adam through the arrival of our master Muhammad [s]. And all praise is due to God, Lord of all the worlds.

Question 3:

We have heard that those who convert to Islam marvel at this religion. How does Islam evoke such passion in its new members?

The beauty of Islam dazzles the senses and its lofty morals, originating in revelation and divine teachings and manifested in the conduct of its adherents, are what overwhelm the heart. Once one is exposed to the inner qualities of Islam through its outward manifestations in daily life, one is compelled to at least respect its moral teachings, if not be drawn to incorporate them into one's own practices. Islam is a religion of mercy, peace, and good will. The Messenger of God [s] said, "The believer is even-tempered, accommodating, openhanded, magnanimous, and has good manners."[12] Through noble ethics, the fulfillment of contracts, honesty, equity, and the affirmation of truth, Islam has over time made such a good impression on people that many have joined. And all praise is due to God, Lord of the worlds.

One may also consider Islam as the practical application of the divine attributes of God, the message of the Quran, and the teachings of the Prophet Muhammad [s]. This practical application has shaped the way in which Muslims interact with the world; they were provided with a firmly rooted experiential model that guided them to become members of the world in which they live. With this practical application Muslims have been able to answer the first key question facing humanity: Where did we come from? This question has to do with the past, and it has arisen due to humanity's confusion and ignorance of their genesis. We are like the child who asks, 'Where did I come from?' for the child does not recall the day he was born, nor does he have the capacity to recollect what came before him. God says, *I called them not to witness the creation of the heavens and the earth, nor their own creation, nor do I take misleaders as helpers* [18:51]. Muslims answer with firm conviction that God is the creator and sustainer of the heavens and the earth as He is the creator of everything; God says, *The Beneficent, He has made known the Quran, He has created man,* [55:1-3].

---

12. Ahmad ibn Hibban AL-TAMIMI. *Sahih Ibn Hibban*. Mu'assisah al-Risalah, 2:215. Sulayman ibn Ahmad b. Ayyub AL-TABARANI. *Al-Mu'jam al-Kabir*. Maktabat al-'Ulum wa-l-Hikam, 10:231.

The Muslim's faith is infused by the concept of divine unity (*tawhid*). Muslims believe in an all-embracing unity that encompasses everything found in their creed. For example, their Prophet [s] is singular because he is the seal. The Most High says, *Muhammad is not the father of any man among you, but he is the messenger of God and the Seal of the Prophets*, [33:40]. Their book is also one; God made only one version without multiplicity and thus He protected it from tampering and foolish talk. God says, *Indeed We have revealed the reminder [Quran] and verily We are its guardian*, [15:9]. The community is one. In this regard the Most High says, *Indeed this community of yours is one and I am your Lord so worship me.* [21:92]. The direction of Muslim prayer, Mecca, is also one. God says, *So turn thy face toward the Inviolable Place of Worship [Mecca], and wheresoever you may be, turn your faces toward it [when you pray]*, [2:144]. Lastly, the message of all the prophets is one and the same. God says, *It is the creed of your forefather Abraham. It is He who has named you Muslims both before and in this [Revelation]; so that the Messenger may be a witness upon you, and you be witnesses upon humanity* [22:78]. As this concept of unity has distinguished Islam and Muslims throughout the ages, it should be even more intrinsic to the contemporary Muslim outlook. It should be the basis of Muslims' understanding of life and all of their interactions with creation, especially with other human beings.

Muslims believe that God has not left people without responsibility. On the contrary, there exist for our guidance revealed laws, scriptures, and divine revelation. God says, *To each of you We prescribed a law and a way* [5:48]. In spite of this, He made Islam the name of the religion that He desired throughout history from Adam until our master, Muhammad [s]. The Most High says, *Verily, religion with God is submission [islam]* [3:19]. The Most High also says, *And those who seek other than submission as a religion, it will never be accepted from them* [3:85]. And God says, *This day I have perfected your religion for you, completed My favor upon you, and I have chosen for you Islam as your religion* [5:3].

The concept of legal responsibility should answer the second question, which is "What are we to do here?" Legal responsibility is based on three principles. The first is the worship of God. That is, the worship of God that gives birth to human beings who are cultivated and civilized. God says, *I created the jinn and humankind only that they might worship Me. I seek no sustenance from them, nor do*

I ask that they should feed Me. Indeed God is He that gives sustenance, the firm Lord of might [51:56-58].

The second principle of legal responsibility is the positive development of the earth. This is accomplished through activity that makes the earth livable and by refraining from what leads to its ruin. The Most High says, *He brought you forth from the earth and has made you husband it,* [11:61]. He also says, *And do not do evil in the earth,* [11:85]. In other words, He commands us to engage in its positive development.

The third principle of legal responsibility is purification of the self. The Almighty says, *And [I swear] by the soul and He who has perfected it, who inspired it [with conscience of] what is wrong for it and [what is] right for it. Those are indeed successful who cause it to grow. And those are indeed failures who stunt it* [91:7-10]. This belief necessitates belief in the hereafter, the time when all of humanity will be taken to account for their deeds on earth. God says, *And whoever does an atom's weight of good will see it then. And whoever does an atom's weight of ill will see it then* [99:7-8]. Muslims also believe in the last day of reckoning, when reward and punishment will be determined. God says, *To God belong the most beautiful names so invoke Him by them,* [7:180]. This basic belief influences every impulse and action of the believer. One might observe the believer embarking on a difficult task or a task that subjects him to the loss of a comfort whenever he feels that such an act will bring him closer to Paradise, or will produce a divine recompense. The believer may also give up something pleasurable because she sees that it will only draw her nearer to Hell. This is all connected to the belief in God and the belief in legal responsibility. This belief also has an effect on life and it should affect it positively, otherwise hope and fear will become obstacles to life. But hope and fear have been legislated by God to protect and encourage life; therefore, actions that turn these emotions into obstacles to life oppose the goal of the Shari'ah.

These three major questions have produced intellectual qualities that shape the identity of Muslims and we hope that Muslims will manifest them in the manner that God intended, just as we hope that they may understand God's intent from His revelation.

Muslims also believe in absolutes since God has no limits and boundaries, and the belief in what has neither limits nor boundaries comes from the belief in God's names and attributes. God's most beautiful names that have come from the Quran and Sunnah

(Prophetic tradition) provide a model of growth for Muslims. God says, *To God belong the most beautiful names so invoke Him by them,* [7:180]. The names that God has used to describe Himself number more than one hundred and fifty in the Quran, and more than one hundred and sixty in the *hadith* literature, which makes the total two hundred and twenty names after excluding those that are repeated. These attributes and names are classified as: names of Divine Beauty, such as the Merciful, the Infinitely Good, the Compassionate, and the Oft-Forgiving; and names of Divine Majesty, such as the Avenger, the Omnipotent, and the Severe in chastisement. They are also divided into names of Divine Perfection, such as the First, the Last, the Manifest, the Hidden, and every other description by which God is characterized.

Muslims adorn their character with only the attributes of Divine Beauty. The attributes of Divine Majesty are for God alone, although Muslims attach themselves to these attributes. Therefore Muslims forgive and withhold their anger. The Most High says, *Let not hatred of any people seduce you to deal unjustly; be just, this is nearer to piety and God consciousness* [5:8]. God also says, *Many of the people of the scripture long to make you disbelievers after your belief, through envy on their own account, after the truth has become manifest to them. Forgive and be indulgent [toward them] until God gives His command. Indeed God is Able to do all things. Establish worship, and pay the poor-due; and whatever of good you send before [you] for your souls, you will find it with God. Indeed God sees all that you do* [2:109-110].

Believers see human beings as ennobled creatures, not merely as part of the universe. The Most High says, *Verily we have honored the Children of Adam. We carry them on the land and the sea, and have made provision of good things for them, and have preferred them above many of those whom We have created with a marked preferment* [17:70]. Humans are unique beings in this universe because we bear the responsibility to cultivate and civilize the earth. The Most High says, *Indeed We offered the trust unto the heavens and the earth and the hills, but they shrank from bearing it and were afraid of it. And humans assumed it. Indeed they have proven to be tyrants and fools* [33:72] The believer affirms that human beings are masters in this universe; therefore they march forth in the service of God in a way that inanimate objects are not capable of. God says, *[God] has made of service unto you whatsoever is in the heavens and whatsoever is in the earth; it is all from Him. Indeed in this are portents for a people who reflect* [45:13]. This relationship enables Muslims to see that time, place, individuals, and states are all sacred. Muslims dignify and revere the night of power because of God's words, *Indeed, We have revealed it during the Night of Power* [97:1], and *Indeed we revealed it during a blessed night* [44:3]. Muslims show reverence to the Kaaba in following His revelation, *The first house [of worship] appointed for humanity was that at Bakka; full of blessing and of guidance for all the worlds,* [3:96]. It is narrated that the Messenger of God [s] addressed the Kaaba, saying:

> How pleasant you are and your scent! How great you are and how great your sanctity! By the One in whose hand is the soul of Muhammad, the sanctity of a believer is greater to God than your sanctity. Their wealth and life are likewise, and let one only think good of another believer.[13]

In addition to the Kaaba, Muslims honor the sanctity of the Quran and the elevated status of the Messenger of God. In reference to the Quran, the Most High says, *None but the pure touch it* [56:79]. Regarding the Prophet, God says, *Make not the calling of the messenger among you as your calling one of another* [24:63].

This intellectual paradigm should serve as the starting point for making a value judgment. It is a rubric to guide one in accepting human ideas and perspectives, and it is a principle by which we may renew a discourse that facilitates comprehension of the current state of affairs. Through a combination of its intellectual paradigm, its concept of the human being who has been fashioned by God through His revealed law, and the behavior of its adherents, Islam has astounded hearts and minds because it is the religion chosen by the Lord of the worlds. And God is most high and knows best.

---

13. Muhammad ibn Yazid (Ibn Majah) AL-QIZWINI. *Sunnan Ibn Majah.* Dar al-Fikr, u.k. 2:1297.

Question 4:

Does the corruption of Muslims bring about the corruption of the world? Why is this so?

Indeed, the corruption of Muslims is equated with the corruption of the world, just as their righteousness is equated with the righteousness of the world. This statement does not reflect sectarianism or bias; rather, it is a clarification of the role of humanity in this world. Islam is the last of all revealed religions and their seal, and the Prophet Muhammad [s] is the seal of the prophets. The Muslim community, which believes in all of the prophets as well as the seal of the prophets, is God's final community. Accordingly, God has appointed this community to call others to their way just as He has commissioned them to remedy the ills of the world and by so doing create a better society for humanity. God says, *Thus, We have appointed you a middle community, that you may be witnesses to humanity, and that the messenger may be a witness to you,* [2:143]. God also says, *You are the best community that has been raised up for humanity. You enjoin right conduct and forbid indecency; and you believe in God* [3:110]. The Muslim community is thus enjoined to observe the condition of the world and to improve it; to uphold the right and to forbid the wrong. Therefore, if this community is corrupted then the world will be corrupted. The early generation of Muslims understood this concept well. Rabi'i ibn 'Amir [r], when asked "What has brought you here?" by the commander of the Persian army, replied, "God has! By God, we are a people who have been sent to take those who wish from the servitude of human beings into the service of God alone, from the narrowness of this world into the expansiveness of this world and the afterlife, and from the tyranny of false religions into the justice of Islam."[14]

This responsibility placed upon Muslims and the light that God has given them define their role in the world, which is ultimately to save humanity by leading people to the path of God and bringing them from darkness into light. If Muslims were to abandon their role by allowing themselves to be corrupted, God forbid, then the world would fall into disarray. This is because Muslims bear the light that illuminates the path for humanity. Were they to fall into

---

14. Muhammad ibn Jarir b. Yazid AL-TABARI. *Tarikh al-Tabari*. Dar al-Kutub al-'Ilmiyyah, u.k. 2:401 2:401.

darkness by extinguishing that light, who then would illuminate the path? But God protects His light, as He says, *They seek to put out the light of God with their mouths, but God will manifest His light however much the disbelievers hate it* [61:8]. We ask God for safety, and God is Most high and knows best.

Question 5:

What is the place of moral conduct in Islam? What is the Muslim concept of moral conduct?

Moral conduct is central to Islam, as indicated by the words of the Messenger of God [s], "I have been sent only to perfect moral character."[15] He also said,

> The most beloved of you to me and the nearest seated to me on the Day of Resurrection are the best of you in character, and the most despised of you to me and the furthest seated from me on the Day of Resurrection are the prattlers, the boasters, and the prolix. The companions responded, "By God we understand the prattlers and the boasters, but who are the prolix ones? The Messenger of God said, "Those who are arrogant."[16]

The Messenger of God [s] also stated, "God is most generous and He loves generosity and high character, but He despises base character."[17]

These three hadiths, as well as numerous others, highlight the utmost importance of character in Islam. Indeed, the first *hadith* cited above summarizes the Prophet Muhammad's [s] prophetic mission as the endeavor to elevate the character of humanity. The *hadith* employs the word "only" to constrict the meaning of the verb "sent" and thus emphasize the reason for his prophethood. Such eloquent expression awakens Muslims to the prodigious standing that God intends moral character to occupy. However, moral conduct is important not only by virtue of the Prophet's [s] words. The admira-

---

15. Ahmad ibn Muhammad IBN HANBAL. *Musnad Imam Ahmad.* Mu'assisah Qurtuba, u.k. 2:382, Malik ibn ANIS. *al-Muwatta'.* Dar Ihya al-Turath, 2:904 and Malik's wording is, "To perfect the best of character," Muhammad ibn 'Abdullah AL-HAKIM. *al-Mustadarak 'ala al-Sahihayn.* Dar al-Kutub al-'Ilmiyyah, 2:670 and his wording is, "to perfect the most virtuous character," Ahmad ibn al-Hussein b. 'Ali AL-BAYHAQI. *al-Sunan al-Kubra.* Maktabat Dar al-Baz, 10:191, al-Qada'i in Muhammad ibn Salamah b. J'afar AL-QADA'I. *Musnad al-Shihab.* Mu'assisah al-Risalah, 2:192.

16. IBN HANBAL, *Musnad Imam Ahmad*, 4:193, Muhammad ibn 'Isa al-Sulami AL-TIRMIDHI. *Sunan al-Tirmidhi.* Dar Ihya' al-Turath al-'Arabi, 4:370, AL-QIZWINI, *Sunan Ibn Majah*, 2:231.

17. Ahmad ibn al-Hussein Ali AL-BAYHAQI. *Shu'ab al-Imam.* Dar al-Kutub al-'Illmiyyah, 6:241.

tion of moral conduct is an intrinsic characteristic of mankind. All intelligent people agree that honesty, diligence in fulfilling promises, openhandedness and generosity, patience, valor, and goodwill are all positive character traits that warrant respect and praise, just as they agree that traits such as dishonesty, deceit, cowardice, and miserliness are all negative traits that warrant condemnation. Muslims aspire to adorn themselves with positive character traits and strive to rid themselves of negative character traits. The Messenger of God [s] advised his companion 'Uqba ibn 'Amir [r], "O 'Uqba! Shall I not inform you of the best character traits of the people of this life and the hereafter? Maintain ties with those who have severed them with you, forgive those who transgress against you, and give to those who do not give to you."[18]

A number of traits signify good character: modesty, righteousness, honesty, speaking little and working diligently, ignoring that which does not concern one, filial piety, maintaining family ties, patience, thankfulness, forbearance, and chastity. However, all of these traits are encompassed by the qualities of humility and high aspirations.

Moral character also plays a role in reinvigorating societies. Whenever positive and honorable traits are common, society flourishes. The source of true civilization is the elevated moral character of humanity. The famous Egyptian Prince of Poets, Ahmad Shawqi, summarized this concept:

Communities are but morals as long as they last,
As morals dissipate, so do they.

Moral conduct is what emanates from a sound heart, a pure soul, the healthy belief system of a strong mind, and a balanced psychological and spiritual state. Moral character is therefore the outward manifestation of these traits, just as immoral character is an indication of deficiency in one or more of these areas. We ask God to protect us all from immoral character. Our final supplication is: all praise is due to God, Lord of the worlds. And God is most high and knows best.

---

18. IBN HANBAL, *Musnad Imam Ahmad*, 3:438, AL-HAKIM, *al-Mustadrak 'ala al-Sahihayn*, 4:178, Sulayman ibn Ahmad b. Ayyub AL-TABARANI. *al-Mu'jam al-Awsat*. Dar al-Haramayn, 5:364 and in his AL-TABARANI, *al-Mu'jam al-Kabir*, 17:279, AL-BAYHAQI, *al-Sunan al-Kubra*, 10:235.

Question 6:

Is the statement, "Glad tidings to those whose blemishes preoccupy them from focusing on the blemishes of others," a Prophetic statement (*hadith*)? Is the statement "You see the speck in your brother's eye, but forget the bough in your own" a *hadith*? If so, then what are the social implications of these statements?

The statement, "Glad tidings to those whose blemishes preoccupy them from focusing on the blemishes of others," is part of a *hadith* as narrated by Bayhaqi (Shu'ab al-Iman, 7:355), Quda'i (Musnad al-Shihab, 1:358), al-Daylami al-Hamdhani (al-Firdaws bi ma'thur al-khitab, 2:447/1), and Haythami (Majma' al-Zawa'id, 10:229). The *hadith* is narrated on the authority of Anas ibn Malik [r], who said,

> The Messenger of God [s] addressed us while he was on his camel *al-'Adaba'*, not *al-Jada'a'*,[19] saying, "O people, it is as if death has been prescribed for other than us, and it is as if the obligation to fulfill rights has been ordained for other than us, and it is as if those whom we bid farewell to among the dead are on a short journey soon to return to us: we place them into their graves and then devour their inheritance as if we are destined to live on forever after them. We have forgotten every admonition and feel safe from every calamity, glad tidings to those whose blemishes preoccupy them from focusing on the blemishes of others . . . ."[20]

Al-Haythami comments in his volume *Majma' al-Zawa'd*, "Bazzar narrated it, but its chain of transmission contains al-Nasr ibn Muhriz and other weak transmitters."[21]

---

19. These were the names for two of the female camels that the Messenger of God had. *Al-'Adaba'* means the sharp and caustic one and *al-Jada'a'* means the mutilated or amputated one. However, these were simply their names and did not reflect a specific quality of the camels. See: Nabahani, Yusuf, *al-Anwar al-Muhamidiyya min al-Mawahib al-Laduniyya* (Dar al-Fikr n.d.) p. 178. [Trans.]

20. AL-BAYHAQI, *Shu'ab al-Iman*, 7:355, AL-QADA'I, *Musnad al-Shihab*, 1:358, Shiriway ibn Shahrdar b. Shiriway AL-DAYLAMI. *Musnad al-Firdous bi ma'thur al-Khitab*. Dar al-Kutub al-'Ilmiyyah, 2:447, and 'Ali ibn Abi Bakr AL-HAYTHAMI. *Majma' al-Zawa'id*. Dar al-Kitab al-'Arabi, 10:229.

21. Ibid.

Al-'Ajluni also mentions this *hadith* in the text *Kashf al-Khafa'* (2:59),

> Al-Daylami related it on the authority of Anas [r] as a statement of the Prophet [s]. Al-Najm says, "And its completion of the narration is, " . . . and who spend from the surplus of their wealth, find sufficiency in the Sunnah, and do not stray from it into reprehensible innovation. Similar reports have been narrated by al-Hasan ibn Ali [r] and Abu Hurayrah [r]. The author of *al-Tamyiz* said, "al-Bazzar narrates it on the authority of Anas as a statement of the Prophet with a fair chain of transmission."[22]

Lastly, the scholar of *hadith* al-Dhahabi referred to this *hadith* in his *Siyar 'Alam al-Nubala'* (13:557), "The chain of this *hadith* is tenuous, and al-Nadir and al-Walid are unknown, as is mentioned by Abu Hatim. Furthermore, there is no sound chain for this text."[23]

From this discussion we gather that the scholars of *hadith* disputed the sound ascription of this *hadith* to the Prophet [s]. Some have graded it as rigorously authentic (*sahih*) and others have said it is weak (*da'if*). Nevertheless, the scholars have deemed the weak *hadith* permissible to use in matters of righteous actions, in following the guidelines set by the scholars of *hadith*. There is no doubt that this *hadith* is amongst those that encourage virtue and good character. Consequently, Muslim scholars have agreed that its meaning is sound because it promotes honorable characteristics and asceticism, but they have disagreed on its attribution to the Prophet [s].

Regarding the statement of the Messenger of God [s], "You see the speck in your brother's eye, but forget the bough in your own," this *hadith* has been narrated by Ibn Hibban (*Sahih* 13:73), al-Bayhaqi (*Shu'ab al-Iman* 5:311), and Bukhari. Bukhari narrated it twice in *al-Adab al-Mufrad*, once with the wording '*yubsiru*' (to perceive) (1:207) and another time with the wording '*yara*' (to see) (1:305), and also in al-Mundhiri (*al-Targhib wa'l-Tarhib*, 3:167).[24]

---

22. Isma'il ibn Muhammad al-Jarrahi AL-'AJLUNI. *Kashf al-Khafa'*. Mu'assisah al-Risalah, 2:59.

23. Muhammad ibn Ahmad b. 'Uthman AL-DHAHABI. *Siyar 'Allam al-Nubala'*. Mu'assisah al-Risalah, 13:557.

24. AL-TAMIMI, *Sahih Ibn Hibban*, 13:73, AL-BAYHAQI, *Shu'ab al-Iman*, 5:311, Muhammad ibn Isma'il BUKHARI. *al-Adab al-Mufrad*. Beirut: Dar

In his *Hilyat al-Awliya'* (4:99), Abu Nu'aym al-Asfahani said after mentioning this *hadith*, "It is of singular origin from the *hadith* narrated by Yazid, it has been singularly narrated by Muhammad ibn Himyar on the authority of J'afar. However, Ibn Hibban graded it as rigorously authentic (*sahih*)."[25] Hafiz al-Munawi expressed his views that the report is weak, and that it is but fair in Fayd Al-Qadir (6/457).

This *hadith*, like the previous, has debatable authenticity. However, as already mentioned, a weak report may be acted upon when it encourages virtue. There is no doubt that the meaning of this *hadith* is sound as it reflects the fundamentals of the sacred law and virtuous conduct. Therefore the community in its entirety has agreed upon its value.

Through these two hadiths, the Messenger of God [s] has provided us with a method for improving the overall condition of society. He has also taught us how to identify those who claim to be improving society in order to distinguish those who are honest in their desire for reformation from those who intend to impose authority and influence over others, either with or without explicit intention. Therefore, if one is obsessed with the faults of others and neglects introspection, he should take a critical look at himself and seek reform. If one has already improved herself, then she may endeavor to improve the state of those closest to her. The following verses by Imam Shafi'i[26] apply to those who act contrary to this approach:

> O you who seek to teach others,
> Why not be a teacher to yourself?

> You prescribe the medicine to the sick amongst the weak
> For their health to improve, while you yourself, are ill.

> Do not forbid people from certain traits that you in turn engage in,
> Shame on you if you commit this grave sin.

---

al-Kutub al-'Ilmiyyah, 1:207, 1:305, and 'Abd al-'Azim ibn 'Abd al-Qawi AL-MUNDHIRI. *al-Targhib wa al-Tarhib*. Dar al-Kutub al-'Ilmiyyah, 3:167.

25. Abu Na'im Ahmad ibn 'Abdallah AL-ASFAHANI. *Hilyat al-Awliya*. Dar al-Kutub al-'Arabi, 4:99.

26. Imam Muhammad ibn Idris al-Shafi'i (d. 820 CE) was the epinomous founder of the Shafi'i school of Islamic Jurisprudence.

Begin with yourself, and forbid it from following its desire,
If your self can seize this, then you are truly wise.

Then what you say will be accepted, and you will be followed
In what you say, and you will be efficient in teaching.

If one is sincere in helping society then let him begin with himself. This will form a center that is sound which can radiate out to all corners of society. And our final prayer is all praise is due to God. And God is most High and knows best.

Question 7:

Is the statement "The *isnad* (the chain of transmission) is part of religion," a *hadith*, and what does it mean?

The statement, "The *isnad* (chain of transmission) is part of religion," is not a *hadith* of the Prophet [s], it is not a weak *hadith* or any other grade of *hadith*. This statement is attributed to 'Abdallah ibn Mubarak who used to say, "The *isnad* (chain of transmission) is part of religion, and were it not for the chain of transmission anyone would say whatever they wanted to say." He also declared, "Between us and other peoples are the pillars," in reference to the chains of transmission.

The second half of the first quote, "If it were not for the chain of transmission then anyone would say whatever they wanted to say," may answer our question because here is summarized the importance of ascertaining reliability and authentication; the *isnad* is used in the transmission of Islam so that the religion does not become clouded by a collection of legends and mistaken assumptions. Indeed, the matter of authentication is one of the most important building blocks of a Muslim's identity and intellectual perspective. The Muslim community is characterized in particular by its authentication of sources as Islam continually authenticates the Book of God by teaching the correct way to write and recite the revealed text. The fact that Muslims have concerned themselves with the authentication of this book generation after generation has greatly impressed other communities.

In the realm of the Sunnah, chains of transmission have been and continue to be the most important means by which God has protected the *hadith* and prevented fabrication and lies. The *isnad* is the first reference by which narrations are evaluated and reports are weighed, in order to know the sound from the unsound and the strong from the weak. In our present time, however, chains of transmission are no longer a basis for preservation so much as a source of blessings and knowing historical dates.

We hope this has clarified of the meaning of Ibn al-Mubarak's statement, "The *isnad* is part of religion." We ask God to protect our religion and faith, and our final prayer is all praise is due to God.

Question 8:

What is the role of the prohibitory phrase ("Do not do such and such") in Islam?

The phrase, "Do not do such and such," falls under the category of prohibition in our religion, and the phrase, "Do such and such," is a command. The prohibited acts are few in Islam and are therefore easy to avoid. The obligation to avoid certain foods was the first test given by God to our father Adam and our mother Eve. The eating of the forbidden fruit was the first act of transgression against God, as the Quran makes clear in more than one place: *O Adam! Dwell you and your wife in the Garden and eat from what you desire, but do not come near this tree lest you become wrong-doers. Then Satan whispered to them that he might manifest unto them that which was hidden from them of their shame, and he said: Your Lord forbade you from this tree only lest you should become angels or become of the immortals. And he swore to them [saying]: Indeed I am a sincere adviser unto you. Thus did he lead them on with guile. And when they tasted of the tree their shame was manifest to them and they began to hide [by heaping] on themselves some of the leaves of the Garden. And their Lord called them, [saying]: Did I not forbid you from that tree and tell you: Indeed Satan is an open enemy to you?* [7:19-22]

These verses illustrate the extent of Divine mercy as God forbade Adam and Eve to eat from only one tree and made all the others permissible for them. Likewise, out of His infinite mercy God has made few prohibitions in order to facilitate our obedience to Him. God says, *O mankind! Eat of that which is lawful and wholesome in the earth, and follow not the footsteps of the devil. Indeed he is an open enemy for you,* [2:268]. Therefore the entire universe is the table of God, created for the benefit of mankind and as a place for His worship. The duty to worship God has also been made easy by the small number of prohibited things that God has obliged people to avoid. God has also promised forgiveness for those who commit the prohibited and then turn to Him in sincere repentance. This statement of the Messenger of God [s] emphasizes God's command to avoid sin, "Leave to me that which I have brought to you as those before you were destroyed by their excessive questions and quarrels with their prophets. If I command you to do something then strive to obey as much as is possible, and if I forbid you from something then leave it alone."[27]

This is the significance of the phrase "Don't do such and such" in the religion of Islam, so may God grant us the grace to obey Him and our final prayer is all praise is due to God.

27. IBN HANBAL, *Musnad Imam Ahmad*, 2:428, AL-BUKHARI, *Sahih Bukhari*, 6:3658, and AL-NAYSABURI, *Sahih Muslim*, 2:975.

Question 9:

How can Muslims respond to the claim that women are oppressed through Islam's system of inheritance?

It is commonly stated in contemporary times that Islam oppresses women by making their inheritance half that of men. As Muslims, we have firm conviction in God's immutable attributes and this conviction keeps such claims from affecting our hearts. We believe that God is a fair judge and that His justice is absolute: no injustice towards humans or any other creature is found in His sacred law. The Quran says, *And your Lord wrongs no-one* [18:49]; *God is no oppressor of His servants* [22:10]; and *It was not for God to wrong them* [29:40]. Therefore, such a statement does not shake our conviction, but rather calls for an in-depth analysis of the inheritance law stipulated by the Quran.

The difference in inheritance is not based on the gender of the heir, but on three primary conditions:

1. The degree of kinship to the deceased: Regardless of whether the heir is male or female, the closer the relationship to the deceased, the more an individual will inherit. For example, a deceased woman's daughter is entitled to half the inheritance while the husband of the deceased only receives one fourth. This is because the daughter, as an immediate blood relative, is closer in relation than the husband. Therefore the amount of inheritance she receives is greater.

2. The generation to which the heir belongs: Grandchildren usually receive more inheritance than grandparents because they will confront future financial responsibilities, whereas others usually maintain the financial upkeep of grandparents. The system functions this way regardless of gender: despite the fact that they are both women, the daughter of the deceased inherits more than the deceased's mother because they belong to different generations. Likewise, the daughter of the deceased inherits more than the deceased's father. This is so even if she has a living brother who inherits with her.

3. Financial Responsibility: It is in this category alone that shares of inheritance differ according to gender. However, this disparity causes no injustice to the female. When a group of inheritors, such as the children of the deceased, are equal in

46

Sheikh 'Ali Gomaa

the first two aforementioned factors, then their shares are affected by the third. In this specific scenario the misunderstood Quranic verses alluded to in the original question come into play. The Quran has not made the disparity between men and women a general condition, but rather has confined it to this specific situation. When the individuals in a group of heirs are equal in both their relation to the deceased and their age, the male son of the deceased receives twice as much as the female daughter of the deceased. The wisdom behind this arrangement is as follows: the male is responsible for the financial upkeep of his wife and children, whereas his sister's financial upkeep is the responsibility of an individual other than herself, such as her husband or father. Thus, for all practical purposes, the disparity favors the woman because the wealth she inherits is not applicable to the household expenses and is hers to dispense with as she pleases. This financial advantage also protects her from any circumstances that would place her in financial difficulty. Unfortunately, few today understand this finer point of the Muslim inheritance system.

The financial responsibilities of men include:

1. In the beginning of a man's marital life he is obliged to provide a dowry for his spouse: *And give unto the women [whom you marry] free gift of their marriage portions*, [4:4]. This is an obligation that falls on men, not women, and no man has the right to demand such a dowry from a woman.

2. After the initial marriage process, the man is obliged to financially support his spouse even if she is extremely wealthy. The man has no right to ask his wife to support herself or them both. This further illustrates the protection of women's rights, especially their financial rights, by Shari'ah law.

3. Men are also required to financially support the members of their extended family if the situation demands. This is particularly true if they inherit money, since they then become an extension of the deceased and must assume his societal and familial role.

These scenarios, and others, force us to conduct a more objective examination of property and wealth. Wealth is a broader concept than income. Income becomes part of wealth but is not wealth itself, since wealth is that which remains after all expenditure. In the scenarios where a woman receives half of the man's inheritance, the woman's new income is protected by the Shari'ah and is hers to dispense with as she wishes. The man's new income, on the other hand, is to aid him in supporting family members that have now come under his care. This is why we are able to say that Islamic inheritance laws protect the wealth of women and grant preference to them over men.

In other scenarios, men and women inherit the same amount. For example, the children of a deceased women inherit the same amount; as God says, *And if a man or a woman have a distant heir [having left neither parent nor child], and he [or she] have a brother or a sister [only on the mother's side] then to each of them twain [the brother and the sister] the sixth, and if they be more than two, then they shall be sharers in the third* [4:12]. This equality of males and females in this case owes to the fact that they sprung from the same womb but do not share the same father. Sharing the same father would cause the male child to inherit the father's financial responsibilities, to the exclusion of the female child. In the situation explained above, the son does not have those financial burdens so therefore his sister is equally entitled.

By investigating and classifying numerous scenarios of Islamic inheritance, researchers have compiled statistics that surprise many people. Among these facts are the following:

1. There are only four scenarios in which a women inherits half that of a man.

2. In about thrice the number of scenarios a woman inherits the same amount as her male counterpart.

3. There are many scenarios in which a woman inherits more than a man.

4. There are some situations in which a woman inherits and her male counterpart does not inherit at all.

The scenarios in which a woman inherits half that of a man:

1. A daughter who inherits with her brothers along with the granddaughter and grandson of the deceased.

2. The mother who inherits with the father, when the deceased has neither children nor spouses.

3. A sister who inherits alongside her brothers.

4. A daughter with brothers from the same father and a different mother.

The scenarios in which a woman inherits a share equal to that of a man:

1. The mother and a father who inherit with the son of the deceased.

2. Brothers and sisters who share a mother but have different fathers.

3. Brothers and sisters who share the same mother but have different fathers.

4. A daughter who inherits with her paternal uncle or the closest agnate of the father, in the absence of another child who would bar her from inheriting.

5. The woman's father who inherits with the woman's mother's mother or with the woman's son's son.

6. When a husband, mother, and two sisters of the same mother but different fathers inherit along with a male sibling. This ruling is based on the verdict given by 'Umar in which he argued that the two sisters of one mother and different fathers, and the male sibling are to share one third of the inheritance.

7. When a man or a woman is the sole heir. For example, the son inherits the entire estate if he is the sole heir based on agnation, while a daughter would inherit one half of the legacy based on cognation, but then receive the remainder by default because she is the sole heir. This shows equality between the genders: were the deceased to leave his/her father as the sole heir, he would inherit the entire legacy by agnation. Likewise, were the deceased to leave behind a mother, she would inherit one third of the legacy based on cognation and the rest would be hers by default due to the absence of any other heirs.

8. If a woman leaves behind a husband and a female sibling. In this case the sibling takes what a man would; meaning that if a woman left behind a husband and a male sibling, the husband would take a half of the legacy and the brother would take the rest by agnation. If she, however, leaves behind a husband and a sister, the husband takes half, as does the sister.

9. When the woman leaves behind a sister who shares her mother but has a different father, and a male sibling. This scenario occurs when the deceased woman leaves behind a hus-

band, a mother, and a sister and brother from the mother's side. The husband takes a half, the mother takes a sixth, and the sister of the deceased takes a sixth. The rest, which is a sixth, is the inheritance of the brother.

10. If there are no direct descendants of the deceased, then those of blood relation on the mother's side of the deceased inherit the same amount regardless of gender. The Egyptian civil law number 77 article 31 of 1943 has adopted this opinion. For example, if the deceased is survived by his or her daughter's daughter, a son of a daughter, a maternal uncle, and a maternal aunt, then they all would inherit the same amount.

11. There are six people who are never barred from inheritance, three male and three female. The male are: the husband, the son, and the father. The females are: the wife, the daughter, and the mother.

In these scenarios a woman inherits more than a man:

1. When the husband inherits with his only daughter.
2. When the husband inherits with his two daughters.
3. When the daughter inherits with her paternal uncles.
4. If a women dies leaving behind sixty acres of land and the heirs are her husband, her father, her mother, and two daughters, then the two daughters will inherit thirty-two acres (sixteen each). However, if instead of the two daughters the deceased women left two sons, each son would inherit twelve and a half acres each. In other words, the daughters' share is one third each of the inheritance, while the portion of the two sons is simply the inheritance that remains after distribution of the designated shares.
5. If a women dies leaving behind forty-eight acres of land, and the inheritors are her husband, two female siblings, and her mother, then the two sisters inherit a combined two thirds of the inheritance, meaning that each sister would inherit twelve acres. However, if the deceased leaves behind two brothers instead of two sisters, they would each inherit eight undesignated acres after the husband and mother received their designated shares.
6. The situation would be the same if the deceased left behind two sisters from the father's side: they would inherit more than two brothers from the father's side.

7. If a woman dies and leaves behind her husband, father, mother, and daughter, and her inheritance is one hundred fifty-six acres, then the daughter will inherit half (seventy-two acres). However, if she had left behind a son instead, he would only inherit sixty-five acres by default, after shares of the inheritance were disbursed to the husband, father, and mother.

8. If a woman dies and leaves behind her husband, mother, and sister, and the deceased's inheritance is forty-eight acres, for example, then the sister inherits eighteen acres. However, if instead of the sister there had been a brother, he would only inherit eight acres as a universal inheritor after the distribution of the inheritance to the husband and mother. In this case a sister inherits more than double her brother.

9. If a man dies and leaves behind a wife, a mother, two sisters from his mother's side, and two brothers, and his inheritance is forty-eight acres, then the two sisters from his mother's side would inherit around sixteen acres total (eight each). However, the brothers would only receive twelve acres total (six each).

10. If a women dies and leaves behind her husband, her sister from her mother's side, and two brothers, and her inheritance was one hundred twenty acres, the sister from the mother's side would inherit one third, which is equivalent to forty acres. The two brothers inherit a total of twenty acres. In this situation the two sisters from the mother's side, who are further in relation than two full brothers, inherit four times the brothers.

11. If a man dies and leaves behind his father, mother, and a wife, then the wife inherits half, the mother inherits one third, and the rest (one-sixth) goes to the father. This scenario is in accordance with the opinion of Ibn 'Abbas.

12. If a woman dies and leaves behind her husband, mother, a sister from the mother's side, and two full brothers, and the inheritance is sixty acres, then the sister from the mother's side would inherit ten acres while each brother inherits five acres. Here the sisters take double their brothers even though they are further in relation from the deceased.

13. If a man dies and leaves behind his wife, father, mother, two daughters, and a son's daughter, and the inheritance is five hundred sixty-eight acres, then the daughter of the son

inherits ninety-six acres. If the deceased had left a son of his son, then he would only inherit twenty-seven acres.

14. If a deceased leaves behind his or her mother, maternal grandmother, and paternal grandmother, and the inheritance is sixty acres, then the mother would inherit one sixth as her allocated share, and the rest would be forfeited to her. However, if the deceased left his or her father, maternal grandmother, and paternal grandmother, then the maternal grandmother would still inherit one sixth (ten acres) and would not be canceled by anyone. The rest of the inheritance (fifty acres) would go to the father. This means that the mother took the entire inheritance and the father, if he were in her place, would only take fifty acres.

Scenarios in which a woman inherits and the male equivalent does not inherit:

1. If a woman dies and leaves behind her husband, father, mother, daughter, and the daughter of her son, and her inheritance is one hundred ninety-five acres, for example, then the daughter of the son would inherit one sixth (twenty-six acres). But if the son had a son instead of a daughter, then he would not inherit at all.

2. If a woman dies and leaves behind her husband, a full sister, and a sister from her father's side, and the inheritance is eighty-four acres, for example, then the sister from the father's side would inherit one sixth (twelve acres). However, if instead of this sister there were a brother from the father's side, he would inherit nothing, since half goes to the husband, the other half goes to the full sister, and the rest, which is nothing, would go to the son of the father.

3. In many scenarios, grandmothers inherit while grandfathers do not inherit. A grandfather who inherits is one who does not have a woman between him and the deceased. For example, the father of the father of the father and so on. However, the father of the mother or the father of the mother of the mother, and so on, do not inherit. The grandmother who inherits is one who does not have between her and the deceased a person who does not inherit. In other words, it is every grandmother who does not have between her and the deceased a father between two mothers. So, for example, a mother of the

father of a mother does not inherit, but a mother of a mother, or a mother of a mother of a father does inherit.

4. If a person dies and leaves behind a maternal grandfather and a maternal grandmother, then the grandmother inherits the entire inheritance, as she takes a sixth by inheritance and the rest is forfeited to her. The grandfather, as explained in number three above, does not inherit.

5. If a person dies and leaves behind the father of the mother of his or her mother, and the mother of the mother of his or her mother, then the great-grandmother inherits the entire inheritance; she takes one-sixth by inheritance, and the rest is forfeited to her.

In summary, there are more than thirty scenarios in which a woman inherits either the same amount as a man or more than him. In some cases she inherits while her male equivalent does not inherit at all. There are only four scenarios, however, in which a woman inherits half the share of a man. With this detailed response we are confident that we have answered the question. And all praise is due to God, most high.

Question 10:

What is the reality of polygamy in Islam, and how does one respond to the controversy surrounding it?

Polygamy is the practice by which a man has more than one wife. This practice has been the subject of broad discussion, both within and outside the Muslim world. In order to correct misconceptions, we must note that Islam did not proscribe polygamy but rather put limits on this custom that long predated Muhammad [s]. Polygamy was common in the ancient world, but was mostly practiced without guidelines or limitations. The Shari'ah circumscribed and legitimized this practice. Such legislation reveals the inventiveness of the Islamic legal system. For example, on the authority of his father, Salim narrates that Ghaylan ibn Salama al-Thaqafi had ten wives when he converted to Islam. The Messenger of God [s] told him, "Choose four from amongst them to keep."[28] The primary texts discussing polygamy are of this nature, meaning they limit the number of wives to four. There are no texts, however, commanding a man to marry more than one woman. Therefore, in Islam polygamy is not sought out without good reason. It is sought out for specific needs mentioned in conjunction with polygamy. For example, the famous Quranic verse says, *And if you fear that you will not deal fairly by the orphans, marry of the women, who seem good to you, two or three or four; and if you fear that you cannot do justice [to so many] then one [only] or [the captives] that your right hands possess* [4:3]. The exegetes of the Quran say that polygamy occurs in conjunction with situations involving widows and orphans. This meaning is entirely lost when modern examiners partially quote the verse and ignore the context of the discussion. The verse specifically speaks of orphans and widows, and uses an "if-then" clause to stress the conditional nature of polygamy. Many modern readers miss this; however, the Quran does not openly invite polygamy without conditions attached.

There is a huge difference between Islam commanding the marriage of four wives, as some claim today, and Islam bringing under strict legislation an already common and unfettered practice. If one delves into ancient history, it is common to read of rul-

---

28. IBN HANBAL, *Musnad Imam Ahmad*, 2:13, AL-QIZWINI, *Sunan Ibn Majah*, 1:628.

ers who had hundreds of wives, and of these same rulers giving wives to other rulers as gifts. Similar to Islam, Jewish law permitted men to marry more than one wife.

The intention of the Shari'ah is to examine this practice and insure the marital rights of all spouses. Thus it is strange to hear detractors of Islam targeting polygamy, while ignoring other social phenomena that present a great threat to the unit of the family. Many non-Muslims in Western countries chastise Muslim polygamy, yet their own supposedly monogamous society is ridden with single-parent homes, depression, and high abortion rates. Adultery in the West is a type of polygamy occurring outside the institution of marriage. Both the legal wife and the mistresses of an adulterous man suffer. The man's entire family suffers, as his acts are a form of treachery and emotional abuse.

We ask God to grant us insight into our religion, and our final prayer is all praise is due to God.

Question 11:

Some claim that Islam harms women by allowing men to strike their wives. What does the Shari'ah actually rule on this matter?

The subject of "striking" one's wife appears only once in the Quran: *As to those women on whose part you fear disloyalty and ill-conduct, admonish them, refuse to share their beds, and hit them [lightly]* [4:34]. The marital discord (*nushuz*) referred to in this verse is specifically that which arises from the violation of social norms and etiquette that occurs when a woman refuses to carry out her marital obligations. A wife's obligations are considered her husband's rights, just as a husband's obligations towards his wife are her rights.

A man is given three options to bring marital discord back to harmony. First he should admonish his wife with words. If that does not bring results, the second step is to refuse her sexually. The third step is the subject of this discussion, as it allows a man to "hit" or "strike" his wife in a way that does not leave a trace or cause any harm.[29] The action does not aim to cause physical distress; rather, it reveals the intensity of the man's frustration and concern for their relationship. It is an emphatic way of communicating anger when no other measures have been heeded. The act of "striking" is not mandatory; on the contrary, it is a last resort. Jurists have ordered men to avoid this option as much as possible and to communicate their anger in alternative ways.

While most people focus on the aforementioned verse, rulings on this issue are based on other sources as well. In accordance with the books of Islamic jurisprudence, under some circumstances men are beaten for abusing or otherwise mistreating their wives. The books of jurisprudence state, "If a man deflowers his wife by using his hand, it is considered prohibited [as it causes unnecessary pain], and he is punished for such an act."[30] We find further

29. Although the wording we have used here, "one that does not leave a trace or cause any harm," does not appear in the verse itself, this is the phrase commonly used by both jurists and Quranic exegetes to define the term "strike." They are taken from the description of the Prophet during his Farewell Sermon. See AL-NAYSABURI, *Sahih Muslim*, 8:54, #3009. Also see Isma'il ibn 'Amr IBN KATHIR, *Tafsir al-Quran al-'Azim*. Dar al-Fikr.

30. Islamic Endowment Ministry of KUWAIT. *al-Mawsu'ah al-Fiqhiyyah al-Kuwaytiyyah*: Wizarat al-Awqf al-Kuwaytiyyah, harf ba, 8:181, bakkarah,

condemnation of abuse in the books of *hadith*; the women of Medina complained to the Messenger of God [s] that their husbands hit them, and he responded by saying, "Many women have come to the wives of Muhammad complaining of their husbands' actions. Such men are not the best among you."[31]

It is also pertinent to note that not a single source mentions that the Messenger of God [s] struck his wives. Therefore, in deference to the Sunnah of the Messenger of God [s], it is best to refrain altogether from striking one's wife even though the Quran sanctions the act under certain circumstances.

In some cultures, women expect men to display a certain amount of bravado, and a wife enjoys that manly quality in her husband. This cultural attitude is not prevalent in the West and to many it is completely foreign. Yet because the Quran was revealed for all times and circumstances until the Final Hour, it has included and addressed all types of cultures and mentalities that, if left unaddressed, would lead to imbalance and potential dissolution of the family. In order to prevent cultural tensions, these different norms and mentalities are addressed for the benefit of all societies.

Finally, spousal abuse is absolutely rejected by Islam. Islam's intense aversion to this behavior is best captured by the statement of the Messenger of God [s] in which he asks rhetorically, "Do any of you beat their wives like a slave is beaten and then seek intimacy with them at the end of the day?"[32]

We hope that this brief discussion has sufficed to answer the question at hand, and God is Most High and knows best.

---

which cites Dasuki:Hashiyat Sharh Kabir, 6:495, 'Abdallah ibn Ahmad b. Qudmah AL-MAQDISI. *al-Mughni*. Dar Ihya al-Turath al-'Arabi, 6:495, Mansur ibn Yusuf AL-BUHTI. *Kashf al-Qina'*. Dar al-Kutub al-'Ilmiyyah, 5:47 RIYADH, Jalal al-Din AL-MAHALLI. *Sharh Minhaj al-Talibin*. Dar Ihya al-Kutub al-'Arabiyyah, 3:223, Muhammad Amin ibn 'Omar IBN 'ABIDIN. *Rad al-Muhtar 'ala al-Dur al-Mukhtar*. Dar al-Kutub al-'Ilmiyyah, 2:302, al-Kamal IBN AL-HUMAM. *Fath al-Qadir*. Dar Ihya al-Turath al-'Arabi, 3:169, and 'Uthman ibn 'Ali AL-ZAYLA'I. *Tabyin al-Haqa'iq Sharh Kanz al-Daqa'iq*. Dar al-Kitab al-Islami, 2:120 with al-Anqani's *hashiyah*.

31. Sulayman ibn al-Ash'ath (Abu Dawud) AL-SIJISTANI. *Sunan Abi Dawud*. Dar al-Fikr, 2:245, 'Abdullah ibn 'Abd al-Rahman AL-DARMI. *Sunan al-Darami*. Dar al-Kutub al-'Ilmiyyah, 2:198.

32. AL-BUKHARI, *Sahih Bukhari*, 5:1997, AL-BAYHAQI, *al-Sunan al-Kubra*, 7:305 and the wording is Bayhaqi's.

Question 12:

Islam enjoins all people to display good will to one another. Is it therefore permissible for Muslims to give gifts to non-Muslims and to send them special greetings during their holidays?

Maintaining ties, giving gifts, making visits, and congratulating non-Muslims are acts of goodness. God has enjoined us to say good things to everyone, without exception. He states, *Speak fairly to people*, [2:83] and *God commands justice and the doing of good*, [16:90]. God has not prohibited us from being good to non-Muslims, from visiting them, giving them gifts, nor from accepting their gifts. God says in the Quran, *God forbids you not, with regard to those who fight you not for [your] Faith nor drive you out of your homes, from dealing kindly and justly with them: for God loves those who are just* [60:8].

The Messenger of God [s] incorporated these teachings into his everyday behavior, for he was a walking Quran, making its moral code his own.[33] Many hadiths recount that the Messenger of God [s] accepted gifts from non-Muslims. These hadiths were transmitted through corroborative continuity and are therefore of the highest authenticity. For example,

The Messenger of God [s] sent Hatib ibn Abi Balta'a to the Christian ruler of Alexandria with a message for him, and the Patriarch accepted the letter, honored Hatib, and made his stay comfortable. The Patriarch then sent him back with a garment for the Messenger of God [s], a mule with its saddle, and two slave girls as gifts. One slave girl was the mother of Ibrahim,[34] and the other one, the Messenger of God [s] gave as a gift to Jahm ibn Qays al-'Abdari.[35]

Another incident occurred when Salman, the Persian, became Muslim:

---

33. IBN HANBAL, *Musnad Imam Ahmad*, 6:90, AL-BAYHAQI, *Shu'ab al-Iman*, 2:15.

34. Her name was Mariya al-Qibtiyya and she bore the Messenger of God a son whose name was Ibrahim. [Trans.]

35. Yusuf ibn Muhammad AL-HANAFI. *Mu'tasar al-Mukhtasar*. 'Alim al-Kutub, 1:226. al-Hafidh mentioned this *hadith* in Ahmad ibn 'Ali b. Hajar AL-'ASQALANI. *al-Isabah*. Dar al-Jil, 2:450 and Yusuf ibn Muhammad IBN 'ABD AL-BARR. *al-Isti'ab*. Dar al-Jil, 1:314.

Salman the Persian came to the Messenger of God [s] when he first entered Medina with a platter of dates. He placed this in the hands of the Messenger of God [s] and the Messenger of God [s] said to him, "What is this Salman?" He replied, "Charity for you and your companions." The Messenger of God [s] said, "Take it back! For, we do not eat from charity." Salman took it and returned the next day with a similar platter and gave it to the Messenger of God [s] who asked him, "What is this Salman?" Salman replied, "Charity for you and your companions," and the Messenger of God [s] told him, "Take it back! For we do not eat from charity." So Salman took it and came the following day with a similar platter and gave it to the Messenger of God [s] who said to him, "What is this Salman?" He replied, "A gift," so the Messenger of God [s] told his companions, "Indulge as you like!"[36]

Al-Hafidh al-'Iraqi commented on this *hadith*, "This is proof that accepting gifts from non-Muslims is permissible since Salman was still not a Muslim at that time."[37] Thus, accepting gifts from non-Muslims is not only an act of goodness toward humanity, but it is also an emulation of the Sunnah of the Prophet [s]. Shaykh al-Islam Zakariyyah al-Ansari confirms, "It is permissible to accept a gift from a non-Muslim in emulation of the Messenger of God [s]."[38]

Imam al-Sarakhsi further emphasizes this :

It has been mentioned on the authority of Abu Marwan al-Khuza'i who said, "I told Mujahid that there are blood ties between me and a certain non-Muslim, and I owe him money. Should I repay him?" Mujahid said "Yes, and you should keep family ties with him." Thus we deduce that there is nothing wrong with a Muslim maintaining ties with non-Muslims, whether they are family or not. Ties should also be maintained regardless of whether they have a peace accord or are at war with Muslims, in accordance with the *hadith* of Salma ibn al-Akw'a who said, "I prayed behind the Messenger of God [s] one

---

36. IBN HANBAL, *Musnad Imam Ahmad*, 5:354, AL-HAYTHAMI, *Majma' al-Zawa'id*, 9:336.

37. 'Abd al-Rahim ibn al-Hussein AL-'IRAQI. *Tarh al-Tathrib*. Dar Ihya al-Turath al-'Arabi, 4:35-36.

38. Zakariya ibn Muhammad AL-ANSARI. *Asna al-Matalib*. Dar al-Kitab al-Islami, 3:479.

morning and I felt a tap on my shoulders. I turned and saw the Messenger of God [s] who asked me, "Will you gift me the daughter of Umm Qarfa?" I said, "Yes," and gave her to him. The Messenger of God [s] sent her to his maternal uncle Huzn ibn Abi Wahb who was a polytheist, and she was a polytheist. The Messenger of God [s] also sent 500 dinars to Mecca during a time of famine and ordered that it be given to Abu Sufyan ibn Harb and Safwan ibn Umayya to disperse among the needy of Mecca. They accepted the money and said, "Muhammad only seeks to trick our youth with this." Maintaining ties of kinship is praised in every culture and religion. Similarly, giving gifts is a trait of good character as the Messenger of God [s] said, "I was only sent to perfect moral character." So we have come to understand that this act is something good as far as Muslims and non-Muslims are concerned.[39]

After mentioning the verse, *God forbids you not, with regard to those who fight you not for [your] Faith nor drive you out of your homes, from dealing kindly and justly with them: for God loves those who are just* [60:8], Ibn Muflih the great Hanbali jurist recounts that Ibn Jawzi said,

> The exegetes have stated that this verse is a dispensation to maintain ties with those who are not hostile to Muslims, and a dispensation to be kind to them even if one shares no kinship with them. Some have stated that this verse has been abrogated by 'The Verse of the Sword,' but Ibn Jarir says that there is no validity in this statement since it is not prohibited for Muslims to show goodwill towards those at war with them, whether they be family members or otherwise, unless that goodwill aids the enemy in battle against the Muslims ....

He then mentioned the *hadith* in which 'Umar gives a silk garment to his polytheist brother, as well as the *hadith* in which Asma' says that these instances are examples of maintaining family ties with those at war with Islam."[40]

According to Al-Mardawi the Hanbali, the soundest opinion on the matter permits one to extend condolences to non-Muslims

---

39. Muhammad ibn Ahmad b. Abi Sahal AL-SARAKHSI. *Sharh al-Siyar al-Kabir*. al-Sharikat al-Sharqiyyah li-l-'Illanat, 1:96.

40. Muhammad Ibn Muflih AL-MAQDISI. *al-Adab al-Shari'iyyah*. Riyad:'Alim al-Kutub, 1:437.

when necessary, and to offer them well-wishes on their holidays.[41]

> The *al-Fatawa al-Hindiyyah* mentions, There is nothing wrong with being guests to non-Muslims . . . and there is nothing wrong with having non-Muslims as guests, even if you are only acquaintances. . . . There is nothing wrong with a Muslim maintaining ties with a non-Muslim (close relative or not), a person at war with Islam and Muslims, or someone living under the protection of non-Muslims.[42]

The textual evidence and opinions of prominent jurists mentioned in this answer prove that it is an act of good will when Muslims keep ties with non-Muslims. This includes visiting them when they are sick, sending condolences for death, giving gifts, accepting gifts, and entertaining them in one's home. Such exhibitions of good character invite people to Islam by giving them a positive impression of the religion. God is Most High and knows best.

---

41. Ali ibn Sulayman b. Ahmad AL-MARDAWI. *al-Insaf.* Dar Ihya al-Turath al-'Arabi, 4:234-35.

42. LAJNAT AL-'ULAMA'. *al-Fatawa al-Hindiyyah.* Ed. By Nidham al-Din AL-BALKHI. Dar al-Fikr, 5:347.

Question 13:

We heard that a woman gave a Friday sermon and led the prayer. What is the Islamic legal opinion on what occurred?

Prayer is an act of worship legislated by God. It is not the result of anybody's personal interpretation. God prescribed both its form and its content, and made the validity of prayer conditional to certain precepts. For the congregational prayer to be valid, it is a condition that the imam be a man.[43] This is not a special privilege given to men, and it does not diminish the status of women. This is rather a matter of worship in the first degree.

Muslims are in agreement that women should be honored. They consider it an honor, not a form of belittlement, that women are prevented from leading men in prayer. With their honor as His objective, God ordered women to stand behind the rows of men during devotional prayers because such prayers contain prostrations. The aim of this injunction is of the same nature as the old Arab saying, "He only held you back in order to put you forward." Positioning women in the posterior rows of prayer does not diminish their honor, but instead declares their elevated status. It constitutes a consideration of high morals and modesty, as well as an act of cooperation between believers—both men and women—to follow the commandment that one should lower one's gaze.

The issue of women leading men in prayer can be looked at from two vantage points. The first considers the reality of Muslim practice and its manifestations throughout the ages. The second vantage point is that of the tradition of jurisprudence and the theoretical reality upon which Muslims rely.

Muslims in both the East and West, in both early and recent times, have agreed in practice that women do not give the call to prayer, lead congregational prayers, or lead the Friday communal prayer. A woman giving the Friday sermon and leading men in prayer is unknown to the history of Islam even during the times when Muslims had female rulers. Shajarah al-Dur ruled Mamluk Egypt, yet she did not give the Friday sermon or lead men in prayer.

---

43. i.e., when the prayer is composed of both men and women. [Trans.]

As for the theoretical reality, the jurists defined the leading of prayers as, "The linking of one's prayer to another person according to conditions made clear by the law." An individual becomes an imam only when the prayers of his followers are linked to his own. This link is the reality of leadership in prayer, and it is the objective of following somebody in prayer.

The legal texts relate two hadiths concerning this issue. Both are widely considered weak, but for the purpose of scholarly thoroughness we will address them. The first *hadith*, reported by Umm Waraqah bint 'Abdallah ibn al-Harith, states, "The Prophet [s] appointed a *mu'adhdhin* for her[44] and ordered her to lead the people of her home [in prayer]."[45] The second *hadith* comes from one of the Prophet's [s] sermons. Jabir ibn 'Abdallah's narrates, "The Messenger of God [s] said in a sermon, ' . . . a woman does not lead a man in prayer, nor does [an ignorant] Bedouin lead one of the companions who emigrated from Mecca, nor does a heretic lead a believer, unless they be compelled to do so by an authority whose sword and whip they fear.'"[46]

Some of the foremost *hadith* scholars, such as Ibn Hajar al-'Asqalani, have considered the first *hadith* to be weak. He said, "'Abd al-Rahman ibn Khallad is in its chain of narration and he is unknown."[47] As for the second *hadith*, most scholars have considered it to be even weaker than the first. Concerning one of the transmitters of this *hadith*, 'Abdallah ibn Muhammad al-'Adawi, *hadith* scholars have said, "Waki' accused him of forging hadiths, and 'Ali ibn

---

44. A *mu'adhdhin* is someone who is designated to make the call to prayer. [Trans.]

45. IBN HANBAL, *Musnad Imam Ahmad*, 6:405; AL-SIJISTANI, *Sunan Abi Dawud*, 1:161; AL-BAYHAQI, *al-Sunan al-Kubra*, 3:130; 'Ali ibn 'Amr al-Baghdadi AL-DARAQUTNI, *Sunan al-Daraqutni*. Dar al-Kitab al-'Arabi, 1:403; AL-TABARANI, *al-Mu'jam al-Kabir*, 25:134; Muhammad ibn Ishaq al-Sulami AL-NAYSABURI, *Sahih Ibn Khuzamah*. al-Maktab al-Islami, 3:89; and the phrasing in Ibn Khuzamah reads, "The Prophet would say, 'Let us go visit the martyr.' And he gave her permission for the call to prayer to be made for her and for her to lead the people of her home in obligatory prayers, and she had memorized the Quran."

46. AL-QIZWINI, *Sunan Ibn Majah*, 1:343; Ahmad ibn al-Hussein b. 'Ali AL-BAYHAQI, *Kubra*, 3:90; AL-TABARANI, *al-Mu'jam al-Awsat*, 2:64.

47. AL-'ASQALANI, *al-Talkhis al-Habir*, 2:26-27.

Zayd b. Jad 'an, his Shaykh from whom he narrates, is also weak."[48]

The juristic tradition of the Muslims represents the proper understanding of the general principles of the law, especially if there is a consensus. In this regard, all of the knowledgeable people from the eight schools of law,[49] as well as the seven jurists of Medina,[50] have formed a consensus that it is impermissible for a woman to lead a man in an obligatory prayer, and that the prayer performed by a man being led by a woman is invalid. A few scholars such as Abu Thawr, al-Muzani, and Ibn Jarir held the minority opinion that the prayer of a man behind a woman is valid as an obligatory prayer.[51] Muhyi al-Din Ibn al-'Arabi from the Zahiri school also adopted this aberrant opinion.

The vast majority of scholars also consider it impermissible for a woman to lead men in supererogatory prayers and in *tarawih*.[52] Some adherents of the Hanbali school disagreed, asserting that it is in fact permissible. For example, Ibn Muflih says of women leading prayer, "It is valid in supererogatory prayers, and on this premise it is also valid in *tarawih*. It has been said, '[This is valid only] if she is the best reciter.' It has also been said, '[It is valid even] if she is not as good a reciter as the men are.' Another view states, '[She may lead them] if she is related [to them] by birth.' It is also said, '[She may lead them] if she is advanced in age.' In any case, she should stand behind them, for that is more modest. Based on these

---

48. Ibid.

49. i.e., The Maliki, Hanafi, Shafa'i, Hanbali, Ja'fari, Zaydi, Zahiri, and Ibadi schools of Muslim jurisprudence. [Trans.]

50. Sa'id ibn al-Musayyib, 'Urwah ibn al-Zubayr, 'Ubaydillah ibn 'Abdullah b. 'Utbah al-Hudhali, Abd Bakr ibn 'Abd al-Rahman b. al-Harith b. Hisham b. al-Mughirah, Kharijah ibn Zayd b. Thabit, Sulayman ibn Yasar al-Hilali, and al-Qasim ibn Muhammad. [Trans.]

51. See KUWAIT, *al-Mawsu'ah al-Fiqhiyyah al-Kuwaytiyyah*, harf dhal (dhu-kurah), starting at 21:266-67, which cites Yahya ibn Sharf AL-NAWAWI, *al-Majmu'ah*. Matb'ah al-Muniriyyah, 4:254, Muhammad ibn Muhammad b. 'Abd al-Rahman AL-HATTAB, *Muwahib al-Jalil fi Sharh al-Khalil*. Dar al-Fikr, 2:92, JawahirIklil, 1:78, Ahmad ibn Ghunaym b. Salim b. Muhanna AL-NAFRAWI, *al-Fawakih al-Dawani*. Dar al-Fikr, 1:238, Mas'ud ibn Ahmad AL-KASANI, *Bada'i' al-Sana'i'*. Dar al-Kutub al-'Ilmiyyah, 1:157, and Ibn Qudmah AL-MAQDASI, *al-Mughni*, 2:198.

52. The supererogatory prayers performed in congregation during the nights of Ramadan. [Trans.]

descriptions, she follows the men she is leading in all but the recitation, while one [of the men] makes the intention of being imam. Most [of the Hanbali scholars] have considered such a prayer valid in its entirety due to the general and particular report of Umm Waraqah."[53]

So we give our fatwa in accordance with the consensuses of the community, past and present, in their words and their deeds, due to strength of the evidence and the depth of their perception. We related the minority opinion of the juristic tradition not to sanction it, but simply to preserve intellectual integrity. Calling for the implementation of this minority opinion would constitute a censure of the community both past and present. The Muslim community never agrees upon misguidance. Consensus is legal evidence, and it is through consensus that the legal issues transmitted in the religious sources have been regulated.

The wisdom in placing women at a distance when it comes to leading prayers has to do with upholding the commandments concerning modesty, the lowering of one's gaze for believing men and women equally, and the concealing of those parts of the body meant to be concealed (for a woman this is her entire body except for her face and hands). Because Muslim prayer includes prostration, a motion that defines and reveals the form of a woman's body, God has ordained that women should stand behind the lines of men in prayer in order to maintain their modesty.

As for the confounding of the two issues of a woman leading a congregation in prayer and a woman giving a Friday sermon, nobody has ever permitted the latter. Those who condone the practice are confused and adhere to a schismatic school of thought which takes many forms, some of which deny the Sunnah and consensus, some of which toy with Arabic words, and some of which call for the permissibility of homosexuality, illicit intercourse, wine, abortion, the changing of the shares of inheritance, and similar topics that reemerge every century or so. Despite these confusions, Muslims continue on the path that God commanded them to follow, carrying the message of felicity in both this world and in the Afterlife, to all the worlds. God says, *Then, as for the foam, it passes away as scum upon the banks, while, as for that which is of use to humanity, it*

---

53. Muhammad Ibn Muflih AL-MAQDISI, *Kitab al-Furu'*. Dar al-Kutub al-'Ilmiyyah, 2:16.

remains on earth. Thus God coins the similitude [13:17].

Hopefully this short explanation has clarified the legal ruling concerning this issue. And God is Most High and Knows Best.

Question 14:

Does a son have to obey his father if he orders him to divorce his wife?

Children are a fruit of the relationship between a man and a woman. They in turn forge relationships and become a source of fatherhood and motherhood themselves. It may be hard to imagine that marriage and its continuity, with all the good that it brings to humanity, could come into conflict with the rights of parents and the obedience that they are due. From the first age of prophecy, when 'Umar ibn al-Khattab [r] ordered his son 'Abdallah [r] to divorce his wife whom he loved dearly, reality has born witness to the conflict between the rights of parents and the continuation of marital life. Muslim jurists have dealt with this issue through explanation and analysis, so that we can understand the boundaries of filial obedience and disobedience as they apply to ending marital life.

The jurists clearly state that a son should not obey his parents unless the parent is righteous and pious, but they do not address the question of whether it is preferred for them to do so when it comes to divorce. Ibn Taymiyah mentioned, "[Imam] Ahmad's view, that it is mandatory for a man to divorce his wife if his father commands him to do so, is restricted by the condition that the father be righteous."[54] Ibn Taymiyah asserts his own opinion that it is impermissible for a son to obey his mother concerning the divorce of his wife, especially if they have children. He was also specifically asked if it is permissible for a man with children from his wife to divorce her on the insistence of his mother who dislikes her. He answered, "It is not permissible for him to divorce her because of what his mother says. It is incumbent upon him to obey his mother, but divorcing his wife is not part of the obedience he owes her. And God knows best."[55]

Ibn Muflih also held the view that it is not compulsory to obey one's parents when it comes to divorce. He said, "[When Ahmad was asked about the ruling] on the situation of one's mother ordering him [to divorce his wife], he said: 'I dislike such a divorce.'

54. Ahmad ibn 'Abd al-Halim IBN TAYMIYYAH, *al-Fatawa al-Fiqhiyyah al-Kubrah*. Dar al-Kutub al-'Ilmiyyah, kitab al-talaq, 5:490.

55. Ahmad ibn 'Abd al-Halim IBN TAYMIYYAH, *Majmu' al-Fatawa*. Majma' al-Malik Fahd, kitab talaq, 3:573.

And our shaykh forbade him from it . . . . He ruled in the same manner when such a man's parents forbid him to marry."[56] Ibn Muflih mentions in *al-Adab al-Shar'iyyah*, "It is not the right of parents to force their son to marry someone he does not want to marry, and if he were to refuse to do so he would not be disobedient. If no one has the right to force him to eat what he finds repulsive while being able to eat that for which he has an appetite, it is even more emphatically his right when it comes to marriage. For the bitterness of eating something distasteful lasts but an hour, while the bitterness of living with someone disliked brings a perpetual harm which is nearly impossible to avoid."[57] The great Hanbali scholar al-Buhuti also held the opinion that it is not obligatory for a son to obey his parents when it comes to divorcing his wife. He said, "(It is not mandatory) for the son (to obey his parents) even if they are (just, when it comes to divorcing) his wife, because that is not part of the obedience due to them (or), meaning it is also not mandatory for a son to obey his parents if (they prevent him from marrying) based on clear textual evidence due to the preceding."[58] The author of *Ghidha' al-Albab* seconds this opinion by saying, ". . . (and) like their ordering him (to divorce wives) of his, or to sell a slave of his (due to an opinion) i.e., a belief (alone) without relying on any legal basis. It says in *al-Qamus*: An opinion (*ra'y*) is a belief (*'itiqad*) and its plural is *ara'*. It says in *al-Adab al-Kubra*: If his father orders him to divorce his wife, then it is not obligatory to do so, as has been mentioned by the majority of the legal authorities of our school. A man told Imam Ahmad, 'My father ordered me to divorce my wife.' The Imam told him, 'Do not divorce her.' The man said, 'But did not 'Umar order his son 'Abdallah to divorce his wife?' The Imam replied, 'Not until your father is like 'Umar.'"[59] In *Sharh al-Nil wa Shifa' al-Alil*, Ibn Atfish al-Ibadi said that a son is not required to divorce his wife if one or both of his parents ask him to: "If he vows to divorce his wife, or his parents ask him to, he is not required to fulfill the vow, nor is

56. Ibn Muflih AL-MAQDASI, *Kitab al-Furu'*, Kitab al-Talaq, 5:363.

57. IBN MUFLIH, *al-Adab al-Shar'iyyah*, 1:502-3.

58. Mansur ibn Yusuf AL-BUHITI, *Daqa'iq Uli al-Nuha Sharh Muntaha al-Iradat*. 'Alim al-Kutub, Kitab al-Talaq, 3:74.

59. Muhammad ibn Ahmad b. Salim AL-SAFARINI. *Ghidha al-Albab*. Mu'assisah Qurtuba, Birr al-Walidayn, 1:383. See also Ibn Muflih AL-MAQDASI, *al-Adab al-Shar'iyyah*, 2:56-57.

there anything that binds him to obey them in that."[60]

Based on the aforementioned elucidation it is clear that it is not compulsory for a son to obey his father if he orders him to divorce his wife. Likewise, it is not a sinful act to disobey one's father in this matter. And God is Most High and Knows best.

60. Abd al-'Aziz ibn Ibrahim AL-THAMINI, *Kitab al-Nil wa Shifa' al-'Alil.* 3rd ed. Jiddah: Maktabat al-Irshad, 1985, al-kitab al-tasa' fi al-huquq, bab fi haq al-walidayn wa man nazala manzilahuma bi-l-jawarih wa al-lisan wa al-qalb 5:22.

Question 15:

Does Islam give a father the right to force his daughter to marry someone that she does not want to marry? Can a woman terminate a marriage in Islam or is that solely the right of the man?

Islam treats men and women equally when it comes to choosing a spouse. Parents do not have the authority to compel their children of either gender to marry someone they do not want to marry. The parents' role in the marriage process involves giving advice, direction, and guidance. The final say belongs to the children themselves.

Marriage is one of a person's private affairs, thus it would be an oppressive infringement upon the rights of others for parents to force their daughter to marry someone she does not desire. In Islam, a woman has complete freedom to accept or reject whoever proposes to her. Neither her father nor her legal guardian has the right to force her to marry someone she does not want, for marriage cannot result from compulsion and coercion because these concepts contradict the love and mercy that God has placed between man and wife.

Many legal texts from our tradition indicate this firmly established ruling, and actual events further reinforce the ruling by showing how the Prophet [s] treated women and their legal guardians. The Prophet [s] confronted the oppressive norms of the pre-Islamic era by affirming the right of women to choose their husbands, and by nullifying marriages that women were forced to enter into, even if it was their fathers who were forcing them. By contravening the norms of the Arabs at that time, the Prophet [s] tested the believers' hearts. He challenged them to be satisfied with the pure law that honors women and respects their choice and free will, while freeing themselves of the practices that devalued, belittled, and oppressed women.

All of the prophetic traditions referring to this matter affirm the right of a woman to choose her husband. The Prophet [s] said, "A formerly married woman may not be married off without being consulted, and a virgin's consent is to be sought." He was asked, "O Messenger of God, how does she give consent?" He said, "By remaining silent."[61] Similarly, he dealt justly with the young woman who came to him complaining that her father had forced her to get married. It is related in his Sunnah, "A young woman who was a virgin came to the Prophet [s] and told him that her father had married her off and that she was averse to it, so the Prophet [s] gave her the choice of whether or not to remain married."[62]

Another woman brought before him a similar case. In addition to being married off without her consent, she said, "And my cousin was betrothed to me." The Prophet [s] said, "He has no special right to marry you. Marry whomsoever you wish."[63]

Khansa' ibn Khudham said, "My father married me off when I was a virgin, and I was averse to the marriage, so I complained of it to the Prophet [s] who said, "Do not marry her off if she is averse to it."[64] A woman of the Ansar[65] was married to a man of the Ansar. When the man was killed in the Battle of Uhud he left behind a son from their marriage. Her son's paternal uncle, as well as another man, asked her father for her hand in marriage, so he married her to the man and disregarded her son's uncle. She came to the Prophet [s] and said, "My father married me to a man that I do not want and disregarded my son's uncle, so my son is going to be taken from me." The Prophet [s] called her father and said, "Did you marry your daughter to this man?" He said, "Yes." The Prophet [s] said, "You have no right to initiate a marriage in such a case." Then he said to the woman, "Go marry your son's uncle."[66]

A *hadith* of the Prophet, narrated by al-Bukhari and Muslim, says, "A'isha [r] asked the Prophet [s] if a young woman whose family marries her off should be consulted. He said, 'Yes, she should

61. IBN HANBAL, *Musnad Imam Ahmad*, 2:434; AL-BUKHARI, *Sahih Bukhari*, 5:1974; AL-NAYSABURI, *Sahih Muslim*, 2:1036.

62. IBN HANBAL, *Musnad Imam Ahmad*, 1:117; AL-SIJISTANI, *Sunan Abi Dawud*, 2:232; AL-QIZWINI, *Sunan Ibn Majah*, 1:603.

63. Ahmad ibn Shu'ayb AL-NASA'i, *al-Sunan al-Kubra*. Dar al-Kutub al-'Ilmiyyah, 3:282.

64. Ibid., 3:282; AL-TABARANI, *al-Mu'jam al-Kabir*, 24:251.

65. The early companions of the Prophet were divided into two groups: the Ansar who were the dwellers of Medina who believed in and assisted the Prophet when he emigrated, and the Muhajirun, those who believed in him in Mecca and made the emigration with him. [Trans.]

66. 'Abd al-Razzaq ibn Hisham AL-SAN'ANI, *Musannaf 'Abd al-Razzaq*. al-Maktab al-Islami, 6:147; AL-KHURASANI, *Musannaf al-Khurasani*, 1:184.

be consulted.' A'isha said, 'But she is shy.' He said, 'If she remains silent, that is her consent.'" Concerning this *hadith*, Ibn al-Qayyim says,

> We adopt this fatwa. A virgin must be consulted concerning her marriage. There is a sound tradition that the Prophet [s] said, "The formerly married woman has more right to herself than her guardian, and the virgin's consent is to be sought from her, and her consent is her silence." In one version it reads, "The virgin's permission is sought by her father, and her permission is her silence." It is related in al-Bukhari and Muslim that the Prophet [s] said, "Do not marry off a virgin girl until her permission is sought." They asked, "How is her permission given?" He replied, "By remaining silent." Also, a young virgin woman told him that her father married her off and she was averse to the marriage, so the Prophet [s] gave her the choice of whether or not to remain married. So he ordered guardians to acquire the consent of virgins, forbade marrying them off without it, and gave an option to whoever had been married without having their permission sought. How then can we ignore all of this and go against it?[67]

The attention that Islam pays to choice of spouse is, in effect, a concern for the nucleus of the family. Family begins with a man and a woman who come together with a great deal of mutual understanding. This mutual understanding has an effect on the family when it grows and its members increase. Family is the essential building block of society, and upon this sound basis civilizations are established and values are elevated.

The words of Ahmed Shawqi, the Prince of Poets, bears witness to the importance of women in the foundation of Muslim society,

> Mothers are schools. If you prepare them,
> You prepare a people of goodly origins.

Just as Islam gave women the right to choose their husbands, it gave them the right to choose whether to remain with them. A woman has the choice to part from her husband when relations between them sour and reconciliation cannot be reached. Divorce

---

67. Muhammad ibn Abi Bakr al-Zar'i b. al-Qayyim AL-JAWZIYYAH, *'Ilam al-Mawqa'in*. Dar al-Kutub al-'Ilmiyyah, 4:260-1.

was incorporated into the law for the benefit of women and men alike. One of the widespread misconceptions about Islam's family structure is the assumption that only men have the right to initiate divorce. The truth, however, is quite different.

Islamic law gives women the right to end a marriage just as it gives that right to men. Islamic law allows women to end a marriage in a number of ways: A woman has the right to include a condition in the initial marital contract giving herself the right to pronounce divorce unilaterally whenever she likes. In this case it is as if her husband had divorced her and she remains entitled to all of her rights[68] without her material compensation diminishing in any way. A woman may also request to be separated from her husband due to harm. If the man has inflicted great harm on his wife, a judge will separate them and she will be entitled to all of her rights without exception. A married woman may also seek *khul'*. Only in this case does she separate from her husband and forego her rights to certain monies due to the absence of a reason for ending the marriage. As such, it would not be fair to impose dues on the man when he is still willing to continue the relationship.

Many religious texts point to these different ways of granting women the option to independently determine separation. For example, Ibn 'Abbas [r] related,

> Barira's husband was a slave called Mughith. It is as if I can see him now following her and weeping, the tears moistening his beard. The Prophet [s] told 'Abbas [r], "O 'Abbas, do you not marvel at the love of Mughith for Barira and the dislike of Barira for Mughith?" So the Prophet said to her, "Would you take him back?" She said, "O Messenger of God, are you commanding me?" He said, "I only intercede." She said, "I have no need for him."[69]

When she understood that the Prophet's words were advice and not a command, she chose to leave her husband since that was her right after becoming free.[70]

---

68. Such as her dowry, etc. [Trans.]

69. AL-BUKHARI, *Sahih Bukhari*, 5:2023; AL-SIJISTANI, *Sunan Abi Dawud*, 2:207; Ahmad ibn Shu'ayb AL-NASA'I, *Sunan al-Nasa'i (al-Mujtaba)*. Maktabat al-Matbu'at al-Islamiyyah, 8:245.

70. If a slave woman is married to a slave man and the woman is freed she has the right, according to Islamic law, to choose to separate from her

The wife of Thabit ibn Qays came to the Prophet [s] and said, "O Messenger of God, there is none more steadfast than Thabit when it comes to religion and morals, but I do not love him." He said, "Will you return his garden to him?" She said, "Yes," and gave him back his garden and he was ordered to part with her.[71]

This is a brief clarification of the issue of women choosing their own husbands and having their desires respected if they want to part with them. In conclusion, we reiterate that it is impermissible for a father, or anyone else for that matter, to force his son or daughter to marry someone, and women have the right to end marriage in the ways mentioned. And God is Most high and knows best.

---

husband. [Trans.]

71. AL-BUKHARI, *Sahih Bukhari*, 5:2022.

Question 16:

How can Islamic law be applied in modern times, and what percentage of the entire body of Islamic Law do corporal punishments (*hudud*) represent?

The issue of implementing Shari'ah needs to be understood in a broad context. Unfortunately, both Muslim and non-Muslim contemporary literature restrict their discussion of contemporary Shari'ah to the topic of corporal punishments (*hudud*). In addition, a given society is often unjustly described as not implementing the Shari'ah simply because some of its rulings are absent in daily life. Yet the application of Shari'ah is multifaceted and characterized by different degrees of implementation; for this reason, the absence of rulings have occurred in varying ways and degrees all through the course of Islamic history and in every Muslim land and regime. Not a single Muslim scholar has ever accused a Muslim community of becoming disassociated with Islam for not implementing the Shari'ah. In fact, one might claim that the term "implementation of the Shari'ah" is a modern expression.

Some important facts concerning the Shari'ah:

1) The Shari'ah refers to a worldview based on the beliefs that this universe has a Creator, that human beings are held legally responsible for their actions, that this responsibility arises from the revelation that God sent with His Messengers and revealed in His Books, and that there is a Day of Judgment when rewards and punishments will be meted out. The Shari'ah also includes jurisprudence, which regulates personal, communal, and societal conduct, a system of ethics, the means for spiritual development, intellectual and interpretive methodologies for dealing with revelation in the form of both the Quran and the Sunnah, and methodologies for dealing with the world, no matter how it changes and no matter how complex it becomes.

2) The issue of corporal punishment (*hudud*) has two aspects. The first is the belief in the preeminence of the penal system in deterring crime and asserting the gravity of these sins in their grossness and their negative impact on society. Belief in corporal punishment constitutes a personal rejection of these crimes in all their forms. The extremity of the

punishment underlines the extremity of the crimes for which it is prescribed; the penal system is not inherently unjust or violent in and of itself. This brings us to the second aspect of corporal punishment: Islamic law has set conditions for the implementation of corporal punishments and has also delineated certain situations in which their implementation would be temporarily halted or suspended. The implementation of corporal punishments in these situations or in the absence of its requisite conditions would constitute a departure from the Shari'ah.

3) Anyone who closely examines the Islamic legal sources will find that corporal punishments were not instituted for the purpose of revenge, but to deter crimes before they were committed. One will also find that Islamic law does not aspire to implement punishment as much as it aspires to pardon, forgive, and protect citizens from committing crimes in the first place. Numerous texts attest to this.

4) Corporal punishments have not been implemented in countries such as Egypt for over one thousand years. This is because the legal conditions for their implementation, which describe specific means for establishing guilt and stipulate the possibility of retracting a confession, are not met. The saying of the Prophet [s] sums this up, "Stay the enforcement of corporal punishments when there is doubt."[72] He also said, "To err in pardoning is better than to err in punishing."[73]

5) The characteristics of a certain era may necessitate the general application of exceptions, even though exceptions, by

---

72. Muhammad ibn 'Abd al-Baqi AL-ZURQANI, *Mukhtasar al-Maqasid*, 71:42, AL-'ASQALANI, *al-Talkhis al-Habir*, 4:56.

73. AL-TIRMIDHI, *Sunan al-Tirmidhi*, 4:33; AL-BAYHAQI, *al-Sunan al-Kubra*, 8:238, AL-HAKIM, *al-Mustadrak 'ala al-Sahihayn*, 4:426; and al-Tirmidhi added a comment saying, "We do not know this *hadith* as being ascribed directly to the Prophet except through the *hadith* of Muhamad ibn Rabi'ah according to Yazid ibn Ziyad al-Damishqi according to al-Zuhri according to 'Arwah according to Aishah according to the Prophet [s]. Waqi' narrated a similar *hadith* according to Yazid ibn Ziyad, but did not ascribe it directly to the Prophet [s]. The narration of Waqi' is more authentic and it has been related that one of the Prophet's companions said something similar." And al-Hakim commented, "Its chain of transmission (*isnad*) is authentic, but they [i.e., Bukhari and Muslim] did not narrate it."

their nature, are to be applied only to isolated cases. An age of necessity, an age of doubt and uncertainty, an age of discord, and an age of ignorance are examples of eras whose character-istics have an effect on legal rulings. Necessity permits the im-permissible even if it becomes prevalent and ongoing, which is why scholars permitted burial in crypts (*al-fasaqi*) in Egypt despite its contradiction of Shari'ah. Uncertainty justified a stay of corporal punishment as in the time of 'Umar ibn al-Khattab [r]; during a year of drought, uncertainty became so widespread that the legal prerequisite for enforcing corporal punishments was non-existent. Imam J'afar al-Sadiq and al-Kirkhi from the Hanafi school, among others, maintained that the impermissibility of looking at improperly clothed women was not applicable in the countries of Middle Asia[74] because women do not wear hijab there, and thus lowering one's gaze became difficult, if not impossible. In his book *al-Ghayathi*, Imam al-Juwayni illustrated the different courses of action that people are to take during times of ignorance character-ized by the absence of scholars capable of deriving the law directly from its sources (*mujtahids*), the absence of religious scholars, and the absence of the sources of the law.

Linked to this is what scholars of juristic methodology, like al-Razi in the *al-Mahsul*, referred to in their books as "rational abrogation," which is the result of the disappearance of the ob-ject (*al-mahal*) in the ruling. "The disappearance of the object (*al-mahal*) in the ruling," is a more precise term since, accord-ing to the consensus of the community, reason cannot abro-gate firmly established rulings. The ruling is not implement-ed if its object no longer exists. For example, the command to make ablutions stipulates washing the hands to the elbow, but if one's arm has been amputated this becomes impossible. Similar rulings include those based on having slaves, the Ca-liphate's supreme office of governorship (*al-khilafah al-kubra*), and the use of gold and silver currency.

6) In order to implement the legal rulings as God intended, in obedience to God and His messenger [s], we must under-stand the reality in which we live. Similar advice was given to

---

74. This includes countries such as present-day Kazakhstan, Uzbeki-stan, Turkmenistan, Tajikistan.

David's people, as related in *Shu'ab al-Iman* according to Wahb ibn Munabih, "The intelligent person should have knowledge of his era, hold his tongue, and embrace his role."[75]

The jurists clearly stated that rulings are open to the change of times if they were originally based on custom (see the text of Article 90 of *Majallahh al-Ahkam al-'Adliyyah*). In the sphere of monetary transactions, the Hanafi school permitted legally invalid transactions to be conducted in non-Muslim lands. In this case the ruling changed in accordance with the change in location. An important legal maxim states, "Necessity permits the impermissible." This is derived from God's saying, *But he who is driven by necessity, neither craving nor transgressing, it is no sin for him. Lo! God is Forgiving, Merciful* [2:173]. Thus matters may differ depending on their circumstances. These rulings also change with regard to individuals. Rulings pertaining to an actual person who is a singular entity with communicative capacity are different from those pertaining to a collective legal entity (*al-shakhsiyyah al-'itibariyyah*) that has no singular communicative presence. Al-Qarafi cited time, place, persons, and states as the four aspects of change that must be taken into consideration when rulings are applied to social reality.

In this age of ours, yesterday does not survive and today does not live through tomorrow. There are many reasons for this pace of change; mass communication, transportation, and modern technologies have united the world into a single village. The exponential growth in population, which has not decreased since 1830, also contributes to these changes that many refer to as globalization. Many intellectual disciplines have developed to study the interior states of human beings, their roles as members of society, and their behavior living under the conditions that we have mentioned. The characteristics of this age have changed many concepts, such as the concepts of contracts, liability, delivery of goods, usufruct, and legal politics. We must realize all of this in order to avoid missing the greater goals of the Shari'ah.

7) We can examine the attempts of modern Islamic countries to implement corporal punishments:

---

75. AL-BAYHAQI, *Shu'ab al-Iman*, 4:165.

i) We find that Saudi Arabia implements corporal punishment directly through Islamic courts without legal texts
formulated as laws for a penal code. The Saudi implementation of corporal punishment is firmly established and there
are no effective calls or approaches to cancel or halt it. However, there are some appeals from those who oppose the Saudi
political system and who seek to regulate its procedures. They
describe the current system as unjust and an infringement on
human rights.

ii) Then there is the situation in Pakistan, Sudan, one of
the states of Nigeria, one of the states of Malaysia, and Iran, all
of whose legal codes include Islamic corporal punishment. The
practical application of corporal punishment has been halted
in Pakistan. Its application was suspended in Sudan after the
reign of al-Namiri. It has been suspended in Iran and Malaysia, and is implemented in one state of Nigeria in an extremely
limited manner. In all of these countries, judicial castigation
(*t'azir*) is commonly used instead of the execution of fixed leg-
islative castigation (*hudud*), except in the case of crimes that
necessitate execution.

iii) The penal codes of the remainder of the Islamic countries, which number fifty-six out of the one hundred ninety-six
countries of the world, remain silent on the issue of corporal
punishment (*hudud*). This is because our age is one of general
uncertainty (*shubha*), and the Prophet [s] said, "Stay the enforcement of corporal punishments when there is doubt."[76]
Furthermore, the legally accepted witnesses needed to con-
vict offenders in capital cases necessitating corporal punishment have not existed for a long time. Al-Tanukhi relates in
his book *Mishwar al-Muhadara*, "A judge used to enter a district
or a village and find forty witnesses of the sort with whom we
are satisfied as to their being just and accurate, while today a
judge enters a town and only finds one or two witnesses." Thus
our age could be generally described as one in which there are
no witnesses.

Investigations undertaken to uncover crimes, which lead to the implementation of corporal punishments, are not part of the method

---

76. AL-ZURQANI, *Mukhtasar al-Maqasid*, 71:42, AL-'ASQALANI, *al-Talkhis al-Habrir*, 4:56.

of the Shari'ah. During the lifetime of the Prophet Muhammad [s], Ma'iz confessed to having committed adultery and the Prophet [s] turned his face away from him four times. He then turned him over to his family in the hopes that they would testify that he was mentally impaired or insane. When that could not be established, he sought loopholes for him, and when Ma'iz recanted while the punishment was being carried out, the Prophet [s] said to 'Umar [r], "Why did you not let him go?"[77] From this exchange, the scholars understood that it is permissible to go back on one's confession as long as the crime has to do with transgressing the rights of God, as opposed to the rights of human beings. It must also be noted that the Prophet [s] never asked about the other party participating in the crime, nor did he seek her out even to complete the investigation. Along similar lines, Abu Bakr, 'Umar, Abu Darda', and Abu Hurayra would say to the thieves brought before them, "Have you stolen? . . . Say, 'No!'"[78]

The textual evidence for corporal punishments essentially points to the gravity of the sin for which the punishments were legislated and that they require this severe form of punishment. This results in preventing people from committing these crimes. God says, *In this way does God imbue His servants with fear. O My servants, be then conscious of Me!* [39:16]. Corporal punishments help maintain the social order born of the dominant culture. This culture views these sins as enormous and repudiates those who have been known to commit them, as well as those who have made their sins public or exhibited pride in committing them. At the same time, the Shari'ah leaves the door of repentance open and encourages the concealment of sin in many texts found in the Quran and the Sunnah.

With this brief overview, we have shown the legal origins of the Shari'ah and provided a description of its implementation, as well as the way in which this is played out in reality, and the place of corporal punishments therein. And God is Most High and knows best.

---

77. The report is found in a shorter form in Bukhari and Muslim, but this version comes from IBN HANBAL, *Musnad Imam Ahmad*, 5:216, AL-SIJISTANI, *Sunan Abi Dawud*, 4:154, and AL-TIRMIDHI, *Sunan al-Tirmidhi*, 4:36 who declared it a fair *hadith*.

78. AL-SAN'ANI, *Musannaf 'Abd al-Razzaq*, 10:224; 'Abdullah ibn Muhammad b. Abi Shaybah AL-KUFI, *Musannaf ibn Abi Shaybah*. Maktabat al-Rushd, 5:519-20.

Question 17:

What is the extent of al-Azhar's authority? To what degree do its rulings agree or disagree with the Shiites?

The Quran and the pure Prophetic Tradition are the basis of authority and judgment in Islam. The average Muslim does not have a critical understanding of the Quran and the Prophetic Tradition because that requires the study of other subjects, such as the branches of the Arabic language including grammar, morphology, and rhetoric; the sciences of the Quran, such as the circumstances of revelation and the rules and different styles of recitation; the sciences of the Shari'ah, such as jurisprudence and juristic methodology; and the sciences of theology and logic. The Muslim scholars of every era are those who have transmitted the religious tradition, and they are the ones entitled to speak in its name because of their knowledge of religious law and its correct transmission. They transmit the Divine Revelation along with its interpretation, the traditions of those who proceeded, and the means of reconciling differing opinions and identifying correct ones.

As the oldest institution of learning that teaches religion, promulgates the Islamic faith, and gathers together a great number of Muslim scholars specializing in various Islamic sciences, al-Azhar is considered one of the most important authorities. It comprises institutions of learning such as the Islamic Research Council, a subsidiary of al-Azhar that is headed by the Grand Imam[79] Dr. Ahmad al-Tayyib. The Sheikh of the Azhar Mosque is considered one of the greatest religious authorities in the Islamic world, alongside the muftis of Islamic countries and the *fiqh* councils such as the Islamic Fiqh Council of Jeddah, which falls under the Organization of the Islamic Conference. Authority belongs to the Quran and the Prophetic Tradition, from which it is given to religious scholars, and from whom it is given to the councils we have mentioned.

The Sunnis and the Shiites have some great differences concerning secondary matters, but there endures a movement to bring the Sunnis and Shiites closer. They are in agreement when it comes to theology: there is no divergence in their convictions concerning God, the Prophet [s], revelation, or belief in the unseen. Shiites have lived alongside Sunnis for centuries in countries like

---

79. This title is traditionally used to refer to the Sheikh al-Azhar.

Saudi Arabia, the Gulf Countries, Iraq, Yemen, and Pakistan. I do not think that Shiites believe that Sunnis are not Muslims, nor, of course, do I think that Sunnis believe that Shiites are not Muslims. At the same time we cannot deny the differences between these schools.

The J'afari and Zaydi schools are the foundations of the Shiite schools, yet Sunni scholars also consult their positions when deriving rulings. These schools have been taught for centuries in al-Azhar, the oldest institution of learning, which has been in the business of education for over one thousand years and is considered to adhere to Sunnism.

We hold that the Shiites are a part of the Muslim community (al-ummah al-islamiyyah) and cannot be separated from it or eschewed. Any appearance that Muslims believe otherwise owes to the lack of understanding of ignorant people and non-specialist zealots. Those who have specialized in the study of theology and social reality know that Islam is vaster than Sunnism alone, encompassing not just the Sunnis and the Shiites but also other categories of believers. And God is Most High and knows best.

Question 18:

Some people claim that Islam infringes on freedom of belief by permitting the execution of apostates. Is this true?

The issue of executing apostates is misunderstood by Westerners who think that Islam compels people to follow it. They disregard the Muslim doctrine of freedom of belief expressed by God's words, *There is no compulsion in religion. Truth stands out clear from error* [2:256].

The issue of executing apostates may be examined from two vantage points. The first is the theoretical legal text that permits the execution of Muslims who leave their religion and divide the community.[80] The second examines both the implementation of the law and the method of dealing with apostasy in the time of the Prophet [s] and the early Caliphs.

In his own time, the Prophet [s] did not have 'Abdallah ibn Ubay executed even though he said, "If we were to return to Medina the mightier would expel the weaker."[81] Likewise, he did not execute Dhu al-Khuwaysirah al-Tamimi for his words, "Be just! You have not been just."[82] He also did not order the execution of the person who told him, "They say you eschew transgression, but transgression is your constant companion,"[83] nor the one who said to him, "God's pleasure was not sought in this allotment."[84] Similarly, he did not execute the one who told him, "You would not have given Zubayr to drink first if he had not been your cousin,"[85] or the others who insulted and disrespected him. All of these utterances constitute apostasy, for they involve accusations that negate the integrity and justice of the Prophet [s].

---

80. IBN HANBAL, *Musnad Imam Ahmad*, 1:381, AL-BUKHARI, *Sahih Bukhari*, 6:2521, AL-NAYSABURI, *Sahih Muslim*, 3:1302.

81. AL-BUKHARI, *Sahih Bukhari*, 6:2636; AL-NAYSABURI, *Sahih Muslim*, 2:1006.

82. AL-BUKHARI, *Sahih Bukhari*, 3:1296; AL-NAYSABURI, *Sahih Muslim*, 4:2140.

83. IBN HANBAL, *Musnad Ahmad*, 5:2.

84. AL-BUKHARI, *Sahih Bukhari*, 3:1249; AL-NAYSABURI, *Sahih Muslim*, 2:739.

85. IBN HANBAL, *Musnad Ahmad*, 1:185, AL-BUKHARI, *Sahih Bukhari*, 2:832, AL-NAYSABURI, *Sahih Muslim*, 4:1829, as well as the rest of the six canonical books of *hadith*.

By not executing those mentioned and others, Islam avoided repelling people and instead attracted more followers both in the Prophet's [s] lifetime and after his passing. If people had heard that he had his companions executed, they would have fled from him; he alluded to this possibility when 'Umar suggested that he should have 'Abdallah ibn Ubayy executed. The Prophet's [s] response was, "Let it not reach people that Muhammad kills his companions."[86] He also did not avenge himself by punishing the hypocrites, although God gave him permission to do so in Surah al-Ahzab, *If the hypocrites, and those in whose hearts is a disease, and the alarmists in the city do not cease, We verily shall urge you on against them, then they will be your neighbors in it but a little while. Accursed, they will be seized wherever found and slain with a [fierce] slaughter* [33:60-61].

Jabir ibn 'Abdallah related that a man from the desert pledged allegiance to the Prophet [s]. The man later fell ill and came to the Prophet [s] saying, "Release me from my pledge," but the Prophet [s] refused. The man came again to him and said, "Release me from my pledge," but he refused. The man came a third time and said, "Release me from my pledge," but he refused. When the man left the Prophet [s] said, "Medina is like a bellows, it removes its filth and makes plain its goodness."[87] The Prophet [s] did not have him executed. Why did he not execute all of these to whom apply the words of our Lord, *They have said words of disbelief and become disbelievers after having accepted the faith* [9:74]?

During the reign of the rightly guided caliphs, and more specifically during the reign of 'Umar al-Faruq [r], it is related that Anas [r] returned from Tustar and was approached by 'Umar who asked him, "What happened to the six men from Bakr ibn Wa'il, who apostatized from Islam and joined the polytheists?" He responded, "O Commander of the Faithful, a group of people apostatized from Islam, joined the polytheists, and were killed in battle." 'Umar said, "Verily we are unto God, and to Him we are returning." Anas asked, "Was their fate other than to be killed?" 'Umar replied, "Yes. I would have given them the chance to renew their Islam, and if they refused I would have put them in prison."[88] 'Umar did not

---

86. AL-BUKHARI, *Sahih Bukhari*, 6:2636; AL-NAYSABURI, *Sahih Muslim*, 2:1006.

87. AL-BUKHARI, *Sahih Bukhari*, 6:2540.

88. AL-BAYHAQI, *al-Sunan al-Kubra*, 8:207.

think it was necessary to have them executed even though they were apostates and fought against the Muslims.

These examples from the age of legislation caused Muslim jurists to understand the issue of "executing apostates" as being unrelated to freedom of belief, freedom of thought, or persecution. The source texts that strictly called for the imposition of such a punishment do not refer to leaving Islam as much as coming out against Islam. Coming out against Islam is considered a crime against the public order of the state, just as it represents a coming out against the rulings of the religion that have been embraced by the community. In this case apostasy is tantamount to high treason, which is forbidden by all legal systems, constitutions, and laws.

Sheikh Shaltut, former Sheikh of the al-Azhar Mosque (may God have mercy on him), held the opinion that the execution of apostates was not a corporal punishment (*hadd*). He said,

> The perspective from which this issue is looked at may change under the consideration that many scholars uphold that corporal punishments cannot be affirmed by reports lacking corroborative continuity, and that disbelief (*kufr*) alone does not make the shedding of one's blood permissible. The ruling on apostates targets those who fight against the Muslims, attack them, and attempt to separate them from their religion. The apparent meaning of the verses of the Quran rejects compulsion in religion.[89]

The execution of apostates was not just for apostasy. Rather, it was due to an additional factor that divides the Muslim community: using apostasy to cause Muslims to leave their religion. This act of dividing the community is considered an act of war against the religion, as God said, *And a party of the People of the Scripture says: Believe in that which has been revealed at the opening of the day, and disbelieve at the end thereof, in order that they may return* [3:72]. This is also supported by Ibn Taymiyyah's statement, "The Prophet [s] accepted the repentance of some apostates and ordered the execution of others whose apostasy was compounded by doing wrong and causing harm to Islam and Muslims. For example, he ordered the

---

89. Muhammad SHALTUT, *al-Islam 'Aqidah wa Shari'ah*. Dar al-Qalam, p. 103.

execution of Miqyas ibn Hubabah the day Mecca was conquered because, in addition to his apostasy, he had killed Muslims and taken property without repenting before his capture. The Prophet [s] ordered the execution of Al-Quraniyyun when they compounded their apostasy with similar crimes. He ordered the execution of Ibn Khatal when he compounded his apostasy with cursing the Prophet and the murder of Muslims. He also ordered the execution of Ibn Abi al-Sarh when he compounded his apostasy with defamation and slander."[90]

It is clear that the issue of executing apostates is not actually applied in the reality of everyday life. This ruling is found in the sources of law not as a punishment preventing freedom of thought and belief, but rather as something that is subject to administrative law. And God is Most High and knows best.

---

90. Ahmad ibn 'Abd al-Halim IBN TAYMIYYAH, *al-Sarim al-Maslul*. Maktabat al-Tajj, p. 368.

Question 19:

Western media often blames Islam for terrorism instead of focusing on the specific circumstances and individuals responsible for the acts. How has Islam dealt with the issue of terrorism?

Terrorism cannot be born of religion. Terrorism is the product of corrupt minds, hardened hearts, and arrogance, and these attributes are unknown to the heart attached to the Divine.

Islam is a religion of tolerance that espouses peaceful coexistence with all of humanity both as individuals and as communities. Islam views people as honored creatures regardless of their religion, race, or color. God says, *Verily We have honored the Children of Adam. We carry them on the land and the sea, and We have made provision of good things for them, and We have preferred them above many of those whom We have created with a marked preferment* [17:70]. Islam puts forth a code of ethics for Muslims to apply towards their non-Muslims neighbors with whom they live in the same society: *God forbids you not, with regard to those who fight you not for [your] Faith nor drive you out of your homes, from dealing kindly and justly with them: for God loves those who are just,* [60:8]. God commands us in this verse to act well towards non-Muslims and to avoid harming them. He says, "Show them kindness," for kindness (*birr*) is all that is good. In this sense God commands cooperation with non-Muslims in all avenues of good.

Anyone who truly knows Islam is aware of its concern for global peace. Peace (*al-Salam*) is one of the main pillars of Islam and it is one of the names and attributes of God Most High. He said, *He is God, other than Whom there is no god, the Sovereign Lord, the Holy One, Peace, the Keeper of Faith, the Guardian, the Majestic, the Compeller, the Superb. Glorified be God from all that they ascribe as partner [unto Him]* [59:23]. He made "peace" His salutation to His servants and enjoined them to make it their salutation as well. Peace has been the distinguishing mark of Muslims in the East and the West from the advent of Islam to this day. Whether in mosques, schools, factories, or the marketplace, Muslims say "Peace be upon you" both when they greet each other and when they part company. Paradise is named the Abode of Peace: He said, *For them is the Abode of Peace with their Lord. He will be their Protecting Friend because of what they used to do,* [6:127]. "Peace" is mentioned in numerous verses of the Quran.

This peace and security is not limited to Muslims alone. Muslims believe that all people, regardless of their faith, always posses the right to live in peace and security in Muslim lands. Protecting others from oppression within one's borders is not just emphasized in Islam but is mandatory. Muslims are forbidden to harm or display animosity, either by word or deed, towards those under their protection. God does not love or guide oppressors; He punishes them for such transgressions while they are still on earth, or else leaves them to be punished doubly in the Afterlife.

The Quranic verses and hadiths that mention the impermissibility, grossness, and the ill effects of oppression are many. There are hadiths that specifically warn against oppressing non-Muslims who are under the protection of Muslims or possess treaties with them. The Prophet [s] said, "Whoever wrongs someone with whom the Muslims have a treaty, denies them their rights, burdens them beyond their capacity, or takes something from them without their consent, I am that person's witness on the Day of Judgment."[91]

Islam encourages peace and security in order to make life stable for humanity and promote advancement in all fields. To fully comprehend the role of peace and security in the advancement of humanity, we need only to consider the destructive effects of war on peoples' advancement and development. As the saying goes, "The good of something is revealed by its opposites." Some of the most basic components of community development and advancement are the health and physical well being of the individuals of the society that allow them to fulfill their roles. Wars and economic sanctions have a devastating effect on the prosperity of a community.

Prior to Islam, tolerance for adherents of other religions by a victorious people devoted to a particular religion was uncommon. This is something to which Westerners themselves bear witness and many Europeans who have studied the history of the Arabs have realized the extent of Muslim tolerance. It is both false and unjust to brand Islam the cause of terrorism just because some acts of violence are perpetuated by groups who associate themselves with Islam. If an individual's actions were always considered to represent his faith, then this claim would be a call for the destruction of all religions.

---

91. AL-SIJISTANI, *Sunan Abi Dawud*, 3:170; AL-BAYHAQI, *al-Sunan al-Kubra*, 5:205.

For example, we know that Christianity calls for love and that its followers were oppressed at a time when they were weak. Thus we cannot consider the repression and torture of Muslims and Jews by the Church in Spain to be the result of Christian teachings. The Church took out its anger on the Jews and Muslims due to the spread of the philosophy and thought of Ibn Rushd (Averroes), especially among the Jews, and ruled that all Jews who were not baptized were to be expelled from the country. They were allowed to sell their property if they wished, but they were not permitted to take any gold or silver with them when they left, thus they were forced to accept trade-goods in return for their property. The Jews left their properties behind in order to escape with their lives, and even so many were overcome by hunger and the hardship of the journey due to their poverty. The Church also ruled in 1052 CE that all Muslims should be expelled from Spain and its outlying lands if they did not submit to being baptized. Upon their departure, the Church forbade them from taking roads leading to Muslim lands, and whoever went against this order was killed.[92]

We are also loath to blame the teachings of Christianity for the Crusades; we attempt to differentiate between the true teachings versus the practices of certain Christian extremists and terrorists. Christians were targeted by the Spanish Inquisition as well. Sheikh Muhammad 'Abduh wrote, "The cruelty of the Inquisition was such that people of that time said it was nearly impossible to be a Christian and die at home in one's bed." He also says, "Between the years 1481 and 1808 CE the courts of the Inquisition judged 340,000 people, 200,000 of whom were burned alive."[93]

Of the examples much closer to us today are the number of Afghan villages that were completely destroyed in order to punish one person, and the fires that are still burning in Baghdad in order to punish one person who was falsely accused of possession of weapons of mass destruction. Similarly, the clear and unabashed terrorism carried out in the name of Zionism cannot be blamed on the teachings of Judaism, for all religions came as a mercy to people and a means of spreading justice and forgiveness among them.

---

92. Muhammad 'Abduh, *al-Islam wa al-Nasraniyyah*. 2nd ed. Dar al-Haddathah, p. 36-37.
93. Ibid., p. 715.

We cannot deny the acts of decimation and terror that occur in our secure lands. But these acts are merely the result of perverse minds, corrupted hearts, and arrogance. God says, *Behaving arrogantly in the land and plotting evil; and the evil plot only encloses the men who make it* [35:43]. In fact, the words of God seem to comment directly on terrorism when He says, *And of humanity there are those whose conversation of the life of this world please you [Muhammad], and they call God to witness as to that which is in their hearts; yet they are the most rigid of opponents. And when they turn away [from you] their effort in the land is to make mischief therein and to destroy the crops and the cattle; and God does not love mischief. And when it is said to them: "Fear God," pride takes them to sin. Hell will settle their account, an evil resting-place* [2:204-206].

We ask God to inspire us with guidance and to give peace to our children, our countries, and the entire Muslim community. And God is Most High and knows best.

Question 20:

Westerners repeatedly claim that Islam was "spread by the sword." How do Muslim scholars respond to this accusation? What is the truth concerning the jihad carried out by the Prophet [s], and what are the characteristics of Islamic jihad?

God Most High says, addressing His prophet Muhammad [s], *We have not sent you but as a mercy for all the worlds* [21:107]. This statement in the Quran is broad in its meaning. It encompasses all places so that no one place is specified to the exclusion of another. It encompasses all time so that no era is specified to the exclusion of another. It encompasses all conditions, those of peace and those of war, so that no condition is specified to the exclusion of another. It also considers all people, believers and non-believers, Arabs and non-Arabs, so that no one group of people is specified to the exclusion of another. Thus we are challenged to meditate on the meaning of this verse. *We have not sent you but as a mercy for all the worlds*; a mercy that is general and all-embracing, which is manifested in every incident in the Prophet's [s] life relating to creation and the people around him.

Jihad in Islam is warfare that is extremely pure, just, and noble. This is clear in both the theory and practice of Islam. Despite the great clarity of this reality, however, bigotry, a disregard for the reality of Islam, and the insistence to make it a party to conflict and an object of struggle has caused confusion regarding the meaning of jihad among Muslims to the point that it is popularly said that Islam was spread by the sword and that it calls for war and violence. The justice and evenhandedness, the distinguishing of matters from each other, the search for truth as it is, and the desisting from slandering others, all of which God has commanded in the Quran, collectively serve as a sufficient response to these allegations: *O People of the Scripture! Why do you confound truth with falsehood and knowingly conceal the truth?* [3:71].

The Prophet spent thirteen years calling people to God with wisdom and goodly exhortation, the result of which was that only the most outstanding of his followers entered Islam. Most of those who embraced Islam at this time were poor, and the Prophet did not have great wealth with which to seduce them. He had nothing but the call to God. The Muslims (especially the poor, slaves, and those without protectors) suffered such torture and hardship that not even the most sturdy of mountains could have borne it. But this did not turn them away from their religion, nor did it shake their faith. Rather, it made them hold more strongly to the truth, and they withstood their torments like heroes in spite of the paucity of their numbers and their abject poverty. There are no accounts of early Muslims abandoning their religion or being seduced by the polytheists to withdraw their belief. They were like pure gold, which is only made purer by fire, and like iron, which is only made stronger by being melted. Some of them even reached a state wherein they found pleasure in torment and sweetness in what was bitter. In light of these historical truths, is it correct to say that Muhammad could have coerced people and forced them to accept his religion through the use of force, terrorism, and the sword?

An examination of the verses of the Quran makes it clear that Islam stipulates only the fairest forms of warfare:

1) From the perspective of its means and goals.

2) From the perspective of its preconditions and guidelines.

3) From the perspective of the results that come from it.

Firstly, the goals of war in Islam are:

1) Self-defense and the suppression of military aggression.

2) To secure the freedom to call people to God and provide the opportunity for the weak who want to embrace it.

3) Seeking the retrieval of usurped rights.

4) Championing truth and justice.

Secondly, the conditions of jihad are:

1) Having nobility and clarity in both means and ends.

2) Fighting only with combatants and not aggressing against civilians.

3) If the enemy inclines towards peace with the Muslims and leaves off fighting, then aggression is impermissible except towards oppressors.

4) Prisoners must be protected and treated humanely.

5) The ecosystem must be preserved. This includes a pro-

hibition against killing animals without reason, burning trees, ruining crops and waters, polluting wells, and destroying homes.

6) Freedom of belief must be preserved for the residents of monasteries and temples, and they must not be attacked.

Thirdly, the effects of jihad are that:

1) It teaches a person to be bold, courageous, and chivalrous.

2) It removes the tyrants who are crouching on peoples' chests, which is an evil that leads to corruption on earth after its having been reformed.

3) It ensures justice and freedom for all humanity regardless of their religion.

4) It puts the greater good before one's own personal benefit.

5) It produces a preventative force that can protect people and their lands.

The truths about the battles of the Prophet [s] and the Islamic conquests are that:

1) The military expeditions of the Prophet [s] include approximately 80 military mobilizations, but actual fighting only occurred about seven times.

2) All of the enemy combatants were from the tribe of Mudar, paternal cousins of the Prophet, and none of the members of the Rabi'ah or Qahtan tribes fought.

3) The number of Muslims killed in all of these battles was 139. The number of polytheists killed was 112. Combined they come out to 250 deaths, which is the number of people killed in car accidents every year in a city of moderate size today. So the number of people killed on average in each of these eighty battles was 3.5. It is impossible that these numbers could have been a cause for the Arabs to change their religion and enter Islam with all that they possessed of strength and obstinacy in the face of war.

4) Islam spread organically thereafter, and the sword and coercion played no role in it whatsoever. The formation of family ties between Muslims and non-Muslims and emigration from the Hijaz to other parts of the world was largely responsible for Islam's spread.

The following are some facts concerning the spread of Islam: During the first one hundred years after the Prophet's emigration to Medina the extent of the spread of Islam outside the Arabian Peninsula was the following: In Persia (Iran) the Muslim population was 5%, in Iraq it was 3%, in Syria it was 2%, in Egypt it was 2%, and in Andalusia it was less than 1%.

The dates in which the Muslim population in these countries reached 25% are the following: Persia: 185 AH; Iraq: 225 AH; Syria: 275 AH; Egypt: 275 AH; Andalusia: 295 AH.

The dates in which the Muslim population in these countries reached 50% are the following: Persia: 235 AH; Iraq: 280 AH; Syria: 330AH; Egypt: 330AH; Andalusia: 355 AH.

The dates in which the Muslim population in these countries reached 75% are the following: Persia: 280 AH; Iraq: 320 AH; Syria: 385 AH; Egypt: 385 AH; Andalusia: 400 AH.

The circumstances of the spread of Islam include:

1) No genocide was committed.

2) Captives were treated well, given education, trained, and even placed in roles of political leadership during the period of Islamic history known as the Mamluk Period.

3) The religious pluralism of the Jews, Christians, Zorrastrians, as well as Hindus and other religions of South East Asia was preserved.

4) Freedom of opinion was acknowledged. Muslims never held a court of inquisition to try those who held opinions that differed from their own.

5) The Arabian Peninsula, the source of Islam's call, remained poor until oil was discovered in modern times.

These truths have remained throughout history and to this day. Contrarily the Islamic World has been the victim of occupation, genocide, displacement of its population, courts of inquisition, the crusades, and having people stolen from West Africa and being made slaves in North America. This is only mentioned for the purpose of comparing the purity of Islam and the wars carried out by others both historically and today.

This is the truth about the spread of Islam and the characteristics of jihad, and God is Most High and knows best.

Question 21:

There have been many recent calls to implement democracy in countries that lack it. What is the Islamic view of democracy?

The conventions of the Islamic state evolved from its beginning up until the end of the Ottoman Caliphate. Society became increasingly complex as academic institutions multiplied and knowledge became more specialized. Muslims initiated systems of administration that were in keeping with these developments. 'Umar ibn al-Khattab [r], the second Caliph, instituted the accounted book of the treasury (*Diwan*), and the minting of coins commenced with the Umayyad Dynasty in the 7th century CE. The Muslim state began to organize its military and paramilitary forces, separating them from the judicial and the administrative powers. Islam's clear framework is relevant to every era: the first Muslims to govern were guided by Islam despite their simplicity of societal structure and limited number of political offices, while Muslims of later eras also applied Islamic principles despite the complexity of their societies and the increased number of political offices.

Islam provided Muslims with political rights, the most apparent of which are the following:

1) The right to choose their own leaders and be satisfied with them. The legal tradition calls this "pledging allegiance" (*bay'a*).

2) The right to participate in matters concerning the entire community. Islam encourages this principle of council (*shura*).

3) The right to be appointed to political positions in the government or its agencies.

4) The right to advise their rulers, insisting that they do good, and forbidding them from doing wrong.

Political systems differ in their arrangement and implementation of political rights. Islam addresses the objectives of these rights, but it allows the system of application to be formed in accordance with the needs of each specific time and place. As for democracy, it is unthinkable that the democracy for which peoples in the West fought for so fiercely and struggled so bitterly in order to rid themselves of tyrants and despots could be evil or unbelief. Rather, the essence of democracy is the heart of Islam.

Islam is in agreement with the principle of choosing one's own ruler, as is evidenced by the right of the people to reject their imam, or "prayer leader." If Islam does not permit someone whom the people despise to lead them in prayer, then certainly it does not permit such a person to lead them in the political arena. People came up with various functions of democracy, such as elections, the solicitation of legal rulings, majority rule, multiple political parties, freedom of the press, an independent judiciary, and the right of the minority to protest. Western governments, who preceded us in this regard, invented all of these forms. However, it would have been more fitting for us as Muslims to have preceded them. Islam laid down the principles upon which the essence of democracy is based one thousand years before the first modern democracy.

Islam does not forbid taking a theoretical notion or practical solution from non-Muslims. The Prophet [s] got the idea to build a trench around Medina from the Persians. He had the idol-worshipping captives taken during the battle of Badr teach Muslims how to read and write. He adopted the practice of worldly kings and began to place a seal on his letters. The caliph 'Umar observed and replicated the account system of the public treasury and the taxation of land. We must understand that wisdom is the lost camel of the believer; wherever he finds it, he is most deserving of it.

Thus, calling for democracy does not necessarily involve considering the rule of the people as a substitute for the rule of God, for there is no contradiction between them. The type of democracy envisioned for Islamic countries manifests the governing principles of Islam by promoting the fair selection of a ruler, a system of consultation, the advising of leadership, the enjoinment of good and the forbidding of evil, and the resistance of tyranny. When Muslims demand democracy, they seek a means that aids them in the realization of a noble lifestyle and thus attracts others to God. It does not harm Muslims to employ Western terminology, such as "democracy," because the name itself does not determine the Islamic ruling on the matter. The ruling revolves around the deeper meaning comprised by the term and its signification.

In spite of all of this, we cannot consider the Islamic concept of council (*al-shura*) to be an exact duplicate of democracy. Muslims should not apply every aspect of Western democracy without careful consideration. They should accept truth in the ideas of others while rejecting anything that is false. Muslims should not simply imitate. They should benefit from the experiences of others while weighing those experiences against their sacred standards. That is, Muslims should weigh any new knowledge by the standards of the Shari'ah.

Both the proponents of Western democracy and Muslims agree that the products of human intellect are not all divinely sanctioned. Man's knowledge is subject to additions, changes, and refinement. Democracy, as it is understood in the West, must be adjusted to the Arab-Islamic context in order to better serve the people of this region. An Arab-Islamic democracy would be in accordance with the cultures and traditions of those implementing it and would thus assure them safety and stability.

The democracy that Islam approves and to which it calls does not make the fixed aspects of the community, like faith and custom, a point of debate and possible disposal. Just as Western democracy mandates the preservation of secularism, Muslims consider Islamic faith and the other fixed aspects of their society's religion and culture non-negotiable and necessary conditions for the democratic process.

As long as democracy does not infringe upon the rights of the population by undermining their identity and faith, and destabilizing their community values, it serves Islam and actualizes its goals. If, however, democracy is imposed by outsiders who seek to dominate populations and their systems, then it is just a tool of loathsome occupation. We ask God for security for our countries and ourselves. God is Most High and knows best.

Question 22:

Much debate surrounds the issue of female circumcision. Some claim that it cannot be prohibited by Islamic law. What is the truth?

Many people think that the issue of female circumcision was just raised recently, and some even claim that it was only brought up after the Population Conference in Cairo.[94] This is not the case. Sheikh Rashid Rida addressed the issue female circumcision in the journal *Al-Manar* in 1904 because even at that time people were asking whether or not it is mandatory. In an article titled "The Obligatory and Recommended Nature of Circumcision," he wrote, "Ibn al-Mundhir said, 'There are no reports upon which circumcision can be based, and no Prophetic example that can be followed. Those who say that it is Sunnah base this on the tradition reported by Usama found in the collections of Ahmad and al-Bayhaqi: Circumcision is recommended (*sunnah*) for men and it is an adornment (*makramah*) for women. But the transmitter of this tradition, al-Hajjaj ibn Artah, is a fabricator (*mudallis*).'"

In 1951, the Egyptian Minister of Health contacted Sheikh Mahmud Shaltut, asking him about the issue of female circumcision. Sheikh Shaltut was a member of the Association of Distinguished Scholars and a professor of Islamic Law at al-Azhar University who would later become Sheikh al-Azhar. He answered the Minister of Health on May 28, 1951 and his answer was published in the *al-Azhar* journal on page 21 of the 23rd issue of the year 1371 AH. Sheikh Shaltut clearly states, "The Shari'ah has established a general principle: if it has been proven by extensive research, and not by way of temporary opinions that are given in response to a particular conflict or in following the cultural practices of a specific group of people, that something is harmful to health or is a moral corruption, then it is mandatory, according to Islamic law, that the action in question be prevented in order to protect against the harm or the corruption. Until this is proven with regard to female circumcision, the practice should remain at the people's discretion, for that is what they have become accustomed to in the shade

---

94. The author is referring to The United Nations International Conference on Population and Development, which was held in Cairo, Egypt in September 1994. [Trans.]

of Islamic law and the teachings of religious scholars from the time of the Prophet [s] until our own times; that female circumcision is an adornment, not an obligation or a recommended action."

Other relevant comments follow this passage, but in the quote above we have an important maxim that displays the intellectual capabilities of a knowledgeable Muslim jurist. Earlier events led up to Sheikh Shaltut's article. In May of the same year, the journal *al-Duktur* printed a supplement on female circumcision in which they asked a group of doctors for their opinions and recommendations regarding the topic. The doctors all agreed that there is no need for female circumcision and also specified the harm that may result from the operation. However, truth be told, this opinion was based on the norms of their society and not on proven medical knowledge.

In the first issue of the fifth volume of *al-Liwa' al-Islami*, dated June 1951 (Ramadan 1370 AH), the journal carried out a survey of distinguished scholars. Following an extended discourse on the boundaries of commonly accepted knowledge, Sheikh Ibrahim Hamrush, a member of the Association of Distinguished Scholars and president of al-Azhar's fatwa committee, said, "And that which has to do with worldly matters are as we have been commanded, 'You are more knowledgeable about your worldly affairs,' thus it is permissible for her to not be circumcised, but in this case she would not have carried out the act of adornment (*makramah*). If one seeks a decision to prevent female circumcision, it must be known, according to correct means, that science establishes that there is harm in circumcising women; then it would be possible to say that it is forbidden." Professor 'Abd al-Wahhab Khalaf, Professor of Islamic Law at the Cairo University Law School, said, "Doctors need to expand the field of the survey and not judge the circumcision of girls to be harmful based on individual cases. They should compare the health of girls who have been circumcised and girls who have not been circumcised and, if at the completion of this survey the results are that the circumcision of girls is harmful to them and the doctors recommend prohibiting it, then there would be nothing in this prohibition that would contradict the evidence of religious texts or the consensus of Muslim jurists." Another distinguished scholar, Muhammad Bey al-Banna, delivered a long discourse in which he explained the difference of opinion between doctors. He said, "If a greater number took part in the manner that I have set forth—meaning in the form of a conference—the research would be more complete and substantial. The summation is that Muslims have a choice from a religious point of view and so the matter is left up to benefit, and sufficient research needs to be carried out by experts."

In the 10th issue of the 24th volume of *al-Azhar*, dated June 11, 1953 (Shawal 1372 AH), Sheikh Muhammad 'Arafah, the journal's editor-in-chief and a member of the Association of Distinguished Scholars, wrote on female circumcision, "Science says that it harms marital life and leads to the spread of drug use among men. If this is all established, then the matter is quite simple. There is nothing wrong with women who have not been circumcised, and as for those who have, the organ should not be entirely removed. If it were prohibited in Egypt, as is the case in a number of Muslim countries such as Turkey and Morocco, then there would be nothing wrong with that. And it is God who grants righteousness."

From this string of commentaries we see that female circumcision is an old issue. Sheikh Hasanayn Muhammad Makhluf spoke on the subject, as did Sheikh Sayyid Sabiq, and Sheikh Mahmud Shaltut reiterated his legal opinion in his 1959 book *al-Fatawa*, where he again mentions that there is nothing in law, morality, or medicine that calls for female circumcision or makes it necessary.

In the view of distinguished scholars, this matter clearly engages certain medical knowledge. Since medical knowledge of the past asserted that female circumcision is beneficial, the jurists of that era said that it was an adornment (*makrama*). The term "adornment" indicates that the practice was considered a cultural custom, to be followed by people in accordance with the scientific knowledge current to their era. The early scholars referred to female circumcision as an "adornment" not to promote it, but to deny it the status of a religious obligation or recommended action.

Female circumcision procedures fall into four categories. The doctors of the past, whose opinions formed the basis for Muslim jurists' "adornment" ruling, were referring to the first category in which a small incision is made but nothing is removed. As already stated, this first category of circumcision is a custom, and not one of the essential symbols of Islam. It is an "adornment" in that it has no place in Islamic law; it is based, rather, on the accepted scientific knowledge of a given time.

Therefore doctors today need to announce the findings of

their research and academic conferences. The decisions of the World Health Organization and the current practices of specialized doctors should also be consulted. All together, these sources would form the consensus of specific knowledge that Muslim legal scholars requested over fifty years ago, may God be pleased with them. If we follow the position established by proven medical discoveries, then we are also following those scholars who laid down our principles and led us to the clear path.

When we deal with an issue whose roots stretch back into history, and especially an issue as opaque as female circumcision, we require more clarity in order to affirm the truth. We elucidate the issue through the following arguments:

1) The scholars of *hadith* have affirmed that there are no sound hadiths enjoining female circumcision. All of the hadiths that have been related concerning this issue are weak and therefore cannot be used as evidence. It is sufficient to mention the valuable studies carried out by Shams al-Haqq al-ʿAdhim al-Ibadi in his commentary on *Sunan Abu Dawud* entitled *ʿAwn al-Maʿbud,* and by Imam al-Shawkani in his book *Nayl al-Awtar.* Al-ʿAdhim al-Ibadi said, "The *hadith* of female circumcision has been related by many different chains of narration, but all of them are weak and flawed and cannot be used as evidence."[95] Al-Shawkani says, "With the *hadith* being unsuitable as evidence, there is no evidence for it [female circumcision]."[96] A third commentary by Ibn al-Mundhir said, "There are no reports that can be relied on, and there is no Sunnah that can be followed in regards to female circumcision." Ibn al-Hajj made similar statements in *al-Madkhal.* All of these scholars make clear that female circumcision is a custom, and not an act of worship.

2) When we are asked about the legal status of female circumcision, we respond that it is an adornment, thus indicating that we have denied it the status of being obligatory or recommended. By denying the practice legal standing, we have designated it as a custom. If female circumcision is a customary practice, then it is up to the experts and the cultural milieu to determine its associated benefits or harms. Prior medical

95. Shams al-Haqq al-ʿAdhim ABADI, *ʿAwn al-Maʿbud.* 14:126.

96. Muhammad ibn ʿAli AL-SHAWKANI, *Nayl al-Awtar.* Dar al-Hadith, 1:191.

practitioners have said that is not harmful, while others stated there is no benefit in it, and still others held the opinion that it provided some benefit. Based on these medical opinions, the jurists said that female circumcision is an adornment. Some people mistook the jurists' term "adornment" to mean that the practice is desirable, but this is not the case. Jurists' use of the term adornment was based on medical opinion, not on Islamic law. Female circumcision cannot be substantiated by Islamic law because the *hadith* that mentions it is weak. If they were to use this *hadith* as evidence, then it would prove that the practice does not stem from the Shari'ah. The *hadith* that I am referring to is the one narrated by Ahmad and al-Bayhaqi that says, "Circumcision is recommended (*sunnah*) for men and is an adornment for women."

3) Medical knowledge has advanced such that specialists have now come to the consensus that female circumcision causes great harm. Doctors who go against this consensus are not specialists. We find them speaking in a non-scientific manner, and it may be that their opinion is the result of an unscientific attachment to prevalent cultural practices or the misconception that female circumcision is commanded by the Shari'ah.

We know that jurists, in many cases, link rulings to the position of medical experts. Imam al-Shafi'i says, speaking of the aversion to making ablutions with water that has been sitting in the sun, "I do not consider it to be disliked except from the perspective of medicine."[97] Similarly, when the jurists spoke of matters such as women's menstrual cycles and childbirth, they did so on the basis of medical investigation and empirical examinations. As is mentioned on page ninety-seven of the book *Fath al-Mannan Sharh al-Zubad li-Ibn Raslan*, that which does not have a guiding rule in law or in language derives its guide from the world as it is.

4) Our methodology is that we respect the knowledge that God has bestowed upon human beings. We do not desire to find fault with our predecessors, or to detract from their achievements. We respect them to the utmost, for they carried out their duties with a sound intellectual approach that was con-

---

97. Muhammad ibn Idris al-Shafi'I, *Kitab al-Umm*, Dar al-Qutaybah, 1:7.

sistent with the knowledge that God granted them.

We previously spoke of four kinds of circumcision. The first is that which the doctors of old endorsed. It is the kind referred to by the weak *hadith* in which the Prophet [s] commanded a woman who was carrying out circumcisions not to remove the organ. As stated by al-Mawardi in the quote that was mentioned by Ibn Hajar al-'Asqalani and followed by al-Nawawi, the intention is to incise, not to cut off the organ. The other three forms of circumcision constitute attacks on the female body and warrant punishment or compensation equal to that required for killing a person. While the first form is a custom associated with medical knowledge of the past, medical specialists have now come to the consensus that even the least invasive of the circumcision procedures causes harm. Thus it has become necessary to prevent female circumcision by saying that it is forbidden and to criminalize its practice. Contrary to some claims, this is not a criminalization of the Sunnah that has been left to us by the Prophet [s].

5) Some object that a number of great legal scholars of recent times, such as Sheikh Jad al-Haqq 'Ali Jad al-Haqq and Sheikh 'Atiyyah Saqar, issued fatwas decreeing that female circumcision is *sunnah* or obligatory. I say, with all assurance, that their approach was an attempt to maintain continuity and refrain from the blind following of others' opinions or desires. These scholars wanted to avoid abandoning something that we have inherited. If, however, they had seen the recent studies upon which I am basing my opinion, then they would have conceded to the agreement of the medical community just as they taught us to do.

6) Based on what I have said, I consider it necessary that scholars deem female circumcision forbidden according to the Shari'ah. We asked the medical community to look into this matter over fifty years ago. We asked them to come to agreement based on sound research rather than opinion and blind imitation, so they performed research and reached a consensus. We advised them to have conferences, so they gathered together and reconfirmed their position.

Our teachers have taught us that scholars of the Shari'ah must lift confusion and come together in agreement. The issue of female circumcision does not allow for much difference of opinion now that its facts have been brought to light. And God is Most High and knows best.

Question 23:

We read in the newspapers that you permit legally invalid transactions when they are undertaken in non-Muslim lands. If this is true, then what is the evidence for this fatwa?

Regarding this fatwa, I was asked about this matter a number of years before the newspapers reported on it. The fatwa had to do with Hajj and the wording of the question was as follows: Is it permissible to make Hajj with money that has been gained through invalid transactions like selling alcohol to non-Muslims and engaging in interest-based transactions with non-Muslims in their lands?

I answered:

Imams Abu Hanifa and Muhammad, as opposed to Abu Yusuf, maintained that the prohibition of *riba* (usurious interest) does not apply to transactions between Muslims and non-Muslims in non-Muslim lands. In addition, Muslims in non-Muslim lands may acquire the property of non-Muslims through any kind of transaction, including transactions prohibited by Islam, such as gambling, selling meat that has not been ritually slaughtered, or selling alcohol. Muhammad al-Shaybani said, "If a Muslim enters non-Muslim lands (*Dar al-Harb*) in safety, there is nothing wrong with him acquiring ownership of their property through any means to which they agree."[98] Then he said, "If a Muslim with safe passage amongst them were to trade a non-Muslim one dirham for two dirhams to be paid in one year, then return to our lands and then go back to them, or go back to them and take the dirhams after the passing of the year, then there is nothing wrong with that."[99] After mentioning the *mursal hadith*[100] narrated by Makhul, al-Sarakhsi said, "The ruling against engaging in interest-based transactions is inapplicable to transactions between Muslims and non-Muslims in non-Muslim lands. The *mursal hadith* narrated by Makhul serves as Abu Hanifa and Muhammad's evi-

---

98. AL-SARAKHSI, *Sharh al-Siyar al-Kabir*, 4:141.

99. Ibid., 4:148.

100. A *mursal hadith* is a tradition attributed to the Prophet [s] that lacks a chain of transmission reaching back to him. [Trans.]

dence for the permissibility of a Muslim selling a non-Muslim a dirham for two dirhams in non-Muslim lands . . . . Similarly, if the Muslim were to sell them meat that had not been ritually slaughtered, or had gambled with them and won money, that money would be acceptable according to Abu Hanifa and Muhammad."[101]

The position of Imams Abu Hanifa and Muhammad is the standard and accepted opinion of the Hanafi school of jurisprudence. After the preceding passage, Al-Sarakhsi said on behalf of the Hanafis, "Our evidence for this derives from what we have narrated and that which has been mentioned on the authority of Ibn 'Abbas and others: the Prophet [s] said in his sermon, 'All interest that occurred before Islam is invalid, and the first interest to be invalidated is that of al-'Abbas ibn 'Abd al-Muttalib.' After he embraced Islam, al-'Abbas returned to Mecca and engaged in interest. He did not conceal his actions from the Prophet [s], so the fact the Prophet did not forbid the transactions indicates that they had been permissible. He only invalidated what had not been collected before the conquest of Mecca."[102]

Al-Marghinani, al-Kamal ibn Humam, al-Haskafi, and Ibn 'Abdin all asserted, "There is no interest between Muslims and non-Muslims in non-Muslim lands."[103] They also mentioned that Muslims in non-Muslim lands may acquire the property of non-Muslims in any manner that does not involve deception.

The evident meaning of the Hanafi position is that the ruling is general and refers to Muslims both giving and receiving interest in non-Muslim lands. However, according to al-Kamal ibn Humam, in their lessons the Hanafi imams restricted the permissibility of interest to Muslims in non-Muslim lands receiving interest from non-Muslims and not to paying it. Ibn Humam explains, "But it is clear that this requires the permissibility of the transaction, meaning the transaction involving interest, only if the advantage goes

101. Muhammad ibn Ahmad b. Abi Sahal AL-SARAKHSI, *al-Mabsut*. Dar al- Ma'rifah, 14:56.

102. Ibid.

103. Abi Bakr ibn 'Ali al-Rashdani AL-MIRGHIANI. *al-Hidayah ma' al-Binayah*. Dar al-Fikr, 7:784-5; IBN AL-HUMAM, *Fath al-Qadir*, 6:177, Muhammad ibn 'Ali AL-HASFAKI, *al-Durr al-Mukhtar*. Dar al-Kutub al-'Ilmiyyah, 4:188, and IBN 'ABIDIN, *Rad al-Muhtar 'ala al-Dur al-Mukhtar*. 4:188.

to the Muslim. Interest, however, is more general than this as it includes cases wherein the two dirhams in return paid on one dirham go the Muslim as well as when they go to the non-Muslim. Addressing the issue as permissible is general and it includes both cases. Similarly, gambling might lead to a non-Muslim winning the wagered money. The evident meaning is that the permissibility only applies to situations in which a Muslim acquires the advantage. The disciples of Abu Hanifa stated in their lessons that their intention in permitting interest and gambling is for cases when a Muslim acquires financial advantage considering the *ratio legis,* even if the unqualified response indicates otherwise."[104] Ibn 'Abidin also reported this from Ibn Humam.[105] Rather, the ruling even includes the permissibility of selling alcohol, and the unqualified response, which includes the permissibility of the advantage going to a non-Muslim in these transactions, is the appropriate ruling for our age.

In support of their position, the Hanafis relied on the following evidence:

1) That which is mentioned according to Makhul that the Prophet [s] said, "There is no interest between a Muslim and a non-Muslim in non-Muslim lands."[106] Al-Sarakhsi said, "Even if the *hadith* is *mursal,* Makhul is a trustworthy jurist and *mursal* hadiths related by the likes of him are accepted."[107] Al-Marghinani also used this as evidence,[108] as did al-Kamal ibn Hum-

---

104. *Fath al-Qadir* vol. 6, p. 178.

105. *Hashiyah Ibn 'Abidin*, vol. 4, p. 188.

106. The *mursal hadith* of Makhul is mentioned by: Muhammad ibn Idris AL-SHAFI'I, *al-Umm.* Dar al-Kutub al-'Ilmiyyah, 7:359; Abu Yusuf in ABU YUSUF, *al-Radd 'ala Siyyar al-'Awza'i.* Dar al-Kutub al-'Ilmiyyah, 1:97; al-Hafidh in Ahmad ibn 'Ali b. Hajar AL-'ASQALANI, *al-Diriyah fi Takhrij Ahadith al-Hidayah.* Beirut: Dar al-Ma'rifah, 2:158; 'Abdallah ibn Yusuf AL-ZAYLA'I, *Nasb al-Rayah fi Takhrij Ahadith al-Hidayah.* Dar al-Hadith, 4:44; Ibn Qudmah AL-MAQDASI, *al-Mughni,* 4:47, but he said, "The best of them is *mursal* whose authenticity we do not know, and it could be interpreted as indicating a command to not engage in the act." It was used as evidence by the author of AL-SARAKHSI, *al-Mabsut,* 14:56.

107. Ibid., 14:56.

108. In the *al-Hidaya* (Muhammad ibn Ahmad 'AYNI and 'Ali ibn Abi Bakr AL-MARGHINANI, *al-Binayah Sharh al-Hidayah,* 7:384).

am.[109]

2) Muhammad used the hadith of Bani Qaynuqa' as evidence. When the Prophet [s] expelled this tribe from Muslim lands, they said, "We have debts whose payments are not yet due." He replied, "Take partial payment now or let them go." And when Bani al-Nadir were driven out, they said, "We have debts owed to us by the people." The Prophet told them, "Let them go or take partial payment now."[110]

Al-Sarakhsi clarified the evidentiary aspect of this hadith: "It is known that these kinds of transactions[111] are not permissible between Muslims. So if one is owed a debt by another for a certain period of time, it is not permissible to release the debt on the condition that some of it is paid before it is due. Umar, Zayd ibn Thabit, and Ibn Umar disliked this, so the Prophet [s] permitted it for them, since they had been people of war at the time, and for that reason they were driven out; then the Prophet [s] permitted it for them because they were people of war at the time, and it was for this that they were expelled. So we see that there are some things permissible between non-Muslims and Muslims which are not permissible between Muslims."[112]

3) The fact that the Prophet [s] wrestled Rukanah in Mecca supplies more evidence in support of the position above. Each of the three matches, the Prophet [s] wrestled him for a third of his small livestock, and if that sort of wager had been disliked, then the Prophet [s] would not have done it. When he wrestled him for the third time, Rukanah said, "Nobody has ever defeated me. It was not you who wrestled me." So the Prophet [s] returned his herd to him.[113] Al-Sarakhsi said, "Returning the

---

109. IBN AL-HUMAM, Fath al-Qadir, 6:178, and he related what al-Sarakhsi said concerning the hadith.

110. AL-TABARANI, Mu'jam al-Awsat, 1:249; AL-DARAQUTNI, Sunan al-Daraqutni, 3:46. It is related by al-Hakim in AL-HAKIM, al-Mustadrak 'ala al-Sahihayn, 2:60, and he said, "This hadith has an authentic chain of transmission, but they [Bukhari and Muslim] did not relate it."

111. Referring to the riba described by his words, "let them go or take partial payment now."

112. AL-SARAKHSI, Sharh al-Siyar al-Kabir, 4:1412.

113. The original hadith of the wrestling, without mention of it having been for sheep, was related by al-Hakim in AL-HAKIM, al-Mustadrak

sheep to him was graciousness on his part. The Prophet [s] did many such things with the polytheists to endear himself with them so that they would believe."[114]

4) Ibn 'Abbas and others related the Prophet's [s] words, "All interest that occurred in the pre-Islamic era is void, and the first interest to be voided is that of my uncle Al-'Abbas ibn 'Abd al-Muttalib."[115] After al-'Abbas was taken prisoner in the battle of Badr, and consequently embraced Islam, he asked the Prophet's [s] permission to return to Mecca as a Muslim. The Prophet [s] granted him permission, and Al-'Abbas engaged in interest-based transactions until the conquest of Mecca. His doing so was not kept secret from the Prophet [s], so his not having forbidden him from doing it indicates that it was permissible. Only the interest accrued in *Dar al-Harb,* and not collected before the conquest of Mecca, was voided, since Mecca had become an abode of Islam. This is why the Prophet [s] voided interest when Mecca was conquered.[116]

5) Before the emigration to Medina, Abu Bakr al-Siddiq gambled with the polytheists of Quraysh when God revealed

---

'ala al-Sahihayn, 3:511; Abu Dawud in AL-SIJISTANI, *Sunan Abu Dawud,* 4:55; AL-TIRMIDHI, *Sunan al-Tirmidhi,* 2:427; al-Bayhaqi in AL-BAYHAQI, *al-Sunan al-Kubra,* 10:18. The following scholars narrated it with the mention of sheep: AL-'ASQALANI, *al-Talkhis al-Habir,* 4:162 and he said, "The *hadith* about Rukanah was narrated by Abu Dawud and al-Tirmidhi through Abi al-Hassan al-'Asqalani, from Abu J'afar ibn Muhammad b. Rukanah." Ma'mar ibn RASHID, *Jami' Ma'mar ibn Rashid,* 11:427, Sulayman ibn al-Ash'ath (Abu Dawud) AL-SIJISTANI, *Marasil Abi Dawud.* Mu'assisah al-Risalah, 1:235, Ibn Mulaqqin AL-ANSARI, *Khulasat al-Badr al-Munir.* Riyadh: Maktabat al-Rushd, 2:405; AL-SHAWKANI, *Nayl al-Awtar,* 8:256 and he commented on it by saying, "It includes permission for Muslims and non-Muslims to wrestle as well as just Muslims, especially if a Muslim is challenged, not the challenger, and he wants to achieve some kind of good by putting down an arrogant person."

114. AL-SARAKHSI, *Sharh al-Siyar al-Kabir,* 4:1412; AL-SARAKHSI, *al-Mabsut,* 14:57.

115. AL-NAYSABURI, *Sahih Muslim,* 2:889; AL-SIJISTANI, *Sunan Abi Dawud,* 2:185; AL-BAYHAQI, *al-Sunan al-Kubra,* 8:5.

116. AL-SARAKHSI, *Sharh al-Siyar al-Kabir,* 4:1488, with its commentary, and AL-SARAKHSI, *al-Mabsut,* 14:75.

the verse, *Alif lam mim The Romans have been defeated* [30:1-2].[117]
The Quraysh asked, "Do you think that Rome will be defeated?"
Abu Bakr replied, "Yes." They said, "Do you want to bet on it?"
He assented and told the Prophet [s], who instructed him, "Go
back to them and increase the wager." Abu Bakr did so, and the
Romans were defeated by the Persians. Abu Bakr took his win-
nings and the Prophet [s] approved. This example shows that
gambling was sanctioned between Abu Bakr and the polytheists of Mecca when Mecca was an abode of polytheism.[118]

6) Also, because the property of non-Muslims is permissible, so it is a Muslim's right to acquire their property as long
as the acquisition is free from deceit, since the Shari'ah forbids
the acquisition of property through deceit.[119]

It should be noted that the Muslim jurists' use of the terms *Dar
al-Kufr* (the land of disbelief) and *Dar al-Harb* (the land of war) was
descriptive based on a specific historical context. The countries
referred to by these terms were hostile enemies of the Muslims,
waging war against them and driving them from their lands. This
happened during the Crusades, and again in Andalusia when the
Muslims were ethnically cleansed—forced either to convert or
leave the lands they had inhabited for hundreds of years. Some
countries were referred to as *Dar al-Kufr* because they prevented
Muslims from residing within their borders while practicing Islam.
The situation, however, has changed. Today we see that the world
does not prevent Muslims from taking up residence, practicing
their religion, expressing their beliefs freely, and establishing their
practices. There is also no open declaration of war against Islam
and the Muslims.

Therefore, today we prefer to use the term non-Muslim Lands
(*bilad ghayr al-Muslimin*) in order to reaffirm that the division is

---

117. This is the story of Abu Bakr wagering with Quraysh. It was related
by al-Tirmidhi in his AL-TIRMIDHI, *Sunan al-Tirmidhi*, 5:342, and he said
it was *hasan gharib*.

118. IBN AL-HUMAM, *Fath al-Qadir*, 6:178; also see AL-SARAKHSI, *Sharh
al-Siyar al-Kabir*, 4:1411 and AL-SARAKHSI, *al-Mabsut*, 14:57.

119. AL-SARAKHSI, *Sharh al-Siyar al-Kabir*, 4:1410; 'AYNI and AL-MARHI-
NANI, *al-Binayah Sharh al-Hidayah*, 7:385; AL-SARAKHSI, *al-Mabsut*, 14:58;
IBN AL-HUMAM, *Fath al-Qadir*, 6:178; IBN 'ABIDIN, *Rad al-Muhtar 'ala al-Dur
al-Mukhtar*, 4:188.

historical rather than technical and legalistic. This must be kept in mind when reading the texts of our predecessors from which we have quoted. A proper understanding of the terms will prevent the derivation of rulings that lead to conflict, and will thus protect Islam from being described as a religion of conflict as a result. Muslims resorted to conflict only when others initiated it by treating them with animosity.

The upshot of the Hanafi school's position is that it is permissible for Muslims to engage in invalid transactions with non-Muslims in non-Muslim lands, whether one is selling meat that has not been slaughtered in accordance with Islamic law, selling pork or alcohol, or engaging in gambling. In addition, readers should also consider that the other schools of law have principles according to which one can deal with situations of necessity and affliction, and one can create a link between the Hanafi position and the opinions of the other schools regarding the same issue. These principles include:

1) Adopting the position of those who permit something in times of necessity in order to alleviate hardship: Al-Shayruwani said, "Those who are challenged by such circumstances, as often happens, may follow that which has preceded in order to remove the ruling of impermissibility."[120]

2) Condemnation is only justified when there is consensus on a matter: Al-Suyuti said, "Only that which is agreed upon can be denounced, not that concerning which there is a difference of opinion."[121] This means that if the schools of law have different opinions concerning an issue, it is not permitted for the followers of a particular school to denounce those from another school who take a different position, because it is an issue concerning which there is a legitimate difference of opinion.

3) One must differentiate between the realms of jurisprudence (*fiqh*), rulings (*hukm*), and scrupulousness (*war'*): The ju-

---

120. 'Abd al-Hamid AL-SHARWANI, Ahmad ibn Muhammad b. 'Ali b. Hajar AL-HAYTHAMI, and Yahya ibn Sharf AL-NAWAWI, *Hashiyah al-Shayruwani 'ala Tuhfah al-Muhtaj*, 1:119.

121. 'Abd al-Rahman ibn Abi Bakr b. Muhammad Jalal al-Sin AL-SUYUTI, *al-Ashbah wa al-Naza'ir fi Furu' al-Shafi'iyyah*. Dar al-Kutub al-'Ilmiyyah, p. 158.

rists have agreed that the realm of scrupulousness is broader than the realm of legal rulings. This is because Muslims may often refrain from doing things that are permitted out of scrupulousness. The Companions of the Prophet would refrain from nine-tenths of that which is permissible out of scrupulousness fearing that they might do something forbidden. However, this does not mean that they forbade the permissible. Scrupulousness is so vast that it could lead to a person giving up all of his possessions out of fear that he might acquire something forbidden.

Based on the position of the Hanafi school, performing the Hajj with money gained through invalid transactions between Muslims and non-Muslims in non-Muslim countries is permissible because this money is pure. As al-Sarakhsi has clearly stated, "And if he were to sell them meat that was not slaughtered according to Islamic law, or gambled with them and won money, that money would be pure."[122]

If the money is pure, then it is permissible to perform Hajj with it according to all of the jurists. And God is Most High and knows best.

---

122. AL-SARAKHSI, *al-Mabsut*, 14:56.

Fatwas Related to Creed and Belief

Question 24:

What is the meaning of the declaration of faith, "There is no god but God?"

The phrase of divine unity (*tawhid*), "There is no god but God," means there is none deserving of worship but God, and all that is worshipped other than Him is false. This phrase first denies everything the right to be worshipped, then it exempts God from this so that it is only He that is worshipped for He alone is the Creator and it is He alone that acts.

Atheists deny everything the right to be worshipped; they have not known God so they say, "There is no god." Polytheists give the right to be worshipped to both God and other beings, saying, "There is no god but God, and the idols," or "the stars," and other beings that polytheists hold to be divine. Likewise, the Christians consider their Messiah divine, while the Buddha is also held to be divine by some schools of his followers. The Muslim monotheists are upon right guidance. They deny all created beings the right to be worshipped and they believe that everything other than God is created by Him. God alone is the Creator. None but He deserves to be worshipped. He is the One deserving of all forms of worship and devotion, both inward and outward.

The meaning of the phrase of divine unity is that you should only trust in God, rely solely on God, seek assistance from God alone, make God your singular aim, desire nothing but God, and perceive only God. May God bless us with the realities of divine unity (*tawhid*), and God is Most High and knows best.

Question 25:

In Islam, how does the phrase, "There is no god but God," relate to the phrase, "Muhammad [s] is the Messenger of God?"

Islam connects the two phrases "There is no god but God" and "Muhammad is the Messenger of God" in order to make clear the accepted manner of worship. The phrase, "There is no god but God," means that nothing in existence deserves to be worshipped and turned to except for God. Once internalized, this belief logically leads to the question, "How can I worship and turn to God?" The answer is to worship God according to the Shari'ah of our Master Muhammad [s]. God alone has the right to be worshipped, and there is no worship of God except according to the way of Our Master Muhammad [s]. God does not accept an act unless it is sincere (meaning that it is done for His sake alone) and correct (meaning that it is in accordance with the Shari'ah of His Prophet [s]). God Most High says, *Say, [O Muhammad]: If you love God, follow me; God will love you and forgive you your sins. God is Forgiving, Merciful,* [3:31]; and He also said, *Whoever obeys the messenger has obeyed God, and whoever turns away: We have not sent you as a warder over them,* [4:80].

The Prophet [s] taught us that acts of worship are unacceptable unless they are done in the manner in which he carried them out. For this reason he said, "Pray as you have seen me pray."[123] And he said, "Take the rites of pilgrimage from me."[124]

This short explanation of the connection between the phrase of divine unity, "There is no god but God," and the declaration of prophethood, "Muhammad is the Messenger of God," clarifies the significance of worship. And God is Most High and knows best.

---

123. AL-BUKHARI, *Sahih Bukhari,* 1:226.

124. IBN Hanbal, *Musnad Imam Ahmad,* 3:318; AL-NAYSABURI, *Sahih Muslim,* 2:943; AL-BAYHAQI, *Kubra,* 5:125.

Question 26:

What is the meaning of the phrase, "Whoever knows their Lord will not be concerned with other than Him?"

The saying, "Whoever knows their Lord will not be concerned with other than Him," refers to the person who perceives the Majesty, Might, and Perfection of God Most High. Whoever truly knows God will not find anything better than Him with which to concern him or herself. If, in spite of the desire to be in His presence, one becomes distracted from Him, one will have a feeling of constriction and will feel alone until one returns and becomes intimate with God, which is the only true intimacy. This intimacy is accomplished through constant remembrance of Him. Whoever tastes, knows, and whoever who knows, drinks. Those who taste the sweetness of God's intimacy will not find pleasure with other than God, and those who remember God constantly will attain intimacy with Him. Even if they outwardly appear concerned with other than Him, the hearts of God's intimates are always with Him. And God is Most High and knows best.

Question 27:

How should Muslims believe in the angels?

Muslims must believe in the existence of the blessed angels and know that they are God's creation. Muslims accept as true the angels' names related by the Shari'ah, such as Jibril [Gabriel]: *Say [O Muhammad, to mankind]: Who is an enemy to Gabriel! For it is he who has revealed [this Scripture] to your heart by God's leave, confirming that which was [revealed] before it, and a guidance and glad tidings to believers; Who is an enemy to God, and His angels and His messengers, and Gabriel and Michael! Then, lo! God is an enemy to the disbelievers*, [2:97-98]. And God refers to the angels as his helpers in a verse directed towards the wives of the Prophet who rallied against him (with the aim of winning his full attention to the exclusion of his concubine): *If you two turn unto God repentant, [you have cause to do so] for your hearts desired [the ban]; and if you aid one another against him [Muhammad] then lo! God, even He, is his Protecting Friend, and Gabriel and the righteous among the believers; and furthermore the angels are his helpers*, [66:4]. And our Lord mentioned the Angel of Death in the Quran, *Say: The angel of death, who has charge concerning you, will gather you, and afterward unto your Lord you will be returned*, [32:11]. God also names the gatekeeper of the Hellfire, called Malik: *And they cry: O Malik! Let your Lord make an end of us. He says: Lo! here you must remain*, [43:77]. He describes the angels of the Hellfire, *Ah, what will convey unto you what that burning is!—It leaves naught; it spares naught. It shrivels the man. Above it are nineteen. We have appointed only angels to be wardens of the Fire, and their number have We made to be a stumbling-block for those who disbelieve; that those to whom the Scripture has been given may have certainty, and that believers may increase in faith; and that those to whom the Scripture has been given and believers may not doubt; and that those in whose hearts there is disease, and disbelievers, may say: What does God mean by this similitude? Thus God sends astray whom He will, and whom He will He guides. None knows the hosts of thy Lord save Him. This is naught else than a Reminder unto mortals*, [74:27-31].

Authentic hadiths describe various orders of angels. Though they are not mentioned in the Quran, one must believe in these orders as well. For example, the Prophet [s] told of an angel who blows children's spirits into their mothers' wombs. The Prophet [s] said, "Your creation comes together in your mother's belly in forty days. Then it is a clot for a similar period. Then it is a lump of flesh for a similar period. Then God sends an angel to blow into it the spirit, and the angel is commissioned with four things: to record its sustenance, life span, deeds, and whether it will be wretched or felicitous. I swear by He other than Whom there is no divinity, a person may do the works of the people of Paradise until there is but an arm's length between him and Paradise, then destiny will catch up with him and he will end with the works of the people of Hell and enter their realm. And a man may do the works of the people of Hell until there is but an arm's length between him and Hell, then destiny will catch up with him and he will end with the works of the people of Paradise and enter their realm."[125]

A Muslim must believe in all of the angels, but particularly those about whom God, through the Quran and the Prophet [s], has taught us in detail. Belief in the angels guides believers closer to their Lord: constantly feeling the presence of blessed creatures makes us shy away from disobedience. And our final prayer is, "All praise is due to God, Lord of the Worlds."

---

125. IBN HANBAL, *Musnad Imam Ahmad*, 1:382; AL-BUKHARI, *Sahih Bukhari*, 6:2423; AL-NAYSABURI, *Sahih Muslim*, 4:2036.

Question 28:

What should Muslims believe concerning the books revealed by God?

Our belief in the divinely revealed books is one of the pillars of our religion, and without it a Muslim's faith is not valid. The divinely revealed books are a manifestation of God's care for humanity, and His Lordship over creation. Our Lord revealed books to us and commanded His Messengers to convey them, and it is the responsibility of Muslims to believe in the entire body of divinely revealed books. Muslims must believe that God revealed books in order to make Himself known to humanity and teach us how to worship Him. Before our Lord revealed the Quran to Muhammad [s], He revealed other books: *He has revealed unto you [Muhammad] the Scripture with truth, confirming that which was revealed before it, even as He revealed the Torah and the Injil* [3:3]. Muslims must believe what the divine law informs us concerning these previous revelations.

Muslims believe that God revealed pages to Abraham, and the Tablets and Torah to Moses: *Lo! This is in the former scrolls. The Books of Abraham and Moses* [87:18-19]; *Or has he not had news of what is in the books of Moses. And Abraham who paid his debt* [53:36-37]; *Has there not come unto them the proof of what is in the former scriptures?* [20:133].

We also believe that God revealed a part of everything to Moses in the Tablets. He said: *O Moses! I have preferred you above the rest of humanity by My messages and by My speaking to you. So keep that which I have given you, and be among the thankful. And We wrote for him, upon the tablets, the lesson to be drawn from all things and the explanation of all things, then [bade him]: Hold it fast; and command your people [saying]: Take the better [course made clear] therein. I shall show you the abode of evil-livers* [7:144-145]; *Again, We gave the Scripture unto Moses, complete for him who would do good, an explanation of all things, a guidance and a mercy, that they might believe in the meeting with their Lord* [6:154]; *We gave unto Moses the Scripture, and We appointed it a guidance for the children of Israel, saying: Choose no guardian beside Me* [17:2].

We also believe that God revealed the *Zabur* (the Psalms) to David, as mentioned in the Quran: *And your Lord is Best Aware of all who are in the heavens and the earth. And we preferred some of the prophets above others, and unto David We gave the Psalms* [17:55]; *Lo! We inspire you as We inspired Noah and the prophets after him, as We inspired Abraham and Ishmael and Isaac and Jacob and the tribes, and Jesus and Job and Jonah and Aaron and Solomon, and as We imparted unto David the Psalms* [6:163].

We believe that God revealed the *Injil* to Jesus, the son of Mary. The Quran says, *And We caused Jesus, son of Mary, to follow in their footsteps, confirming that which was [revealed] before him in the Torah, and We bestowed on him the Injil wherein is guidance and a light, confirming that which was [revealed] before it in the Torah—a guidance and an admonition unto those who ward off [evil]* [5:46]; *When God says: O Jesus, son of Mary! Remember My favor unto you and unto your mother; how I strengthened you with the holy Spirit, so that you spoke to mankind in the cradle as in maturity; and how I taught you the Scripture and Wisdom and the Torah and the Injil* [5:110].

Muslims do not deny or affirm the names of any books revealed to the prophets unless revelation informs them to do so. As illustrated by the previous verses, the Quran guides Muslims to believe that God revealed "pages" to Abraham, the Torah to Moses, the *Zabur* to David, and the *Injil* to Jesus. However, for two reasons Muslims do not believe that God preserved these books or that they contain legislation that is to be followed by Muslims.

First, in the Quran God does not say that He preserved those books to this day. In verses concerning other revelation, He reminds Muslims that the books were revealed to the Children of Israel before the coming of Islam, and that the Children of Israel altered them: *Therefore woe be unto those who write the Scripture with their hands and then say, "This is from God," that they may purchase a small gain therewith. Woe unto them for what their hands have written, and woe unto them for what they earn thereby* [2:79]; *And because of their breaking their covenant, We have cursed them and made hard their hearts. They change words from their context and forget a part of that whereof they were admonished* [5:13]; *Have you any hope that they will be true to you when a party of them used to listen to the word of God, then used to change it, after they had understood it, knowingly?* [2:75]; *Say O People of the Scripture! You have naught [of guidance] till you observe the Torah and the Injil and that which was revealed unto you from your Lord. That which is revealed unto you [Muhammad] from your Lord is certain to increase the contumacy and disbelief of many of them. But grieve not for the disbelieving folk* [5:68].

The second reason is that even if the pre-Islamic revelations existed in their unaltered form, the Quran would still abrogate the validity of acting in accordance with their dictates. The Quran says: *And unto you have We revealed the Scripture with the truth, confirming whatever Scripture was before it, and a watcher over it. So judge between them by that which God has revealed, and follow not their desires away from the truth which hath come to you* [5:48]; *Follow that which is inspired in you from your Lord; there is no God save Him; and turn away from the idolaters* [6:106]; *And this is a blessed Scripture which We have revealed. So follow it and ward off [evil], that you may find mercy* [6:155]; *Follow that which is sent down unto you from your Lord, and follow no protecting friends beside Him. Little do you recollect!* [7:3].

In summary, Muslims should believe in the divinely revealed books generally, and particularly those whose revelation to specific prophets is mentioned by the sources of our tradition. Muslims do not, however, follow these books, because we believe the Quran is God's final message to humanity. Nothing abrogates or disproves the Quran. All Praise is due to God, Lord of the Worlds, and God is Most High and knows best.

Question 29:

What should Muslims believe concerning the Messengers of God?

Belief in the Messengers is one of the tenets of faith. Muslims believe that God did not leave creation to its own devices. Rather, He cared for our needs by sending revelations to at least one person in every time and place. Muslims consider Muhammad [s] the seal of the prophets: there is no prophet after him.

In particular, Muslims believe in the twenty-five Messengers mentioned in the Quran, eighteen of whom God mentions in Chapter 6 of the Quran, *That is Our argument. We gave it unto Abraham against his folk. We raise unto degrees of wisdom whom We will. Lo! your Lord is Wise, Aware. And We bestowed upon him Isaac and Jacob; each of them We guided; and Noah did We guide aforetime; and of his seed [We guided] David and Solomon and Job and Joseph and Moses and Aaron. Thus do We reward the good. And Zachariah and John and Jesus and Elias. Each one [of them] was of the righteous. And Ishmael and Elisha and Jonah and Lot. Each one [of them] did We prefer above [Our] creatures* [6:83-86].

The remaining seven are, Muhammad, Adam, Hud, Salih, Dhu al-Kifl, Shu'ayb, and Idris [alayhim al-salam] all of whom God mentions in the Quran: *Muhammad is not the father of any man among you, but he is the messenger of God and the Seal of the Prophets; and God is ever Aware of all things* [33:40]. And He mentions Adam in numerous verses of the Quran: *And He taught Adam all the names, then showed them to the angels, saying: Inform Me of the names of these, if you are truthful. They said: Be glorified! We have no knowledge saving that which You have taught us. Lo! You, only You, are the Knower, the Wise. He said: O Adam! Inform them of their names, and when he had informed them of their names, He said: Did I not tell you that I know the secret of the heavens and the earth? And I know that which you disclose and which you hide* [2:31-33]; *Then Adam received from his Lord words [of revelation], and He relented toward him. Lo! He is the relenting, the Merciful* [2:37].

Dhu'l-Kifl is named as a prophet twice in the Quran, *And [mention] Ishmael, and Idris, and Dhu'l-Kifl. All were of the steadfast* [21:85]; *And make mention of Ishmael and Elisha and Dhu'l-Kifl. All are of the chosen* [38:48]. God mentions Idris in multiple verses, including: *And make mention in the Scripture of Idris. Lo! he was a saint, a prophet; And We raised him to high station* [19:56-57]. Of Hud, God says, *And unto [the tribe of] A'ad [We sent] their brother, Hud. He said: O my people!*

Serve God. You have no other god save Him. Will you not ward off [evil]?
[7:65]. Salih is also mentioned in more than one place, such as in
the following verse, *And We verily sent unto Thamud their brother Salih, saying: Worship God. And lo! they then became two parties quarrelling*
[27:45]. God says of Shu'ayb, *And unto Midian [We sent] their brother
Shu'ayb. He said: O my people! Serve God. You have no other god save Him!
And give not short measure and short weight. Lo! I see you well-to-do, and
lo! I fear for you the doom of a besetting Day* [11:84].

Muslims must believe in these prophets named by the Quran,
meaning they should not deny the prophethood of any one of
them. Muslims must also affirm that God sent prophets in addition
to those mentioned in the Quran: *Verily We sent messengers before
you, among them those of whom We have told you, and some of whom We
have not told you; and it was not given to any messenger that he should
bring a portent save by God's leave, but when God's commandment comes
[the cause] is judged aright, and the followers of vanity will then be lost*
[40:78].

The Prophet [s] said, "I am the seal of one thousand or more
prophets. No prophet has ever been sent except that he warned his
community of the *Dajjal* (the ant-Christ)."[126] Abu Dharr asked the
Prophet [s], "O Messenger of God, how many prophets are there?"
The Prophet [s] replied, "One hundred twenty-four thousand
prophets." Abu Dharr then asked, "How many of them are messengers?" The Prophet said, "Three hundred thirteen."[127]

Just as one believes in the scriptures, so one must believe in
the messengers. A Muslim may not cease to follow the Prophet
Muhammad [s] in favor of another messenger. Muslim faith in the
prophets [alayhim al-salam] is underpinned by the belief that God
sent the prophets to the people of their respective communities. It
is not permissible for us to follow the prophets sent to other communities for the same reasons that we do not follow the divinely
revealed books of other times and places. First, we cannot be sure
that the content concerning prophets in the books of other peoples
has not been altered. And even if the content could be proven unaltered, it is not permissible for us to follow those prophets because

126. IBN HANBAL, *Musnad Imam Ahmad*, 3:79; AL-HAKIM, *al-Mustadrak
'ala al-Sahihayn*, 1:588.
127. Ibid., 2:652; AL-BAYHAQI, *al-Sunan al-Kubra*, 9:4, and in AL-BAY-
HAQI, *Shu'ab al-Iman*, 1:49.

God abrogated their lessons by sending the Prophet Muhammad [s], the Seal of the Prophets. Muhammad [s] said, "I have brought it to you white and pure, and if Moses were alive he would have no choice but to follow me."[128]

This is but a brief summary of the Muslim belief in the Messengers. We ask God to provide us with true faith and good works. Our final prayer is: all praise is to God, Lord of the Worlds, and God is Most High and knows best.

---

128. IBN HANBAL, *Musnad Imam Ahmad*, 3:387; AL-KUFI, *Musannaf ibn Abi Shaybah*, 5:312; AL-BAYHAQI, *Shu'ab al-Iman*, 1:200.

Question 30:

What does it mean to believe in the Last Day?

The Last Day is the Day of Resurrection: the day when God will raise all of humanity to stand before Him and be judged for their actions. God reminds us in the Quran, *Do they not think that they will be called to account on a mighty day, a Day when [all] humanity will stand before the Lord of the Worlds?* [83:4-6]. God has sworn by the great day, *I do call to witness the Day of Resurrection,* [75:1]. On this day God will gather everyone's remains and clothe our bones with flesh once again, so all bodies will return to their earthly state. Then God will give these bodies life. God reminds us that He is capable of this: *Does humanity think that We cannot assemble their bones?* [75:3]. God describes the signs indicating the arrival of this day. He warns in the Quran, *At length, when the sight is dazed, and the moon is buried in darkness, and the sun and moon are joined together, that Day will man say: 'Where is the refuge?' By no means! No place of safety!* [75:7-11]. God also says, *When the sky is rent asunder, And hearkens to [the Command of] its Lord, and it must needs [do so]; and when the earth is flattened out, and casts forth what is within it and becomes [clean] empty, And hearkens to [the Command of] its Lord, and it must need [do so]; [then will come Home the full reality]* [25:1-5].

Thus every believer must have firm conviction in the final hour, the hour in which God calls forth those who are in their graves: *Again, on the Day of Judgment, will you be raised up* [23:16]. It is incumbent to prepare for this hour by performing righteous deeds. As the Quran says, *And fear the Day when you shall be brought back to God. Then shall every soul be paid what it earned, and none shall be dealt with unjustly* [2:281]. Muslims are obliged to believe in the descriptions of this great event and its horrors. God says, *We shall set up scales of justice for the Day of Judgment, so that not a soul will be dealt with unjustly in the least. And if there be [no more than] the weight of a mustard seed, We will bring it [to account]: and enough are We to take account* [21:47]. Muslims should also believe in the unseen states associated with the final hour, such as heaven, the abode of bliss; hell, the abode of flames; the reckoning; the resurrection, and the intermediate life one lives immediately after death before being resurrected (*al-barzakh*). God says, *Before them is an intermediary state until the Day they are raised up* [23:100]. One must also believe in the grave, and the good and bad that can occur there. God says, *In front of the fire* will they be brought, morning and evening; and [the sentence will be] on the Day when the Hour comes to pass: "Cast the People of Pharaoh into the severest penalty!"* [40:46]. Thus Muslims must hold true both the torment and the pleasure of the grave described by the Shari'ah. At the same time, Muslims should not concern themselves with the manner and form of this torment, for every world has its own governing rules. While in the life of this world we cannot imagine or anticipate the rules that govern other realms of existence, such as the worlds of spirits and Jinn.

Scholars have differed in opinion concerning the pleasure and the torment of the grave: does it affect the spirit alone, or only the body, or both? Ibn Hubayra and al-Ghazali asserted that the spirit alone experiences both the pleasure and torment of the grave. However, the majority of Sunni scholars, theologians and jurists alike, are of the opinion that the soul and the body equally experience the pleasure and torment of the grave. Al-Nawawi said, "Both pleasure and torment in the grave are experienced by the body itself, or by a part of it, after the spirit has been returned to the body or to a part of it. The pain is felt even though the person is not alive."[129] Ibn Jarir differed slightly in his opinion, agreeing that the deceased experience pain without being alive but arguing that this torment occurs in their graves without restoration of the spirit.[130]

This is what Muslims are required to believe in general regarding the Day of Judgment. And God is Most High and knows best.

---

129. Yahya ibn Sharf AL-NAWAWI, *Sharh Sahih Muslim*. Dar Ihya al-Turath al-'Arabi, 17:201.

130. Muhammad ibn al-Hussein b. al-Farra' ABU YA'LA, *al-Mu'tamad fi Usul al-Din*. Dar al-Mashriq, 178.

Question 31:

How should a Muslim correctly understand destiny?

Belief in destiny is an essential tenet of Islam. It is the most important of the outward manifestations of faith in God. The Quran says, *Verily, all things have We created in proportion and measure* [54:49]. 'Ubada ibn Samit further expands on the nature of destiny in these words to his son:

> My son! You will never taste true faith until you realize that what hit you was not going to miss you, and what missed you was not going to hit you. I heard the Messenger of God [s] say, "The first thing that God created was the pen and He said to it, 'Write,' and the pen said, 'What shall I write?' God said, 'Write the destiny of everything up until the final hour.'" My son, I heard the Messenger of God [s] say, "Whoever dies believing something other than this, is not from among my followers."[131]

The Messenger of God [s] made a similar statement to Ibn 'Abbas, "Know that if all the nations gathered to benefit you with something they would not be able to benefit you except with that which God has already written for you, and if they gathered to harm you then they would only harm you with that which God has written for you. The pens have been raised and the pages have dried."[132]

Muslims must have firm conviction that there is no acting agent other than God, that everything that occurs, has occurred, and will occur in the universe arises from God's actions, and God has decreed this action in pre-eternity. The issue of destiny contains great wisdom as it tests one's degree of contentment with the decree of God. Human beings do not know what shall befall them tomorrow, so it is their right to have hope and to strive to attain that which is permissible and legislated. It is when our hopes and dreams are not realized, when what we have planned differs from what the Creator has planned, that true faith is revealed. The sign of the true believer is that what the Creator has decreed is more

---

131. IBN HANBAL, *Musnad Imam Ahmad*, 5:317; AL-SIJISTANI, *Sunan Abi Dawud*, 4:225 and the wording is his, and AL-TABARANI, *al-Muʿjam al-Kabir*, 12:68.

132. IBN HANBAL, *Musnad Imam Ahmad*, 1:293, AL-TIRMIDHI, *Sunan al-Tirmidhi*, 4:667, AL-TAMIMI, *Sahih Ibn Hibban*, 1:355.

beloved than what he or she initially wanted, and the sign of the rebellious sinner is that they reject God's decree and turn away from it disgruntled. Being unsatisfied with God's decree can even lead to one's leaving the faith, and we seek refuge with God from this behavior. Belief in destiny is the active expression of faith in God. If you believe in the existence of God and in His attributes of perfection, majesty, and beauty, then you must also believe in the effects of those attributes, which are His actions. Further, to believe in the actions of God is to believe that there is no agent of action in existence other than Him and to be satisfied with all that issues forth from Him so that one may become a divine servant (*'abd rabbani*).

There is no contradiction between one believing that God is the sole actor in the universe and one's possessing free will. The decisions made by human beings in accordance with their own will are observable and cannot be denied by any rational individual. Anyone who does so has denied both that which is experientially observable as well as that which is revealed in the Quran where God establishes human beings' free will and choice: *We have shown human beings the two paths*, [90:10], and, *Among you are some that hanker after this world and some that desire the Hereafter*, [3:152]. The correct understanding of this issue is to affirm one's own actions and free choice while maintaining that God is the agent of action to whom belongs the command, and that nothing occurs outside of His control. Destiny is God's secret in His creation. This is why some of those who possess knowledge of God, such as Abu 'Abbas al-Harithi, were known to say, "Whoever looks at creation from the eye of the Shari'ah abhors it, and whoever looks at creation from the eye of the *Haqiqah*[133] pardons it." Thus the knowledgeable perceive the world through the secret of God in His creation, and God is Most High and knows best.

---

133. The metaphysical reality behind the Shari'ah. [Trans.]

Question 32:

If the will and decree of God is undetterable, then how does one explain the many hadiths stating that supplication (*du'a*) affects the decree of God, and that filial piety and loyalty to family increases one's success and one's lifespan?

Muslims should not imagine that there are contradictions between the primary texts of the Shari'ah. Supplication is a powerfully effective form of worship. God has commanded us to supplicate to Him: *Call on your Lord with humility and in private, for God loves not those who trespass beyond bounds* [7:55]. The Messenger of God [s] supplicated to God throughout his life. What a great number of troubles have been lifted by supplication! Whoever ceases to perform supplications has closed many doors to good. Imam al-Ghazali wrote:

One may ask, "What is the point of supplication if destiny is set?" Know that part of destiny is the prevention of tribulations through supplication, thus supplication acts to prevent tribulation and attract mercy; just as a shield prevents arrows from striking and water causes plants to sprout forth from the ground. Just as the shield deflects the arrow and they are repelled by one another, supplication and tribulation vie with one another; the acknowledgment of destiny does not mean we should not bear arms to battle.[134]

The hadiths that some people might think contradict orthodox beliefs concerning destiny are actually in perfect accord with them. The great scholars' commentaries on these texts clarify the relationship between divine agency and supplication. A discussion of two example hadiths and their corresponding commentaries suffices to further elucidate the matter.

According to the first *hadith*, the Messenger of God [s] said, "Destiny is not repelled except by supplication, and nothing increases one's lifespan except for piety."[135] Al-Mubarkafuri commented:

---

134. Abu Hamid AL-GHAZALI, *Ihya 'Ulum al-Din*. Al-Tab'ah al-Azhariyyah, 1:100 end of section four Prophetic Invocations.

135. IBN HANBAL, *Musnad Imam Ahmad*, 5:277; AL-TIRMIDHI, *Sunan al-Tirmidhi*, 4:448; AL-QIZWINI, *Sunan Ibn Majah*, 1:35; AL-KUFI, *Musannad ibn Abi Shaybah*, 6:109; AL-TABARANI, *al-Mu'jam al-Kabir*, 6:251; Ahmad ibn

Destiny refers to that which has been ordained. The meaning of this *hadith* is that if one considers destiny to be those unpleasant things that one fears may happen and that one expects to occur, and one is blessed to make supplications, then God prevents those things from happening. In this case the word destiny is used figuratively to refer to what a person thinks may befall them. This is also made clear by the *hadith* of the Messenger of God [s] concerning healing through Quran, which says, "It is from the destiny of God." God has also commanded us to use medicine and to make supplications, even though that which is destined to be will be, but this is hidden from humanity. When 'Umar ibn al-Khattab reached the Levant and was told of a great plague, he returned to Medina. Abu 'Ubaydah said to him, "Do you flee from the destiny and decree of God, O leader of the faithful?" 'Umar replied, "If only someone else had made this statement! Yes, we flee from the destiny and decree of God to the destiny and decree of God."

If taken literally, "repels destiny," may also mean that it lightens the situation, making it easy to the point that it seems to have never occurred. This meaning is supported by the *hadith*, narrated by al-Tirmidhi from the *hadith* of Ibn 'Umar, that states that supplication aids in that which has occurred as well as with that which has not occurred . . . . *Al-Kashshaf* mentions that the increase or decrease of a person's lifespan is written. For example, it is written that if so and so does not perform the pilgrimage, or if so and so engages in this certain battle, their lifespan will be forty years, and if so and so performs the pilgrimage and engages in this certain battle, then their lifespan will be sixty years. If the person does both, they will have a long lifespan of sixty years, and if they engage in one without the other, they will shorten their lifespan from sixty to forty years. *Ma'alim al-Tanzil* touches on the same theme. As for piety, it is mentioned that if someone is pious, then his or her life will not be wasted, which is as if their life has been extended. It is also said that the destiny and decree of piety is a cause for an extended lifespan, just as the destiny and decree of supplication is a cause for repelling harm.

'Amr b. 'Abd al-Khaliq AL-BAZZAR, *Musnad al-Bazzar*. Mu'assisah 'Ulum al-Quran, 6:502.

Supplication for parents and relatives increases one's lifespan, in the sense that it adds extra grace to one's own life, so that in a short time one is able to engage in a number of good works that another person, having a longer lifespan, will not be able to engage in. In this case, the extra life is only figurative since an actual extension of life is impossible. Al-Tayyibi stated, "Know that, if God most high knows that Zayd will die in the year 500, it is impossible for him to die before or after it, so it is impossible for life spans, which are in God's knowledge, to increase or decrease. It becomes necessary then to interpret the increase as something that happens with respect to the Angel of Death, or another who has been commissioned to take souls, and has been ordered to take the souls after a determined period."[136]

In the second *hadith* of our discussion, the Messenger of God [s] relays God's words, "The son of Adam does not vow to do anything that I [God] have not already determined. Destiny meets them as I have made their destinies. Thereby do I draw out the miserly."[137]

Al-Hafiz Ibn Hajar comments on this *hadith*:

Al-Baydawi says that people have the habit and custom of making vows conditional to the occurrence of something good or the avoidance of something bad. This has been forbidden, as it is an act of the miserly. If generous people desire good then they hurry to accomplish it, but miserly people do not volunteer themselves unless they first receive something in compensation, and then they give only out of obligation. This does not affect destiny because nothing good will come their way except that which has been destined, and nothing will deter a harm that was destined to befall them. The vow, however, can match something destined, so that the miserly person gives something they would not normally give.

Ibn al-'Arabi stated, "This *hadith* proves that one who makes a vow must adhere to what he has vowed, as the *hadith* says, 'Thereby do I draw out the miserly,' because if they were

---

136. Muhammad ibn 'Abd al-Rahman AL-MUBARAKFURI, *Tuhfat al-Ahwidhi Sharh Sunan al-Tirmidhi*. Dar al-Kutub al-'Ilmiyyah, 6:289.

137. IBN HANBAL, *Musnad Imam Ahmad*, 2:314; AL-BUKHARI, *Sahih Bukhari*, 6:2437.

not obliged to do what they had vowed, then the description of being miserly would have no meaning concerning the act that they had vowed to do. If one were free to act or not act upon a vow, then the person would continue to withhold action because of their miserliness."

As for the *hadith* of al-Tirmidhi, narrated from Anas, which says, "Charity repels a calamitous death," seemingly contradicting the *hadith* that says, "Vows do not repel destiny," one can bring the two hadiths together to mean that charity is a cause to repel bad states, and causes are destined and decreed, just as effects are. The Messenger of God [s] was asked about healing through Quran, "Does it repel anything from the destiny of God?" He responded, "It *is* from the destiny of God." Hakim and Abu Dawud narrated this *hadith*.

Ibn al-'Arabi has stated, "Vows are similar to supplication in that they do not repel destiny, but are instead a part of it. Vows, however, are discouraged, while supplications are recommended. This is because supplication is a form of worship that manifests one's impotence and utter powerlessness before God, while vows involve delaying an act of worship until something happens first."[138]

Thus we have clarified how one can reconcile these prophetic reports with unwavering belief in the destiny of God. May God grant us true faith and good works, and God is Most High and knows best.

---

138. Ahmad ibn 'Ali b. Hajar AL-'ASQALANI, *Fath al-Bari*. Dar al-Ma'rifah, 11:577.

Question 33:

Who are the Ash'aris: are they true upholders of the Sunnah (*Ahl al-Sunnah*), possessing sound theological doctrines, or are they a sect involved in reprehensible innovation?

The Ash'aris are those who ascribe to Imam Abu al-Hasan al-Ash'ari's school of theology. Before we understand this school of theology, we should introduce Abu al-Hasan al-Ash'ari himself.

Imam Abu al-Hasan Ali ibn Isma'il b. Abi Bishr Ishaq b. Salim b. Isma'il b. 'Abdallah b. Musa b. Bilal b. Abi Burdah 'Amir b. Abi Musa al-Ash'ari, the last being the famous companion of the Messenger of God [s].

He was born in either 260 or 270 AH in Basra. The date of his death is also disputed by scholars. Some say it was 333 AH, while others claim he died in 324 AH, and still others say he died in 330 AH. He died in Baghdad and was buried between *al-Kurkh* and *Bab al-Basra.*

Abu al-Hasan al-Ash'ari was a Sunni Muslim from a Sunni household. When he was young he studied Mu'tazalite theology with Abu 'Ali al-Jubba'i, but later in life he renounced the Mu'tazalites. One day he ascended the teaching chair in the mosque and announced at the top of his voice, "He who knows me, knows me, and as for he who does not know me, let me introduce myself. I am so and so and I once taught that the Quran was created and that God cannot be perceived by sight. I am the perpetuator of my own evil actions, and I repent. I will respond to the teachings of the Mu'tazilites and expose their falsehood."[139] The jurist Abu Bakr al-Sayrafi said, "The Mu'tazilites were prominent until Abu al-Hasan halted their efforts."[140]

Qadi 'Iyad the Maliki said of him:

He composed the seminal works of the Ash'ari school and established proofs affirming the Sunnah and the attributes of God that the people of innovation had negated. He affirmed the vision of God, and the beginning-less character of His speech, His will, and the matters explained in revelation . . . . The people of the Sunnah held fast to his books, learned from him, and studied under him. They became intimately familiar with his school of

139. IBN NADIM, *al-Faharas*, 231, *Wafayat al-'Ayn*, 3:275.
140. AL-DHAHABI, *Siyar 'Allam al-Nubala'*, starting at 15:85.

thought and it grew in its number of students and adherents wishing to learn his way of defending the Sunnah and adducing arguments and proofs to give victory to the faith. These students, as well as his students' students, adopted his ascription, and so they all became known as Ash'aris. They were originally known as the *muthbitah* (the affirmers), a name given to them by the Mu'tazalites, since they affirmed parts of the Sunnah and the Shari'ah that the Mu'tazalites negated . . . . Therefore, the people of the Sunnah from the East to the West championed al-Ash'ari's arguments and methodology. Many of them have praised and commended his school and approach.[141]

Al-Taj al-Subki said of him:

The way of Abu al-Hasan al-Ash'ari has been adopted by those considered the most notable scholars of Islam from the four schools of law; those who know the permissible from the prohibited and who are the defenders of the religion of Muhammad [s].[142]

Al-Isnawi said of him:

Abu al-Hasan al-Ash'ari was the one who stood to defend the people of the Sunnah and suppressed the Mu'tazalites and others of grave innovation with both his tongue and his pen. He authored great works, and his fame is too vast to elucidate here.[143]

Qadi Ibn Farhun al-Maliki said of him:

Abu al-Hasan al-Ash'ari was a follower of the Maliki school of law. He authored works for the people of the Sunnah and adduced arguments for the establishment of the Sunnah and for those things that the people of innovation refuted . . . . He established clear arguments and proofs from the Quran and the hadiths, as well as from sound rational arguments. He dispelled the sophism of the Mu'tazilites and the atheists who came after them. He wrote detailed works on the subjects with

---

141. Abu Fadl AL-QADI 'IYYAD, *Tartib al-Madarik*. Dar Maktabat al-Hayat, 5:24-25.

142. Taj al-Din AL-SUBKI, *Idah al-Burhan fi al-Radd 'ala Ahl al-Zaygh wa al-Tughyan*.

143. *Al-Idrak fi Funun*, al-Isnawi.

which God benefits Muslims. He debated the Mu'tazilites and was victorious over them. Abu Hasan al-Qabisi used to praise him and he even authored a treatise about him, for those who inquired about his school, in which he spoke very highly of him. Abu Muhammad ibn Abi Zayd and others from the leaders of the Muslims also praised him.[144]

UNDERSTANDING THE CRITICIZED ASPECTS OF ASH'ARI THOUGHT

The orthodox school of Sunni Islam, including both the Ash'ari and Maturidi schools, clearly expresses all aspects of theology. Those who criticize these schools are ignorant of their tenets of belief in God. Misunderstandings mostly have to do with the "possessive attributes of God" or what are technically referred to as "reported attributes."

The confusion stems from certain Quranic expressions that God uses to refer to Himself in His book. Some people seek to affirm these expressions according to their literal linguistic meaning, which leads to God having similarities with creation. People of truth, however, understand that, since they are ambiguous, the literal meanings of these attributes are not to be affirmed. They believe that these attributes of God's have been established through revelation, not through reason, so their approach is to accept these possessive phrases and reported attributes used by the Quran in reference to God as they are, without believing in the literal meaning of their linguistic expression. They do not say that they affirm them according to their literal linguistic meanings because the apparent meaning of these phrases refers to known realities that contradict the transcendence of God. This was the approach of the early theologians of Ahl al-Sunnah who would later become known as the Ash'aris.

The later Ash'ari theologians took the approach of interpretation because they thought that affirming attributes in an ambiguous manner led some to anthropomorphic beliefs and all that they necessitate. Both the early and the later Sunni theologians agree that the best approach entails accepting these passages without denying the expression, but also without affirming the literal meaning that likens God to His creation. The later theologians,

---

144. al-Qadi al-Maliki IBN FARHUN, *al-Daybaj al-Mudhhib*. al-Maktabah al-Turathiyyah, 194.

however, added that we may only understand these attributes in ways that are appropriate for God. It is as if they are saying to their opponents, "If you must understand these attributes, then do so only in a way that is appropriate for God. So say, 'The eye of God is His care for His creation,' as in His statement *in order that thou may be reared under Mine eye*, [20:39]. Never say that the eye of God is literal!" Thus one could say that the early theologians' approach was one of acceptance and belief, while the later theologians' approach was one of debate.

This is the nature of Sunni theology's methodology for dealing with ambiguous words and expressions that, if taken literally, would lead to anthropomorphism. Al-Hafiz al-'Iraqi commented on the frequently occurring expression, "the face or countenance of God," saying: "There are two opinions on how to understand this expression: one approach accepts it as it is without asking how. So one believes in it fully, leaving its meaning to the One who possesses this meaning, with firm conviction that there is none like unto God. The second approach involves interpreting the expression in a manner appropriate for God's essence, so the 'face' or 'countenance of God' is understood to refer to His existence."[145] Al-Hafiz al-'Iraqi designates those possessing these opinions as the people of truth.

Perhaps the best commentary on this topic appears in Ibn Qudama al-Maqdisi's book *Lum'a al-'Itiqad*:

One is obliged to believe in and accept without reservation all that has come in the Quran or has been soundly narrated by the Messenger of God [s] concerning the attributes of the most Merciful One. One should refrain from rejecting them, indulging in their interpretation, or drawing comparisons and likenesses between God and His creation. One should affirm whatever expressions may be problematic without addressing their meaning. We are to refer the knowledge of its actual meaning to the one who said it (God) and place the burden of its truthfulness or falsehood upon the shoulders of the one who transmitted it, following the path of those who are firmly grounded in knowledge, whom God has extolled in His Book, saying, *And those who are firmly grounded in knowledge say: "We believe in the Book; the whole of it is from our Lord"* [3:7]. God also said, in condemnation of those who try to interpret the meaning of the

145. AL-'IRAQI, *Tarh al-Tathrib*, 3:107.

ambiguous verses of His revelation, *But those in whose hearts is perversity follow the part thereof that is ambiguous, seeking discord, and searching for its meanings, but no one knows its meanings except God* [3:7]. He has therefore designated the desire to interpret as an indication of sickness in a person's heart, and He has likened this desire to seeking discord, and then He barred them from what they hope to discover with His saying that, *only God knows their meaning*. Imam Ahmad ibn Hanbal said, regarding the statements of the Messenger of God [s] such as, "God descends to the sky of this earth," and "God is seen on the Day of Resurrection,": "We believe in these texts and we verify their truth without asking how, or without seeking a meaning, and we do not reject any of them. We believe that the Messenger of God [s] brought truth and we do not reject his words, nor do we describe God with words other than those He uses to describe Himself without ascribing any limits or ends to Him: *There is none like unto Him and He is the All-Hearing, All-Seeing* [11:11]. We simply state what He has stated concerning Himself, and we describe Him with that which He has described Himself. We do not add to this, as He is exalted beyond anyone's description. We believe in the Quran in its entirety, its clear parts and its ambiguous parts. We do not exclude any aspects of it simply because they displease us. We never go beyond the Quran and *hadith*, and we cannot comprehend them except by believing in the Messenger of God [s] and the Quran. Imam al-Shafi'i said, "I believe in God and what has been revealed concerning God, in accordance with God's intention, and I believe in the Messenger of God [s] and in that which has been revealed concerning him, in accordance with the Messenger of God's [s] intention." This is the path that both the pious ancestors and later scholars have followed. They all agree that the reports in the Quran and the Sunnah are to be accepted as they are and affirmed without interpretation.[146]

THE RELATIONSHIP BETWEEN THOSE WHO FOLLOW THE ASH'ARI SCHOOL AND ABU AL-HASAN AL-ASH'ARI HIMSELF.

Detractors might ask: "If the Ash'aris claim to be people of the Sun-

---

146. Abu Muhammad Ibn Qudmah AL-MAQDASI, *Lumat al-'Itiqad fi Hadi ila al-Rashad*. al-Maktab al-Islami, 8:5.

nah, then why do they not simply call themselves the people of the Sunnah? Why do they call themselves Ash'aris instead of ascribing themselves to the Prophet [s] and his companions?" This question, however, is asked only amongst the ignorant. The scholars know that objections to the technical use of language (*istilah*) are invalid objections; their proofs, not their name, determine the legitimacy of a certain school.

After Muslims began to disagree on theological issues, reprehensible innovation emerged and it became necessary to correct misconceptions and purify the theology of the Messenger of God [s] and his companions. It is not that Abu al-Hasan al-Ash'ari started a new school of thought, rather he successfully restated and emphasized the theology and creed of Ahl al-Sunnah. Al-Subki wrote:

> Know that Abu al-Hasan al-Ash'ari did not innovate a new theological position or start a new school. Rather, he restated the school of the pious ancestors, fighting for the cause that was the way of the Messenger of God [s]. Those who follow his way do so because he gave a voice to the way of the pious ancestors and he established firm proofs and arguments for this voice. Therefore, those who follow this system of proofs and arguments call themselves Ash'ari . . . . al-Mayarqi the Maliki said, "Abu al-Hasan was not the first to argue the theology of the people of the Sunnah. Rather, he traversed an already established path and added to its proofs and clarity. He did not innovate a new position or school. Is it not clear that the school of the people of Medina was ascribed to Malik and those of this school call themselves Malikis? Malik, however, simply followed the example of the pious ancestors who came before him and he was strict in following them. When his school increased in proofs and clarity it became ascribed to him. The school of Abu al-Hasan al-Ash'ari evolved in the same way. He did nothing but clarify the positions of the pious ancestors, and his writings gave them victory."[147]

In another of his writings, al-Subki says: "All of the Hanafis, Shafi'is, Malikis, and Hanbalis are one in their creed, following the way of the Sunnah in the manner established by Abu al-Hasan

---

147. Taj al-Din AL-SUBKI, *Tabaqat al-Shafi'iyyah*. Maktabat 'Isa al-Babi al-Halabi, 3:367.

al-Ash'ari . . . . Generally speaking, the theology of the Ash'aris is gathered in the writings of Abu J'afar al-Tahawi, who has been received and accepted by the various schools."[148]

The great Hanafi jurist Ibn 'Abidin said, "His statement 'according to our creed,' means that which we believe which, aside from secondary matters of creed, every legally responsible individual must believe for themselves without uncritically following somebody else's opinion (taqlid). This set of beliefs is found amongst the people of the Sunnah who are none other than the Ash'aris and Maturidis, and both are in agreement, except for a few minor points, most of which merely amount to a difference in expression, as is clarified in the relevant places."[149]

According to this lengthy discussion and the opinions of the formidable scholars that we have considered, it would be correct to say that the creed of the Messenger of God [s] is the creed of the Ash'ari school. This is an affirmation of the reality of the situation just as we say that the Messenger of God [s] mostly recited according to the narration of Nafi' even though Nafi' never met the Messenger of God [s], and it is, in fact, Nafi' who recites like the Messenger of God [s], not the other way around. However, since Nafi' gathered together and compiled this recitation, it is said that the Prophet usually recited the recitation of Nafi', and based on this we can say that the creed of the Prophet [s] and his companions was the creed of the Ash'aris.

In conclusion, the theological position of the pious ancestors was to affirm the Quranic expressions as they are without addressing the linguistic meanings that may give the impression of a likeness between God and His creation. This was explicitly expressed by Imam al-Shafi'i, Imam Ahmad, and others, and it is the creed and theology of the Ash'aris. And God is Most High and knows best.

---

148. Taj al-Din AL-SUBKI, *Mu'id al-Ni'am wa Mubid al-Niqam*. Dar al-Kitab al-'Arabi, 62.

149. IBN 'ABIDIN, *Rad al-Muhtar 'ala al-Dur al-Mikhtar*, 1:49.

FATWAS RELATED TO
THE MESSENGER OF GOD [s]

Question 34:

What is the extent to which one should love the Messenger of God [s]? Are there limits? Can one's love for the Messenger of God [s] conflict with one's love for God?

Love for the Messenger of God [s] is a sign indicating one's love for God. He who loves a king will love his messenger. The Messenger of God [s] is God's beloved. He brought all goodness to us, and he endured great hardship for the sake of Islam and in the hope of our entering Paradise. He also taught us the extent to which we should love him: "By the One in whose hand is my soul, none of you believe until I become more beloved to him than his parents, his children, and all of humanity."[150] Zahra ibn M'abad reported on the authority of his grandfather, "We were with the Messenger of God [s] and he was holding the hand of 'Umar ibn al-Khattab and he ['Umar] said, 'By God, you are more beloved to me, O Messenger of God, than everything except my own self.' The Messenger of God [s] then said, 'None of you believe until I become more beloved than your own self.' 'Umar responded, 'Then you are now more beloved to me than my own self,' and the Messenger of God [s] said, 'Now 'Umar.'"[151]

Ibn Rajab al-Hanbali said, "Love for the Messenger of God [s] is one of the basic tenets of faith, and it is comparable to the love of God, which is a comparison that God Himself has made. He has also threatened those who place other loves, such as the natural love for relatives, wealth, or one's homeland, above their love for God and His Messenger [s]."[152]

One does not achieve true faith until his or her love for the

---

150. IBN HANBAL, *Musnad Imam Ahmad*, 3:177 and AL-BUKHARI, *Sahih Bukhari*, 1:14.

151. IBN HANBAL, *Musnad Imam Ahmad*, 4:233 and AL-BUKHARI, *Sahih Bukhari*, 5:2445.

152. 'Abd al-Rahman ibn Ahmad IBN RAJAB, *Fath al-Bari*. Maktabat al-Ghuraba' al-Athariyyah, 1:48.

Messenger of God [s] has reached the level that the Messenger himself indicated to 'Umar. This is the level of love that every Muslim should strive for. It does not conflict with one's love for God, as we love the Messenger of God [s] because he was sent from God, and the essence of our love for the Messenger of God [s] is our love for God. No human being better manifests God's attributes of beauty and perfection than the Messenger of God [s]. Therefore, in effect one loves the Divine manifestations reflected in the person of the Messenger of God [s]. This love, in essence, is for God alone.

We have briefly explained the extent to which we should love the Messenger of God [s]. May God bless us with this love and help us follow the Messenger of God [s], and may we be near him on the final day. God is Most High and knows best.

Question 35:

Is the Messenger of God [s] the best of creation as far as lineage is concerned? What proves this?

The Prophet Muhammad [s] is the best of humanity. He said, "I am the master of the children of Adam, without boasting."[153] He is the best of all creation, ranking higher than even the throne of God. Therefore, no human should be considered better than him in any aspect worthy of praise, and lineage is one of those aspects. God praises and honors his lineage by saying, *and your movements among those who prostrate themselves* [26:219]. Ibn 'Abbas commented on this verse, "His '*movements among those who prostrate themselves*' refers to his movements in the loins of the forefathers—Adam, Noah, and Abraham—until God brought him out as a prophet [s]."[154] Therefore, his lineage is the best among the prophets, as well as the best among humanity overall. The Messenger of God [s] said of himself, "God has chosen Isma'il from the children of Abraham, and He has chosen Bani Kinana from the children of Isma'il, and He has chosen Quraysh from Bani Kinana, and He has chosen Banu Hashim from the children of Quraysh, and He has chosen me from Banu Hashim."[155] The Messenger of God [s] also said, "God made all of creation, and He has created me from the best of them, from the best generation. Then He made them into tribes and made me from amongst the best of these tribes. Then He made them into families, and He made me from amongst the best of families. So I am the best of souls and the best of families."[156]

He is our master, Abu Qasim Muhammad, the son of 'Abdallah, the son of 'Abd al-Muttalib, the son of Hashim, the son of 'Abd al-Manaf, the son of Qusayy, the son of Kilab, the son of Murra, the son of Ka'b, the son of Lu'ayy, the son of Ghalib, the son of Fihr, the son of Malik, the son of al-Nadar, the son of Kinana, the son of

153. IBN HANBAL, *Musnad Imam Ahmad*, 1:4 and AL-NAYSABURI, *Sahih Muslim*, 4:1782.

154. Muhammad ibn Jarir b. Yazid AL-TABARI, *Tafsir al-Tabari*. Dar al-Fikr, 7:287 and Muhammad ibn Ahmad b. Abi Bakr AL-QURTUBI, *Tafsir al-Qurtubi*. Dar al-Shu'ab, 13:144.

155. IBN HANBAL, *Musnad Imam Ahmad*, 4:107 and AL-NAYSABURI, *Sahih Muslim*, 4:1782 and the wording is Muslim's.

156. IBN HANBAL, *Musnad Imam Ahmad*, 4:165 and AL-TIRMIDHI, *Sunan al-Tirmidhi*, 5:584 and the wording is his.

Khuzayma, the son of Mudrika, the son of Ilyas, the son of Mudar, the son of Nazar, the son of Mu'ad, the son of Adnan.

His mother was Amina, the daughter of Wahb, the son of 'Abd al-Manaf, the son of Zuhra, the son of Kilab, who was the Messenger of God's [s] fifth grandfather.

A lineage as if it has the sun of the early morning as its
Light, and the morning of daybreak as its support.

The lineage holds none but master upon master
Who have acquired noble qualities, piety, and magnanimity.

Thus we have learned that the Messenger of God [s] is the absolute best of creation. May God bring us benefit through him in this life and in the Hereafter, and may He guide us to his path. Our final prayer is that all praise is to God, and God is Most High and knows best.

Question 36:

"If it were not for our Master Muhammad [s], then God would not have made creation." What is the true meaning of this statement? Does it contradict the foundation of the Islamic creed?

The rule regarding phrases uttered by believers is that we should understand them in a way that does not contradict the principles of divine unity (*tawhid*). We should not hasten to judge people and label them as disbelievers (*kafirs*), sinners, or misguided innovators. A person's identification with Islam carries greater weight than the apparent meaning of his or her words. We must not immediately take at face value a statement implying disbelief and error. All Muslims should learn this rule and apply it to what they hear from their coreligionists.

For example, Muslims believe that Jesus [*alayhi al-salam*] brought the dead back to life only by the permission and aid of God, and that he was not able to do this on his own but only through the power and capacity of God. Christians, on the other hand, believe that Jesus brought the dead back to life through his own power and that Jesus was God, the son of God, or a hypostasis of the Divine. With this in mind, if we were to hear both a Muslim and a Christian say, "I belief that Jesus brought the dead back to life," then we cannot think that the Muslim has become a Christian through this statement. Rather, we must interpret the Muslim's statement in a way that is consistent with his being a Muslim and a believer in divine unity.

As for the statement framing this discussion, neither its outer nor its inner meaning indicates disbelief. If a person believes that all of creation was made for one person, then this does not remove him from the fold of Islam, even if this belief were to prove incorrect.

The statement, "If it were not for our Master, Muhammad [s], God would not have made creation," reaffirms our Muslim beliefs, especially when understood properly. God says in the Quran, *I have not created humans and jinn except to worship Me* [51:56], so the wisdom behind creation and its purpose is the worship of God, which cannot occur without the one who engages in worship, so worship is an attribute that dwells in the worshipper, and the best of worshipers is the Messenger of God [s] who is the paragon of worship and the perfect embodiment of divine unity. This is reinforced by the fact that the verse talks about humans and jinn, but not the rest of creation, for the rest of creation has been created for humanity: *He has made of service to you all that is in the heavens and all that is in the earth; it is all from Him. Indeed in this are portents for a people who reflect* [45:13].

This discussion has established that the statement in question is perfectly congruent with the principles of the Shari'ah. As the embodiment of divine unity and servitude to God, The Messenger of God [s] is the one who actualized the purpose behind creation since he is the paragon of embodying divine unity and servitude to God. He is the perfect human being and the model of humanity, and God created all that is in the heavens and earth for humankind. God is Most High and knows best.

Question 37:

Is the Messenger of God [s] light, or is he human like us, as
the Quran mentions?

The Messenger of God [s] is light. This is correct according to the
Quran, *Now has there come to you light from God and a plain Scripture*
[5:15]. God also says, *He [the Messenger of God] calls to the cause of God
by His permission as a lamp that gives light* [33:46]. The Messenger of
God [s] is both a light and a source of illumination from God. There
is nothing wrong with referring to him as a light, since this is how
God has referred to him.

The Sunnah has established that the companions used to say,
"His face is as the moon."[157] In addition, the Messenger of God [s]
recounted that, when his mother was pregnant with him, "she saw
a light that lit up the palaces of Basra in the lands of the Levant."[158]
His companions stated, "When the Messenger of God [s] entered
Medina, he illuminated everything, and when he passed everything became darkened in Medina."[159] We should not deny that his
light was actual and perceptible, for his possessing physical light
does not contradict any principles of faith or the Quran's reference
to him as being human.

It is, however, impermissible to negate the Messenger of God's
humanity [s], because this would conflict with the Quran's words,
Say: I am but a human being like you who receives revelation [41:6]. The
safe approach is to affirm all that God has affirmed concerning the
Messenger of God [s], such as him being light as well as being human, without going into details and debate. There is no contradiction in believing that the Messenger of God [s] was actually a light
and a source of illumination while affirming his human nature as
a created being. The nature of the moon is that it is stone, but it is
also a light and gives off a tangible light, and the Messenger of God
[s] is better than the moon, and he is the best of all creation [s]. We

157. AL-NASA'I, *al-Sunan al-Kubra*, 5:187, 6:155; AL-TABARANI, *al-Mu'jam
al-Kabir*, 10:147, Ahmad ibn Hajar AL-'ASQALANI, *Idah*, 6:180.

158. 'Abd al-Malak ibn Hisham AYYUB, *al-Sirah al-Nabawiyyah*. Dar
al-Jayl, 1:302; TABARANI, *Tarikh*, 1:458, AL-ASFAHANI, *Hilyat al-Awliya'*,
10:374.

159. IBN HANBAL, *Musnad Imam Ahmad*, 3:268; AL-TIRMIDHI, *Sunan
al-Tirmidhi*, 5:588; AL-QIZWINI, *Sunan Ibn Majah*, 1:522; AL-TAMIMI, *Sahih
Ibn Hibban*, 14:601.

ask God to guide us to the straight path. All praise is due to God, and He is Most High and knows best.

Question: 38:

"Jabir, the first thing created was the light of your Prophet [s]." Is this a sound *hadith*? Does it contradict any aspect of our beliefs concerning the Prophet [s]?

The *hadith* scholars have rated this statement as an objectionable *hadith* (*munkar*), and some have even labeled it a forgery (*mawdu'*). The notable scholar 'Abdallah ibn Siddiq al-Ghumari noted, "It has been ascribed to 'Abd al-Razzaq in error as this statement does not appear in his collection of hadiths, his writings, or his Quranic exegesis. Al-Suyuti states in his book *al-Hawi fi'l-Fatawi* (1:325), 'This statement has no chain that can be relied upon.' This is certainly a forged *hadith* . . . in general, hadiths that are objectionable and forged have no basis in the authentic books of *hadith*."[160] Some of the major *hadith* scholars, such as al-Saghani[161] and al-'Ajluni,[162] have categorized the *hadith* as a forgery.

However, we can consider the meaning of the *hadith* to be sound if we understand it to be referring to a primacy of lights, i.e., that his light was the first light. This interpretation would not be farfetched. As for the absolutely first creation, there is a well-known scholarly debate concerning whether it was the pen or the throne. Al-'Ajluni said, "It is said that the primacy of things is considered with regards to their own categories. So [the meaning of the *hadith* is], 'The first light created by God was my light.' In the *Ahkam* of Ibn Qattan, there is the *hadith* mentioned by Ibn Marzuq related on the authority of 'Ali, the son of Husayn, on the authority of his father ('Ali), on the authority of his grandfather (the Prophet Muhammad[s]) 'I was a light between the hands of my Lord 14,000 years before Adam was created.'"[163]

The great Maliki scholar al-Dardir reiterated this interpretation, "His light [s] is the source of all lights and material objects; as he said to Jabir, 'The first thing God created was the light of your Prophet from His light.'" Thus he is the intermediary for all of

160. Abdullah ibn Siddiq AL-GHUMARI, *Murshid al-Ha'ir li-Bayan Wad' Hadith Jabir*. Maktabat al-Qahira, 2.

161. al-Hasan ibn Muhammad b. al-Hasan al-Qurashi AL-SAGHANI, *al-Mawdu'at*. Dar al-Ma'mun li-l-Turath, 25.

162. AL-'AJLUNI, *Kashf al-Khafa'*, 2:232.

163. Ibid., 1:311-312.

creation."[164] God created numerous realms. He made the terrestrial kingdom, which is the realm of perception, as well as the celestial kingdom, which is the realm of the imperceptible. He created the realm of the spirit, the realm of the Jinn, and the realm of the angels. God also created lights, and nothing would have prevented Him from creating the Messenger of God [s] as the first light from which lights shone onto humanity in the realm of the spirit.

In conclusion, the *hadith* we have discussed is a forgery falsely ascribed to the Messenger of God [s]. The meaning, however, may be considered sound for the reasons we have explained. And God is Most High and knows best.

---

164. Ahmad ibn Muhammad b. Ahmad al-Dardir AL-'ADAWI, *al-Sharh al-Saghir*. Dar al-Ma'arif, 4:778-79.

Question 39:

And if, when they had wronged themselves, they had but come to you and asked forgiveness of God, and asked forgiveness of the Messenger, they would have found God Forgiving, Merciful [4:64]. Is this verse still in effect today, or did its relevance cease with the passing of the Messenger of God [s]?

This verse from Surah al-Nisa (the Chapter of Women) is absolute in its meaning. No restrictions, neither textual nor rational, limit its applicability. Nothing in the Sunnah restricts the verse's relevance to the earthly life of the Messenger of God [s], thus it remains in effect until the Day of Resurrection. The meaning of the Quran is in the generality of its wording, not the contextual specificity of the verse's revelation. Whoever claims that this verse is specified as being during the life of the Messenger of God [s] must produce evidence. General applicability of verses does not require evidence, for it is the basis of verses. Specifying a meaning, however, requires evidence.

This is what the scholars of Quranic exegesis have understood, particularly those who have relied on traditions for their commentaries such as Ibn Kathir. He commented on this verse saying, "Many notable scholars, among them Abu Nasr al-Sabbagh in his book *al-Shamil*, narrate the following well-known story on the authority of 'Utba, who said:

> I was sitting in the *Rawdah* of the Prophet[165] [s] and a bedouin came and said, "Greetings of praise O Messenger of God, I heard God say, *And if, when they had wronged themselves, they had but come to you and asked forgiveness of God, and asked forgiveness of the Messenger, they would have found God Forgiving, Merciful*, and I have come to you seeking forgiveness for my transgressions and seeking your intercession with God."

He then recited the following lines of poetry:

---

165. The *Rawdah* is the section between the Messenger of God's [s] grave and the pulpit from which he used to deliver sermons. It is considered to be a portion of heaven in accordance with the statement of the Messenger of God [s] "What is between my home and my pulpit is a garden from the gardens of Paradise." [Trans.]

O best of those whose bones are buried in the earth,
So that the earth was made sweet by the presence of his
bones,

My soul is a ransom for the grave in which you dwell,
In it is forgiveness, and in it is generosity and virtue.

Then he departed. My eyes became heavy with sleep and I
saw the Messenger of God [s] and he told me, "Utba, catch
that bedouin and give him the glad tidings that God has forgiven him."[166]

This is not to say that visions can serve as evidence. The evidence
here is that Ibn Kathir did not object to this story, which he narrated in the context of explaining the meaning of this verse. Additionally, the great companion 'Utba tacitly approval of the bedouin's statement and did not condemn his asking the Prophet [s]
for forgiveness after his passing from this world.

The jurists of Islam have used this verse to encourage the visitation of the Messenger of God's [s] grave. They have even deemed
it an encouraged act to recite this same verse when visiting the
Rawdah.[167] The al-Fatawa al-Hindiyyah says concerning the etiquette
of visiting the grave of the Messenger of God [s], "Then the visitor
should stand facing the head of the Messenger of God [s] and say,
'God, you have said, and your statement is truth, *And if, when they
had wronged themselves, they had but come to you and asked forgiveness
of God, and asked forgiveness of the Messenger, they would have found
God Forgiving, Merciful.*'"[168]

Ibn Hajj al-'Abdari represents the Maliki school's opinion,
"Seeking intercession (al-tawassul) through him [s] provides a
place to put down the burdens one carries, and the weight of sins
and mistakes; for the blessing of his intercession [s] and its high
standing with God is not exceeded by any sin, for it is greater than
all of them. So whoever visits him [s] should take glad tidings, and
those who have not visited him [s] should turn to God through the

---

166. IBN KATHIR, *Tafsir al-Quran al-'Azim*, 1:521. al-Bayhaqi also narrates
this story: AL-BAYHAQI, *Shu'ab al-Iman*, 3:496.

167. The area in the Prophet's mosque in Medina between his house
and his pulpit.

168. LAJNAT AL-'ULAMA, *al-Fatawa al-Hindiyyah*, 1:266, compiled by a
committee that Nidham al-Din Balkhi headed.

intercession of His Prophet[s]. Do not prevent us from attaining his intercession, O God, and we ask this by the sanctity he has with You. Whoever believes otherwise has been deterred. Have they not heard the statement of God, '*And if, when they had wronged themselves, they had but come to you and asked forgiveness of God, and asked forgiveness of the Messenger, they would have found God Forgiving, Merciful*'? Whoever comes to him [s] and stands at his door and seeks his intercession with God, they will find God most forgiving and most merciful. This is because God is too great to contradict His promise, and He has promised forgiveness to those who stand at the Prophet's [s] door and seek God's forgiveness. Only one who denies the true faith and rebels against God and His Messenger [s] doubts its permissibility. May God protect us from being barred from these blessings."[169]

As for the position of the Shafi'i school, Imam al-Nawawi stated that, "[after completing the visitation] one should return to stand in front of the head of the Messenger of God [s] and make a supplication by calling to God through him and to ask for his intercession. The best of what can be said is the story narrated on the authority of 'Utba that has been mentioned by al-Mawardi, Qadi Abu Tayyib, and the rest of the Shafi'i scholars."[170] Imam al-Nawawi then recounts the story mentioned by Ibn Kathir.

Imam Ibn Qudama puts forth the Hanbali school's position on the matter. He instructs us to recite the verse in question, using it to address the Messenger of God [s] and ask him for forgiveness. He continues:

> Then you come upon the grave and turn your back to the *qibla* and face the grave of the Messenger of God[s] and say, "Peace be upon you O Messenger of God and blessings from God and His grace be with you. Peace be upon you O Messenger of God, O chosen one from amongst His creation and His servants. I bear witness that there is no divinity but God alone, and that he has no partners; and I bear witness that Muhammad is his servant and Messenger. I bear witness that you delivered the message of God, sincerely advised the Muslim community, called to the way of God with wisdom and good council, and

169. Muhammad ibn Muhammad al-'Abdari IBN AL-HAJJ, *al-Madkhal*. Maktabat al-Turath, 1:260.

170. AL-NAWAWI, *al-Majmu'*, 8:256.

worshiped and served God until you passed. May God send you abundant prayers to His pleasing. O God, give reward to our Prophet on our behalf, more than you have rewarded anyone from the Prophets and Messengers, and bring him, O God, to reside in the praiseworthy station that you promised him and which will exult him above the first and last of creation. O God, send prayers to Muhammad and the kin of Muhammad as you bestow prayers on Abraham and on the kin of Abraham; and bless Muhammad and the kin of Muhammad as you have blessed Abraham and the kin of Abraham. Indeed, You are the praiseworthy, the Exalted. O God, you have spoken and your words are true: *and if, when they had wronged themselves, they had but come to you and asked forgiveness of God, and asked forgiveness of the Messenger, they would have found God Forgiving, Merciful.* I have come, seeking forgiveness for my sins and seeking the intercession of the Messenger of God, so I ask you, O God, to give me forgiveness as you gave those who came to him during his lifetime. O God, make him the foremost interceder, and the most successful of those who ask, and the most noble of the first and the last of creation by your mercy, O the most Merciful of the merciful." One should then make supplications for their parents, their companions, and all Muslims.[171]

The notable scholar al-Rahibani, from the Hanbali school, emphasized the importance of reciting this verse while visiting the grave of the Messenger of God [s]. He also advised one to say during the visit,

O God, reward the Prophet Muhammad on our behalf more than you have rewarded any of the Prophets and Messengers, and grant him the praiseworthy station which you promised him, and by which he will be exalted above the first and the last of creation. O God, bestow prayers on Muhammad and on the kin of Muhammad, as you bestow prayers on Abraham and on the kin of Abraham; and bless Muhammad and the kin of Muhammad as you bless Abraham and the kin of Abraham. Indeed, you are the praiseworthy, the exalted. O God, you said, and your statement is true, *and if, when they had wronged themselves, they had but come to you and asked forgiveness of God, and*

---

171. IBN QUDAMA AL-MAQDISI, *al-Mughni*, 3:298.

asked forgiveness of the Messenger, they would have found God Forgiving, Merciful. I have come seeking forgiveness for my sins, seeking the intercession of the Messenger of God, so I ask you, O God, to give me forgiveness as you gave those who came to him during his lifetime. O God, make him the first interceder, and the most successful of those who ask, and the most noble of the first and the last of creation by your mercy, O the most Merciful of the merciful." One should then make supplication for their parents, their companions, and all Muslims.[172]

From the preceding evidence, we know that all the schools of Islamic law encourage the recitation of this verse upon visiting the *Rawdah,* and that they believe that its meaning is still in effect. This is what the pious ancestors did and believed, as well as the scholars who followed in their footsteps, and the opinions of those who deviate from this have no weight. The Messenger of God's [s] ability to request forgiveness for us after his passing does not contradict any rational or textual evidence. The Messenger of God [s] said, "My life is good for you; you speak to me and I respond. And my death is better for you; your actions are presented to me, and I praise God for that which I find good, and I seek your forgiveness for you for that which I find bad."[173] And God is Most High and knows best.

172. Mustafa ibn Sa'd b. 'Abduh AL-RAHYABANI, *Matalalib Uli al-Nuha,* 2:441.

173. AL-BAZZAR, *Musnad al-Bazzar,* 1:379; AL-HARITH IBN USAMAH and 'Ali ibn Abi Bakr AL-HAYTHAMI, *Musnad al-Harith bi-Zawa'id al-Haythami.* Markaz Khidmat al-Sunnah wa al-Sirah, 2:884; AL-DAYLAMI, *Musnad al-Firdous bi Ma'thur al-Khitab,* 2:137; AL-HAYTHAMI, *Majma' al-Zawa'id,* 9:24 and he commented on it by saying, "its narrators are all sound." AL-'IRAQI, *Tarh al-Tathrib,* 3:297 and he commented by saying, "its chain is good." 'Abd al-Ra'uf AL-MANAWI, *Fayd al-Qadir.* Al-Maktabat al-Tijariyyah al-Kubra, 3:401 and he was astonished at those who said this *hadith* was *mursal.* Other hadith masters graded it as rigorously authentic such as Nawawi, Ibn al-Tin, Qurtubi, Qadi 'Iyad, and Ibn Hajar.

Question 40:

What is the importance of loving the Prophet's [s] kin? Are there limits to this love?

God says, *Say: I ask of you no fee, save loving kindness among kinsfolk* [42:23]. Sa'id ibn Jubayr commented on this verse, "There was not a single sub-tribe within the Quraysh that did not have kinship with the Prophet [s]; therefore God said, 'Only that you respect the ties of kinship that are between you and me.'"[174] The verse is a directive concerning the Prophet's kin [s], and God commanded him to convey it to people.

The Messenger of God [s] commanded us to love his kin and hold fast to them. He has advised us concerning them, may peace be upon them all, in many hadiths. For example, he said, "O people I am but a mortal, and soon the angel of death will come to me and I must obey him. I am leaving two weighty legacies with you. The first is the book of God. In it is guidance and light, so take it and hold fast to it. The second is the people of my household (*ahl bayti*). I remind you of God when it comes to the rights of the people of my household." Husayn then said, "Who are his kin, O Zayd (the narrator of the *hadith*). Are not his wives from his kin?" He said, "His wives are from his kin, but his kin are all those for whom charity has been forbidden to accept." Husayn said, "Who are these?" He said, "They are the kin of Ali, the kin of 'Aqil, the kin of J'afar, and the kin of 'Abbas." Husayn said, "All of these are forbidden from accepting charity?" He said, "Yes."[175] The Messenger of God [s] also stated, "O people, I have left with you that which, if you hold fast to it, you will never go astray: the book of God and my progeny, the people of my household."[176]

We love God immensely, and through our love for God we have come to love the Messenger of God [s]. The goodness with which God has blessed the whole world flows to us by way of the Prophet [s]. Through our love for him, we love the people of his household whom the Messenger of God [s] described as possessing virtues and good traits great in both number and quality. Therefore, love

---

174. AL-BUKHARI, *Sahih Bukhari*, 4:1289.

175. IBN HANBAL, *Musnad Imam Ahmad*, 4:366 and AL-NAYSABURI, *Sahih Muslim*, 4:1873.

176. IBN HANBAL, *Musnad Imam Ahmad*, 3:26 and AL-TIRMIDHI, *Sunan al-Tirmidhi*, 5:662.

for the Messenger of God's [s] kin resides deep in the recesses of
the Muslim heart. It signifies love for the Messenger of God [s], just
as loving the Messenger of God [s] signifies one's love for God. By
loving God we have loved all goodness. Therefore, we are all directed to the same source of aid in order to realize the same goal,
and we ask God to teach us what He wills.

There is no excess when it comes to love, but there can be excess in beliefs. We believe in no deity except God, and we uphold
that our master Muhammad [s] is the Messenger of God. We believe that the Prophets are infallible, and that none but the Prophets, not even their pure progeny or companions, are infallible like
them, though they are protected in the way that God protects the
righteous. If a Muslim's belief is sound concerning these issues,
then he should love the people of the Prophet's household with
all his heart. One's love, in actuality, reaches degrees to which God
elevates whomsoever He wills. The more one loves the kin of the
Messenger of God [s], the more he or she advances in rank amongst
the righteous. Love for the kin of the Messenger of God is a sign of
love for the Messenger of God [s], and love for the Messenger of
God [s] is a sign of one's love for God. And God is Most High and
knows best.

Question 41:

Is it possible to physically see the Prophet [s] while awake?
How should these visions be understood?

Seeing the Messenger of God [s] while awake is not related to legislation and does not result in an increase or decrease of how religious a person is. This matter pertains to one's experience of the world, and whoever claims to have had such a vision bears the responsibility for it. Seeing the Messenger of God [s] in a waking state is a good tiding and a marvel. It does not conflict with the Messenger's passing from this life, nor does it mean that one has become a companion of his.

To analyze this issue beyond our introductory remarks, we must first ask whether or not this phenomenon is rationally possible. What is rationally impossible is that one entity be simultaneously present in two locations. Seeing the Messenger of God [s] in a waking state does not depend on his being present in two locations, for his location is the *Rawdah* where he is alive in his grave, praying to his Lord and enjoying His good company, as do all of the deceased prophets. Anas reported that the Messenger of God [s] said, "The Prophets are alive in their graves praying."[177] In another statement, the Messenger of God [s] recounted, "I passed by Moses on the night of my ascent near the red dune, and he was standing praying in his grave."[178]

Seeing the Prophet [s] while in a waking state is considered nothing more than a disclosure of the Prophet's state in his grave. Interpreting these visions as such is not denied by reason, and textual proof also supports it. 'Umar ibn al-Khattab was delivering a sermon when God revealed to him Sariya's condition. This was a marvel because Sariya was in Nahawand, Persia at that time. 'Umar called out, "O Sariya, the mountain, the mountain!" and

---

177. Abu Ya'ala Ahmad ibn 'Ali b. al-Muthanna AL-TAMIMI, *Musnad Abu Ya'ala.* Dar al-Ma'mun li-l-Turath, 6:147; AL-DAYLAMI, *Musnad al-Firdous bi Ma'thur al-Khitab*, 1:119; AL-HAYTHAMI, *Majma' al-Zawa'id*, 8:21 and he commented by saying, "Abu Ya'ala and al-BAzzar narrated it and the narrators of Abu Ya'ala are reliable."

178. IBN HANBAL, *Musnad Imam Ahmad*, 3:148; AL-NAYSABURI, *Sahih Muslim*, 4:1845; AL-NISA'I, *Sunan al-Nisa'I (al-Mujtabah)*, 1:419; AL-TAMIMI, *Sahih Ibn Hibban*, 1:241.

Sariya heard him.[179] As long as this can happen to others besides the Prophet [s], then it is not restricted to 'Umar ibn al-Khattab or the Companions. The same goes for the one who was seen: it was not exclusive to Sariya.

The vision can be an actual sighting of the Messenger of God [s], meaning that one perceives an image of his living state in the *Rawdah*. These images from the realm of reflection result from that person's immense love and contemplation of the Messenger of God [s]. A person may see multiple forms due to the many planes of reflection, such as mirrors and the like.

One particular *hadith*, transmitted on the authority of Abu Hurayra, clearly indicates the possibility of seeing the Messenger of God [s] in a waking state. Abu Hurayra reportedly heard the Messenger of God [s] say, "Whoever sees me in their dreams, they will see me in a waking state, and Satan does not take on my form."[180] The Prophet's [s] claim, "they will see me in a waking state," predicts potential visions of him during one's life. Restricting visions of the Messenger of God [s] to the Day of Resurrection is difficult for two reasons. First, everyone will see the Messenger of God [s] on the Day of Resurrection, regardless of whether they have seen him in dreams. Secondly, the *hadith* itself mentions no restriction of its meaning; therefore imposing limits on these occurrences would be unjustified.

Questions about seeing the Messenger of God [s] in a waking state were asked during the time of Imam al-Suyuti, who composed a treatise on the issue entitled *Tanwir al-Halak fi Imkan Ru'ya al-Nabi wa'l-Malak* (Illuminating the Darkness Concerning the Possibility of Seeing the Prophet and Angels). He says in the introduction, "There have been many questions regarding those gnostics who have seen the Prophet [s] in a waking state. Those who have no firm grounding in knowledge have exaggerated by denouncing this act and acting surprised upon hearing it, claiming that it is impossible. In light of this, I composed this treatise."[181] Imam al-Suyuti goes on to provide textual evidence proving that it is pos-

179. TABARANI, *Tarikh*, 2:553; IBN 'ABD AL-BARR, *al-Isti'ab*, 4:1605; and AL-'ASQALANI, *al-Isabah*, 3:6.

180. AL-BUKHARI, *Sahih Bukhari*, 6:2567 and AL-SIJISTANI, *Sunan Abi Dawud*, 4:305.

181. 'Abd al-Rahamn ibn Abi Bakr b. Muhammad Jalal al-Din AL-SUYU-TI, *Tanwir al-Halak fi Ru'yat al-Nabi wa al-Malak*. Jawami' al-Kalam, p. 10.

sible to see and hear the Prophet [s] in a waking state. He also addresses hearing the voice of the angels.

Ibn Hajar al-Haythami said:

> [This matter] has been denied by some and deemed possible by others who are correct. This has been mentioned by the righteous, whose integrity cannot be questioned. In addition, the *hadith* found in Bukhari reports, "Whoever has seen me in their sleep will see me in a waking state," meaning with their eyes or their heart. The meaning, as deduced by some, is it refers to the Day of Reckoning, but that is a stretch. There is no point in constricting the meaning, as all of us will see the Prophet [s] on the Day of Reckoning, including those who have seen him during sleep and those who have not. Ibn Abi Jamrah, in his commentary on the hadiths he selected from the collection of Bukhari, held this particular *hadith* to have a general meaning applicable to both the Prophet's [s] life and after. This vision is for the one who is able to follow the Sunnah. He said "Whoever claims that this *hadith* is specific, without the Prophet [s] having specified it himself, has made a baseless assumption." He went on to say that anyone who denies this, denies the trustworthiness of the Prophet [s] and is ignorant of the power of God. Such a person is a denier of the marvels of the saints, which have been confirmed by sound proofs of the Sunnah.[182]

The noble scholar al-Nafrawi al-Maliki has written:

> It is possible to see the Prophet [s] in a waking state, as well as in one's sleep, according to an agreement of the *hadith* masters. The debate is, however, whether one sees his noble essence or an image of it. The first is the opinion of some, while the second is held by al-Ghazzali, al-Qarafi, al-Yafi'i, and others. The first opinion is supported by the fact the Prophet [s] is the lamp and light of guidance and the sun of the gnosis. Therefore, as one sees the light, the lamp, and the sun from afar, and what is seen is the body of the sun and its accidental characteristics, so is it with the Prophet's [s] noble body. He does not leave his blessed grave; instead, God removes the veils so that

---

182. Ahmad ibn Shihab al-Din al-Makki AL-HAYTHAMI, *al-Fatawa al-Hadithiyyah*. 3rd ed. Musata al-Babi al-Halabi, 1989, p. 298.

one can see him in his location no matter where that person might be, whether in the East or West. Or the veils remain but are made transparent so as not to veil what is behind them. What al-Qarafi has argued, however, is that seeing the Prophet [s] in a night vision is accomplished by the heart, which is not blocked by the deadening aspects of sleep. Therefore the vision is through one's inner perception, not one's actual vision. The proof of this is that even a blind person can see him.

Some people have claimed that they have seen and met the Prophet [s] in a waking state, such as Ibn Abi Jamrah and others. Their proof is the well-known *hadith*, "Whoever sees me in their sleep will see me in a waking state." The person that denies this is truly at a great loss; if he or she is amongst those who deny the marvels of the saints, then discussing such a matter with that individual is fruitless since he or she deny what the Sunnah confirms. The teacher of our teachers, Imam al-Laqqani, has addressed all these matters in his didactic poem *Sharh Jawharah al-Tawhid*.[183]

Ibn al-Hajj wrote in his book *al-Madkhal*: "Some have claimed that they have actually seen the Prophet [s] in a waking state. However, this is a rare phenomenon. Those who can claim it are few and require a level of purity that is rare in this age. Rather, it is near extinction. We do not, however, deny it from happening to those whom God protects in their outer and inner states."[184]

Sheikh 'Ilaysh has even spoken of seeing the Prophet [s] in a waking state as a support for the opinions of the scholars. He says, quoting from the gnostic al-Sh'arani,

I heard my sheikh, 'Ali al-Khawas say, "According to the people of gnosis and insight without exception, nothing that the mujtahid Imams say can ever contradict the Shari'ah. How can what they say stray from the Shari'ah when they have examined and weighed their words with the Quran and Sunnah and the statements of the Companions, as well as their meeting the Messenger of God [s] and asking him concerning all the issues regarding proofs they have come across. They would ask him, 'Is this from your statement, O Messenger of God?' in a waking

183. AL-NAFRAWI, *al-Fawakih al-Dawani*, 2:360.
184. IBN AL-HAJJ, *al-Madkhal*, 3:194.

state and orally. Likewise, they would ask him concerning everything related to the Quran and Sunnah before incorporating it into their books making it religious knowledge by which they worship God, and they would ask him, 'O Messenger of God, we have understood such and such from your statement in *hadith* such and such. Are you content with this or not?' They would act according to his statements and suggestions. Whoever questions the gnosis and insight of the Imams, and their meeting with the Messenger of God [s] in the realm of the soul, we shall say to them 'This is one of the marvels of the saints.'[185]

The above discussion establishes that the pious do indeed see the Messenger of God [s] in waking states. There is no rational or scriptural opposition to this occurrence. But it is a rare occurrence, and the door is not open to everyone. It is the responsibility of one who has visions of the Prophet [s] to not relate their experience to those who cannot understand it, because this could cause them to deny the possibility altogether. Speaking to people of that which they can comprehend is better, and God is Most High and knows best.

---

185. Muhammad ibn Ahmad b. Muhammad 'ILLAYSH, *Fath al-'Ali al-Malik*. Dar al-Ma'rifah, 1:92-93.

Question 42:

Every year Muslims who celebrate the birth of the Messenger of God [s] are criticized by those who condemn the celebrations as reprehensible innovation (*bid'a*). What is the correct understanding of this matter?

The birth of the Messenger of God [s] was an outpouring of Divine Mercy within human history. The Quran describes the presence of the Prophet [s] as a "mercy to all the worlds." Divine mercy affects personal growth, self-purification, knowledge, guidance to the straight path, and progression in one's material and spiritual life. This mercy is not limited to specific historical circumstances. Mercy stretches through the entirety of history: *Along with others of them who have not yet joined them. He is the Mighty, the Wise* [62:3].

Celebrating the birth of the Messenger of God [s] is one of the best ways to draw near to God. As an expression of happiness and love for the Prophet [s], celebration of the Prophet [s] is fundamental to faith. According to a rigorously authentic *hadith*, he said: "By the One who holds my soul, none of you truly believes until I am more beloved to you than your parents and children."[186] He also said, "None of you truly believe until I am more beloved to you than your parents, your children, and all people."[187]

Ibn Rajab wrote:

Love of the Prophet is one of the fundamentals of faith, and it is equivalent to loving God, as the two are associated. God has also warned those who place love of anything else that is natural to love such as kin, wealth, and homeland above this love, by saying, *Say: If your fathers, and your sons, and your brethren, and your wives, and your tribe, and the wealth you have acquired, and merchandise for which you fear that there will be no sale, and dwellings you desire, are dearer to you than God and His Messenger and striving in His way, then wait until God brings His command to pass. God guides not wrongdoing folk.* When 'Umar said to the Prophet [s], "You are more beloved to me than anything else except myself," the Prophet [s] responded, "'Umar, until I am more beloved than even yourself." 'Umar then said, "By God,

---

186. AL-BUKHARI, *Sahih Bukhari*, 1:14 and AL-NAYSABURI, *Sahih Muslim*, 1:76.

187. AL-BUKHARI, *Sahih Bukhari*, 1:14.

you are more beloved to me than myself." The Prophet [s] said, "Now 'Umar."[188]

To celebrate the Prophet's birth [s] is to celebrate him [s] and it is absolutely legitimate as he is one of the fundamentals of the religion. God made known to the world the rank of His Prophet [s] informing everything in existence of the Prophet's name, his prophetic commission, his spiritual rank, and his status. All of creation is in a state of joy and bliss due to the Light of God, His relief from hardship, His blessing, and His proof.

Since the fourth and fifth Islamic centuries, our pious ancestors have celebrated the birth of our beloved by enlivening the eve of his birth with various virtuous acts such as feeding the poor, reciting the Quran, reciting litanies, and singing religious odes, particularly those praising him. Many historians, such as al-Hafiz Ibn Jawzi, Hafiz Ibn Kathir, Hafiz Ibn Dihya al-Andalusi, Hafiz Ibn Hajar, and the seal of the hadith masters, Imam al-Suyuti, have documented these happenings, may God be pleased with them all.

Numerous scholars and jurists have composed treatises describing the favorability of celebrating the Prophet's [s] birth. They discuss the textual proofs in such a manner that anyone who is intelligent and of sound mind cannot deny the nature of our pious ancestors' activities. In al-Madkhal, Ibn al-Hajj enumerated the uniqueness of this celebration in such a way that reading his words gladdens any believer's heart, especially since we know that Ibn al-Hajj wrote al-Madkhal to criticize reprehensible innovations unfounded by the Shari'ah.

Following an inquiry concerning the ruling on celebrating the birth of the Prophet [s] during the month of Rabi' al-Awwal, Imam Jalal al-Din al-Suyuti wrote in his book Husn al-Maqsad fi 'Amal al-Mawlid:

> My answer is: the basis for celebrating the birth of the Prophet [s] is the gathering of the people, recitation of the Quran, and reciting reported traditions concerning the noble beginnings of the Prophet [s] and the signs that appeared at his birth. After recitations, they eat food that has been prepared and the celebrations are brought to a close. This is a praiseworthy in-

---

188. IBN RAJAB, Fath al-Bari, 1:22 and AL-BUKHARI, Sahih Bukhari, 6:2445.

novation and the person performing it is rewarded, as it is a way of magnifying the rank of the Prophet [s] and a form of expressing happiness and joy at his noble birth.

Al-Suyuti responded to those who say, "We have no knowledge of the basis of this act from the Quran or Sunnah," by asserting, "The lack of knowledge of something does not require its non-existence." Al-Suyuti goes on to highlight the opinion of Ibn Hajar, who found a basis for celebrations in the Sunnah. Al-Suyuti himself found further evidence in the Sunnah. He also distinguished reprehensible innovations as the ones that have no legal basis and therefore cannot be praised. If, however, legal proof is found for them, they cease to be reprehensible innovations.

Al-Bayhaqi has narrated on the authority of Imam al-Shafi'i, "Newly invented matters are of two kinds: one is something that contradicts the Quran, Sunnah, a tradition, or scholarly consensus. This is the reprehensible innovation. The second is a newly invented matter of goodness of which there is no doubt amongst anyone. This is a newly invented matter that is not reprehensible. 'Umar ibn al-Khattab said, concerning the night prayers of Ramadan, 'What a great innovation this is!' meaning that nightly prayers were a newly invented practice that was not in existence before, and in its implementation there is no negation of prior practices."[189]

Al-Suyuti said, in light of Imam al-Shafi'i's quote cited above, "Celebrating the birth of the Messenger of God [s] does not contravene the Quran, the Sunnah, traditions, or scholarly consensus, and therefore is not a reprehensible innovation, as is clear from al-Shafi'i's statement. Rather, this act is one of the pious acts that were not present during the early generations. Likewise, feeding people from food not acquired through unlawful means is a pious act. It is therefore one of the recommended innovations, as stated by the prince of scholars, Al-'Izz ibn 'Abd al-Salam."

The Prophet's birth is God's greatest blessing, and the Shari'ah encourages us to openly display gratitude to God for His blessings upon us. Thus gathering to celebrate the birth of the Messenger of God [s] in order to publicize the occasion is a recommended act and a means of attaining proximity to God. Ibn al-Hajj opined in his book *al-Madkhal*: "In this month God has blessed us with the

---

189. Ahmad ibn al-Hussein b. 'Ali AL-BAYHAQI, *al-Madkhal ila al-Sunan al-Kubra*. Dar al-Khulafa' al-Makatib al-Islamiyyah, 206.

greatest of the first and the last. Therefore, it is proper that there be an increase in good works, acts of devotion, and thanksgiving for what God has given us."[190]

As textual proof, Ibn Hajar uses a *hadith* found in the two Sahih collections. The *hadith* recounts that the Messenger of God [s] came to Medina and found the Jews fasting 'Ashura. He asked about this practice and they explained, "This is the day that God caused pharaoh to drown and saved Moses, so we fast this day out of thanks to God." Ibn Hajar said, "One can derive from this text the permissibility of annually thanking God for a blessing He bestowed on a certain day, the bestowal of favor, or the removal of a tribulation. Showing thanks to God takes many forms, such as prostration, fasting, giving charitably, and reciting the Quran. And what could be a greater blessing than the manifestation of this Messenger of mercy [s] on this day?"

Ibn Hajar further expounds on the types of celebration that can occur on this specific day, "We should limit ourselves to those things which are known to be a sign of giving thanks to God, such as the recitation of the Quran, feeding the poor, and singing odes in praise of the Messenger of God [s] that cause the heart to move towards good works in preparation for the Last Day. There is nothing wrong with including whatever is permissible as a way of showing joy."

Al-Suyuti has quoted the Imam of Quranic recitation, al-Hafiz Shams al-Din ibn al-Jazari, from his book *'Urf al-T'arif bi'l-Mawlid al-Sharif*:

It is rigorously authenticated that Abu Lahab's punishment in the hellfire is reduced every Monday due to his freeing Thuwayba (his slave girl) as a sign of thanksgiving for the birth of the Messenger of God [s]. If this is Abu Lahab, the disbeliever whom the Quran has damned, and his punishment is allowed to be lessened as a result of his happiness for the birth of the Messenger of God [s], then what is the state of the believer from the followers of the Prophet [s] who is happy because of his birth and spends all he can in expressing this love? Indeed, his reward would be to be admitted to paradise by God.

In his book *Mawrid al-Sadi fi Mawlid al-Hadi*, Al-Hafiz Shams al-Din al-Dimashqi composed lines of poetry on this subject:

190. IBN AL-HAJJ, *al-Madkhal*, 480.

If this one [Abu Lahab] is a disbeliever whose damnation has
  been proclaimed,
And whose hands have perished while in Hell, abiding therein
  forever,

And it has come to us that on Monday of every week
His punishment is made lighter for being delighted by the
  birth of Ahmad.

What does one think, then, of the servant whose entire life
Is made joyful by the birth of Ahmad, and who dies as a
  monotheist?[191]

God's statement, *And remind them of the days of God* [14:50], also
serves as proof because there is no doubt that the birth of the Messenger of God [s] is one of the days of God. Celebrating this day is
nothing but a way of obeying this command, and cannot be considered a reprehensible innovation. Rather, it is a good sunnah, even
if it did not occur during the time of the Messenger of God [s].

We celebrate the birth of the Messenger of God [s] because
we love him. How can we not love him as all of creation knows
and loves him? Even the tree stump, which is an inanimate object,
loved the Messenger of God [s] and was attached to him and longed
to be with him to the point that it cried extensively out of longing. This story was passed down to us by corroborative continuity,
meaning that it possesses a sound chain of narrators and its veracity is unquestioned. Many of the companions reported,

The Prophet [s] used to deliver his sermons standing, while
leaning on the stump of a palm tree that was standing straight. If his
sermon was long, he would place his blessed hand on that stump.
When the number of people praying increased, the companions
built him a pulpit. When he left his blessed room one Friday going
to the pulpit he passed the stump he used to use for his sermons,
and the tree stump let out a great cry, and it moaned a great moan,
until the entire mosque was shaking and the tree stump split. It did

---

191. All of the preceding are quotations taken from 'Abd al-Rahman ibn
Abi Bakr b. Muhammad Jalal al-Din AL-SUYUTI, *Husn al-Maqasid fi 'Amal
al-Mawlid*. Jawami' al-Kalam, 5-15, and all of this has also been quoted in
toto by Ibn Qasim in his gloss on Ahmad ibn 'Ali b. Hajar AL-HAYTHAMI
and Yahya ibn Sharf AL-NAWAWI, *Tuhfat al-Muhtaj Sharh al-Minhaj*. Dar
Ihya' al-Turath al-'Arabi, 7:424.

not stop until the Messenger of God [s] descended from the pulpit, went to it, wiped his hands over it, hugged it, brought it close to his chest, and it quieted. He then allowed it to make a choice: either it could be planted in paradise and drink from the waters of paradise, or it could be planted in this world. The tree stump chose paradise, and the Messenger of God [s] said 'So be it, God willing, so be it, God willing, so be it, God willing.' The tree stump ceased, and the Messenger of God said, 'By the One who holds my soul, if I did not attend to it, it would have cried and moaned until the coming of the Hour out of longing for the Messenger of God [s].'[192]

From the words of the great scholars, such as Ibn Hajar, Ibn al-Jawzi, al-Suyuti, and others preceding them, it is clear that the Prophet's [s] birth has been celebrated by the greater Muslim community since the 5th Hijri century. Celebrating his birth by reciting the Quran, performing invocations, and feeding the poor is an encouraged act in accordance with scholarly opinion. Certain celebratory expressions and practices, such as dancing lewdly and playing the *tablah* drum, are worthy of blame and should be avoided. No consideration should be given to those who depart from this consensus of communal practices and the statements of the scholars. This celebration is not too much for the Prophet of Mercy, the beloved of God the Lord of all the worlds [s]. We conclude with the words of Imam al-Busiri's poem *al-Burdah*:

His form and meaning both were made complete,
Then life's Creator chose him as beloved.

In beauty, he transcends all earthly partners,
In him is beauty's very essence, whole.

From what the Christians for their prophet claim
Abstain, and wisely praise him as you like.

Ascribe whatever honors to his essence,
To his status, any greatness that you wish:

---

192. This *hadith* has been narrated by many of the hadith masters using similar language. It can be found in: IBN HANBAL, *Musnad Imam Ahmad*, 3:293; AL-BUKHARI, *Sahih Bukhari*, 3:1313; AL-TIRMIDHI, *Sunan al-Darami*, 1:30; AL-TAMIMI, *Sahih Ibn Hibban*, 14:435; AL-KUFI, *Musannaf ibn Abi Shaybah*, 6:319; AL-TABARANI, *al-Mu'jam al-Awsat*, 2:367; AL-TAMIMI, *Musnad Abi Ya'ala*, 6:114.

Sheikh 'Ali Gomaa

The Messenger's superiority
Is boundless, so it cannot be expressed.

And God is Most High and knows best.

Question 43:

Some claim that the parents of the Messenger of God [s] were polytheists (*mushrikun*) and are now in the hellfire. Is this true?

Previously we stated that love for the Messenger of God [s] is amongst the greatest acts by which one draws near God. We have also discussed the place of this love in Islam in question thirty-four. This *hadith* of the Prophet [s] serves as sufficient review: "By the One in whose hands lies my soul, none of you truly believes until I become more beloved to you than your parents, your offspring, and all of humanity."[193] Love is counter to the feeling of wanting to harm and insult the beloved object or person. There is no doubt that negative comments about the parents of the Messenger of God [s] hurt him. God states in the Quran: *Those who vex the messenger of God, for them there is a painful doom* [9:61], and *Lo! those who malign God and His Messenger, God has cursed them in the world and the Hereafter, and He has prepared for them the doom of the disdained* [33:57]. God has clearly forbidden us to hurt and insult the Messenger of God [s]; He reminds us of this by mentioning the story of the Israelites and their relationship with Moses, *O you who believe! Be not as those who slandered Moses, but God proved his innocence of that which they alleged, and he was well esteemed in God's sight* [33:69]. Qadi 'Iyad stated, "We do not say anything that is displeasing to God and His Messenger [s], and we do not violate his noble state and insult him with words that he would find negative."

Since they were not recipients of a messenger from God, the parents of the Prophet [s], as well as his grandparents, are not polytheists, even if a sound tradition indicates that they engaged in practices outwardly resembling polytheism. The scholars of Sunni Islam are entirely in agreement that those living between the appearances of two messengers, who engaged in polytheism by changing the laws of pure monotheism, are not punished in the hellfire. The proof text regarding this issue is in the statements of God, *We do not punish anyone until a messenger is sent to them* [17:15]; *This is because your Lord destroys not the townships arbitrarily while their people are unconscious [of the wrong they do]* [6:131]; *And We de-*

---

193. IBN HANBAL, *Musnad Imam Ahmad*, 3:177 and AL-BUKHARI, *Sahih Bukhari*, 1:14.

stroyed no township but that which was warned [26:208]. Judgment can be levied against humanity only once a messenger has been sent to them.

These verses point to what the people of the truth, the people of the Sunnah, believe: that God, out of His mercy and generosity, does not punish anyone until He sends them a messenger. One might say that the parents of the Messenger of God [s] were sent a messenger, and that they apostatized after firm proofs were established against them. However, the texts do not support such a claim, and in fact many refute this claim: *And We have given them no scriptures which they study, nor sent We unto them, before you, any harbinger* [34:44]; *That you may warn a folk unto whom no harbinger came before you, that haply they may give heed* [28:46]; *And never did your Lord destroy the townships, until He had raised up in their mother[town] a messenger reciting unto them Our revelations. And never did We destroy the townships unless the folk thereof were evil-doers* [28:59]. These verses prove that the parents of the Messenger of God [s] are not amongst those who are punished in the hellfire; not just because they are his parents, but also because they are from the "people of the intermission," meaning they lived in the period between two messengers defined above. Al-Shatibi has written, "It has been part of God's Sunnah that He does not take anyone to account for their bad deeds until a messenger has been sent to them. If firm proofs have been established and delivered, then whoever desires let them believe, and whoever rejects let them reject, and each is appropriately recompensed for their choice."[194] Al-Qasimi has said regarding the exegesis of the verse, *And We do not punish anyone until a messenger is sent to them* [17:15], "Otherwise it would not be right, rather it would be impossible according to our habits and customs, which are based on clear wisdoms, that we would punish a people before a messenger be sent to them to guide them to truth and to keep them away from darkness so that the proofs can be established for them without excuse."[195] Ibn Taymiyyah stated, "Both the Quran and the Sunnah have demonstrated that no one is taken to account for their misdeeds except after a message from God has been sent to them. So whoever does not receive any mes-

---

194. AL-SHATABI, *al-Muwafaqat*. Matb'ah Muhammad 'Ali Subayh, 3:377

195. Muhammad Jamal al-Din AL-QASIMI, *Mahasin al-Ta'wil (Tafsir al-Qasimi)*. Dar Ihya' al-Kutub al-'Arabiyyah, 10:312.

sage is not punished at all, and whoever receives a message in summary form lacking details is not punished unless they deny the core of the message (the belief in God and His messenger)."[196]

One of God's verses specifically describes the parents of the Messenger of God [s] as being free of punishment, *And your turning over and over among those who prostrate themselves before God* [26:219]. Ibn 'Abbas said regarding this verse, "Through the progeny of the children of Adam, Noah, and Abraham you were delivered into this world as a prophet."[197] On the authority of Wathilah ibn al-Asqa', the Prophet [s] said, "God has chosen Ishmael from the children of Abraham, and He has chosen Banu Kinana from the children of Ishmael, and He has chosen Quraysh from Banu Kinana, and He has chosen Banu Hashim from Quraysh, and He has chosen me from Banu Hashim."[198] On the authority of al-'Abbas, the Prophet [s] said, "God made creation and created me from the best of them, from the best generation. Then He distinguished them as tribes and made me from the best tribe, and this tribe He made into families and made me from the best of families. So, I am from the best of the tribes and from the best of families."[199] The Messenger of God [s] therefore described himself and his lineage as pure and unsurpassed in quality. These two traits are counter to disbelief and polytheism, as God said regarding the polytheists: *Indeed the polytheists are filth* [9:28].

There are those who unfortunately hold a conflicting view, citing two reports in support of their claim. The Messenger of God [s] says in the first report, "I approached God seeking forgiveness for my mother and He refused, and He permitted me to visit her grave."[200] The second report narrates, "A man asked, 'O Messenger of God, where is my father?' and the Messenger of God [s] replied, 'In the hellfire.' As the man left, the Messenger called him back and said, 'My father and yours are both in the hellfire.'"[201] The first

196. IBN TAYMIYYAH, *Majmu' al-Fatawa*, 13:493.

197. AL-TABARI, *Tafsir al-Tabari*, 7:287 and AL-QURTUBI, *Tafsir al-Qurtubi*, 13:144.

198. IBN HANBAL, *Musnad Imam Ahmad*, 4:107 and AL-NAYSABURI, *Sahih Muslim*, 4:1782, and the wording is Ahmad's.

199. IBN HANBAL, *Musnad Imam Ahmad*, 4:165 and AL-TIRMIDHI, *Sunan al-tirmidhi*, 5:584.

200. AL-NAYSABURI, *Sahih Muslim*, 2:671.

201. Ibid., 1:191.

report contains nothing stipulating that the Prophet's mother is in the hellfire, because the lack of permission to seek forgiveness for her does not indicate that she was a polytheist. If this were the case, he would not have been given permission to visit her grave, as it is not permissible to visit the graves of the polytheists or to show them good will after death. As for the second report, it is possible that the Prophet [s] was referring to his uncle, not his father, as Abu Talib died after the advent of the prophetic mission, and did not become a Muslim. It is commonly known that the Arabs call their uncles father, as in the Quranic verse where Abraham refers to his uncle as such: *Remember when Abraham said unto his father Azar: Do you take idols for gods?* [6:74]. The father of Abraham was Tarih, or Tarikh, as is mentioned by Ibn Kathir and by other great Quranic exegetes.

If our detractors hold to their claim through the literal meaning of these two reports, even though a literal understanding does not aid them in the first report, and the second report is interpreted to mean that the parents of the Prophet [s] are not saved from hellfire, then we are still obliged to reject the two reports as they contradict the clear Quranic verses that have already been discussed. This principle is well known. Al-Hafiz al-Baghdadi ruled, "If reliable narrators narrate a report with a connected chain of transmission, it will be rejected based on certain conditions: if it contradicts a verse from the Quran or a *hadith* reported with corroborated continuity. If this is the case, then know that the report in question has no basis, or it has been abrogated."[202] This principle has been applied elsewhere. For example, consider the following report, "God created the earth on Saturday, on Sunday He created mountains on it, on Monday He created trees on it, on Tuesday He created minerals, on Wednesday He created light, on Thursday He created the animals, on Friday afternoon He created Adam, and He created the rest of creation in the final hour of Friday, during the time between afternoon and evening."[203] This report has been rejected, as Ibn Kathir says, because it contradicts God's statement, *Lo! your Lord is God Who created the heavens and the earth in six days.*[204]

202. Abu Bakr al-Khatib AL-BAGHDADI, *al-Faqih wa al-Muttafaqih*, Dar al-Kutub al-'Ilmiyyah, 132.

203. AL-NAYSABURI, *Sahih Muslim*, 4:2149.

204. IBN KATHIR, *Tafsir al-Quran al-Azim*, 2:230.

With similar reasoning, Imam al-Nawawi rejected the outward meaning of 'Aisha's statement, "The prayer was prescribed for us in cycles, two while at home and while traveling. The prayer of the traveler was kept the same and it was increased for the one at home."[205] Although this report is agreed upon, Nawawi commented, "The report appears to mean that the two units of prayer during traveling constitute the original prayer, not a dispensation in shortening, and the prayer of a non-traveler is extended. However, this contradicts the text of the Quran, and the consensus of the Muslims, in that the traveler's prayer is called a 'shortened prayer.' Whenever a non-concurrent report contradicts the text of the Quran, or the consensus of the Muslims, it is obligatory to depart from its apparent meaning."[206]

Let the detractors either adopt a deeper explanation of the mentioned texts, which is better since it does not entail rejecting a text, or they can reject these texts as they contradict sound texts from the Quran, which is the path of the great Imams. In either case, it should be clear that the parents of the Prophet [s] are saved from the hellfire, as are all of his forbearers. May God grant us love for him and a sound knowledge of his rank. As our final prayer: all praise is due to God. And God is Most High and knows best.

205. AL-BUKHARI, Sahih Bukhari, 1:137 and AL-NAYSABURI, Sahih Muslim, 1:478.
206. AL-NAWAWI, al-Majmu', 4:222.

Question 44:

Is it permissible to ask for things by way of supplicating through the Prophet [s] after his death (*al-tawassul*)?

The Islamic concept of intermediary supplication (*tawassul*) has been misunderstood in the modern age. We must return to the original linguistic and legal meanings of this term before we can discuss the ruling concerning intermediary supplication through the Prophet [s].

First, we will clarify the linguistic and legal meaning of a go-between (*wasilah*). Linguistically, *al-wasilah* is a rank that one possesses with the king, or it is a degree, or proximity. Someone acts as an intermediary to God for someone by acting in a way that draws that person closer to Him. The *wasil* is the one who desires God. The poet Labid said:

I see people unaware of their worth,
In fact, all who have an opinion are desirous (*wasil*) of God.

Someone *tawassala* to someone else with a *wasilah* if they draw closer to that person by some act or another. The phrase, "He *tawassala* to him with such and such," means that he drew closer to him with the sanctity of a bond that makes him endeared. *Al-wasilah* is a connection and a type of nearness.[207]

The legal meaning of *al-wasilah* does not depart from the linguistic definition. The main objective of a Muslim's life is to draw closer to God and attain His pleasure and reward. As part of God's mercy to us, He has given us acts of worship and opened the door to His presence. Muslims draw near to God through the various means that God has legislated for this purpose. When Muslims pray, they approach God, meaning they establish nearness to Him (*yatawassal*) with their prayer. The entirety of the Quran commands us to seek nearness to God (*wasilah*).

God mentions *al-wasilah* in two verses of the Quran. In the first, He commands *al-wasilah*: *O you who believe! Be mindful of your duty to God, and seek the way of approach unto Him [al-wasilah]* [5:35]. The second verse praises those who seek His proximity through their supplications, *Those unto whom they cry seek the way of approach*

---

207. Jamal al-Din Muhammad IBN MANSUR, *Lisan al-'Arab*. al-Matba'ah al-Amiriyyah bi-Bulaq, 11:724, wa-s-la.

[al-wasilah] *to their Lord, which of them shall be the nearest; they hope for His mercy and they fear His doom. Lo! the doom of your Lord is to be shunned* [17: 57].

The four schools of Sunni jurisprudence agree that performing *tawassul* through the Prophet [s] is permissible and even preferable, and they make no distinction between that performed during his life and after his passing. The only person who differed in opinion was Ibn Taymiyah, who claimed that there is a distinction between making *tawassul* through the Prophet [s] during his life and after his passing. However, his lone opinion holds no weight. We call upon the community to maintain that which its great Imams have established through their agreement. In our answer to question thirty-nine concerning the verse that states, *And if, when they had wronged themselves, they had but come to you and asked forgiveness of God, and asked forgiveness of the Messenger, they would have found God Forgiving, Merciful* [4:64], we sought to determine if this verse's advice is still effective, or if its relevance ended with the passing of the Prophet [s]. We related evidence affirming that making *tawassul* through the Prophet [s] is preferable, as is asking him to seek forgiveness on one's behalf. We will now provide the evidence from the Quran and the Sunnah upon which the consensus of the four schools relied.

Quranic evidence:

1) *O you who believe! Be mindful of your duty to God, and seek the way of approach unto Him, and strive in His way in order that you may succeed* [5:35].

2) *Those unto whom they cry seek the way of approach to their Lord, which of them shall be the nearest; they hope for His mercy and they fear His doom. Lo! the doom of your Lord is to be shunned* [17:57].

3) *And if, when they had wronged themselves, they had but come to you and asked forgiveness of God, and asked forgiveness of the Messenger, they would have found God Forgiving, Merciful* [4:64].

The first verse commands the believers to draw near to God through the various means of approaching Him. Performing *tawassul* through the Prophet [s] in supplication is a means of drawing near to God, which we will explain in detail when we discuss the evidence from the Sunnah. Nothing indicates that this verse refers to one particular *wasilah* to the exclusion of another. The verse's command is general and applies to all forms of *wasilah*, which please God. Supplication is accepted as an act of worship, so long as it does not sever familial ties, request something that is sinful, or consist of phrases that are in contradiction with theological principles and the fundamentals of Islam.

In the second verse, God praises those believers who have responded to Him and drawn closer to him through the *wasilah* of supplication. We will show how Muslims are to make *tawassul* to God in their supplications, according to the Sunnah.

In the third verse, God clearly calls upon believers to go to the Prophet [s] and seek God's forgiveness in his presence, stating that one's repentance is more likely to be accepted this way. This verse still holds true, as we clarified in our answer to question thirty-nine.

Evidence from the Sunnah:

1) According to Uthman ibn Hanif, a blind man came to the Prophet [s] and said, "Ask God to cure me." The Prophet [s] said, "If you like, you can be patient [and suffer your blindness], for that would be better for you." The blind man said, "Ask Him." So the Prophet [s] told him to make thorough ablutions and say this supplication, "O God, I ask You, and I turn to You through Your prophet Muhammad, the Prophet of Mercy. O Muhammad, I have turned to my Lord through you concerning this need of mine so that it may be taken care of. O God, let him intercede on my behalf."[208] Both al-Hakim and al-Tirmidhi ruled that this *hadith* is authentic, and we do not know of anyone from the modern period, even from among those known for being stern (*tashaddud*), who has ruled that it is weak. Even Sheikh al-Albani ruled that it is authentic.[209] Nobody objects to this *hadith*, neither to its chain of transmission, nor to its text. This *hadith* evidences that this formulation in supplication is

---

208. IBN HANBAL, *Musnad Imam Ahmad*, 4:138; AL-TIRMIDHI, *Sunan al-tirmidhi*, 5:569 who said, "This *hadith* is hasan sahih"; AL-NASA'I, *al-Sunan al-Kubra*, 6:169; AL-QIZWINI, *Sunan Ibn Majah*, 1:441; AL-HAKIM, *al-Mustadrak 'ala al-Sahihayn*, 1:458; Sulayman ibn Ahmad b. Ayyub AL-TABARANI, *al-Mu'jam al-Saghir*, 1:306; AL-TABARANI, *al-Mu'jam al-Awsat*, 2:105, and AL-TABARANI, *al-Mu'jam al-Kabir*, 9:30.

209. This comment is found in AL-NAYSABURI, *Sahih Ibn Khuzaymah*, 2:225 where al-Albani says, "It's chain is authentic."

preferable, since the Prophet [s] taught it to one of his companions. God made the miracle of His prophet [s] known by accepting the prayer of the blind man in the very same sitting.

In fact, we should not have to relate this *hadith* from the reign of Mu'awiyah ibn Abi Sufyan in order to prove the permissibility of this formulation's use in supplication after the Prophet's [s] passing. If the Prophet [s] taught one of his companions a formula for supplication, and it is transmitted to us with a sound chain, then this proves that using this supplication at all times is preferable until the day when God inherits the earth and all who are upon it. Nothing restricts the supplication to only that companion, or to solely the Prophet's [s] lifetime. Legal rulings are presumably absolute without exception, unless a specific condition or restriction has been explicitly established. Al-Shawkani[210] said, "There is evidence in this *hadith* for the permissibility of making *tawassul* to God through the Prophet [s] with the belief that the one who acts is God. It is God alone who is the Giver and the Preventer. Whatever He wills, happens, and whatever He does not will, does not happen."

However, today many people are unaware of these methodological concepts, and thus we find it necessary to give the context of the above *hadith* which clarifies that this great companion advised those who are in need to use this formula for supplication after the passing of the Prophet [s].

2) The story of the *hadith*: A man used to come to 'Uthman ibn 'Affan with a problem, but 'Uthman would not pay any attention to him or address his problem. The man encountered 'Uthman ibn Hanif and complained to him. 'Uthman ibn Hanif told him, "Go to the place of making ablutions and make your ablutions, then go to the mosque and pray two cycles of prayer. Then say the following: 'O God, I ask You, and I turn to You through Your prophet Muhammad, the Prophet of Mercy. O Muhammad, I turn to my Lord through you, to have my need fulfilled.' Then mention your need." The man departed and did as he had been told. Then he went to 'Uthman ibn 'Affan's door. The doorkeeper came, took him by the hand, presented him to 'Uthman ibn 'Affan, and seated him with him on the carpet.

210. Muhammad ibn 'Ali AL-SHAWKANI, *Tuhfat al-Dhakirin*. Matb'ah al-Babi al-Halabi, 208.

'Uthman asked him, "What is your need?" The man mentioned his need, and 'Uthman took care of it. Then he told him, "You did not mention your need until this moment. Whenever you are in need come to us." The man left and met 'Uthman ibn Hanif and said to him, "May God reward you, he used to not pay attention to my need or pay me any attention until you addressed him." 'Uthman ibn Hanif said, "By God, I did not speak to him, but I saw the Messenger of God [s], and a blind man came to him . . . ."[211] Then he related the *hadith* mentioned above.

'Abdallah ibn al-Siddiq al-Ghumari said, "This narration has been related by al-Bayhaqi in *Dala'il al-Nabuwwah* from the chain of Ya'qub ibn Sufyan [who said]: Ahmad ibn Shabib b. Sa'id related to us, my father informed us on the authority of Ruh ibn al-Qasim from Abu J'afar al-Khatami from Abu Umama ibn Sahl b. Hanif from his uncle, 'Uthman ibn Hanif, who said that a man used to go to 'Uthman ibn 'Affan . . . ." Then he mentioned the *hadith* in its entirety. Then he said, "Ya'qub ibn Sufyan is al-Nisawi, al-Hafiz al-Imam the trustworthy. Rather, he was even more than trustworthy, and this chain of transmission is authentic, so the story is very authentic. Its authenticity has also been agreed upon by al-Hafiz al-Mundhiri in *al-Targhib* 3/606, and al-Hafiz al-Haythami in *Majma' al-Zawa'id* 3/379."[212] This story confirms what is proven by the *hadith*, while correcting those who claim that it only applies to the lifetime of the Prophet [s].

3) The *hadith* concerning going out to the mosque to pray: According to Abu Sa'id al-Khudri, the Prophet [s] said, "Whoever says, when going to prayer, 'O God, I ask You by the right of those who ask of You, by the right of my walking, for I have not gone out of insolence, pride, ostentation, or for a reputation. I have gone out of fear of Your displeasure and seeking Your contentment. I ask You to guard me from the fire and

---

211. AL-TABARANI, *al-Mu'jam al-Saghir*, 1:306; Ahmad ibn Hissein b. 'Ali AL-BAYHAQI, *Dala'il al-Nubuwwah*. Dar al-Rayan li-l Turath, 6:167-8; AL-MUNDHIRI, *al-Targhib wa al-Tarhib*, 1:273; and al-Bayhaqi mentioned it in AL-HAYTHAMI, *Majma' al-Zawa'id*, 2:279; and AL-MUBARAKFURI, *Tuhfat al-Ahwudhi*, 10:24.

212. Abdullah ibn Siddiq AL-GHUMARI, *Irgham al-Mubtada' al-Ghabi*. Maktabat al-Qahira, p. 6.

forgive my sins, for none forgives sins except You.' God commands seventy angels to ask for forgiveness on their behalf and He turns towards them with His face until they finish their prayers."[213]

This *hadith* has been referenced as authentic by al-Hafiz Ibn Hajar al-'Asqalani,[214] al-Hafiz al-'Iraqi,[215] Abu al-Hasan al-Maqdisi the Sheikh of al-Mundhiri,[216] al-Hafiz al-Dumyati,[217] and al-Hafiz al-Baghawi.[218] The *hadith* indicates the permissibility of making *tawasal* to God through good deeds, namely the steps taken by the person walking to the mosque in a state of ritual purity, and by the right of those who ask.

4) Further evidence is provided by the *hadith* of Anas, delivered upon the death of Fatimah bint Asad, the mother of 'Ali. At the end of this long *hadith* he narrates, "and he said, 'O God who gives life and death, and who is the living who never dies, forgive my mother Fatimah bint Asad. Help her to pronounce her proofs to her testimony and make her entranceway wide, by the right of Your Prophet and the prophets before. Verily You are the Most Merciful of the Merciful.'"[219] There is some discussion concerning this *hadith*'s chain of transmission because it relies on Ruh ibn Salah as a transmitter. Ibn Hibban considered him trustworthy, but Ibn al-Jawzi counted him

213. IBN HANBAL, *Musnad Imam Ahmad*, 3:21; AL-QIZWINI, *Sunan Ibn Majah*, 1:256; AL-MUNDHIRI, *al-Targhib wa al-Tarhib*, 1:135; Abu Bakr IBN AL-SUNNI, *'Amal al-Yawm wa al-Laylah*. Maktabat al-Turath, p. 42; Ahmad ibn Abi Bakr b. Isma'il AL-BUSAYRI, *Misbah al-Zujajah*. Dar al-'Arabiyyah, 1:98; Ahmad ibn al-Hussein b. 'Ali AL-BAYHAQI, *al-Da'wat al-Kabir*. Markaz al-Makhtutat, p. 47; AL-KUFI, *Musannaf ibn Abi Shaybah*, 6:25; Abu Na'im al-Fadl ibn Dakin transmitting it from Ibn Hajar in Ahmad ibn 'Ali b. Hajar AL-'ASQALANI, *Amali al-Adhkar*. Mu'assisah Qurtubah, 1:273.

214. Ibid., 1:272.

215. 'Abd al-Rahman ibn Hussein AL-'IRAQI, *Takhrij Ahadith al-'Ihya'*. Riyad: Dar al-'Asimah, 1:291.

216. AL-MUNDHIRI, *al-Targhib wa al-Tarhib*, 3:273.

217. Abu Muhammad Sharaf al-Din AL-DUMYATI, *al-Mutajar al-Rabih fi Thawab al-'Amal al-Salih*. Dar al-Fikr, 471-72.

218. AL-BUSAYRI, *Misbah al-Zujajah*, 1:98.

219. AL-TABARANI, *al-Mu'jam al-Awsat*, 1:68; AL-TABARANI, *al-Mu'jam al-Kabir*, 24:351; AL-ASFAHANI, *Hilyat al-Awliya'*, 3:121; and it was mentioned by al-Haythami in AL-HAYTHAMI, *Majma' al-Zawa'id*, 9:257.

among those of unknown status. Thus scholars differ in opinion concerning the *hadith*'s authenticity or lack thereof. Its meaning, however, is indeed correct, as it is supported by the authentic hadiths that have preceded.

5) Adam asked forgiveness by performing *tawassul* through our Prophet [s]. In the *hadith* of 'Umar ibn al-Khattab, the Prophet said, "When Adam committed the sin he said, 'O Lord, I ask You by Muhammad to forgive me.' God asked, 'Adam, how did you know about Muhammad if I have not yet created him?' Adam replied, 'Because when You created me with your hands and blew into me from Your Spirit, I raised my head and saw written on the pillars of Your throne, 'There is no god but God, and Muhammad is the Messenger of God.' God said, 'You speak truthfully, Adam: he is the most beloved of creation unto Me. You supplicated to Me by him so I have forgiven you. If not for Muhammad, I would not have created you.'"[220]

Al-Hakim ruled that the *hadith* is authentic: "This *hadith*'s chain of transmission is authentic, and it is the first *hadith* that I mentioned to 'Abd al-Rahman ibn Zayd b. Aslam in this book."[221] When he cited the story of Adam in his book *Stories of the Prophets* (*Qisas al-Anbiya'*), al-Hafidh Ibn Kathir said that it was false.[222] Al-Hafidh al-Dhahabi exaggerated when he ruled that it is a fabrication based on the inclusion of 'Abd al-Rahman in its chain of transmission. 'Abd al-Rahman is not a liar, nor is he accused of falsehood. He is merely weak, and so he does not cause a *hadith* to be considered a fabrication. At the most, his presence would make a *hadith* weak. In any case, we mention the differences between the *hadith* scholars out of academic duty. The *hadith*, if it is authentic, includes clear evidence that it is permissible to make *tawassul* through the Prophet [s] in supplication. As for the statement at the end of the *hadith*, "If not for Muhammad, I would not have created you," refer to question thirty-six for clarification.

6) The *hadith*, "Assist me servants of God." According to

---

220. AL-TABARANI, *al-Mu'jam al-Awsat*, 6:313; AL-HAKIM, *al-Mustadrak 'ala al-Sahihayn*, 2:672; AL-DAYLAMI, *Musnad al-Firdous bi Ma'thur al-Khitab*, 4:59; AL-ASFAHANI, *Hilyat al-Awliya'*, 10:222; and it was mentioned by AL-HAYTHAMI, *Majma' al-Zawa'id*, 8:253.

221. AL-HAKIM, *al-Mustadrak*, 2:672.

222. Isma'il ibn 'Amr IBN KATHIR, *Qisas al-Anbiya'*, 1:29.

Ibn 'Abbas, the Prophet [s] said, "God has angels on the earth other than the guardian angels who record the seeds that fall from trees. If one of you is afflicted by lameness in a deserted place he should call out, 'Assist me servants of God.'"[223] Al-Hafiz al-Haythami commented on its chain of transmission, "It was related by al-Tabarani, and its narrators are trustworthy."[224] The *hadith* contains evidence in support of seeking the aid of beings that we cannot see, such as angels. It assures us that God can cause them to aid us, and that we may make *tawassul* through them to our Lord in order to achieve that end. It is not farfetched to make an analogy between the angels and the spirits of the righteous, for they are bodies of light that remain in our world.

7) The story of praying for rain through the Prophet [s] by his grave during the rule of 'Umar. According to Malik al-Dar, who was 'Umar's treasurer, "People were afflicted with a drought during the reign of 'Umar. A man went to the grave of the Prophet [s] and said, 'O Messenger of God, pray for rain on behalf of your community, for they have been destroyed.' The Messenger of God [s] came to him in a dream and said, 'Go to 'Umar and greet him with peace from me. Inform him that they will be given water. Tell him: 'You must employ intelligence, employ intelligence.' The man went to 'Umar and told him. 'Umar said, 'O Lord, I will not fall short unless I have no capacity.'"[225]

This *hadith* has been authenticated by al-Hafiz Ibn Hajar, who said, "Ibn Abi Shaybah related, with an authentic chain of transmission from the narration of Abu Salih al-Samman according to Malik al-Dar that, "People were afflicted with a draught during the reign of 'Umar. A man went to the grave of the Prophet [s] and said, 'O Messenger of God, pray for rain on behalf of your community for they have been destroyed.' The Messenger of God [s] came to him in a dream and said, 'Go to Umar . . . .' And in *al-Futuh* of Sayf, the person who had

___

223. AL-KUFI, *Musannad ibn Abi Shaybah*, 6:91; AL-BAYHAQI, *Shu'ab al-Iman*, 1:183; and it was metnioend by AL-HAYTHAMI, *Majma' al-Zawa'id*, 10:132.

224. *Majma' al-Zawa'id*, vol. 10 p. 132.

225. AL-KUFI, *Musannaf ibn Abi Shaybah*, 6:356; IBN 'ABD AL-BARR, *al-Isti'ab*, 3:1149.

the dream was one of the Companions, Bilal ibn al-Harith al-Muzani."[226] This narration was also mentioned by al-Hafiz Ibn Kathir who said, "This chain of transmission is authentic."[227] The *hadith* has been authenticated by major scholars of *hadith*, therefore it is accepted evidence that praying through the Prophet [s] for rain and performing supplication after his passing from this world are both permissible actions.

8) The story of the Caliph al-Mansur with Imam Malik: When the second Abbasid Caliph, Abu J'afar al-Mansur al-'Abbasi, asked Malik, "O Abu Abd Allah, should I face the Messenger of God [s] and supplicate, or should I face the *qiblah* and supplicate?" Malik told him, "Why would you turn your face away from him when he is your means of drawing near (*wasilah*) to God and the means of drawing near to your father Adam until the Day of Judgment? Face him and seek intercession through him, and God will allow him to intercede on your behalf."[228] This signals that Malik took the *hadith* of Adam's *tawassul* into consideration, and that he considered it a good thing to face the grave of the Prophet [s] and seek intercession through him.

This quantity of authentic and explicit evidence from the Quran and the Sunnah has enabled the scholars of the community, from the four schools and others, to form a consensus concerning *tawassul* through the Prophet [s] during his lifetime and after his pass-

---

226. AL-'ASQALANI, *Fath al-Bari*, 2:495-96.

227. Isma'il ibn 'Amr IBN KATHIR, *al-Bidayah wa al-Nihayah*. Matba'ah al-Sa'adah, 7:90.

228. This story has been related by Abi al-Hasan Ali ibn Fahr in his book *Fada'il Malik*. It includes a decent chain of transmission. It has been narrated by al-Qadi 'Ayad in *al-Shifa'* from many sheikhs from amongst the trustworthy ones. It was also mentioned by al-Subki in Taj al-Din AL-SUBKI, *Shifa' al-Siqam*. Dar al-Kutub al-'Ilmiyyah, al-Samhudi in 'Ali ibn al-Sayyid al-Sharif AL-SAMHUDI, *Wafa al-Wafa*. Matba'ah al-Adab, and al-Qastalani in AL-QASTALANI, *al-Mawahib al-Laduniyyah*. In *al-Jawhar al-Munadhim* Ibn Hajar said, "This has been related with an authentic chain of transmission." In Muhammad ibn 'Abd al-Baqi AL-ZURQANI, *Sharh al-Mawahib*. al-Matba'ah al-Azhariyyah. al-Zurqani said, "Ibn Fahr mentioned this with a good (*hasan*) chain of transmission, and al-Qadi 'Ayad mentioned it with an authentic chain of transmission."

ing. They have agreed that *tawassul* through the Prophet [s] is not only preferable (*mustahabb*), but is also counts as an encouraged (*mandub*) genre of supplication to God. No consideration is given to those who break with the consensus of the scholars, such as Ibn Taymiyah, and those who repeat their words. And God is Most High and knows best.

Question 45:

Is the Prophet alive in his grave? To what extent does his ongoing life influence our world?

First, we must clarify the technical terms involved in this issue, for the simple explanation of terms dissipates most misunderstanding. If the phrase "alive in his grave" means to claim that he did not depart from the life of this world, and that God did not bring the Prophet [s] to Him, then that is a false statement according to the Quranic verses, *We appointed immortality for no mortal before you. What! if you die, can they be immortal!* [21:34]; *Lo! you will die, and lo! they will die* [39:30].

The Prophet [s] left the life of this world, but his departure did not cut him off from us. He has another life, which is the life of the prophets. This is called life after death. The Prophet [s] referred to it when he said, "My life is good for you, you speak and I speak to you; and my death is good for you, your actions are brought before me and whatever I see of good I praise God, and whatever I see of bad I ask for God's forgiveness on your behalf."[229]

And he said, "Every time somebody greets me with peace, God sends it to my spirit and I respond to him or her with peace."[230] This *hadith* indicates that his spirit is perpetually connected to his

229. AL-BAZZAR, *Musnad al-Bazzar*, 1:379; AL-HARITH IBN USAMAH and 'Ali ibn Abi Bakr AL-HAYTHAMI, *Musnad al-Harith bi-Zawa'id al-Haythami*. Markaz Khidmat al-Sunnah wa al-Sirah, 2:884; AL-DAYLAMI, *Musnad al-Firdous bi Ma'thur al-Khitab*, 2:137; AL-HAYTHAMI, *Majma' al-Zawa'id*, 9:24 and he commented on it by saying, "its narrators are all sound." AL-'IRAQI, *Tarh al-Tathrib*, 3:297 and he commented by saying, "its chain is good." 'Abd al-Ra'uf AL-MANAWI, *Fayd al-Qadir*. al-Maktabat al-Tijariyyah al-Kubra, 3:401 and he was astonished at those who said this *hadith* was *mursal*. Other hadith masters graded it as rigorously authentic such as Nawawi, Ibn al-Tin, Qurtubi, Qadi 'Iyad, and Ibn Hajar.

230. IBN HANBAL, *Musnad Imam Ahmad*, 2:527; AL-SIJISTANI, *Sunan Abi Dawud*, 2:218; AL-TABARANI, *al-Mu'jam al-Awsat*, 3:262; AL-BAYHAQI, *Kubra*, 5:245; AL-BAYHAQI, *Shu'ab al-Iman*, 2:216; AL-DAYLAMI, *Musnad al-Firdous bi Ma'thur al-Khitab*, 4:25; AL-MUNDHIRI, *al-Targhib wa al-Tarhib*, 2:326; it was mentioned by AL-HAYTHAMI, *Majma' al-Zawa'id*, 10:162; AL-'ASQALANI, *Fath al-Bari*, 6:488 al-Hafidh Ibn Hajar said, "Its narrators are trustworthy," and he responded to the intellectual issues brought up concerning it.

blessed body, because at every moment someone is greeting the Prophet [s] with peace. The life of the Prophet [s] after his passing is not like the life of other people after their passing, because the spirits of people other than prophets do not return to their bodies again. Theirs is an imperfect life of the soul without the body. Even if they connect to the life of this world, such as by returning greetings of peace, the prophets enjoy a life that is more complete than their lives before passing, and more complete than the lives of the rest of creation after passing.

It has been firmly established that the prophets worship God in their graves. According to Anas, the Prophet [s] said, "I passed by Moses on the night of my night journey by the red dune, and he was standing praying in his grave."[231] Also according to him, the Prophet [s] said, "The prophets are alive in their graves praying."[232] By specifying that they are "in their graves," this *hadith* indicates that the prophets are alive in both body and spirit. If they possessed ongoing life of the spirit alone, then he would not have mentioned their physical dwelling. They are as alive in their graves as they were before passing from this life; the afterlife is not an endurance of the spirit alone. Their bodies are protected, and it is forbidden for the earth to devour them. The Prophet [s] said, "God has forbidden the earth to devour the bodies of the prophets."[233]

The Prophet, then, is alive in his grave in both body and spirit, and his body is preserved like the bodies of the rest of his broth-

---

231. Ahmad vol. 2, p. 315; Muslim vol. 4, p. 1845; al-Nasa'i in *al-Kubra* vol. 1, p. 419; Ibn Hibban in his *Sahih* vol. 1, p. 242; Ibn Abi Shaybah in his *Musannaf* vol. 7, p. 335; al-Tabarani in *al-Awsat* vol. 8, p. 13.

232. Abu Ya'ala Ahmad ibn 'Ali b. al-Muthanna AL-TAMIMI, *Musnad Abu Ya'ala*. Dar al-Ma'mun li-l-Turath, 6:147; AL-DAYLAMI, *Musnad al-Firdous bi Ma'thur al-Khitab*, 1:119; AL-HAYTHAMI, *Majma' al-Zawa'id*, 8:21 and he commented by saying, "Abu Ya'ala and al-Bazzar narrated it and the narrators of Abu Ya'ala are reliable."

233. IBN HANBAL, *Musnad Imam Ahmad*, 4:8; AL-SIJISTANI, *Sunan Abi Dawud*, 1:275; AL-NASA'I, *Sunan al-Nasa'i (al-Mujtabah)*, 3:91; AL-QIZWINI, *Sunan Ibn Majah*, 1:524; AL-DARAMI, *Sunan al-Darami*, 1:445; AL-HAKIM, *al-Mustadark 'ala al-Sahihayn*, 1:413 and he commented on it by saying, "It is authentic according to the condition of Bukhari and he did not narrate it; it was narrated by Ahmad ibn al-Hussein b. 'Ali AL-BAYHAQI, *Sunan al-Bayhaqi al-Sughra*. Maktabat al-Dar, 1:372 and in AL-BAYHAQI, *Kubra*, 3:428.

ers, the prophets. He enjoys the company of his Lord, worshipping Him in his grave. He is connected to his community, seeking their forgiveness, interceding with God on their behalf, and returning their greetings of peace, among many other things.

Whoever denies the Prophet's [s] life after death in his grave has contradicted his sayings that we have related. And whoever denies his departure from the life of this world has belied the Quranic verses cited here. One must affirm his passing from this world and his life in his grave. We believe that which the most trusted one has informed us: the Prophet [s] worships his Lord, returns the greetings of those who greet him with peace, intercedes on behalf of his community, and seeks forgiveness for them. And God is Most High and knows best.

Question 46:

What is the general ruling on visiting graves, and particularly on visiting the grave of the Prophet [s]? Is it permissible to travel (*shadd al-rihal*) with the intention of visiting the grave of the Prophet [s] and the graves of the righteous?

This question requires an answer in two parts. First, we need a ruling on visiting the graves of righteous Muslims, including the grave of the Prophet [s]. Secondly, we need a ruling on traveling with the intention of visiting the grave of the Prophet [s] or the graves of the righteous.

The entire Muslim community is in agreement concerning the permissibility of visiting graves. Most scholars consider visiting graves preferable only for men, but the Hanafis consider it preferable for women as well. The Hanafi position differs from the majority opinion that general female visitation of graves is permissible, but discouraged. The Prophet [s] explained the value of this practice: "I used to forbid you to visit graves, [but now] visit them, for it is a reminder of the afterlife."[234] In contrast to general grave visitation, the majority of scholars do not discourage women from visiting either the Prophet's [s] grave, or the graves of the other prophets. The reasoning behind this exception is based on the benefits of visiting the Prophet [s].

No intelligent Muslim can be unaware of the value behind visiting the grave of the Prophet [s]. If the Messenger of God [s] were among us now and had not passed on to his Lord, would we visit him? Surely we would not hesitate! And visiting the Prophet [s] after his passing is accomplished through visiting his noble grave.

The Muslim community has come to a consensus concerning the permissibility of visiting the Prophet [s]. The majority of scholars who are qualified to issue fatwas in their schools of jurisprudence have adopted the position that visiting the Prophet [s] is an encouraged Sunnah. Some legal experts emphasize this Sunnah nearly to the point of making it mandatory, such as exemplified by the fatwas of certain Hanafis. Other experts, such as the Ma-

---

234. IBN HANBAL, *Musnad Imam Ahmad*, 1:145; AL-NAYSABURI, *Sahih Muslim*, 2:672, 3:1563; AL-SIJISTANI, *Sunan Abi Dawud*, 3:333; AL-TIRMIDHI, *Sunan al-Tirmidhi*, 3:370; AL-NASA'I, *Sunan al-Nasa'i (al-Mujtabah)*, 4:89; AL-QIZWINI, *Sunan Ibn Majah*, 1:501.

liki jurist Abu 'Umran Musa ibn 'Isa, consider visiting the Prophet mandatory.

The opinion that mandates visiting the grave of the Prophet [s] derives from various pieces of evidence, including the Quranic verse, *And if, when they had wronged themselves, they had but come to you and asked forgiveness of God, and asked forgiveness of the Messenger, they would have found God Forgiving, Merciful* [4:64]. The verse applies generally; no textual or rational evidence limits its applicability to the worldly life of the Prophet [s]. The significance of the phrase is eternal. The import of the Quran is in the general meaning of the phrase, not in the specific occasion of its revelation. Further proof of the immutability of paying homage to the Prophet [s] comes from his words: "Whoever visits me after my death, it is as if they visited me during my life."[235] Another *hadith* says, "Whoever visits my grave is guaranteed my intercession."[236]

Particular etiquette should be observed in the presence of the Messenger of God [s] when visiting his grave. One should lower one's voice, stand with reverence (*waqar*) and humility (*khushu'*), and keep the image and the magnanimity (*haybah*) of the Prophet [s] in mind, while refraining from trespassing on the noble grave by touching it or circumambulating it. Touching his blessed pulpit is permissible, according to Ahmad Ibn Qudamah: "It is not preferable to touch or kiss the wall of the Prophet's [s] grave. Ahmad said, 'I do not know of this.' Al-Athram said, 'I saw that the people of knowledge who reside in Medina do not touch the grave of the Prophet [s]. Rather, they stand to the side and greet him.' Abu 'Abdallah said, 'That is what Ibn 'Umar used to do.' Ibrahim ibn 'Abd al-Rahman b. 'Abd al-Qari' related that he saw Ibn 'Umar put his hand on the Prophet's [s] seat on the pulpit and then touched his face."[237]

The following section addresses the issue of traveling to visit the grave of the Prophet [s] and graves in general:

"Tightening the saddles" (*Shadd al-rihal*) is a metaphor for traveling, which in itself is not an act of worship, nor is it intended for its own sake when carrying out acts of worship. If it were not permissible to travel to visit graves in general or the grave of

---

235. AL-BAYHAQI, *Shu'ab al-Iman*, 3:488.

236. AL-BAYHAQI, *al-Sunan al-Kubra*, 5:245, and in AL-BAYHAQI, *Shu'ab al-Iman*, 3:489; AL-TABARANI, *al-Mu'jam al-Kabir*, 12:406; AL-DARAQUTNI, *Sunan al-Daraqutni*, 2:278.

237. Ibn Qudmah, *al-Mughni*, 3:298.

the Prophet [s] in particular, then the preferable nature of visiting graves would only apply to residents of the countries in which those graves are found. In this case, the residents of Medina would be the sole Muslims permitted to leave their homes with the intention of visiting the grave of the Prophet [s], and anyone else needing to travel in order to do the same thing would be committing a sin. This idea is extremely farfetched and blatantly false.

The scholars of legal theory have agreed that the means have the same rulings as their ends. Therefore, if the pilgrimage (hajj) is mandatory, then traveling in order to make the pilgrimage is mandatory. If visiting the grave of the Prophet [s] and the graves of the righteous, one's relatives, and the Muslims in general is preferred, then traveling in order to visit them is preferred. How can the act be preferable and the means of carrying it out forbidden?

Based on overwhelming evidence, the scholars are of the opinion that it is permissible to travel in order to visit graves, especially the graves of the prophets and the righteous. The hadith, "One is not to tighten one's saddle unless one is traveling to one of three mosques: this mosque of mine, the mosque in Mecca, and the Masjid al-Aqsa,"[238] specifically refers to mosques, so one does not travel except to those three. This exclusivity derives from the fact that it is permissible to travel in order to seek knowledge and for trade.

The scholars have agreed upon this meaning. Sheikh Sulayman ibn Mansur, known as al-Jamal, explained:

"Saddles are only to be tightened," means in order to pray in the mosques, so it does not oppose traveling for another purpose . . . al-Nawawi said, "It means there is no preeminence in traveling to a mosque other than these three," and he related this according to the majority of scholars. Al-'Iraqi said, "One of the best interpretations of the hadith is that it only refers to rulings of mosques, so one does not travel to a mosque other than these three. As for seeking other than mosques by traveling for the sake of knowledge, to visit the righteous and one's comrades, for trade, or pleasure, and the like, this is not re-

238. IBN HANBAL, Musnad Imam Ahmad, 2:234, 3:64; AL-BUKHARI, Sahih Bukhari, 1:398; AL-NAYSABURI, Sahih Muslim, 2:1014; AL-SIJISTANI, Sunan Abi Dawud, 2:216; AL-TIRMIDHI, Sunan al-Tirmidhi, 2:148; AL-NASA'I, Sunan al-Nasa'i (al-Mujtaba), 1:258; AL-QIZWINI, Sunan Ibn Majah, 1:452.

ferred to in the *hadith*."

This was made explicit in the narrations of Imam Ahmad and Ibn Abi Shaybah with a good (*hasan*) chain of transmission according to Abu Sa'id al-Khudri who ascribed it to the Prophet [s], "The one performing prayer should not travel to a mosque in order to pray except the mosque in Mecca, the al-Aqsa mosque, and this mosque of mine," and in another narration, "The one praying should not travel . . . ." Al-Subki said, "There is no place on earth that is preferred above others in and of itself for one to travel to it seeking its preferred nature except these three cities." And he said, "What I mean by preferred is what the sacred law has taken into consideration and upon which legal rulings have been based. As for other places, one does not travel to them for their own sake, one rather travels to them for the sake of making a visit, acquiring knowledge, or the like from among the things that are recommended or permissible. Some people have been confused by this and they have claimed that traveling to visit other than these three, like Sidi Ahmad al-Badawi and others like him, is included in the prohibition. This is an error because the exempted object can only be excluded from a category of the same species from which they are being exempted. The meaning of the report then is that one should not travel to a mosque from among mosques, or a place among places for the sake of that place in and of itself, except to the three mentioned. Traveling in order to make a visit or to acquire knowledge is not traveling to a place. Rather, it is traveling to the person in the place, so understand."[239]

Based on this evidence, traveling in order to visit the grave of the Prophet [s] is recommended because it is the only means to accomplish the recommended visit. Similarly, traveling in order to visit the graves of the righteous and one's relatives is recommended, and traveling in order to carry out permissible actions is permissible. And God is Most High and knows best.

---

239. Sulayman ibn Mansur al-'Ajili AL-JAMAL and Zakariya ibn Muahmmad Al-ANSARI, *Futuhat al-Wahhab bi Tawdih Sharh Minhaj al-Tulab*. Dar al-Fikr, 2:361, known as *Hashiyat al-Jamal*.

Question 47:

Many utter oaths (*al-taraji*) evoking the Prophet Muhammad [s], his family, the Kaaba, or the Quran, such as when
someone says, "By the Prophet do this," or "By Sayyidna
al-Husayn and his worth with you." We know that making
oaths to other than God associates partners with Him, but
what if the person intends to simply convey hope? Some
people are surprised when they are told, "This is forbidden. This is associating partners with God. Say, 'There is no
god but God.'" What is the ruling on this matter?

Before of the rise of Islam, the people of the pre-Islamic era swore
by their gods in order to worship and venerate them as we do God,
may He be exalted over all partners they associated with Him. The
Quran says, *Yet of human beings there are some who take unto themselves [objects of worship which they set as] rivals to God, loving them
with a love like [that which is the due] of God [only]—those who believe are
stauncher in their love for God—Oh, that those who do evil had but known,
[on the day] when they behold the doom, that power belongs wholly to
God, and that God is severe in punishment!* [2:165]. The Prophet [s] forbade this in order to protect the purity of divine unity (*tawhid*); he
said, "Whoever swears by other than God has committed disbelief
or polytheism."[240] By this he meant that they have said something
akin to the polytheists, and not that they have left the religion,
may God protect us. The scholars agree that one who swears by
other than God is not a disbeliever unless he venerates the subject
of his oath as one venerates God. In this instance, their disbelief
would be due to the veneration, and not the swearing alone.

The Prophet [s] also forbade swearing by one's forefathers.
This was done in the pre-Islamic period out of pride for the ancestors, to sanctify them, to put their lineage before the brotherhood
of Islam, and in order to differentiate their friends and enemies
on that basis. The Prophet [s] said, "God forbids you to swear by
your forefathers. Whoever swears should swear by God or remain
silent."[241] He clarified the rationale for this ruling in another re-

240. IBN HANBAL, *Musnad Imam Ahmad*, 2:67; AL-SIJISTANI, *Sunan Abi Dawud*, 3:223; AL-TIRMIDHI, *Sunan al-Tirmidhi*, 4:110.

241. IBN HANBAL, *Musnad Imam Ahmad*, 2:11; AL-BUKHARI, *Sahih Bukhari*, 5:2265; AL-NAYSABURI, *Sahih Muslim*, 3:1267.

port, "A people who are prideful because of their forefathers who have died should desist. They are but coals for the hellfire, or they are more debased in the eyes of God than the dung beetle that rolls feces around with its nose. God has removed from you the trivialities of the pre-Islamic age. Now there is nothing but the pious believer and the sorrowful one without morals. All of humanity are the sons of Adam, and Adam was created from dust."[242] The Quran says, *And when you have completed your devotions, then remember God as you remember your fathers or with a more lively remembrance* [2:200]. The commentators wrote, "The people of the pre-Islamic age would stand during the Hajj season and one of them would say, 'My father used to feed and carry goods.' The only form of remembrance they had was the mention of the actions of their forefathers."

Swearing by that which has been venerated in the legal tradition, such as the Prophet [s], Islam, and the Kaaba, has no likeness whatsoever to the oaths of the polytheists. Those scholars who forbade it did so only out of consideration for the apparent meaning of the general command of the Prophet [s] to not swear by other than God. Those scholars who permitted it, as Imam Ahmad did in one of his positions, considered the fact that the Prophet [s] is one of the two integrals of the testimony of faith, and without him the testimony is not complete. Nothing suggests that the Prophet [s] poses a rivalry to God. Rather, by venerating him one venerates God. The prohibition of swearing by other than God is not meant definitively because scholars hold a consensus concerning the permissibility of swearing by God's characteristics. Therefore the prohibition, while general in apparent meaning, actually refers to more specific circumstances.

Ibn al-Mundhir said,

> The people of knowledge have differed concerning the meaning of the prohibition of swearing by other than God. One group of them said that it is particularly related to the oaths sworn by the people of the pre-Islamic age: aggrandizing other than God like Alat, al-'Uzza, and their forefathers. Someone who swears by one of these oaths is commiting a sin, although there are no expiations to be paid. As for that which results in the aggrandizement of God such as someone saying, by the

---

242. IBN HANBAL, *Musnad Imam Ahmad*, 2:361; AL-TIRMIDHI, *Sunan al-Tirmidhi*, 5:734.

Prophet [s], by Islam, by the pilgrimage, by the lesser pilgrimage, by the sacrifice, by charity, by the freeing of slaves, and similar things by which the aggrandizement of God and drawing near to Him is intended, such are not included in the prohibition. Included amongst those who held this position is Abu 'Ubayd and a number of people that we met. They supported the position with that which is narrated according to the companions of the Prophet that they would hold someone to an oath made on freeing a slave, sacrifice, or charity, even though they perceived the prohibition mentioned. This indicates that they did not understand it to be general, for if it were general they would have prohibited such oaths and not held people to them.[243]

Mentioning the Prophet [s] or others in hopes of emphasizing a point, and not in a way that intends an actual oath, is not included in the prohibition at all. This is permitted without objection because the practice is displayed by the speech of the Prophet [s] and his Companions. According to Abu Hurayrah, a man came to the Prophet [s] and said, "O Messenger of God, which act of charity is greatest in reward?" He replied, "By your father! You shall be informed of it! It is for you to give charity while you are healthy, although you are greedy, fear poverty, and wish for permanence."[244] In another report, a man from Najd recounts the time when he asked the Prophet [s] about Islam. The end of the report says, "The Messenger of God [s] said, 'He will be successful, by his father, if he be honest,'" or, "He will enter Paradise, by his father, if he be honest."[245]

According to Abu Hurayrah, a man came to the Prophet [s] and said, "O Messenger of God, inform me: of all people who has the most right over me concerning keeping good company?" The Prophet [s] said, "Yes, by your father, I will tell you: your mother."[246] Abu al-'Ushara' related his father's words, "O Messenger of God, is the ritual slaughter only to be done by cutting the gullet or must

---

243. AL-'ASQALANI, *Fath al-Bari*, 11:535.

244. IBN HANBAL, *Musnad Imam Ahmad*, 2:231; AL-NAYSABURI, *Sahih Muslim*, 2:716.

245. Ibid., 1:41; AL-SIJISTANI, *Sunan Abi Dawud*, 1:107.

246. AL-NAYSABURI, *Sahih Muslim*, 4:1974; AL-QIZWINI, *Sunan Ibn Majah*, 2:903.

it include the jugular vein?" He replied, "By your father, if you stabbed it in the thigh it would count."[247]

It has been narrated that the Prophet [s] was brought a meal of meat and bread. He said, "Pass me the foreleg." So he was passed the foreleg and he ate it. Then he said, "Pass me the foreleg." So he was passed the foreleg and he ate it. Then he said once again, "Pass me the foreleg." Someone replied, "O Messenger of God, there are only two forelegs." He said, "By your father, if you had remained silent you would have kept passing me forelegs as long as I asked for them."[248]

The story of the amputee who stole a necklace from Asma' ibn 'Umays conveys a similar lesson. Abu Bakr said to the theif, "By your father, your night is not the night of a thief."[249] It has been established by the authentic collections that Abu Bakr's wife told him, referring to the food of their guests, "No, by the light of my eyes, it is now three times more than what it was before."[250]

Imam al-Nawawi said, "This is not an oath. Rather, it is a phrase from Arab custom that entered their speech without intending an actual oath. The prohibition only applies to those who intend actual oaths, because of the veneration of that which is sworn by and the comparison with God. That is the satisfactory answer."[251]

Al-Hafiz Ibn Hajar related the position of al-Baydawi: "Al-Baydawi said, 'This phrase is one of those that are added to speech merely for purposes of reassurance and emphasis. Oaths are not intended by this phrase; just as interjectional exclamations are added only for the purpose of particularization, not with the intention of summoning."[252]

Based on the evidence we have presented, there is nothing wrong with evoking the Prophet [s] and his family, or others such as one's father, in order to simply express hope and add emphasis to speech. This turn of phrase is found in the speech of the Prophet

247. AL-BAYHAQI, *al-Sunan al-Kubra*, 9:246.

248. IBN HANBAL, *Musnad Imam Ahmad*, 2:48; AL-HAYTHAMI, *Majma' al-Zawa'id*, 8:312.

249. ANIS, *al-Muwatta'*, 2:835; AL-BAYHAQI, *Kubra*, 8:273; Ahmad ibn al-Hussein b. 'Ali AL-BAYHAQI, *Musnad al-Shafa'I*, 1:326.

250. IBN HANBAL, *Musnad Imam Ahmad*, 1:198; AL-BUKHARI, *Sahih Bukhari*, 1:27; AL-NAYSABURI, *Sahih Muslim*, 3:1627.

251. AL-NAWAWI, *Sharh Sahih* Muslim, 1:168.

252. AL-'ASQALANI, *Fath al-Bari*, 11:534.

[s] and his Companions, and over the course of history people have adopted it in a way that does not counter the legal tradition. It is not considered an act of associating partners with God, and Muslims should not make allegations about God without knowledge. The Quran says, *And speak not, concerning that which your own tongues qualify [as clean or unclean], the falsehood: "This is lawful, and this is forbidden," so that you invent a lie against God. Lo! Those who invent a lie against God will not succeed* [16:116]. It is not permitted for intelligent people to accuse their brethren of disbelief and polytheism; as the Prophet [s] warned, "If a man judges his brother to be a disbeliever, one of them is."[253]

---

253. IBN HANBAL, *Musnad Imam Ahmad*, 2:112; AL-NAYSABURI, *Sahih Muslim*, 1:79; ANIS, *al-Muwatta'*, 2:984.

Question 48:

What is the ruling on visiting the descendants of the
Prophet [s]?

Visiting the descendants of the Prophet [s] is one of the greatest
acts that bring one closer to God, and it is one of the acts of obedience whose acceptance by the Lord of all creation is most hopeful.
The Prophet [s] advised his community concerning the rights of
his family. Zayd ibn Arqam said: "The Prophet [s] stood among us
one day preaching by a well between Mecca and Medina known as
Qum. He praised God and gave exhortation, admonishment, and
reminder. Then he said, 'O people, I am but a man, and it may be
that God's messenger [i.e., the angel of death] comes for me and I
will answer, but I leave you with two matters of great weight. The
first is the Quran, which contains guidance and light, so take the
Quran and hold fast to it.' And he emphasized the importance of
the Quran and made it enticing to us. Then he said, 'And my descendants. I remind you of God concerning my descendants. I remind you of God concerning my descendants. I remind you of God
concerning my descendants.'"[254] The Prophet [s] also encouraged
the visiting of graves when he said, "Visit graves, for they remind
one of death."[255] And we clarified the ruling on visiting graves in
the answer to question forty-seven, so return to it.

The graves most worthy of visitation, after that of the Messenger of God [s], are the graves of his noble descendants, because
visiting them demonstrates obedience to the Messenger of God [s]
and forges a connection with him. God says in the Quran: *This is
what God announces to true believers who do good works. Say: I ask of
you no recompense, save loving kindness among kinsfolk* [42:23]. In fact,
a person's right to visit the graves of the Prophet's descendants
is more strongly supported than their right to visit the graves of
their own relatives. Abu Bakr al-Siddiq said, "By He in whose Hand
is my soul, the descendants of the Prophet of God [s] are more dear
to me than my own."[256] He also said, "Be vigilant in your care of

254. IBN HANBAL, *Musnad Imam Ahmad*, 4:366; AL-NAYSABURI, *Sahih Muslim*, 4:1873.

255. IBN HANBAL, *Musnad Imam Ahmad*, 2:441; AL-NAYSABURI, *Sahih Muslim*, 2:671; AL-TAMIMI, *Sahih Ibn Hibban*, 7:440.

256. IBN HANBAL, *Musnad Imam Ahmad*, 1:9; AL-BUKHARI, *Sahih Bukhari*, 3:1360; AL-NAYSABURI, *Sahih Muslim*, 3:1380.

Muhammad [s] through his descendants."[257]

Therefore, visiting the graves of the Prophet's [s] descendants is recommended, and they are even more worthy of visitation than the graves of one's own relatives, for the relatives of the Messenger of God [s] are more beloved to us than our own. And God is Most High and Knows best.

---

257. AL-BUKHARI, *Sahih Bukhari*, 3:1361, 1370.

FATWAS RELATED TO BASIC TENETS
OF ISLAMIC LAW AND LEGAL DIFFERENCES

Question 49:

Certain subjects of Islam are characterized by a scholarly difference of opinion. Yet some books try to convince the reader that the author's position is the only correct stance on that subject, and that anyone who disagrees is a heretic who has gone astray. Why is there a difference of opinion concerning these matters, and does this difference of opinion cause the fragmentation of the Muslim community?

The publication of the type of books described above poses a threat to the unity of the Muslim community. These books try to convince people to adhere to the school of thought of their author by describing their opposition as innovators, heretics, and ones who have gone astray. There is no doubt that these books played a role in creating much of the fragmentation that we experience in this day and age. That does not mean that we should stubbornly adhere to our school of thought in opposition to theirs. Everyone has the right to present an opinion and consider it correct, but it is never permissible to accuse the opposition of innovation, going astray, and heresy, especially when the denounced opinions have been accepted by scholars throughout the ages. No one has the right to claim that these respected scholars are astray. The most that one may do is oppose one school and follow another, which does not cause disunity within the community. Discord and conflict occur when people persistently insist that their school is correct and everyone else is wrong.

Nobody in the past or the present, in the East or the West, disagrees on the essentials of Islam, which are those aspects of the religion that are known by necessity. Similarly, nobody disagrees concerning those issues established by community consensus, which reflects the essence of this religion. Everything else is left to interpretation. Muslims are free to follow any school they like, as long as it is led by scholars qualified to examine and interpret evidence. No consideration is given to the interpretations of people who have not fulfilled the conditions and requirements.

Variance of opinion concerning matters that are uncertain has existed since the time of the Companions of the Prophet [s]. Imam Abu al-Qasim ibn Muhammad b. Abi Bakr al-Siddiq said, "God has caused benefit through the variance of opinion among the Companions of the Prophet in their actions. Anybody who acts according to the actions of one of them will find themselves with ample room, and that someone better than they has done the same."[258]

Sufyan al-Thawri said, "If you see a person doing something concerning which there is a variance of opinion, and you hold the opposing position, do not prevent them [from their actions]."[259] Imam Ahmad ibn Hanbal said, "The jurist should not make people follow his school or be harsh with them."[260]

Ibn Qudama al-Maqdisi, the Hanbali Imam said, "There are great Imams from the predecessors within this community through whom the principles of the religion were extracted and problematic rulings were clarified. Their agreement is evidence, and their variance of opinion is a vast mercy."[261] A man wrote a book about variance of opinion and Imam Ahmad told him, "Do not call it variance of opinion, rather, call the book 'Spaciousness.'"[262] He also said, "When a mufti is asked to issue a fatwa, and his fatwa does not accommodate a spacious breadth of opinion for the one requesting the fatwa, he may refer him to someone who does have flexibility."[263]

Even if a scholar is certain that the bearer of an opposing opinion is wrong, it is still not permissible for him to describe that person as an innovator or a heretic, because holding an incorrect opinion based on a correct intellectual methodology is not described as heretical. This is how things have been understood by the great scholars of the past. Imam al-Dhahabi said, "If we were to accuse of innovation every Imam who makes a forgivable error in interpretation, and ostracize him from the community, then Ibn

258. Yusuf ibn Muhammad IBN 'ABD AL-BARR, Jami' Bayan al-'Ilm wa Fadlihi. Al-Maktabah al-Salafiyyah, 4:80.

259. AL-ASFAHANI, Hilyat al-Awliya', 2:368.

260. Ibn Muflih AL-MAQDASI, al-Adab al-Shar'iyyah, 1:166; AL-SAFARINI, Ghidha al-Adab, 1:233.

261. Ibn Qudmah AL-MAQDASI, al-Mughni, 1:1.

262. IBN TAYMIYYAH, Majmu' al-Fatawa, 30:79.

263. Ibid.

Nusayr, and Ibn Mandah, and those even greater than them would not have been safe from us. God guides people to truth, and He is the Most Merciful towards those who show mercy. We seek refuge with God from impulsiveness and impoliteness."[264]

Ibn Taymiyyah said, "Saying that an issue is definitive does not entail an accusation of those *mujtahids* who oppose it. This is like the rest of the issues concerning which the early generations differed and we have certainty of the correctness of one of the positions, such as the fact that the pregnant woman whose husband has died has a waiting period that lasts until she gives birth, intercourse with penetration but without ejaculation necessitates major ritual purification, interest of increase (*riba al-fadl*) is forbidden, and temporary marriage is forbidden."[265]

From the preceding evidence, we understand that the variance of opinion among the scholars and *mujtahids* possessing the requirements for making *ijtihad* in matters allowing variance is a great mercy bestowed by God upon Muslims. God has allowed for broad interpretation and it is permissible for them to follow whatever is appropriate to their circumstances; there is no doubt concerning this.

The fragmentation mentioned in the question is brought about by acts of intellectual terrorism, coercion, and deception that seek to impress upon people one unequivocal truth. This is the characteristic that was enquired about, and it is a blameworthy innovation that is not part of the guidance of the predecessors of this community. May God grant us breadth in our understanding. And God is Most High and knows best.

---

264. AL-DHAHABI, *Siyar 'Allam al-Nubula'*, 14:40.
265. Ibn Muflih AL-MAQDASI, *al-Adab al-Shar'iyyah*, 1:186.

Question 50:

What is the meaning of innovation? How have the scholars dealt with innovation? What is the correct understanding of innovation?

In order to comprehend the meaning of innovation and understand it correctly, we must be aware of both its lexical definition and its technical meaning in Islamic law.

Let us begin with the lexical definition of innovation. Innovation (al-bid'a) means something new (al-hadath) and refers to something invented in the religion after its completion. Ibn al-Sikkit said, "Innovation is every new thing, but its most frequent usage connotes something blameworthy." Abu 'Adnan said, "An innovator is someone who does something in a way other than how it was done originally. When someone is an innovator in something, it means that they are the first to do it and they have not been preceded by anybody else."[266]

The scholars have taken two approaches to defining innovation in Islamic law. The first is that adopted by al-'Izz ibn 'Abd al-Salam, who considered anything not done by the Prophet [s] to fall into a category of innovation. He said, "Innovation is any action that was not known at the time of the Prophet [s]. These are categorized as: obligatory innovation, forbidden innovation, recommended innovation, disliked innovation, and permissible innovation. The way to know which category of innovation a given action falls into is by examining it in light of the principles of Islamic law. If it falls under the rules of obligation, it is obligatory, if it falls under the rule of the forbidden, it is forbidden, if it falls under the rules of the recommended, it is recommended, if it falls under the rules of the disliked, it is disliked, and if it falls under the rules of the permissible, it is permissible."[267] Al-Nawawi verified this understanding when he said, "Anything that was not present during the Prophet's [s] time is called innovation, but it can be praiseworthy or otherwise."[268]

The second approach considers the meaning of innovation in

---

266. IBN MANSUR, *Lisan al-'Arab*, 8:6.

267. Izz ibn 'Abd al-Salam AL-SALAM, *Qawa'id al-Ahkam fi Masalih al-Anam*. Maktabat al-Kulliyyat al-Azhariyyah, 2:204.

268. AL-'ASQALANI, *Fath al-Bari*, 2:394.

Islamic law to be more specific than its linguistic meaning. This approach uses the term innovation to connote only that which is blameworthy, and thus it does not follow al-'Izz's system of calling innovation obligatory, recommended, permissible, or disliked. Rather, the meaning of innovation is strictly relegated to the forbidden. This is the position adopted by Ibn Rajab al-Hanbali, who clarified, "The intended meaning of innovation is what has come about which has no principle in Islamic law that refers to it. As for that which has a principle in Islamic law that refers to it, this is not innovation, even if it is such according to linguistic usage."[269]

In practice, these two approaches only differ in method of argumentation. They reach the same true understanding of innovation: the blameworthy and sinful innovation is that which has no basis in Islamic law. This is the intended meaning of the Prophet's [s] saying, "Every innovation is astray."[270]

This was the opinion of the great jurists and scholars that the Muslim community follows. Al-Bayhaqi relates that Imam al-Shafi'i said, "There are two kinds of innovation. The first is that which contradicts the Quran, the Sunnah, a tradition, or consensus. This is innovation of misguidance. The second is that which is good and does not entail a contradiction of any of these. This is a non-blameworthy innovation."[271]

Abu Hamid al-Ghazali said, "Not everything that is innovated is forbidden. Rather, it is the innovation that contradicts an established Sunnah and removes a ruling of the law that is forbidden."[272]

Imam al-Nawawi relates the position of al-'Izz ibn 'Abd al-Salam, "The Sheikh and Imam upon whose stature, mastery of and proficiency in all kinds of knowledge is a point of agreement, Abu Muhammad 'Abd al-'Aziz ibn 'Abd al-Salam, said at the end of his book *Kitab al-Qawa'id,* 'Innovation is categorized as being obligatory, forbidden, recommended, and permissible . . . .'"[273] On another

---

269. And al-Rahman ibn Ahmad IBN RAJAB, *Jami' 'Ulum wa al-Hima.* Dar al-Ma'arif, p. 223.

270. IBN HANBAL, *Musnad Imam Ahmad,* 3:310; AL-NAYSABURI, *Sahih Muslim,* 2:592.

271. AL-ASFAHANI, *Hilyat al-Awliya',* 9:113.

272. AL-GHAZALI, *Ihya' 'Ulum al-Din,* 2:248.

273. Yahya ibn Sharaf AL-NAWAWI, *Tahdhib al-Sama' wa al-Lughat.* al-Matba'ah al-Muniriyyah, 1:22.

occasion, when discussing shaking hands after prayer (which we will discuss in fatwa sixty-six) he said, "Know that this shaking of hands is recommended at every encounter. As for the shaking of hands after the morning and afternoon prayers that people have grown accustomed to, there is no basis for this practice in the legal tradition, but there is nothing wrong with it since the shaking of hands is a Sunnah. The fact that they have held fast to the practice in some instances and neglected it in many others does not mean the instances in which they do it fall outside the sphere of shaking hands whose basis is reported in the legal tradition."[274]

Ibn al-Athir said, "There are two kinds of innovation: innovation of guidance and innovation of misguidance. That which is in contradiction to what God and His Messenger [s] have commanded is blameworthy and denounced, and that which falls under what is generally recommended and enjoined is praised." He continued, "In reality, praiseworthy innovation is Sunnah, and according to this interpretation the *hadith*, 'Every innovation is astray,' is understood as referring to that which contradicts the principles of Islamic law and is not in accordance with the Sunnah.'"[275]

Ibn al-Manzur also makes important comments concerning the technical meaning of innovation: "There are two kinds of innovation, innovation of guidance and innovation of misguidance. That which is in contradiction to what God or His Messenger [s] have commanded is blameworthy and denounced, and that which falls under what is generally recommended and enjoined is praised. That for which there is no example, like a kind of generosity or munificence, and doing good, are praiseworthy actions. These cannot be in contradiction to that which has been related in the law, for the Prophet [s] made a reward for them saying, 'Whoever initiates a good Sunnah will be given the reward of it and the reward of those who act upon it.' And he said of its opposite, 'Whoever initiates a bad Sunnah will bear the responsibility for it and the responsibility of those who act upon it.'" This applies only to actions contradicting that which God and His Messenger [s] have commanded. 'Umar's saying, "What a great innovation this is," (referring to the *tarawih* prayers in Ramadan) is of the category of

---

274. Yahya ibn Sharaf AL-NAWAWI, *al-Adhkar*. Riyad: Dar al-Huda, p. 382.

275. IBN ATHIR, *al-Nihayah*. al-Matba'ah al-Khayriyyah, 1:80.

innovation of guidance, because the actions he was referring to were good and fell under that which is praised. He called them innovation and praised them because the Prophet [s] did not make it a Sunnah for them. The Prophet [s] prayed them some nights, refrained from praying them regularly, and did not gather the people for them. That was also not the case during the reign of Abu Bakr. 'Umar, however, gathered people for the prayers and urged them to perform them. This is why it is called an innovation, whereas in reality it is a Sunnah, as evidenced by the saying of the Prophet [s], "Keep to my Sunnah and the Sunnah of the rightly guided Caliphs after me," and, "Follow those who come after me, Abu Bakr and 'Umar." The *hadith*, "Every innovation is misguidance," is similarly interpreted to refer to that which contradicts the principles of Islamic law and is not in accordance with the Sunnah.[276]

The majority of scholars have dealt with innovation as falling into categories, as is evident from the quote of Imam al-Shafi'i and his followers: al-'Izz ibn 'Abd al-Salam, al-Nawawi, and Abu Shama; from the Malikis: al-Qarafi and al-Zurqani; from the Hanafis: Ibn 'Abidin; from the Hanbalis: Ibn al-Jawzi; and from the Zahiris: Ibn Hazm. This approach is represented in the definition of innovation given by al-'Izz ibn 'Abd al-Salam: "It is an action that was not known at the time of the Prophet [s], and it is categorized as obligatory innovation, forbidden innovation, recommended innovation, disliked innovation, and permissible innovation."[277]

They also provided examples of these categories: Obligatory innovation includes the act of occupying oneself with the grammar through which the words of God and His Messenger [s] are understood. This is obligatory because it is necessary for the preservation of the Shari'ah, and since the Shari'ah is indisputably necessary, whatever aids its attainment is therefore necessary itself. Examples of forbidden innovation are the schools of al-Qadariyah, al-Jabriyah, al-Murji'ah, and al-Khawarij. Recommended innovations include the establishment of schools, building aqueducts, and praying *tarawih* in a mosque as a group behind a single imam. The decoration of mosques and Qurans is considered a disliked innovation. Permissible innovation includes shaking hands after prayer, consuming extravagant food and drink, and wearing fine clothes.

276. IBN MANSUR, *Lisan al-'Arab*, 8:6.
277. Al-SALAM, *Qawa'id al-Ahkam fi Masalih al-Anam*, 2:205.

The categorization of innovation was distilled into the five legal rulings, based on evidence including the following:

1) 'Umar's saying, "What a great innovation this is!" concerning *tarawih* prayer performed as a group in a mosque during Ramadan. It has been related, according to 'Abd al-Rahman ibn 'Abd al-Qari, that he said, "I went to the mosque with 'Umar ibn al-Khattab one night in Ramadan. The people were in separate groups, some men praying alone and some men praying with a group praying with them. 'Umar said, 'I think it would be better if they all gathered behind one reciter.' Then he made up his mind and gathered them behind Ubayy ibn Ka'b. Then I went out with him on another night and the people were praying behind their reciter. 'Umar said, 'What a great innovation this is, and the part of the night that they sleep through is better than the one in which they stay up.' He meant the end of the night, since people used to stay up in the beginning of the night."[278]

2) Ibn 'Umar, while among the mosque's congregation, called the post-sunrise prayer (*duha*) a praiseworthy innovation. It has been narrated, according to Mujahid, that he said, "Urwah ibn al-Zubair and I entered the mosque and found 'Abdallah ibn 'Umar sitting by Aishah's chamber while people were praying the post-sunrise prayer in the mosque. We asked him about their prayer and he said, 'Innovation.'"[279]

3) The hadiths that inform us of the division of innovation into good and bad, such as that which has been related from the Prophet [s], "Whoever initiates a good Sunnah will be given the reward of it and the reward of those who act upon it until the Day of Judgment; and whoever initiates a bad Sunnah will bear the responsibility for it and the responsibility of those who act upon it until the Day of Judgment."[280]

The preceding explanations clearly define the two points of view. A non-specific point of view, adopted by Ibn Rajab al-Hanbali and others, maintains that commendable actions that have been legislated are not called innovation in the technical language of law,

---

278. AL-BUKHARI, *Sahih Bukhari*, 2:707.
279. Ibid., 2:630; AL-NAYSABURI, *Sahih Muslim*, 2:917.
280. Ibid., 2:705.

even if that name could be used for them according to the linguistic meaning. Therefore only blameworthy innovation is called innovation according to the law. We also discussed in detail the specific point of view mentioned by al-'Izz ibn 'Abd al-Salam.

Muslims must fully comprehend the information provided here because the matter of innovation has become one of the most important issues affecting Islamic thought. It affects how Muslims deal with questions of jurisprudence, as well as how they deal with their Muslim brothers and sisters. Many people fall victim to judging others as innovators and sinners (may God protect us) because they are ignorant of these principles, which were once very clear and today have become obscured by much confusion. We ask God for well-being, and God is Most High and knows best.

Question 51:

Zealots claim that many Muslims do the impermissible by performing actions not done by the Prophet [s] and his companions. Is the fact that the Prophet [s] and his companions did not do something to evidence the impermissibility of that practice?

Sheikh 'Abdallah ibn al-Siddiq al-Ghumari wrote a treatise on this topic called *The Correct Understanding of the Issue of Omission*. He begins the treatise with the following verses:

Omission is not evidence in our law.
It does not necessitate prohibition or obligation.

Whoever seeks prohibition of that which our Prophet has omitted,
And thinks it is a true and correct ruling,

Has strayed from the path of all evidences;
He has belied the correct ruling and is in error.

There is no possibility of prohibition unless a proscription has come,
Promising punishment for he who transgresses it,

Or blame for one who commits [the act] which allows for punishment;
Or a phrase delineating prohibition accompanied by disgrace.

Muslim scholars of past and present, East and West, have agreed that omission alone cannot serve as proof. They established a system of legal rulings that categorizes actions as obligatory, recommended, neutral, disliked, or prohibited, according to the following sources of evidence:

1) A Quranic citation unequivocal in meaning.
2) An unambiguous text from the Sunnah.
3) Consensus on the ruling.
4) Analogy.

The scholars disagreed on the legitimacy of other types of legal evidence, such as:

5) The opinion of a companion of the Prophet [s].
6) The barring of means to evil (*sadd al-dhariʿah*).
7) The actions of the people of Medina.
8) An action ascribed to the Prophet [s] by a successor (known as a *mursal* action).
9) Juristic preference (*al-istihsan*)
10) Weak hadiths.

Scholars employed other sources of evidence in addition to those listed, but omission is not included among them.

All Muslims agree that omission alone cannot serve as the basis for a legal ruling. Textual evidence and traditions show that the companions did not understand the Prophet's [s] omission to indicate prohibition of an action or even his dislike for it. The jurists have maintained this opinion over the centuries. The Malikis and the Hanafis posited that performing two prayer cycles before the sunset prayer is disliked on the premise that Abu Bakr, ʿUmar, and ʿUthman did not pray this way. Ibn Hazm responded to this claim by saying, "Even if this [report] were authentic, it would bear no evidence because it does not assert that they issued a prohibition against it or said it was disliked, and we do not disagree with them that omitting all of the supererogatory acts of worship is permissible:"[281] Ibn Hazm did not pause in the face of the Companions' omitting the two cycles of prayer. Rather, he said that their omission of the prayer meant nothing as long as they did not explicitly say it was disliked, and this has not been reported.

Ibn Hazm's approach to the omission of the Companions is exactly the same as his position regarding the Prophet's [s] omission of a legislated action. When discussing the question of praying two cycles after the afternoon prayer, he said, "The *hadith* of ʿAli ibn Abi Talib contains no evidence. Rather, all it contains is a report of what he was aware of, mainly that he did not see the Prophet [s] pray them. He is truthful in what he says, but there is no prohibition or dislike of them in that. The Prophet [s] never fasted an entire month outside of Ramadan, but that does not necessitate dislike for fasting an entire month voluntarily."[282] Here it is understood that the Prophet's [s] not fasting an entire month outside of

---

281. ʿAli ibn Ahmad b. Saʿid IBN HAZM, *al-Mahala bi-l-Athar*. Dar al-Fikr, 2:22.

282. Ibid., 2:36.

Ramadan does not entail prohibition or dislike for this practice.

It has been established that the Prophet [s] did not deliver the Friday sermon from a pulpit, and that he instead delivered it from a tree stump. But the Companions did not surmise that giving a sermon from a pulpit is reprehensible or forbidden, so they built him a pulpit.[283] They would never have done something that the Prophet [s] had prohibited, and thus we understand from this example that they did not consider omission to be an innovation.

The Prophet [s] did not say "O Lord, praise is Yours . . ." after raising his head from the bowing position in prayer, but the Companions did not interpret the omission as forbidding that supplication. After all, how could they have done something that they believed to be forbidden? The Prophet [s] did not chastise the Companions for performing that supplication. He did not say, for example, "Good, but do not do it again," and forbid them from coming up with other supplications in prayer. Additionally, it is not permissible to delay clarification until after the time in which it is needed. Rifa'a b.Rafi' al-Zurqi narrated, "One day we were praying with the Prophet [s] and when he raised his head from the bowing position he said, 'God hears those who praise Him.' A man said, 'O Lord, praise is Yours, much goodly and blessed praise.' When the Prophet [s] finished he said, 'Who spoke?' The man said, 'I did.' The Prophet [s] said, 'I saw thirty some angels hastening for it, competing for who would record it first.'"[284]

Ibn Hajar commented on this *hadith*, "They have used this as evidence to support the permissibility of coming up with a new invocation in prayer other than that which has been handed down, as long as it does not contradict what has been handed down."[285] If new invocations are allowed in prayer, then they should be even more encouraged outside of prayer.

Bilal did not understand that when the Prophet [s] abstained from praying two cycles of prayer after making ablutions, he meant that it was impermissible to do so. Instead, Bilal prayed the two cycles and did not inform the Prophet [s]. But the Prophet [s]

283. AL-BUKHARI, Sahih Bukhari, 2:908, 3:1314.

284. IBN HANBAL, Musnad Imam Ahmad, 4:340; AL-BUKHARI, Sahih Bukhari, 1:275; AL-SIJISTANI, Sunan Abi Dawud, 1:204; AL-NASA'I, Sunan al-Nasa'i (al-Mujtabah), 1:222; ANIS, al-Muwatta', 1:211; AL-BAYHAQI, al-Sunan al-Kubra, 2:95.

285. AL-'ASQALANI, Fath al-Bari, 2:287.

asked him about his prayer, saying, "Bilal, tell me about the act you have done in Islam for which you are the most hopeful of its acceptance, for I heard the sound of your sandals before me in Paradise." Bilal said, "I have not done anything that is more hopeful than the fact that I have never made ablutions at an hour of the day or night without praying in that state of purity whatever I can."[286]

We know that praying after making ablutions became a Sunnah after the Prophet [s] approved it. For evidence we reference the Companions' understanding that it is permissible to come up with new invocations and prayers at times when the Prophet [s] did not pray. The Prophet [s] did not denounce this approach and did not forbid it in the future.

The preceding evidence confirms that the omission of an action by the Prophet [s], the Companions, or even the first three generations of Muslims, does not imply prohibition, dislike, or anything else. This is what the Companions of the Prophet understood during his lifetime, and because he did not denounce this understanding, scholars have maintained this opinion. We ask God to give us understanding of our religion, and our last prayer is, "All praise is God's, Lord of the Worlds." God is Most High and knows best.

---

286. AL-BUKHARI, *Sahih Bukhari*, 1:366, 4:1910.

Question 52:

What are the main books relied upon by each of the four schools of Sunni law?

The study of Islamic law, as embodied by the different schools of law, must be carried out by trained scholars using a methodology established by centuries-old consensus. In order to become a trained scholar of Islamic law, a student must first study a short text in any of the schools of law. The student then undertakes a medium-length commentary, studying the proofs employed by each of the differing opinions until he or she reaches an extensive knowledge of every school's references. Those interested in simply gaining a general idea of the methodology follow a different path of study. The information in this section summarizes the books relied upon by the various schools, all of which are narrated through authentic chains of transmission, as well as their corresponding commentaries. This summary should suffice to inform the casual learner.

THE HANAFI SCHOOL

The books of the Hanafi school are numerous. Therefore we will limit our discussion to the most popular of those considered reliable by the jurists of this school.

The First Level: The Foundational Works (*Usul*)

The foundational books contain the popular opinions of the school. These are the works of Muhammad ibn Hasan in his book *al-Jami al-Kabir*, *al-Jami al-Saghir,* and his *al-Siyar al-Kabir* and *al-Siyar al-Saghir*, *al-Ziyadat*, and *al-Mabsut*. These works contain the opinions narrated by Muhammad on the authority of Abu Yusuf, who narrates on the authority of Imam Abu Hanifa. Also included are those Muhammad narrated on the authority of Abu Hanifa alone. These works were written in Baghdad and he provided corroborative continuity in his narrations.

The Second Level: The books of rare opinions (*nawadir*)

These works include:

•*Al-Ruqayat*—These opinions were given during Abu Hanifa's term as judge of the Ruqa area, a township south of Baghdad. He was appointed by Harun al-Rashid.

•*Al-Kisaniyat*—These opinions were recorded and narrated by Shu'ayb ibn Sulayman al-Kisani.

•*Al-Jurjaniyat*—These are the opinions of Ali ibn Salih al-Jurjani, narrated by his companions.

The book *al-Muntaqa* by al-Hakim al-Shahid collects the works of Muhammad not found in the foundational works, so these opinions fall in this second category. Other works of this category include *al-Amali wa'l-Jawami'* by Abu Yusuf, *al-Mujarrad* by Hasan ibn Ziyad, and the *Nawadir* by Hisham ibn 'Abdallah al-Razi.

Opinions narrated singularly may be stronger than popular opinions. If a unique opinion is strong in its narration and its meaning is sounder than that of a popular opinion, then it is preferred over the popular opinion, even if it is transmitted singularly. One such example is found in *al-Tuhfa*: the author preferred the unique, singular opinion concerning the sighting of the moon crescent for the Feast of the Sacrifice. He asserted that one report could outweigh the popular opinion: "The correct opinion is that one witness is sufficient."[287] In another example, a popular opinion states that one cannot follow the legal opinions of a successor. However, there is a unique opinion that says the opinion of a successor is equal to that of a Companion, as long as the fatwa of the successor was issued during the lifetime of the Companions and it was approved by them. Fakhr al-Islam leaned toward this unique opinion and then others followed him in making this opinion the sound one.

Therefore, the six foundational books for the Hanafi jurists function like the two *Sahihs* of *hadith* studies, and the books of *nawadir* are akin to the four of *Sunan* collections.

The Third Level: the books of legal responsa (*fatawa*)

These books contain the opinions derived by the jurists who lived after the companions of Muhammad, Abu Yusuf, Zufar, al-Hasan ibn Ziyad and the rest. These opinions are found in books such as *al-Nawazil* by Abu Layth al-Samarqandi, in which he compiled the opinions of his teachers and his teachers' teachers, including Muhammad ibn Muqatil al-Razi, 'Ali ibn Musa al-Quma, Muhammad

---

287. Muhammad Bukhit AL-MUTI'I, *Irshad Ahl al-Milla ila Ahkam al-Ahilla*, p. 345.

ibn Salma, Shaddad ibn Hakim, Nasir ibn Yahya al-Balkini, Abu al-Nasr al-Qasim ibn Salam. There are also the opinions of earlier jurists like 'Isam ibn Yusuf, Ibn Rustum, Muhammad Sama, Abu Sulayman al-Juzjani, and Abu Hafs al-Bukhari. These scholars often agree that they must contradict some of the opinions of the two Imams for reasons that have become apparent to them.

Other books of legal responsa include *Majmu' al-Nawazil wa'l-Hawadith wa'l-Waqi'at*, by Ahmad ibn Musa b. 'Isa al-Kashi; *al-Waqi'at*, by Abu al-'Abbas Ahmad ibn Muhammad al-Razi al-Natifi; and *al-Waqi'at*, by Sadr al-Shahid.

After these main books came collections of miscellaneous legal fatwas. Examples are Qadikhan's collection of legal responsa, the *Khulasa*, *al-Sirajiya*, and *al-Muhit al-Burhani*. In *Muhit*, al-Sarakhsi distinguished between the three levels by first listing the popular opinion, then the singular opinion, and finally the legal responsa.

The books of legal responsa contain the miscellaneous opinions of the latter Hanafi jurists, and are therefore considered weaker than the books of unique opinions. The contents of these books do not necessarily represent the direct opinion of the founder of the Hanafi school, and the opinions do not have chains of narration verifying the statements' supposed sources. In addition, the jurists of these opinions are not at the level of the earlier jurists.

Followers of the Hanafi school should consult its books in the following order. First one must look up the popular opinions. Next one should review the opinions in the small compendiums, such as the compendiums of Tahawi, Kirkhi, and al-Hakim al-Shahid. These works are those most relied upon, as generations of Hanafi jurists have studied them and passed them on. The following is a short list of books that a Hanafi student should study:

1. *al-Bahr al-Ra'iq Sharh Kanz al-Daqa'iq* by Ibn Najim

2. *al-Mabsut* by al-Sarakhsi. This work exists in many editions, the best being that of Abu Sulayman al-Jawzjani, referred to as *al-Asl*. A number of popular commentaries discuss *al-Mabsut*. Al-Tarsusi said regarding Sarakhsi's work, "No one should follow an opinion that counters it. One should rest upon it only, and one should not give legal opinions unless they are based on it." Whenever the work *al-Mabsut* is mentioned, the person is referring to this work.

3. *al-Jawhara al-Nayyira* by Ibn Ali al-Haddadi al-Ibadi

4. *al-'Inaya Sharh al-Hidaya* by Muhammad ibn Mahmud al-Babarti

5. *Bada'i al-Sana'i* by al-Kasani

6. *Rad al-Muhtar 'ala al-Dur al-Mukhtar*, known as the *Hashiyah*, of Ibn 'Abidin

THE MALIKI SCHOOL

The most famous of the Maliki books is the *Mudawwana,* commonly called *al-Umm.* This book contains thousands of legal issues compiled by Imam Sahnun ibn Sa'id in the 3ʳᵈ Islamic century. Imam Sahnun narrates these opinions from Ibn Qasim who in turns narrates from Imam Malik directly. Ibn Qasim is one of Imam Malik's most famous students who lived with him for more than twenty years. Imam Sahnun also included Ibn Qasim's own opinions that he did not hear from Imam Malik, as well as the opinions deduced by Ibn Qasim through analogy of Imam Malik's legal reasoning. Imam Sahnun strengthened these opinions by using narrations found in the *Muwatta* of Imam Malik that were transmitted by Ibn Wahb. Imam Sahnun also included opinions disputed by the companions of Imam Malik. However, the book was never completed in its entirety.

The Malikis of al-Qayrawan based their legal opinions on Imam Sahnun's work, forsaking the work compiled by al-Qadi Asad ibn al-Furat, who derived his opinions from Ibn Qasim. Ibn Qasim reversed many of his opinions later in life and he wrote to al-Furat to rely on the *Mudawwana* of Imam Sahnun. The *Mudawwana* of Imam Sahnun became the Maliki school's foremost book since it contained the opinions of four great *mujtahid* imams: Imam Malik, Ibn Qasim, Asad ibn al-Furat, and Sahnun ibn Sa'id. It became the source of many commentaries, such as the ones by al-Lakhmi, Ibn Mahriz, Ibn Basir, and Ibn Yunus. Ibn Yunus's commentary remains the most comprehensive discussion of the *Mudawwana.* Then came the compendiums of Ibn Abi Zayd al-Qayrawani, Ibn Abi Zamanayn, and Abu Sa'id al-Baradi'i. Al-Baradi'i titled his work *al-Tahdhib,* and it became the most reliable book for the Malikis of Africa.

Another major work of this school, *al-Wadiha* by 'Abd al-Malak ibn Habib, combines the opinions of Ibn Qasim and his companions. This work became popular in Andalusia. Ibn Rushd wrote an extensive commentary on *al-Wadiha* that was also popular in that

SONDING FROM THE TRADITION

region.

Al-'Utbi, the student of Ibn Habib, wrote *al-'Utbiyya*. He took narrations concerning Imam Malik from a combination of Ibn Qasim, Ashhab, and Ibn Nafi', as well as his own narrations from Yahya ibn Yahya. This work came to be highly regarded and was the subject of many commentaries.

During the 4th Islamic century, Ibn Abi Zayd al-Qayrawani, known as 'Little Malik,' decided to combine all the opinions found in the major previous works. He compiled them in a book entitled *al-Nawadir*. This work includes both the legal theory of the Maliki school and its legal injunctions.

These books remained the main subject of study for the school until the 7th Islamic century, at which point Ibn Hajib composed *Mukhtasar Ibn Hajib*. This work replaced all that came before it as it was accepted by most of the Maliki scholars of this time throughout different regions. Both Ibn Rashid al-Qafasi and Ibn 'Abd al-Salam wrote commentaries on this work.

During the 8th Islamic century, Khalil ibn Ishaq b. Musa al-Jundi also wrote a compendium of Ibn Hajib's work, commonly known as *Mukhtasar Khalil*. From this time forward, he relied upon the preferences of Ibn 'Abd al-Salam and he added his own opinions based on the principles of the school. As al-Hattab mentioned, this was the most comprehensive of the commentaries on Ibn Hajib's work. Khalil also wrote a compendium of Ibn Hajib's work. Commonly known as *Mukhtasar Khalil*, from this time forward the compendium became the focus of the school and the main book used to study Maliki jurisprudence. Abu Muhammad al-Hattab said of Khalil's compendium, "It is a book that is small in size, abundant in its knowledge, comprehensive and full. It has surpassed everything else like it. It has become the source for giving legal opinions, as well as the source to decipher what is relied upon and what is not."[288] The compendium of Khalil was so popular that more than one hundred commentaries and glosses have been written on it.[289]

In summary we list the main books of the Maliki school:

1. *al-Mudawwana*, which contains the opinions of Imam Malik narrated by Ibn Qasim

---

288. AL-HATTAB, *Mawahib al-Jalil fi Sharh al-Khalil*, intro.

289. For more details see 'Abdullah ibn Siddiq AL-GHUMARI, *Kitab al-Iklil Sharh Mukhtasar Khalil*. Ed. Muhammad AMIR.

2. *al-Nawadir* by Ibn Abi Zayd al-Qayrawani

3. The compendium of Ibn Hajib entitled *Jami' al-Ummahat* and *al-Mukhtasar al-Fari*

4. The compendium of Khalil entitled *Mukhtasar Khalil*, which is a compendium of the previous work

5. Ahmad Dardir al-'Adawi's *al-Sharh al-Kabir*, which is a famous commentary on Khalil's compendium. Imam al-Dasuqi has also written a gloss on Dardir's commentary.

6. Ahmad Dardir al-'Adawi's *al-Sharh al-Saghir*, a text and commentary on the established positions of the Maliki school. Imam al-Sawi wrote a gloss on this as well.

THE SHAFI'I SCHOOL

Before the time of Ibn Salah, the Shafi'i school consisted of two branches: the school of Khurasan and the school of Iraq. The school of Khurasan was the first of the two. It consisted of Imam al-Shafi'i's companions, including Ishaq ibn Rahuwiya al-Hanzali, Hamid ibn Yahya b. Hani al-Balkhi, Abu Husayn al-Nisaburi, Ali ibn Salama b. Shaqiq, and Abu Sa'id al-Asfahani al-Hasan ibn Muhammad b. Yazid. The latter was the first to take the school of Imam al-Shafi'i to Khurasan. This branch of the Shafi'i school endured nine generations. Among the last scholars of the Khurasan school were Ilkiya al-Harrasi, Abu Sa'id al-Mutawalli, al-Baghawi, al-Ruwiyani, Imam al-Haramayn al-Juwayni, and Imam al-Ghazali.

This branch of the Shafi'i school composed many important works. The most famous of these works are the writings of Abu 'Ali al-Sinji, such as his commentary on the compendium of al-Muzani which Imam al-Haramayn called *al-Madhab al-Kabir*, and his commentary on *al-Talkhis* of Ibn al-Qass. Other famous texts include al-Qadi Husayn's seminal work and collection of legal responsa, the works of al-Juwayni, the *Tahdhib* of al-Baghawi, and the *Ibana* of al-Furani.

As for the Iraqi branch of the Shafi'i school, its early generation consisted of Imam al-Shafi'i's companions Abu Thawr, Ibrahim ibn Khalid al-Kalbi al-Baghdadi, Imam Ahmad ibn Hanbal, Abu J'afar al-Khallal Ahmad ibn Khalid al-Baghdadi, Abu J'afar al-Nahshali, Abu 'Abd Allah al-Sayrafi, Abu 'Abd al-Rahman Ahmad ibn Yahya b. 'Abd al-Aziz al-Baghdadi, and al-Harith ibn Surayj. The latter narrated al-Shafi'i's *Risala* to 'Abd al-Rahman al-Mahdi. The Iraqi branch lasted eight generations. Among the last jurists of this branch were al-Qadi

Abu al-Sa'ib 'Uqba ibn 'Abd Allah b. Musa al-Hamadani, Abu al-Hasan al-Muhamili al-Kabir, Abu Sahl Ahmad ibn Ziyad, al-Faqih al-Bagh-dadi, Abu Bakr Muhammad ibn 'Umar al-Zabadi al-Baghdadi, Abu Muhammad al-Juzjani, and many others.

The Iraqi branch produced many works, such as the *T'aliqa* of Abu Hamid al-Isfarayni, the *Dhakhira* of al-Bandaniji, *al-Dariq* of Abu Hamid al-Ghazali with the comments of al-Bandaniji, both the *al-Majmu'* and *al-Awsat* of al-Muhamili, as well as his *Lubab* and *Tajrid* with the comments of Abu al-Tayyib al-Tabari, both the *Hawi* and *al-Iqna'* of al-Mawardi, and many others.

During the time of Ibn Salah, his father facilitated the union of the two branches of the Shafi'i school. Ibn Salah studied the Iraqi branch under the tutelage of his father, who adopted the school and its tenets from Ibn Sa'id 'Abdallah ibn Muhammad b. Wahb Al-lah. His father also taught him the tenets of the Khurasani branch according to the scholar Abu Qasim ibn al-Bazri al-Jazari who learned from Ilkiya al-Harrasi. Thus Ibn Salah is considered the major unifier of the two branches.

Ibn Salah's main students were: Imam Abu Ibrahim Ishaq ibn Ahmad b. 'Uthman al-Maghribi al-Maqdisi, Abu 'Abd al-Rahman ibn Nuh b. Muhammad b. Ibrahim al-Maqdisi the Mufti of the Le-vant, Abu Hafs 'Umar ibn Asad b. Abi Talib al-'Arabi, and al-Arbali. The only one of these scholars to study and master both branches of the Shafi'i school was Imam al-Nawawi. Imam al-Nawawi said on this subject, "Our colleagues of the Iraqi branch excelled in transmitting the texts of Imam al-Shafi'i and the principles of the school, and our colleagues of the Khurasani branch have excelled in researching the various branches of jurisprudence, organizing the contents of these searches, and basing rulings off of them."[290]

Even though Imam al-Haramayn and Imam al-Ghazali are con-sidered to belong to the last generation of the Khurasani school, the joining of the two branches of the Shafi'i school was initiated by Imam al-Haramayn. In his work *Nihayat al-Matlab fi 'Ilm al-Madhab*, he began to collect the various opinions of the school's compan-ions and advance the strongest of them based on the principles of the school. His most famous student, Imam al-Ghazali, continued on this path in his own works. However, uniting the legal opinions of the two branches and choosing the strongest opinions proved to

---

290. AL-NAWAWI, *al-Majmu'*, 1:69.

be a long process. It did not come to fruition until the efforts of the two great sheikhs, al-Rafi'i and al-Nawawi.

These two illustrious scholars gave their full attention to the major works of both branches. Ibn Hajar al-Haythami said, "The experts of the Shafi'i school are in agreement that the books which appeared before the two great sheikhs (al-Rafi'i and al-Nawawi) cannot be relied upon without conducting extensive research on each issue until one is certain that a particular opinion is the definitive opinion of the Shafi'i school."[291]

The definitive opinion of the Shafi'i school is that agreed upon by the two great sheikhs. If they disagree, and neither opinion appears stronger, then that of al-Nawawi is preferred. If one has an opinion and the other does not, then the existing opinion should be considered the one relied-upon. After the two great sheikhs, Ibn Hajar al-Haythami and al-Ramli both wrote commentaries on the *Minhaj* of al-Nawawi. They each contributed so many works to the Shafi'i school that jurists of the school unanimously recognize al-Haythami and al-Ramli's opinions as second to only those of the two great sheikhs. It is not permissible to substantiate legal responsa with that which counters their opinions. If they disagree, the jurists of Egypt take the opinions of al-Ramli and the jurists of Yemen, the Levant, the Kurds, and the Hijazis take the opinions of al-Haythami. When neither scholar touches upon a subject, one gives legal responsa based on the opinions of Sheikh al-Islam Zakariya al-Ansari. Last, one may turn to the opinions of al-Khatib al-Shirbini.

The books relied upon by the Shafi'i school begin with the writings of al-Juwayni. His book *Nihayah al-Matlab* forms the foundation of all later books. *Nihayah al-Matlab* is considered a compendium of Imam al-Shafi'i's four great legal works: *al-Umm, al-Imla', al-Buwiti,* and *Mukhtasar al-Muzani.* Another opinion maintains that al-Juwayni's seminal work is a summary of *Mukhtasar al-Muzani.* Imam al-Ghazali later condensed al-Juwayni's work into *al-Basit,* which he further condensed into *al-Wasit,* which was summarized in *al-Wajiz,* and finally he summarized *al-Wajiz* in *al-Khulasa.* Imam al-Rafi'i then condensed the content of *al-Wajiz* into his work *al-Muharrar.* He also wrote two commentaries on *al-Wajiz: Sharh al-*

---

291. 'Asqalani, Ibn Hajar, 'Alawi ibn Ahmad AL-SAQQAF, *al-Fawa'id al-Makiyyah.* al-Babi al-Halabi, n.d.

Saghir and *al-'Aziz*. Imam al-Nawawi then summarized *al-'Aziz* in his work *al-Rawda*, and he also summarized *al-Muharrar* in *al-Minhaj*. The *Minhaj* was further summarized by al-Ansari in his book *al-Manhaj*, and by al-Jawhari in *al-Nahj*.

Ibn al-Muqri summarized *al-Rawda* in *al-Rawd* and Zakariya al-Ansari wrote a commentary on *al-Rawd* entitled *al-Asna*. Ibn Hajar summarized this last work in his book *al-Na'im*, but the text was lost during his own lifetime.

The following lists the books relied upon by the Shafi'i school that we have discussed:

1. *al-Muharrar* by al-Rafi'i, a summary of al-Ghazali's *al-Wajiz*
2. *al-'Aziz* by al-Rafi'i, a lengthy commentary on al-Ghazali's *al-Wajiz*
3. *al-Minhaj* by al-Nawawi, a summary of *al-Muharrar*
4. *al-Rawda* by al-Nawawi, a summary of Rafi'i's *al-'Aziz*
5. *Tuhfat al-Muhtaj* by Ibn Hajar al-Haythami, a commentary on Nawawi's *Minhaj*
6. *Nihayat al-Muhtaj* by al-Ramli, a commentary on Nawawi's *Minhaj*
7. *Asna al-Matalib* by Sheikh al-Islam Zakariya al-Ansari, a commentary on Ibn al-Muqri's *Rawd al-Talib*, which is a summary of *al-Rawda*
8. *Mughni al-Muhtaj* by al-Khatib al-Shirbini, a commentary on Nawawi's *Minhaj*

THE HANBALI SCHOOL

There are many books in the Hanbali school. The books that are relied upon and used for giving legal responsa are:

1. *Iqna' li Talib al-Intifa'*. This is a highly beneficial book written by the notable expert Musa ibn Ahmad b. Musa b. Salim al-Hijawi al-Maqdisi al-Dimashqi al-Salihi. This is the main book used by the Hanbalis in the Levant.
2. *al-Insaf fi M'arifah al-Rajih min al-Khilaf*. This book contains the full range of the Hanbali school's different opinions on all legal issues. In this sense, one may rely solely on this work and dispense with all others. The work is unique in that it highlights the strong and definitive opinion, but rarely cites the textual proof used to arrive at the correct conclusion. In his introduction, the author mentions the different narrations of

the Hanbali school as well as the main works used throughout
the book. He highlights his method of deriving the dominant
opinion. This book is based on Ibn Qudamah's *al-Mughni*, which
serves as a commentary and also provides more information as
needed. The author further condensed *al-Insaf* into *al-Tanqih
al-Mushbi' fi Tahrir Ahkam al-Muqni'*.

3. *Dalil al-Talib*: This brief but highly influential conspectus
was written by Mar'i ibn Yusuf b. Abi Bakr b. Yusuf b. Ahmad
al-Karmi. As suggested by his name, the author hailed from
Karm, a small area near Nablus in Palestine.

4. *Ru'us al-Masa'il*: This work was written by Imam 'Abd al-
Khaliq ibn 'Isa b. Ahmad b. Abi Musa al-Hashimi.

5. *al-Ri'ayatan*: Ibn Hamdan authored both of the books referred to by this title. It is written in *Kashf al-Zunun* that both of
these works follow Hanbali jurisprudence and contain important and rare commentaries rarely found elsewhere.

6. *al-'Umda*: Ibn Qudamah, the author of *al-Mughni*, wrote
this as a conspectus. The book compiles select opinions concerning the different branches of law. It is a simple book that
employs simple language.

7. *'Umdat al-Raghib*: This book was written by Sheikh Mansur al-Bahuti for beginners in the Hanbali school. Sheikh Uthman ibn Ahmad al-Najdi wrote a commentary on this work.

8. *Ghayat al-Muntaha*: Written by Sheikh Mar'i al-Karmi,
this book is a combination of the *Iqna'* and *al-Muntaha*. It follows the style of the *mujtahids* and accordingly contains many
of the author's opinions.

9. *al-Ghunya*: 'Abd al-Qadir ibn Abi Salih 'Abd Allah b. Jinki
Dust al-Jili al-Baghdadi composed this work.

10. *al-Furu'*: This work was authored by Muhammad ibn
Muflih b. Mufarraj al-Maqdisi al-Salihi al-Ramini, the Sheikh
of the Hanbali school during his time and one of the great *mujtahids*.

11. *al-Qawa'id*: 'Abd al-Rahman ibn Ahmad b. Rajab al-Baghdadi al-Dimashqi wrote this book.

12. *al-Kafi*: In this work, Muwaffaq al-Din al-Maqdisi, also
the author of *al-Mughni*, provides the various branches of jurisprudence along with their textual proofs.

13. *Muntaha al-Iradat fi Jam' al-Muqni' ma'a al-Tanqih wa al-
Ziyadat*: Written by Taqi al-Din Ahmad ibn 'Abd al-'Aziz 'Ali b.

Ibrahim al-Futuhi al-Misri, this famous book became one of the main resources of the later period. It is the basis of legal responsa.

14. *Sharh Muntaha al-Iradat*: Mansur ibn Yunus b. Salah al-Din b. Hasan b. Ahmad b. 'Ali b. Idris al-Buhuti wrote this book as a commentary on the previous work. There is also a gloss on this work written by Sheikh Mansur.

This discussion has offered a brief insight into the various books of the four Sunni legal schools. We ask God to grant us benefit from what we have learned, and to teach us what is of benefit to us. Our final supplication: all praise is due to God, the Lord of the worlds.

FATWAS RELATED TO INVOCATION (DHIKR)

Question 53:

Is invoking God (*dhikr*) in numbers greater than those found in the Sunnah a reprehensible innovation (*bid'a*) or an impermissible (*haram*) action?

Invoking God in abundance and in numbers greater than those found in the Sunnah is an encouraged act. In fact, it is commanded clearly in the book of God when He says, *O you who believe, remember God with much remembrance* [33:41]. God has praised those who follow this command: *Save those who believe and do good works, and remember God often* [26:227]. God also says, *Indeed in the Messenger of God you have a good example for those who look to God and the Last Day, and remember God often* [33:21], and *Men who remember God often and women who remember—God has prepared for them forgiveness and a vast reward* [33:35]. God has mentioned that infrequent remembrance of Him often characterizes hypocrites, *And they [the hypocrites] do not invoke God except a little* [33:36].

The Prophet [s] said, "The unique ones have advanced." The companions asked, "Who are the unique ones, O Messenger of God?" He replied, "The men and women who make persistent mention of God."[292] He also said, "Let your tongue remain moist with the mention of God."[293] as well as:

> Whoever says, "There is no deity but God. He is alone without partners. His is all domain and all praise, and He has power over all things," one hundred times a day, it is as if they had freed ten slaves, one hundred good deeds are written for them, and one hundred bad deeds are wiped away from their record . . . . No one can bring better than this

---

292. IBN HANBAL, *Musnad Imam Ahmad*, 2:232; AL-NAYSABURI, *Sahih Muslim*, 4:2062; AL-TIRMIDHI, *Sunan al-Tirmidhi*, 5:577; and AL-TAMIMI, *Sahih Ibn Hibban*, 3:140.

293. IBN HANBAL, *Musnad Imam Ahmad*, 4:188; AL-TIRMIDHI, *Sunan al-Tirmidhi*, 5:458; AL-TAMIMI, *Sahih Ibn Hibban*, 2:1246; ibid., 3:96; AL-HA-KIM, *al-Mustadarak 'ala al-Sahihayn*, 1:672.

except someone who does more."[294]

All of these verses and hadiths emphasize that there is no limit to the number of times one may make mention of God (*dhikr*). The Shari'ah has not prescribed a particular number of times to do so. Someone who makes mention of God more than the number of times found in the *hadith* literature is better than someone who does less, as is clearly expressed by the previously quoted *hadith*. Therefore, making mention of God is a recommended act and doing so abundantly is to perform a recommended act abundantly. It is by making mention of God that our hearts become alive, and by forgetting to do so our hearts become dead.

The texts provided prove that it is permissible for a person to make mention of God any number of times that one chooses as a daily practice for themselves, or that has been prescribed by a spiritual guide. We ask God to enliven our hearts through constant remembrance of Him. And God is Most High and knows best.

294. AL-BUKHARI, *Sahih Bukhari*, 5:2315; AL-NAYSABURI, *Sahih Muslim*, 4:2071.

Question 54:

What is the ruling on using prayer beads (*subha*)?

Prayer beads are a string of beads used in one's litanies and invocation. *Subha* is a new word introduced into Islamic discourse, and it is a means to righteous actions. Since means are judged according to their desired goals, the string of prayer beads is a recommended tool as it aids one in making regular mention of God.

Prayer beads are a permissible tool for Muslims to use to count their litanies and invocations (*wird*). It is better to use beads than to count on one's fingers because it more easily prevents mistakes, allowing the heart to focus. The *hadith* narrated on the authority of S'ad ibn Abi Waqqas proves the *hadith*'s authenticity. Alongside the Prophet [s], the narrator entered into the presence of a woman who had in her hands pebbles or date-pits, which she was using to invoke God. The Messenger of God [s] said,

> Shall I inform you of that which is easier and better than this? Say, "Praise be to God equal to the number of His creation in the heavens. Praise be to God equal to the number of His creation in the earth. Praise be to God equal to the number of His creation between the two. Praise be to God equal to the number of all things He has created. God is the greatest equal to the same number. All praise is due to God equal to the same number. There is no deity but God equal to the same number, and there is no power nor strength except by God equal to the same number."[295]

The Prophet [s] did not prohibit her action. Rather, he guided her to that which was easier and better for her to do. If there were something reprehensible or detestable in her actions, he would have pointed this out.

The jurists have understood this report to indicate the permissibility of glorifying God, outside of prayer, with either the hands, pebbles, or with prayer beads, as well as by counting with one's mind or fingers. During prayer, however, it is considered a reprehensible act, as it does not derive from the actions of prayer. Abu Yusuf and Muhammad from the Hanafi school ruled that there was

---

295. AL-SIJISTANI, *Sunan Abi Dawud*, 2:80; AL-TIRMIDHI, *Sunan al-Tirmidhi*, 5:562; and AL-HAKIM, *al-Mustadarak 'ala al-Sahihayn*, 1:732.

nothing wrong with using prayer beads after mandatory or super-erogatory prayers.[296]

There are many hadiths concerning this issue, for example:

1. On the authority of al-Qasim ibn 'Abd al-Rahman, "Abu Darda' used to keep the pits of *ajwa* dates in a bag. When he would pray the dawn prayer, he would take them out and invoke with them until they ran out."[297]

2. On the authority of Abu Nadra al-Ghifari, "An old man from Tufawa said to me, 'Abu Hurayrah settled in Medina, and I have never seen anyone more diligent than him, and I have never seen anyone more honorable towards their guests than him. One day I was with him and he was sitting on a mat with a bag of pebbles or date-pits, which he was using to invoke God. At his feet was a black slave girl who would collect them once he had finished and return them to the bag.'"[298]

3. On the authority of Na'im ibn Muharrar b. Abi Hurayrah, who related that his grandfather Abu Hurayrah had a rope with one thousand knots and he never slept without invoking with it. This *hadith* has been narrated by 'Abd Allah, the son of Imam Ahmad, in *Zawa'id al-Zuhd,* and by Abu Na'im in his *Hilyah al-Awliya'*.[299] The same has been narrated about S'ad ibn Abi Waqqas; Abu Sa'id al-Khudri; Abu Safiyah, the client of the Prophet [s]; and Sayidah Fatimah, the daughter of al-Husayn who was the son of 'Ali ibn Abi Talib.

Many scholars have composed works demonstrating that the use of prayer beads is religiously sanctioned. Among the well-known works are Imam Jalal al-Din al-Suyuti's *al-Minha fi'l-Subha,* Sheikh Muhammad ibn 'Allan al-Siddiqi's *Iqad al-Masabih li Mashru'iyah It-tikadh al-Masabih,* and Abu Hasan al-Laknawi's treatise *Nuzhat al-Fikr fi Subhah al-Dhikr."*

We will also quote the relied-upon jurists from the various schools of law in order to further clarify this issue.

1. From the Shafi'i school: Ibn Hajar al-Haythami was

---

296. AL-ZAYLA'I, *Nasb al-Rayah fi Takhrij Ahadith al-Hidayah,* 2:113.

297. Ahmad ibn 'Amr b. ABU 'ASIM, *al-Zuhd.* Dar al-Rayyan, 1:141.

298. IBN HANBAL, *Musnad Imam Ahmad,* 2:540; AL-SIJISTANI, *Sunan Abi Dawud,* 2:253.

299. AL-ASFAHANI, *Hilyat al-Awliya',* 1:383.

asked, "Do prayer beads have a basis in the Sunnah?" and he replied accordingly:

Yes, and many scholars have composed works concerning this matter, such as Imam al-Suyuti. From the Sunnah we have the following *hadith* from Ibn 'Umar who said, "I saw the Prophet [s] invoking God with his hands." Another is the *hadith* from Safiya who said, "The Messenger of God [s] found me with four thousand date-pits in my hands that I was using to invoke God. He said to me, "What is this, O daughter of Huyayy?" I said, "I invoke God with them." He said, "I have invoked God more than this from the moment I saw you." I said, "Teach me, Messenger of God." He said, "Say 'Praise be to God equal to the number of His creation.'"

Ibn Abi Shaybah, Abu Dawud, and al-Tirmidhi have narrated the following report: "You must glorify God, proclaim His Oneness and sanctify Him, and not be heedless so that you would forget His Oneness. Count by your finger tips, as they will be questioned and asked to speak [on the Resurrection Day]." Invoking God with stones, seeds, and tied ropes has also been documented by many of the Companions and those after them. Al-Daylami has narrated with a chain of transmission reaching back to the Prophet, "How great a device for invoking God is the prayer bead string." Based on the *hadith* of Ibn 'Umar, some of the scholars have opined that invoking with the fingertips is better than prayer beads. Others have preferred prayer beads, while still others have made a more detailed ruling on the issue by saying that if one is safe from making mistakes, then the fingertips are better, and if not, then the prayer beads are better.[300]

2. From the Hanafi school: Ibn 'Abdin has stated:

The proof of the permissibility of using prayer beads is the *hadith* narrated by Abu Dawud, al-Tirmidhi, al-Nasa'i, Ibn Hibban, and al-Hakim (who said it has an authentic chain of transmission) on the authority of S'ad ibn Abi Waqqas [quoted above]. The Messenger of God [s] did not forbid her from this act. Rather, he guided her to that which was easier and better. If this act were reprehensible he would have indicated

---

300. Ahmad ibn Muhammad b. 'Ali b. Hajar AL-HAYTHAMI, *al-Fatawa al-Fiqhiyya al-Kubra*. Maktabah al-Islamiyyah, 1983, 1:152.

this. Prayer beads do not add anything to this *hadith* except connecting the stones by a thread. This sort of addition does not add anything to prevent the act. There is no doubt that it has been related that many of the elect of the Sufis used to have prayer beads, as well as others. However, the ruling changes if it leads to ostentation in using prayer beads. The aforementioned *hadith* also attests to the preferred status of the specifically mentioned glorification of God over unqualified glorifications, even if the unqualified glorification is repeated a small number of times as is stated in *al-Hilya* and *al-Bahr.*[301]

3. Al-Shawkani has also written brilliantly:

The two previously mentioned hadiths [quoted above] indicate the permissibility of counting invocations of God with date-pits and stones as well as prayer beads, as there is no difference in the Prophet's [s] affirming the two women's actions. His lack of condemnation of their action and advising them to say what is better, does not negate the permissibility of the act of using prayer beads.

This same meaning has been found in hadiths narrated in the *Juz'* of Hilal al-Haffar on the authority of M'utamir ibn Sulayman concerning Abu Safiyah the client of the Prophet, that a leather mat would be placed for him and a basket made of palm leaves filled with stones would be brought to him from which he would invoke God until midday when he would get up. After the noon prayer he would return to it and invoke God until late afternoon. This *hadith* was also narrated by Ahmad in his book *al-Zuhd* on the authority of 'Affan, from 'Abd al-Wahid ibn Ziyad from Yunus ibn 'Abid concerning his mother who said, "I saw Abu Safiyah, a companion of the Prophet [s] and he was a treasurer . . . .he used to invoke God with stones."

Ibn S'ad also narrated on the authority of Hakim b .al-Daylam that S'a'd ibn Abi Waqqas used to invoke God with stones. Ibn S'ad also says in his *Tabaqat* that, "We were told by 'Abd Allah ibn Musa from Isra'il from Jabir from a woman who used to serve him concerning Fatimah the daughter of al-Husayn the son of 'Ali ibn Abi Talib that she used to make

---

301. IBN 'ABIDIN, *Rad al-Muhtar 'ala al-Dur al-Mukhtar*, 1:650-51.

glorification of God with a thread that was tied in several knots. 'Abd Allah the son of Imam Ahmad narrated in *Zawa'id al-Zuhd* concerning Abu Hurayrah that he used to have a thread that had one thousand knots and he would not sleep until he finished making mention of God with it.

Imam Ahmad in his book *al-Zuhd* narrated on the authority of al-Qasim ibn 'Abd Al-Rahman who said, "Abu Darda' used to keep pits of the dates of Medina in a bag, and he would invoke God with them after praying the dawn prayer one by one until they ran out. Ibn S'ad also narrates on the authority of Abu Hurayrah that he used to invoke God with date-pits grouped together. Al-Daylami narrates from the *Musnad al-Firdaws* from the chain of Zaynab bint Sulayman b. 'Ali from Umm al-Hazan bint J'afar from her father from her grandfather from 'Ali that the Prophet [s] said, "How great a device for making mention of God the prayer bead is." Imam al-Suyuti has compiled these traditions in a treatise entitled *al-Minha fi al-Subha* which is a portion of a larger work entitled *al-Majmu' fi al-Fatawi*. Imam al-Suyuti stated at the end of this treatise, "None of the pious ancestors or the later scholars has been documented as prohibiting reciting one's litanies while using prayer beads. Rather, most of them used to commonly use prayer beads and they found nothing reprehensible in this."[302]

This discussion has clarified that the glorification of God using prayer beads is a recommended act, and it is especially recommended for those who fear that they will miscount. Using the beads can ease one's counting, thus freeing the heart to be involved and present during the mention of God. God is Most High and knows best.

302. AL-SHAWKANI, *Nayl al-Awtar*, 2:366.

Question 55:

What is the ruling on invoking litanies (*hizb*) and using daily regimens of invocation (*wird*) that have been compiled? What ruling might guide a Muslim selecting a set invocation with which to invoke daily?

In daily regimens of invocation and litanies, a person commits to regularly invoking certain Sunnah invocations or other invocations, of their choice, as a way of drawing nearer to God. Muslims engage in this act voluntarily; it is not something that God has made mandatory. Sheikh Zakariyyah al-Ansari stated, "Voluntary acts are those acts that have no corresponding specific textual evidence; rather, a person initiates it himself by choosing a daily invocation."[303]

Ibn Hajar al-Haythami stated:

A person being vigilant in keeping a daily regimen, whether it be prayer, a portion of the Quran, certain invocations, supplication during the day and night, or otherwise, is a Sunnah of the Messenger of God [s] and the pious from amongst God's servants of the past and present. That which has been sanctioned by the Sunnah in congregation should be done, and that which has been sanctioned by the Sunnah individually should be done, just as the Companions sometimes would gather and one would be asked to read while the others would listen. 'Umar ibn al-Khattab used to say, "O Abu Musa, remind us of God," and he would recite from the Quran and the rest would listen.[304]

The scholars used to discuss litanies as if the issue was agreed upon. They would mention litanies in passing, without explaining a ruling or any relevant scholarly dispute. For example, Ibn Najim said, "Al-Halwani mentioned that there is nothing wrong with one reciting daily litanies between obligatory and supererogatory prayers."[305]

The scholars have indicated the benefit of committing to these

---

303. Zakariya ibn Muhammad AL-ANSARI, *al-Ghurar al-Bahiyyah*. al-Matba'ah al-Yamaniyyah, 1:387.

304. AL-HAYTHAMI, *al-Fatawa al-Fiqhiyya al-Kubra*, 2:385.

305. Zayn al-Din ibn Ibrahim IBN NUJAYM, *al-Bahr al-Ra'iq*. Dar al-Kitab al-Islami, 2:52.

litanies and the necessity of keeping this commitment. Imam al-Nawawi stated, "Anyone missing a daily litany to which he has committed himself, whether it is during the night or day, after prayer, or during any situation, should make it up and should be vigilant and persevere in saying it. If one has made it a habit then one should not miss it. Those lax in making it up will become lax in reciting it during its proper time. Al-Shawkani used to say that the Companions of the Messenger of God [s] would make up what they missed of the invocations that they would make at specific times every day. Ibn 'Allan said, regarding situational as opposed to non-situational invocations, "What is meant by situations are situations related to certain times, not related to certain occurrences as with invocations made when seeing the new moon, upon hearing thunder, and the like. It is not recommended to make these up when their occurrences pass. It is reprehensible to leave a daily litany after establishing it as a habit."[306]

Ibn al-Hajj said,

> An aspirant must be vigilant concerning time. Every moment should be filled with an action that is related to a specific regimen of invocation. One should not suffice with the prayers and fasting as their regimen, every action of the aspirant is a litany.

The pious ancestors used to respond to one who wanted to meet another who was sleeping, "He is engaged in his daily regimen (*wird*) of sleep." Sleep, therefore, and other similar actions, are litanies an aspirant uses to draw nearer to his Lord. If this is so, then one's time of sleep is known; as is the time of his nightly litany, the time when he meets with his friends, and the time he spends with his family and close relatives. All of these are litanies because all of an aspirant's time is spent immersed in obedience to his Lord. He does not engage in anything other than that which is permissible or recommended, except with the intention of drawing nearer to God. This is the reality of litanies. They are intended to bring one into proximity with God. Engaging in serious struggle to rid one's health and well-being of barriers and inhibitions will give someone this proximity. Or this proximity is attained from a spiritual

---

306. KUWAIT, *al-Mawsu'ah al-Fiqhiyyah al-Kuwaytiyyah*, 21:257-58, subject matter *dhikr*.

state that allows one to overcome this struggle.[307]

In conclusion, we find that commitment to litanies and daily regimens of invocation is the only means that aids Muslims in constantly remembering God. The pious ancestors performed these ritualized remembrances, and therefore they are recommended as a means to achieve the desired goals of the rulings. And God is Most High and knows best.

---

307. IBN AL-HAJJ, *al-Madkhal*, 3:179-80.

Question 56:

Is invoking God (*dhikr*) out loud a reprehensible innovation?

Moderately raising your voice during glorification (*tasbih*) and other similar acts is preferred (*mustahabb*) by a majority of jurists. The jurists base their opinion on His statement: "*And be not loud-voiced in your worship nor yet silent therein, but follow a way between,*" [17:110] and the method practiced by the Prophet [s]. According to Abu Qutadah, the Prophet [s] was out one night and witnessed Abu Bakr praying in a low voice. He then passed 'Umar praying in a loud voice. With the two of them before him, the Prophet [s] said, "I passed by you, Abu Bakr, when you were praying in a low voice." Abu Bakr replied, "I made myself heard to the One upon whom I called." He said, "Raise your voice some." Then he addressed 'Umar saying, "I passed by you and you were praying in a loud voice." 'Umar replied, "O Messenger of God, I rouse the drowsy and drive out the Devil." He said, "Lower your voice some."[308]

Some of the pious ancestors believed in the preferability of raising one's voice when saying "Allahu Akbar" and other invocations after the five daily prayers. This opinion was based on the *hadith* narrated by Ibn 'Abbas, "It was by hearing the invocations after the prayer that I knew they had finished."[309] Raising the voice during invocations is conducive to stimulating contemplation and waking the hearts of the unheedful. One of the best statements on the matter is by the author of the commentary on *Maraqi al-Falah* in which he compiles hadiths and scholarly opinions on the merits of raising or lowering one's voice during supplication and invocation. Al-Tahtawi resolved this matter by understanding its usefulness and relativity: "This differs depending on the person, the state they are in, the time, and the purpose. Whenever one fears ostentation or bringing harm to someone else by raising one's voice, lowering one's voice is better, and whenever these conditions are absent, raising one's voice is better."[310]

Raising one's voice during invocation is not a reprehensible

---

308. AL-SIJISTANI, *Sunan Abi Dawud*, 2:37; AL-NAYSABURI, *Sahih Ibn Khuzamah*, 2:189; AL-TABARANI, *al-Mu'jam al-Awsat*, 7:181; AL-HAKIM, *al-Mustadarak 'ala al-Sahihayn*, 1:454.

309. AL-BUKHARI, *Sahih Bukhari*, 1:288; AL-NAYSABURI, *Sahih Muslim*, 1:410.

310. AL-TAHTAWI, *Hashiyat Maraqi al-Falah*, 2:311.

innovation, nor is there anything inherently wrong with the practice. In fact, a raised voice can effectively involve the heart and improve concentration, as long as the practitioner avoids ostentation. And God is Most High and knows best.

Question 57:

What is the ruling on gathering in circles to invoke God (*dhikr*)?

Gathering in circles to make invocations is a Sunnah established by evidence from the Shari'ah. God ordains such gatherings in the Quran, *Restrain yourself along with those who cry unto their Lord at morn and evening, seeking His Countenance* [18:28]. And in the words of the Prophet [s], "God Most High has angels that travel the roads seeking out those who make mention of God. When they find a group of people invoking God, they call out to each other, 'Come to that which you seek!' and they encircle them with their wings pointed toward the lowest heaven . . . . And God says to the angels, 'You are My witnesses, I have forgiven them.' One of angels then says, 'So and so is not one of them, he only came for a personal need.' To which God replies, 'The one who sits with them does not suffer distress.'"[311] According to Mu'awiyah, the Prophet [s] encountered a gathering of his companions and asked them, "What has brought you together here?" They replied, "We have gathered to invoke and praise God for guiding us to Islam and blessing us." He said, "Gabriel came and told me that God is boasting to the angels about you."[312] In his book *Riyad al-Salihin* al-Nawawi entitled the first *hadith* "The Virtue of the Circles of Invocation."

Invocation (*dhikr*) has many meanings in the Shari'ah, including: the mere mentioning of God's Divine Essence, His attributes, His actions, or His judgments; the recitation of the Quran; supplicating and beseeching Him; and praising Him through His sanctity, exaltation, unity, praise, thanks, and glorification. There is no evidence to support the claim that only sessions of religious study are valid invocations.

Al-San'ani mentions the *hadith* narrated by Muslim on the authority of Abu Hurayrah: "The Messenger of God [s] said, 'No group of people gathers to make mention of God except that angels surround them, mercy descends upon them, and God mentions them to those in His presence.'"[313] Al-San'ani also decrees "This *hadith*

---

311. AL-BUKHARI, *Sahih Bukhari*, 5:2353; AL-NAYSABURI, *Sahih Muslim*, 4:2069.

312. Ibid., 4:2075.

313. Ibid., 4:2074.

indicates the virtues of gathering for the purpose of making mention of God." Al-Bukhari narrated, "God Most High has angels that travel the roads seeking out those who make mention of God. When they find a group of people invoking God they call out to each other, "Come to that which you seek!" and they encircle them with their wings pointed toward the lowest heaven . . . ." One of the virtues of gathering to make mention of God is that the angels seek and attend such gatherings. *Dhikr* is the glorification and praise of God, the recitation of the Quran, and similar acts of worship. In the *hadith* narrated by al-Bazzar, God Most High asks the angels, "What are my servants doing?" even though He knows better than they, and they reply, "They magnify your blessings, recite Your Book, pray for Your Prophet, and beseech you concerning their worldly lives and their afterlives."

The literal meaning of *dhikr* is "to mention with the tongue." Whoever practices *dhikr* is rewarded. Being conscious of *dhikr*'s meaning is not required; it is only necessary to solely invoke God. For a more complete practice, invocations of the heart should accompany invocations of the tongue. A higher practice is based in consciousness of the invocation's meaning, glorification of God and His exoneration of imperfection. Mandatory acts of righteousness, such as prayer, jihad, and similar practices, are even more preferable. The highest form of invocation is that performed sincerely for the sake of God.[314]

Gathering together to invoke God by reciting the Quran, to study religious knowledge, to glorify Him [by saying *subhan Allah*], to acknowledge his oneness [by saying *la ilaha illa Alllah*], and to praise Him [by saying *al-hamdu lillah*], is one of the Sunnahs that our Lord encourages us to perform in the Quran. It is a correct and authentic Sunnah of His Prophet [s]. And God is Most High and knows best.

---

314. Muhammad ibn Isma'il al-Kahlani AL-SAN'ANI, *Subul al-Salam*. Dar al-Hadith, 2:700.

Question 58:

What is the proper invocation (*dhikr*) of God? Is it permissible to invoke God with just one of His Names like "Allah, Allah," and, "al-Rahman, al-Rahman," without using complete sentences?

As mentioned by the author of *Mukhtar al-Sihah*, linguistically *dhikr* has the opposite meaning of forgetting.[315] In the Shari'ah, *dhikr* has a more general set of meanings. God referred to the Friday sermon (*khutbah*) as *dhikr*: *O you who believe! When the call is heard for the prayer of the day of congregation, haste unto remembrance [dhikr] of God and leave your trading* [62:9]. He also referred to the Hajj as *dhikr*: *Remember [dhikr] God through the appointed days* [2:203]. Prayer is also named as *dhikr*: *And if you go in fear, then [pray] standing or on horseback. And if you are again in safety, remember [dhikr] God, as He has taught you that which [heretofore] you knew not* [2:239]. Lastly, God identified the Quran as *dhikr*: *This [which] We recite unto you is a revelation and a wise reminder [dhikr]* [3:58]. All of the above acts of worship in which Muslims invoke the name of God are referred to as *dhikr*.

Other than these acts of worship, remembrance (*dhikr*) of God means the invocation of God by Muslims with their tongues and hearts. God differentiates between invocation and prayer saying, *Indeed, prayer preserves from lewdness and iniquity, but verily remembrance [dhikr] of God is greater* [29:45]. God may be invoked individually or in a group, silently or out loud. Invocations may be counted on one's fingers or on prayer beads (as we made clear in the answers to previous questions), and it may be done with or without a phrase from the Quran or a *hadith*. Composing new invocations is permissible as long their comprised meanings do not conflict with Islam.

There is nothing wrong with invoking one of God's names alone, and there is no evidence to indicate that these invocations are forbidden. Rather, the bulk of evidence points to the permissibility of these invocations. Those who differ may object on the grounds that invoking God with one of His names was not related by the Prophet [s]. The answer to question fifty-one clarified that

---

315. Muhammad ibn Abi Bakr b. 'ABD AL-QADIR, *Mukhtar al-Sihah*. al-Matba'a al-Khayriyyah, 1:93.

the Prophet's [s] omission of an action is not evidentiary. An examination of a *hadith* mentioned in fatwa fifty-one proves the permissibility of composing a new form of *dhikr*, even if that invocation is used in the prayer.

Al-Hafiz ibn Hajar mentions the following *hadith* of Rifa'ah ibn Rafi' al-Zarqi: "One day we were praying behind the Prophet [s] and when he raised his head from bowing he said, 'God hears those who praise Him.' A man behind him said, 'O Lord, all praise is Yours with much good and blessed praise.' When the Prophet [s] finished he asked, 'Who was it that spoke?' The man replied, 'It was I.' The Prophet [s] said, 'I saw thirty-odd angels hastening to be the first to write it down.'"[316] Ibn Hajar then said, "This *hadith* has been used as evidence for the permissibility of composing new forms of *dhikr* in prayer. The content does not have to originate in the Quran or the Sunnah, as long as the new form is not contradictory."[317]

Another objection may be that invoking God with one of His names alone is not true to the meaning of exaltation and that one must use complete sentences to convey that meaning. In response to this objection, we wish to clarify that the invocation of God's name alone does carry the meaning of exaltation, and this is what the scholars understood. The Imam of imams Abu Hanifah asserts this opinion when discussing the issue of whether or not one enters prayer by merely mentioning the name of God. The author of *Badai'i* says, "According to Abu Hanifah, the report[318] is understood to mean that the opening of prayer has the meaning of exaltation, and that occurs with the divine name alone. One would enter the prayer if one said, 'There is no deity but God,' which occurs by one's saying 'Allah,' not by the negation of other non-existent deities."[319] Imam Abu Hanifah opined that exaltation occurs with the name of God alone and without requiring the use of a complete sentence.

There are verses in the Quran and citations in the Sunnah that

---

316. IBN HANBAL, *Musnad Imam Ahmad*, 4:340; AL-BUKHARI, *Sahih Bukhari*, 1:275' AL-SIJISTANI, *Sunan Abi Dawud*, 1:204; AL-NASA'I, *Sunan al-Nasa'i (al-Mujtaba)*, 1:222; ANIS, *al-Muwatta'*, 1:211, AL-BAYHAQI, *al-Sunan al-Kubra*, 2:95.

317. AL-'ASQALANI, *Fath al-Bari*, 2:28.

318. He is referring to the *hadith* that says, "God does not accept a prayer unless one is in a state of purification, faces the *qiblah*, and says, 'Allahu Akbar.'" [Trans.]

319. AL-KASANI, *Bada'i' al-Sina'i'*, 1:131.

permit one to pronounce the word, "Allah" on its own, including invoking of the name of God. The Quranic verses include: *Say: Allah. Then leave them to prattle* [6:91], and, *So remember the name of your Lord and devote yourself with a complete devotion* [73:8]. The prophetic hadiths demonstrate that invoking God with His name alone will be practiced and praised before the coming of the Hour, and the cessation of that practice will be one of the final signs: According to Anas, the Prophet [s] said, "The Hour will not come until 'Allah, Allah,' is no longer being said."[320] Another narration declares, "The Hour will not come upon anyone saying, 'Allah, Allah.'" Thabit said, "Salman was in a group invoking God when the Prophet [s] passed by, so they stopped. The Prophet [s] said, 'What were you saying?' We said, 'We were reciting, 'Allah, Allah.' He said, 'I saw mercy descending upon you so I wanted to join you in it.' He then said, 'Praise to God who has placed in my community those with whom I have been commanded to be patient.'"[321]

Muslims do not require textual proof to say "Allah" as long as they feel exaltation, solace, and Godly remembrance. The invocation of the name "Allah" alone is not contradicted by principles of faith and bases of Islam, and the faithful should assert the favorability of invocations transmitted directly from the Prophet [s]. The textual and rational evidence we have mentioned, including the scholarly interpretations, should prompt those of differing opinion to leave those who invoke God by His name alone to invoke Him however their hearts are moved. And God is Most High and knows best.

---

320. IBN HANBAL, *Musnad Imam Ahmad*, 3:107; AL-NAYSABURI, *Sahih Muslim*, 1:131; AL-TAMIMI, *Sahih Ibn Hibban*, 15:263; AL-HAKIM, *al-Mustadarak 'ala al-Sahihayn*, 4:539; AL-KUFI, *Musannaf ibn Abi Shaybah*, 7:452.

321. AL-HAKIM, *al-Mustadarak 'ala al-Sahihayn*, 1:21; AL-ASFAHANI, *Hilyat al-Awliya'*, 1:342.

FATWAS RELATED TO PRAYER

Question 59:

Is it permissible to pray in graveyards? What is the ruling on praying in mosques that contain tombs? Does this equate to treating graves as mosques (*masajid*)?

The question of mosques containing tombs is a secondary matter of jurisprudence that is discussed in the worst of ways by the ignorant and those who wish to sow discord. They have made the issue a cause for division and insults among Muslims. You can see some of them insulting others, calling them grave worshipers, innovators, and idolaters. There is neither might nor power except that of God. We gather the scattered commentaries relevant to this question in the hope that God will open blind eyes and deaf ears with them.

Confusion about different facets of this question has caused misunderstanding, making it difficult to find resolution through discussion. Here we will clarify these matters and differentiate between them. Praying in graveyards is not the same as praying in a mosque containing a tomb, and praying in such a mosque does not constitute making a grave a *masjid*. It is necessary to differentiate between three things:

1) Praying at graves.
2) Praying in mosques containing graves.
3) Making graves *masjids*.

First we will address praying at gravesites. A grave is a place where a person is buried. Islamic law respects graves as a way of honoring the dead. The jurists have agreed that walking on graves is disliked according to the *hadith*, "The Prophet [s] forbade walking over graves."[322] The Malikis considered this *hadith* to refer only to graves that are raised mounds, while the Shafi'is and Hanbalis made an exception for walking over a grave when done out of need, or if walking over a grave is the only way to reach another grave. Rulings on praying in cemeteries differ slightly. The Hanafis disliked the practice, as did al-Thawri and al-Awza'i, due to the

---

322. AL-TIRMIDHI, *Sunan al-Tirmidhi*, 3:368.

fact that cemeteries are likely to be dirty. They also objected to this practice as too similar to certain Jewish practices. However, prayer is acceptable if the cemetery has a clean place designated for prayer.

The Malikis ruled it permissible to pray in cemeteries regardless of whether they are in use, have been dug up, or contain the bodies of polytheists.

Shafi'is hold that prayers performed in unearthed cemeteries are invalid because the earth has mixed with the bodily fluids of the dead. This ruling applies conditionally: if you do not put something between yourself and the earth, or even if you do, the practice is disliked. If the cemetery is deemed intact, then the Shafi'is agreed that prayers are valid because the place of prayer was clean. Even though these prayers are valid, they still are frowned upon because they are performed in a place where decaying matter is buried. When there is doubt concerning the cleanliness of a cemetery, two positions offer guidance. The preferred position says that prayer is valid but disliked because the earth is fundamentally assumed to be pure and cannot be ruled filthy out of simple doubt. The opposing presumption states that the prayer is invalid because the obligation of the prayer is not fulfilled due to the doubt of cleanliness; an obligation is not fulfilled when there is doubt that one has fulfilled it.

The Hanbalis say prayer in a cemetery is never valid regardless of whether the burials are old or new and regardless of whether or not it has been unearthed. There is nothing to prevent one from praying near one or two graves, because technically they do not constitute a cemetery. A cemetery is defined as three or more graves. The Hanbalis' position states that you cannot pray in any area surrounding a group of graves referred to as a 'cemetery.' They unequivocally state that, even if a home possesses more than three graves, it is not forbidden to pray there because the area is not called a cemetery.

The jurists' discourse on praying in cemeteries is separate from the question of praying in mosques surrounded by graves.

Proceeding to the second issue, praying in a mosque that houses the tomb of one of the prophets or the righteous is valid by Islamic law, and is sometimes even recommended. Evidence for this ruling derives from the Quran, the Sunnah, the practice of the Companions, as well as consensus in the actions of the Muslim community.

The Quran states, *They said: Build over them a building; their Lord knows best concerning them. Those who won their point said: We verily shall build a place of worship [masjid] over them* [18:21]. This verse references the story of the people of the cave. Some of those who found them said, "Let's build a structure over them," and others added, "We verily shall build a place of worship (*masjid*) over them." The context of the verse indicates that polytheists made the first statement, while monotheists made the second. Both statements were expressed without any disapproval; if they contained any falsehood it would be appropriate for the verse to indicate it in some way. The verse acknowledging both of these statements evidences the Shari'ah's approval of them. Furthermore, when compared to the polytheists' statement, the monotheists are presented in a fashion that indicates praise; the polytheists express doubt, while the monotheists are decisive, *We verily shall build*, and are possessed of vision and faith. They do not seek merely to build, they seek to build a place of worship (*masjid*). This verse indicates that those people knew God and acknowledged worship and prayer.

In his commentary on the verse, *We verily shall build a place of worship over them*, al-Razi stated the place of worship to be built was a space "in which to worship God and preserve the remnants of the people of the cave."[323]

Al-Shawkani said,

> The mention of building a place of worship gives the impression that 'Those who won their point,' are Muslims. It has also been said that they are the people of the kings and sultans of the people mentioned, for they are those who win their point over others. However, the first interpretation is better. Al-Zuajaji said, 'This indicates that when their matter was made apparent, the believers triumphed through bringing forth and resurrection because mosques are for believers.'[324]

This is what the Quran mentions regarding the construction of mosques on graves.

In the Sunnah we find a *hadith* of Abu Nusayr narrated by 'Abd al-Razzaq from Ma'mar from Muhammad ibn Muslim b. Shi-

---

323. Fakhr al-Din AL-RAZI, *Tafsir al-Razi.* Dar al-Fikr, 1995, 11:106.

324. Muhammad ibn 'Ali AL-SHAWKANI, *Fath al-Qadir fi al-Tafsir.* 'Alam al-Kutub, 3:277.

hab al-Zuhri from al-Muswar ibn Makhramah and Marwan ibn al-Hakam who said, "Abu Basir escaped from the polytheists after the treaty of Hudaybiyah. He went to Sayf al-Bahr and was joined by Abu Jandal ibn Suhayl b. 'Amr who also escaped from the polytheists. Three hundred other Muslims joined them. Abu Basir would say, leading them in prayer, 'God Most High is the Greatest. Whoever defends God is defended by God.' When Abu Jandal joined them, he began to lead the prayers. Not a single caravan of Quraysh passed them without being captured. Quraysh sent a message to the Prophet [s] beseeching him for the sake of God and his relatives to send them Abu Basir and the others, and that if any of them returned they would be safe. The Prophet [s] wrote to Abu Jandal and Abu Basir telling them and those with them to return to their homes and families. The Prophet's [s] letter was brought to Abu Jandal when Abu Basir was on his deathbed. He died reading the Prophet's [s] letter clutched in his hand. Abu Jandal buried him in that very place and built a mosque over his grave."[325]

The companions of the Prophet possessed different opinions regarding where the Prophet [s] should be buried. These differences were related by Imam Malik: "Some people said he should be buried by the pulpit while others said he should be buried in the *Baqi'* cemetery. Abu Bakr arrived and said, "I heard the Messenger of God [s] say, 'No Prophet has been buried except where he died,' so dig a hole for him there."[326] To address our question, we draw evidence from the fact that when the companions of the Messenger of God suggested burying him within the pulpit, which is with all certainty inside the mosque, nobody rebuked them. By adhering to the Messenger's command that he be buried in the place where his blessed spirit was taken, Abu Bakr did not constitute an objection to burying the Prophet in the mosque because that would have

---

325. It was mentioned by IBN 'ABD AL-BARR, *al-Isti'ab*, 4:1614; the author of 'Abd al-Rahman ibn 'Abdullah AL-SUHAYLI, *al-Rawd al-Unuf*. Dar al-Fikr, 4:59; Muhammad ibn Sa'd b. Mani' AL-BASRI, *al-Tabaqat al-Kubra*. Dar Sadir, 4:134; the author of 'Ali ibn Burhan al-Sin AL-HALABI, 2:720; it was also related by Musa ibn 'Uqba in al-Maghazi and Ibn Ishaq in al-Sirah. The al-Maghazi of Ibn 'Uqba is the most reliable book on Sirah. Imam Malik said, "read the maghazi of the righteous man Musa ibn 'Uqbah, it is the most reliable book of maghazi." Yahya ibn Ma'in said, "The book of Musa ibn 'Uqbah according to al-Zuhri is the most reliable book of its kind."

326. ANIS, *al-Muwatta'*, 1:231.

been permissible.

The spirit of the Prophet [s] was taken in Aishah's chamber. Her chamber was attached to the mosque where the Muslims prayed, making the relationship of the chamber to the mosque comparable to that of contemporary mosques where people pray in areas connected to chambers in which saints are buried.

Some object to this comparison, saying the situation is unique to the Prophet [s]. However, particularities of rulings related to the Prophet [s] require evidence, the fundamental assumption being that rulings are general as long as there is no evidence affirming their particularity. Since there is no evidence for particularity in this case, the claimed particularity is invalidated. Even if we accepted the position on the particularity of the Prophet [s] (which we have already shown it is not), we would have to deal with the fact that both Abu Bakr and then 'Umar were buried in the same chamber as the Prophet [s]. Does the particularity include Abu Bakr and 'Umar? The Companions prayed in the mosque connected to this chamber that housed three graves, and Aishah lived and prayed her obligatory and supererogatory prayers in that room. Should we not consider the actions and practical consensus of the Companions?

Turning a grave into a place of worship (*masjid*) differs from using a mosque that houses a grave. The turning of a grave into a place of worship was forbidden by the Prophet [s], while the building of a mosque in the vicinity of, or connected to, a grave, was not forbidden. Aishah related the Prophet's [s] words, "God cursed the Jews and Christians for making the graves of their prophets places of worship."[327] A version narrated by Muslim adds: "the graves of their prophets and righteous."[328] The scholars of the community did not take the intention of this *hadith* to prohibit the connecting of mosques and graves of prophets or righteous persons. They correctly interpreted the turning of a grave into a place of worship to mean turning the grave itself into a place where people make prostrations (*sujud*) in worship of the person in the grave, as some of their Jewish and Christian contemporaries were known to do. The Quran says, *They have taken as lords beside God their rabbis and*

---

327. AL-BUKHARI, *Sahih Bukhari*, 1:446; AL-NAYSABURI, *Sahih Musilm*, 1:376.

328. Ibid., 1:377.

their monks and the Messiah son of Mary, when they were bidden to wor-
ship only One God. There is no God save Him. Be He Glorified from all that
they ascribe as partner [unto Him]! [9:31].

Muslims need to understand what is forbidden and realize that
the above *hadith* does not apply to what Muslims have done in their
mosques. The Khawarij were guilty of such a misapplication, may
God protect us. Ibn 'Umar said, "They [the Khawarij] took verses
of the Quran that were revealed in reference to polytheists, and
applied them to Muslims." No churches or synagogues exist that
are similar to the grave containing mosques to which some people
persist in claiming this *hadith* refers.

Scholarly commentaries on these hadiths are filled with understanding and insight. On the *hadith* concerning graves as sites
of worship, Shaykh al-Sindi says, "He [the Prophet [s]] meant to
warn the community about doing to his grave that which the Jews
and Christians did with the graves of their prophets, which is to
turn them into places of worship, either by prostrating to them as
a form of aggrandizement, or making them a *qibla* towards which to
turn in prayer. It has been said that the mere building of a mosque
in proximity to a righteous person, thereby seeking blessings, is
not forbidden."[329]

Ibn Hajar al-'Asqalani and other commentators on the books of
the Sunnah, related the saying of al-Baydawi:

> Since the Jews would prostrate to the graves of their prophets
> in aggrandizement of their status, and make them their *qibla* to
> which they turned in prayer thereby making them idols, God
> cursed them and forbade the Muslims from doing similarly. As
> for building a mosque in the proximity of a righteous person,
> or praying by his grave thereby seeking support from his spir-
> it and for some of the effects of one's worship to reach him,
> not out of aggrandizement of him nor turning towards him
> in prayer, then there is nothing wrong with this. Do you not
> see that the burial place of Isma'il is in the mosque in Mecca?
> And that mosque is the best mosque in which one can choose
> to pray. And the prohibition of praying in graveyards refers to

---

329. Abu al-Hasan Muhammad ibn 'Abd al-Hadi AL-SINDI, *Hashiyat*
al-Sinid. Maktabat al-Matbu'at al-Islamiyyah, 2:41.

those that are uncovered due to the filth that is there.[330]

In his commentary on the *Jami'* of Imam al-Tirmidhi, Al-Mubarak-furi related al-Tawrabishti's opinion, "Al-Tawrabishti gave the reason for condemning Jews and Christians for prostrating to their prophets in two parts. The first is that Jews and Christians prostrated to the graves of their prophets in aggrandizement of them thereby intending worship. The second is that they prayed in the burial places of their prophets, facing their graves when they were praying and worshipping God. They considered this practice to bring one closest to God since it worshipped God through their prophets."[331]

Praying in mosques in which there are graves is correct if people do not pray separately at the grave; there is nothing fundamentally impermissible or disliked about praying in a mosque adjacent to a grave. If, however, the grave is inside the mosque itself, then the prayer is invalid and forbidden according to the school of Ahmad ibn Hanbal, but permitted and correct according to the other three Imams referenced above. These three Imams are in agreement, however, that it is disliked for the grave to be in front of the one in prayer since that arrangement resembles praying to the individual contained therein. And God is Most High and knows best.

---

330. AL-'ASQALANI, *Fath al-Bari*, 1:524; AL-ZURQANI, *Sharh al-Mawahib*, 4:290; AL-MANAWI, *Fayd al-Qadir*, 4:446.

331. AL-MUBARAKFURI, *Tuhfat al-Ahwudhi*, 2:266.

Question 60:

What is the ruling on making supplication while standing (*qunut*) in the morning prayer?

The question of supplication while standing in the morning prayer is a secondary legal issue that should not divide or cause animosity among Muslims. A variety of juristic opinions address the matter. The Shafi'is and the Malikis deemed the practice preferred, while the Hanafis and the Hanbalis said there is no supplication in the morning prayer.

Al-Nawawi said,

> Know that, according to us [i.e., the Shafi'is] supplication is legislated in the morning [prayer], and it is an affirmed Sunnah. This is based on the narration of Anas ibn Malik who said, 'The Prophet [s] supplicated in the morning prayer until he left this world.' They said [i.e., the Shafi'is]: if you were to neglect to perform it, the prayer is not invalidated, but you should make the prostration of forgetfulness, regardless of whether you neglected to perform it intentionally or out of neglect. As for its position in the prayer, it is after coming up from bowing in the second cycle of the morning prayer. If one were to supplicate before bowing, it does not count, according to the most correct opinion, in which case you would have to do it again after coming up from bowing and then make the prostration of forgetfulness.[332]

The Companions and their followers related different statements and descriptions concerning the ruling of the supplication in the morning prayer. 'Ali ibn Ziyad said the supplication in the morning prayer is obligatory, meaning that the prayer of someone who neglects it is invalid. It is permissible before and after bowing in the second cycle, the most preferred position being before bowing after the recitation and before saying "Allahu Akbar." This timing is preferred because it accommodates those who joined the prayer late. It also facilitates the absence of a gap between supplication and the two integrals of the prayer. In addition, 'Umar practiced this timing in the presence of the companions. According to Qadi

---

332. KUWAIT, *al-Mawsu'ah al-Fiqhiyyah al-Kuwatiyyah*, 23:59-60, under the letter *qaf*, in the entry *qunut*.

'Abd al-Wahhab al-Baghdadi, "It has been related that Abu Raja' al-Ataridi said, 'The supplication used to be after bowing, but 'Umar made it before bowing so that anybody joining the prayer late could catch it.' It has also been related that the emigrants and helpers asked 'Uthman about it and he made it before bowing so that the standing is prolonged, allowing one joining the prayer to catch it. In the supplication there is also a lengthening of standing, and the phase of prayer before bowing is more warranting of this, especially in the morning prayer."

The Shafi'i position on this supplication predominates, due to the strength of their evidence:

> Abu Hurayrah related, "When the Prophet [s] would raise his head from bowing in the second cycle of the morning prayer, he would supplicate with this prayer, 'O God, guide us among those whom You have guided . . . .'" Al-Bayhaqi added, "So unto You is praise for what You have decreed." And al-Tabari added, "None towards whom You have shown enmity gain glory."[333]

The *hadith* of Anas ibn Malik has already been mentioned, "The Prophet [s] supplicated in the morning prayer until he left this world." When Anas was asked, "Did the Prophet [s] supplicate in the morning prayer?" He said, "Yes." When asked, "Before bowing or after bowing?" He said, "After bowing."[334]

Abu Hurayrah said, "By God, I am the closest of you to the Prophet [s] in prayer." Abu Hurayrah used to supplicate during the last cycle of the morning prayer after saying, "God hears those who praise Him," and he would pray for the believers, male and female, and damn the hostile non-believers.[335]

'Abdallah ibn 'Abbas said, "The Prophet [s] taught us a prayer to use during the standing supplication of the morning prayer: O God, guide us among those whom You have guided, and pardon us with those whom You have pardoned, befriend us with those You have befriended, bless us with what You have given, and protect us from the evil You have decreed. Verily, You pass judgment while none judge against You. None You have befriended is humiliated.

---

333. AL-HAKIM, *al-Mustadarak 'ala al-Sahihayn*, 4:298.

334. AL-BUKHARI, *Sahih Bukhari*, 1:468; AL-SIJISTANI, *Sunan Abi Dawud*, 2:68.

335. AL-BUKHARI, *Sahih Bukhari*, 1:275; AL-NAYSABURI, *Sahih Muslim*, 1:468.

Blessed are You, our Lord, and Exalted.'"[336]

Another *hadith* says, "When he raised his head from bowing in the morning prayer in the second cycle he would raise his hands and supplicate with this supplication, 'O God, guide us among those whom You have guided.'" An additional narration tells us, "When he raised his head from bowing in the morning prayer in the last cycle, he would supplicate."[337]

As for the supplication's wording, the best choice is to say that which was narrated according to al-Hasan ibn 'Ali: "The Messenger of God [s] taught me words to say in the *witr* prayer, 'O God, guide us among those whom You have guided, and pardon us with those whom You have pardoned, befriend us with those You have befriended, bless us with what You have given, and protect us from the evil You have decreed. Verily, You pass judgment while none judge against You. None You have befriended is humiliated. Blessed are You, our Lord, and Exalted.'" The scholars have added, "None whom You show enmity gain glory," before, "Blessed are You, our Lord, and Exalted," and after it they added, "So Yours is the praise for that which You have decreed. I seek forgiveness from You, and unto You I repent." Al-Nawawi said in *al-Rawda*, "Our companions [i.e., the Shafi'is] said, 'There is no harm in this addition.' Abu Hamid, al-Bandaniji, and others went so far as to say it is preferred."[338] According to correct and well known opinion, it is Sunnah to say at the end of this supplication, "O God, bless Muhammad and his family and give them peace."

The preferred wording reads, "O God, verily we turn to You for aid. We seek Your forgiveness. We believe in You, we rely on You. We humble ourselves to You, and we cast off and abandon those who disbelieve in You. O God, we worship only You. We pray to You and prostrate, and we hasten towards You and to the worship of You. We hope for Your Mercy, and we fear Your persecution. Verily Your persecution reaches the nonbelievers."

In our opinion, the Shafi'i position predominates. Thus the supplication in the morning prayer is a Sunnah. It is also Sunnah

---

336. AL-BAYHAQI, *al-Sunan al-Kubra*, 2:210.

337. 'Abd al-Rahman ibn Abi Bakr b. Muhammad Jalal al-Din AL-SUYU-TI, *al-Jami' al-Saghir*. Dar Ta'ir al-'Ilm, 1:157; and Sheikh al-Albani said it is sahih. See ALBANI, *Sahih al-Jami'*, #4730.

338. Ahmad ibn Ahmad AL-RAMLI, *Nihayat al-Muhtaj Sharh al-Minhaj*. Dar al-Fikr, 1:503.

for someone missing supplication to make the prostration of forgetfulness. However, their prayer is not invalidated by neglecting it. And God is Most High and knows best.

Question 61:

What is the ruling on using the title Sayyid for the Prophet [s], in prayer and otherwise?

Muslims have reached a consensus affirming the term *sayyid* as an appropriate title for the Prophet [s]. Al-Sharqawi said that the term *sayyidna* (our master) is one of the Prophet's [s] titles. We do not take into consideration the arguments of those who departed from this opinion and adhered to the apparent meaning of some hadiths that seem to contradict this ruling.

These hadiths include one reported by Abu Nadra, who recounted his father's statement, "I went to the Prophet [s] with the delegation of Banu 'Amir and we said, 'You are our master (*sayyidna*).' He said, 'The master (*sayyid*) is God, Blessed and Exalted is He.' We said, 'But you are the best of us in virtue and the greatest of us in graciousness.' He said, 'Say what you have said, or a part of it, may the devil not ridicule you.'"[339] 'Abdallah ibn al-Shukhayr related that his father said, "A man came to the Prophet [s] and said, 'You are the master (*sayyid*) of Quraysh.' The Prophet [s] said, 'The master (*sayyid*) is God.' He said, 'You are the best among them in truthfulness and the greatest of them in graciousness.' The Prophet [s] said, 'Let one of you say as he did, and may the devil not bring him down.'"[340]

The narrators of the *Sunan*, such as Abu Dawud and others, placed these hadiths in the chapter titled "The Dislike of Praising One Another (*al-tamaduh*)." They were interpreted to mean that the Prophet [s] taught his community not to praise, as the hadiths explicitly prohibit praise. According to Abu M'amar, a man stood and praised a prince and as a result he had dirt thrown in his face by Miqdad ibn 'Amr. He said, "The Messenger of God [s] commanded us to throw dirt in the face of those who praise us."[341] Clearly, praising someone in their presence constitutes the type of flattery and dishonorable conduct that all honest Muslims avoid.

In his work *al-Nihayah*, Ibn al-Athir reiterated the scholars' understanding: "It means he is the one who deserves the mastery

---

339. AL-SIJISTANI, *Sunan Abi Dawud*, 4:254; AL-NASA'I, *al-Sunan al-Kubra*, 6:70.

340. IBN HANBAL, *Musnad Imam Ahmad*, 4:24; AL-NASA'I, *al-Sunan al-Kubra*, 6:70; and AL-HAKIM, *al-Mustadark 'ala al-Sahihayn*, 3:213.

341. AL-NAYSABURI, *Sahih Muslim*, 4:2297.

(al-siyadah), so it is as if he disliked being praised to his face and preferred humility. There is also the *hadith* delivered in response to their saying, 'You are our master,' he said, 'Say as you do normally,' by which he meant, 'call me a Prophet and a Messenger as God has called me, and do not call me "master" (*sayyid*) as you call your leaders, for I am not like them who rule you for worldly reasons."[342]

Ibn Muflih said, regarding the meaning of *al-sayyid*, "Al-Sayyid is used to refer to the lord (*al-rabb*), the king (*al-malik*), the noble one (*al-sharif*), the virtuous among you (*al-fadil*), the wise person, the one who bears the harm of his people, the husband, the chief, and the leader."[343] There is no doubt that this title is appropriate for the Prophet [s], based on more than one of the meanings mentioned. Abu Mansur said, "The Prophet [s] disliked being praised to his face and preferred humility before God."[344]

The hadiths speak about reality, and in reality there is no master (*sayyid*) except God. If this title is given to anyone else, then it is merely a metaphor, just as someone might say, "So and so is merciful," even though the truly merciful one is God. It is also akin to the statement of the Quran, *Say: The angel of death, who has charge concerning you, will gather you, and afterward unto your Lord you will be returned* [32:11], when it also says, *God receives souls at the time of their death* [39:42]. In the Quran, God refers to those of a lesser stature than the Prophet [s], such as Yahya (John), as *sayyid*: *God gives you glad tidings of [a son whose name is] John, [who comes] to confirm a word from God, lordly [sayyid], chaste, a prophet of the righteous* [3:39].

The Prophet [s] himself used the term *sayyid* to refer to other than God when he was in the company of his Companions. For example, he used it in reference to S'ad ibn Mu'adh when he told his people, the *Ansar*, "Stand for your master (*sayyid*)."[345] He used the term for himself when he said, "Without pride, I am the master of the children of Adam on the Day of Judgment."[346] In addition, according to a *hadith* he told al-Hasan, "This son of mine is a

---

342. IBN ATHIR, *al-Nihaya*, 2:417.

343. Ibn Muflih AL-MAQDASI, *al-Adab al-Shar'iyyah*, 3:456 in the 'Alam al-Kutub edition.

344. KUWAIT, *al-Mawsu'ah al-Fiqhiyyah al-Kuwatiyyah*, 11:347.

345. Bukhari, *Sahih Bukhari*, 2:900; and AL-NAYSABURI, *Sahih Muslim*, 3:1388.

346. Ibid., 4:1782.

sayyid."[347] It has been related that a number of the Companions addressed the Prophet [s], "O my *sayyid.*" According to Sahl ibn Hanif, "A flood came upon us, so I went to go wash in it and I got a fever from a poisonous bite. This was told to the Messenger of God who said, 'Tell Abu Thabit to seek refuge with God.' I said, 'O my *sayyid*! Is there efficacy in incantations (*al-ruqa*)?' He replied, 'There are no incantations except for three things: poisonous bites, the evil eye, and a scorpion's sting.'"[348] This *hadith* clarifies the aforementioned hadiths. The first references the true mastery (*al-siyadah al-haqiqiyah*), which is only for God. The second indicates the dislike for praising someone to their face, as the commentators of the purified prophetic Sunnah stated. The third *hadith* means that using the title *sayyidna* to refer to the Prophet [s], or as a preface to his name, is an aspect of high etiquette that has been approved by the Prophet [s] and his Companions.

The jurists have different opinions concerning the ruling on calling the Prophet [s] *sayyid* in prayer, the call to prayer, or other acts of worship. The books relied upon by the schools of jurisprudence encourage the use of the title *sayyid* before the Prophet's [s] name, even in acts of worship such as prayer and the call to prayer.

Among the Hanafi scholars, al-Hasfaki, the author of *al-Durr al-Mukhtar*, said,

> Using the title *sayyid* is encouraged because adding a statement of the truth is the very essence of etiquette, so it is better than not using it. This has been mentioned by Al-Ramli the Shafi'i and others. The statement, "Do not call me *sayyid* in prayer," which has been related, is a lie, and their forming the word with the letter *ya'* (*tusayyiduni*) is an error of language. The correct position is with a *waw* (*tusawwiduni*)."[349]

Al-Nafrawi from the Malikis also stated that it is well-liked, "This is an aspect of etiquette, and acting out of etiquette is better than following an order."

Al-Hattab the Maliki said, "Ibn Muflih the Hanbali mentioned

347. AL-BUKHARI, *Sahih Bukhari*, 2:962.

348. AL-SIJISTANI, *Sunan Abi Dawud*, 4:11; AL-NASA'I, *al-Sunan al-Kubra*, 6:71; AL-HAKIM, *al-Mustadrak 'ala al-Sahihayn*, 4:458.

349. AL-HASKAFI, *al-Durr al-Mukhtar*, 1:513.

something similar. Al-'Izz ibn 'Abd al-Salam mentioned that using the title in prayer is substantiated by the difference of opinion concerning whether it is better to follow an order or act out of etiquette. I say that what appears to me [to be correct] and what I act upon, in prayer and outside of prayer, is to use the title *sayyid*, and God knows best."[350]

Representing the Shafi'is, Shams al-Din al-Ramli said, "It is better to use the title *sayyid*. This position, supported by Ibn Zahirah's statements, was explicity declared by a group, and Jalal al-Din al-Mahali has also given this position as a fatwa. This is because it is good etiquette to do what we have been commanded and to add something that is a statement of the truth. Therefore using the title *sayyid* is better than not using it, even if al-Isnawi had doubts about which is better. The *hadith*, 'Do not call me *sayyid* in prayer,' is false and has no source among the canonical *hadith* collections, as has been stated by some of the later *hadith* scholars."[351] He also said in his gloss on *Asna al-Mutalib*, "According to this position, Al-Jalal al-Mahali gave a fatwa and unequivocally stated it saying, 'Because doing what we have been commanded to do and adding something that is a statement of the truth, which is good etiquette, is better than not using it, even if al-Isnawi had doubts about which is better.'"[352]

Al-Shawkani said, "It has been related according to al-'Izz ibn 'Abd al-Salam that he considered it to be a matter of etiquette, and it is based on the idea that acting in accordance with etiquette is better liked than following an example. It is supported by the *hadith* of Abu Bakr when the Prophet [s] ordered him to stay in his place and he did not follow the command saying, 'It is not for the son of Abu Quhafa to step forward in the presence of the Messenger of God.' Also, 'Ali refused to erase the Prophet's [s] name from the pact of Hudaybiyyah after he ordered him to do so, saying, 'I will never erase your name.' Both of these hadiths are in authentic collections and the Prophet's [s] approval of their not obeying his orders out of etiquette indicates that it takes priority."[353]

From the preceding evidence, we know that the preferred

---

350. AL-HATTAB, *Muwahib al-Jalil fi Sharh al-Khalil*, 1:21.

351. AL-RAMLI, *Nihayat al-Muhtaj Sharh al-Minhaj*, 2:86.

352. Ahmad ibn Ahmad AL-RAMLI and Zakariya ibn Muhammad AL-ANSARI, *Hashiyat 'ala Asna al-Matalab*. Dar al-Kitab al-Islami, 1:166.

353. AL-SHAWKANI, *Nayl al-Awtar*, 2:337-38.

opinion supports prefacing the name of the Prophet [s] with the title *sayyidna* in prayer, the call to prayer, and in other acts of worship. Jurists from multiple schools have adopted this practice, such as al-'Izz ibn 'Abd al-Salam, al-Ramli, al-Qalyubi, and al-Sharqawi from the Shafi'i school; al-Haskafii and Ibn 'Abidin from the Hanafi school; and others such as al-Shawkani.

As for prefacing his name with the title *sayyidna* outside of acts of worship, the scholars do not differ in opinion concerning its permissibility. Their unanimity forms a consensus, and no attention is granted those who depart from it and have not been able to come to terms with the evidence. This is the opinion that we choose and to which we give preponderance when it comes to the status of the master (*sayyid*) in creation, the beloved of the God, Muhammad [s]. Etiquette is always given precedence with him. And God is Most High and knows best.

Question 62:

People have different expectations regarding the Ramadan *tarawih* prayer. What is the correct ruling regarding
the number of prayer cycles in *tarawih*?

Every Ramadan we go through the usual yearly conflict between
the unbending members of our community who would like everyone to follow their school, and the remaining majority of Muslims
who do not find anyone to defend them from these people. The
difference of opinion concerns the number of cycles of prayer in
tarawih. Some loud voices claim that the imams and the community as a whole have been in error for centuries. They denounce
them, accuse them of innovation, and make impermissible that
which God has permitted, claiming that one may not pray more
than eight cycles of prayer in *tarawih*.

Tarawih is the plural of the Arabic word *tarwihah*. Ibn Manzur
says, "The *tarwihah* in Ramadan was called such because of the rest
that people take after every four cycles of prayer . . . and it means
a single instance of rest."[354] From the linguistic definition alone,
it becomes clear that the *tarawih* prayer is more than eight cycles
because if there were two rests (*tarwihatan*), then the prayer would
have to be twelve cycles.

In fact, through consensus the community established that
the *tarawih* prayer is comprised of twenty prayer cycles not including the *witr*, or twenty-three prayer cycles including the *witr*. Four
schools of jurisprudence rely on this opinion: the Hanafi, the view
of the Malikis, the Shafi'i, and the Hanbali. Another position, related by the Malikis in opposition to the popular view, states that
tarawih is thirty-six prayer cycles. Until this era, the Muslim community has never known a position claiming that the *tarawih* prayer
is eight prayer cycles. This contradiction arose from a misunderstanding of the Sunnah of the Prophet [s], an inability to come to
terms with differing hadiths, and a disregard for the consensus of
both word and deed that existed from the time of the Companions
to this day. For evidence, the dissenters rely on the *hadith* of Aishah
who said, "The Messenger of God [s] did not exceed eleven cycles
of prayer during Ramadan or at any other time. He would pray four
cycles, and do not ask about their beauty or length. Then he would

354. IBN MANZUR, *Lisan al-'Arab*, 2:462.

pray four cycles, and do not ask about their beauty or length. Then he would pray three cycles. I said, 'O Messenger of God, are you going to sleep without praying *witr*?' He said, 'O Aishah! My eyes sleep, but my heart does not.'" [355]

This *hadith* voices the general guidance of the Prophet [s] concerning his supererogatory prayers during his night vigils, but it does not address *tarawih*. *Tarawih* is a special night vigil unique to Ramadan. It traces its origin to a prophetic Sunnah, and its manner of practice to a Sunnah of 'Umar. The community adopted 'Umar ibn al-Khattab's practice of gathering people together to perform the vigil on all of the nights of Ramadan, praying the same number of cycles for which people gathered with Ubayy ibn K'ab. The Prophet [s] said, "Adhere to my Sunnah and the Sunnah of the rightly guided caliphs. Hold fast to it with your teeth." [356]

If the community were not relying on the actions of 'Umar for guidance, then why do they perform *tarawih* in congregation in mosques behind one imam? It is as if the dissenters are drawing from the Sunnahs of 'Umar when it comes to gathering people together behind one imam for the entire month, which the Prophet [s] did not do, while neglecting the number of prayer cycles recommended by 'Umar, all the while claiming to implement the Sunnah. If this were correct—meaning, if they were strictly adhering to the Prophetic Sunnah and not taking into consideration the actions of 'Umar—then they should pray *tarawih* at home and leave people to practice God's religion as they have inherited it. And there is neither might nor power except that of God, Most High.

Evidence of 'Umar's actions is provided by 'Abd Al-Rahman ibn 'Abd al-Qari, "I went to the mosque with 'Umar ibn al-Khattab one night in Ramadan. People were spread out separately, each person praying alone. A man would pray and a group would pray with him. 'Umar said, 'I think it would be better if we gathered these people together behind one person reciting.' Then he made up his mind and gathered them behind Ubayy ibn K'ab. I went out with him again on another night and people were praying behind their reciter and 'Umar said, 'What a great innovation this is, and the

355. Bukhari, *Sahih Bukhari*, 1:385; and AL-NAYSABURI, *Sahih Muslim*, 1:509.

356. IBN HANBAL, *Musnad Imam Ahmad*, 4:126; AL-TIRMIDHI, *Sunan al-Tirmidhi*, 5:44; and the phrasing is that found in AL-TAMIMI, *Sahih Ibn Hibban*, 1:179.

part of the night that they sleep through is better than the one in which they stay up.' He meant the end of the night, since people used to stay up in the beginning of the night" [357]

The prayer for which 'Umar gathered the people is the *tarawih* prayer, and it is twenty prayer-cycles long. A number of hadiths indicate this number, including the narration of al-Sa'ib ibn Zayd who said, "During 'Umar ibn al-Khattab's reign, they would stand for twenty prayer-cycles during Ramadan. They would recite two hundred verses, and during the time of 'Uthman ibn 'Affan they would lean on their canes from the intensity of the standing." [358] And according to Yazid ibn Ruman, "During the time of 'Umar ibn al-Khattab people would stand for twenty-three prayer cycles in Ramadan." [359]

This is one of the issues concerning which the four schools of Islamic jurisprudence agree completely. It is the opinion of the Hanafis: al-Sarakhsi said concerning *tarawih*, "It is twenty prayer-cycles not including *witr*, and Malik said that the Sunnah is for it to be thirty-six prayer-cycles." [360] Al-Kasani confirms, "As for its length, it is twenty prayer-cycles with ten salams in five sets. Every two salams is a set. And this is the position of the majority of scholars." [361] In his famous gloss, Ibn 'Abidin corroborates, "His saying, (it is twenty prayer-cycles) is the position of the majority, and it is what people act upon in the East and the West." [362]

As for the Malikis, the popular opinion in their school is in agreement with the majority of scholars. Al-Dardir says, "*Al-Tarawih* in Ramadan is twenty prayer-cycles after the night prayer in which salams are made after every two cycles, not including the *shaf'* and *witr*. It is preferred that one complete the recitation of the Quran in *tarawih* by reciting $1/30^{th}$ every night, spread out over the twenty cycles of prayer." [363]

Al-Nafrawi mentioned the strength of the majority position and the agreement of Malik's followers, as well as the final posi-

---

357. AL-BUKHARI, *Sahih Bukhari*, 2:707; AL-BAYHAQI, *Kubra*, 2:492; and ANIS, *al-Muwatta'*, 1:114.

358. AL-BAYHAQI, *Kubra*, 2:496; and ANIS, *al-Muwatta'*, 1:115.

359. Ibid.

360. AL-SARAKHSI, *al-Mabsut*, 2:144.

361. AL-KASANI, *Bada'i' al-Sana'i'*, 1:288.

362. IBN 'ABIDIN, *Rad al-Muhtar 'ala al-Dur al-Mukhtar*, 2:46.

363. AL-'ADAWI, *al-Sharh al-Saghir*, 1:404-5.

tion of Malik, "The Companions [performed it] during the time of 'Umar ibn al-Khattab and at his command, as has preceded [in the mosque in twenty cycles of prayer], which is the preference of Abu Hanifa, al-Shafi'i, and Ahmad, and it is what is acted upon now in the other major cities. After praying twenty cycles, they pray three cycles of *witr*. Referring to all three as one is out of deference for the most noble of the three units which is the last unit, *witr*; not because the three are *witr*, because the *witr* is one cycle, as has preceded. This is evidenced in his saying (and they separate the *shaf'* and the *witr* with a salam) preferably, and it is disliked to combine them except when following someone who is combining. Abu Hanifa said, 'Do not separate them.' Al-Shafi'i left the decision between separating and combining open, and the actions of people continued to be twenty-three cycles in both the east and the west. After the event of al-Harrah in Medina the predecessors prayed similarly, but other than those mentioned above, here the predecessors refers to those who were present during the time of 'Umar ibn 'Abd al-'Aziz. The number that they prayed during the time of 'Umar ibn al-Khattab [thirty-six cycles of prayer; not including the *shaf'* and the *witr*] . . . is what Malik chose in *al-Mudawwana*, and he said it was good and the actions of the people of Medina are in accordance with it. Some of his followers judged that the first number that 'Umar ibn al-Khattab gathered the people for was more correct since all of the cities continued to act upon it." [364]

As for the Shafi'is, they explicitly state that *tarawih* is twenty prayer cycles. Imam al-Nawawi said, "Our position is that it [the *tarawih*] is twenty cycles with ten *taslims* not including the *witr*, which is five *tarwihas* (moments of rest), and a *tarwiha* is four cycles with two *taslims*. That is the position of our school, and it is also held by Abu Hanifa and his companions, Ahmad, Dawud, and others, and according to the majority of scholars it was also related by Qadi 'Iyyad. It is said that al-Aswad b.Yazid used to pray forty cycles and pray seven *witr*. Malik said, '*Tarawih* is nine *tarwihas*, which is thirty-six cycles of prayer; not including *witr*.' His evidence came from the actions of the people of Medina." [365]

The Shafi'is combine the position of Malik with that of the majority; they explain that Imam Malik added the extra cycles as

364. AL-NAFRAWI, *al-Fawakih al-Dawani*, 1:318-19.
365. AL-NAWAWI, *al-Majmu'*, 3:527.

compensation for the circumambulation in the mosque in Mecca. Ibn Hajar al-Haythami said, "In our school it [*tarawih*] is twenty cycles for non-residents of Medina, as was practiced in the time of 'Umar when, through his keen perception, he gathered people behind one imam, and they agreed. And they would pray three cycles of *witr* afterwards. The secret of it being twenty is that the affirmed supererogatory nighttime prayer outside of Ramadan is ten cycles, so they were doubled in Ramadan because it is a time of seriousness and discipline. It is thirty-six only for them [the residents of Medina] because of the honor bestowed on them by being in the vicinity of the Prophet [s]. An additional sixteen cycles was imposed upon them to make up for the four sets of seven circumambulations [around the Ka'ba] performed by the residents of Mecca, seven in between each *tarwiha* of the twenty cycles." [366]

Al-Ramli confirmed this practice: "It is twenty cycles with ten *taslims* in every night of Ramadan. This is based on the narration that they used to perform a vigil of twenty cycles during Ramadan during the reign of 'Umar ibn al-Khattab. In a narration of Malik's in *al-Muwata'*, it is twenty-three. Al-Bayhaqi combined the two with the position that they used to pray three cycles of *witr*. People gathered for vigil during Ramadan; men behind Ubayy ibn K'ab and women behind Sulayman ibn Abi Hathmah. And the people had not been performing it in congregation until that time. Every four cycles were called a '*tarwiha*', because they would rest after them." [367]

As for the Hanbalis, they clearly state that Imam Ahmad preferred the position in support of twenty cycles of prayer. Ibn Qudamah al-Maqdisi said, "The preferred position of Abu 'Abdallah is that it is twenty cycles, and this is the position of al-Thawri, Abu Hanifa, and al-Shafi'i. Malik said it is thirty-six. It has been claimed that it is the ancient practice, and it is connected with the actions of the residents of Medina. For Salih Mawla al-Taw'amah said, 'I found people making vigil with forty-one cycles, making the *witr* with five of them.'" [368]

Al-Buhuti also describes the position relied upon by the Han-

366. HAYTHAMI and AL-NAWAWI, *Tuhfat al-Muhtaj Sharh al-Minhaj*, 2:240-41.

367. AL-RAMLI, *Nihayat al-Muhtaj Sharh al-Minhaj*, 2:127.

368. IBN QUDAMA AL-MAQDASI, *al-Mughni*, 1:456.

bali school, saying that *tarawih* "was called that because they would sit and rest in between every four of its cycles of prayer. It is also said that it is derived from *al-murawaha*, which is the repetition of a given act. And it is twenty cycles of prayer in Ramadan based on Malik's narration according to Yazid ibn Ruman who said, 'People used to make a vigil of twenty-three cycles of prayer during Ramadan during the reign of 'Umar.'" [369]

Even Ibn Taymiyyah, upon whom many zealots rely, confirms the position adopted by the imams and affirms that it is a Sunnah according to many scholars. He says,

> This is similar in some ways to the disagreement of scholars concerning the length of the vigil in Ramadan. It is established that Ubayy ibn K'ab led the people in twenty cycles of the vigil of Ramadan, and made *witr* with three cycles. The opinion of many scholars is that this is the Sunnah since it was done in the presence of the Companions and nobody objected to it. Others preferred thirty-nine cycles of prayer based on the fact that this was the old practice of the residents of Medina. Another group said, "It is established in an authentic tradition according to Aishah that the Prophet [s] never prayed more than thirteen cycles of prayer whether or not it was Ramadan. Some people are confused by this tradition because they think there is a contradiction between the authentic report and the normative practice of the rightly guided caliphs and the broader community of Muslims. The correct position is that all of this is good. [370]

From the preceding evidence, we see that the imams and scholars of the legal schools throughout the ages, in both the east and the west, have held the position that *tarawih* prayer is twenty cycles of prayer. The twenty-cycle *tarawih* is not an obligation, but it is an affirmed Sunnah and thus whoever neglects to perform it is denied a great reward. There is no shame in adding to the twenty cycles, nor is there shame in praying fewer than that number. However, fewer cycles would cause the prayer session to be considered a conventional night vigil (*tahajjud*) instead of the Sunnah of *tarawih*. And God is Most High and knows Best.

---

369. AL-BUHUTI, *Kashf al-Qina'*, 1:425.
370. IBN TAYMIYYAH, *al-Fatawa al-Fiqhiyya al-Kubra*, 2:250.

Question 63:

What is the ruling on holding gatherings to listen to Quranic recitations before the Friday prayer?

It is recommended and praiseworthy that people gather in their mosque to listen to the recital of the Quran on Fridays before the sermon. This includes both listening to someone physically reciting and listening to a recording of the Quran. There is nothing wrong with this act because the Shari'ah has recommended it, especially if the one reciting is gifted with a beautiful voice and recitation. It is soundly narrated that the Prophet [s] said, "The one who recites the Quran and is gifted in it is amongst the pious noble scribes, and the one who recites and it is heavy on him, meaning it is difficult for him, has two rewards."[371] Likewise, listening to the recitation and paying attention to the Quran is ordered by the Shari'ah. God says, *And when the Quran is recited, give ear to it and pay heed, so that you may obtain mercy* [7:204]. Since there is no prohibition of reciting the Quran during the time in question, the ruling is therefore in accordance with the original judgment discussed above, namely it is recommended. God is most high and knows best.

---

371. AL-BUKHARI, *Sahih Bukhari*, 4:1882; AL-NAYSABURI, *Sahih Muslim*, 1:549; and AL-TIRMIDHI, *Sunan al-Tirmidhi*, 5:171 and the phrasing is his.

Question 64:

Zealots claim that having two calls to prayer (*adhan*) during the Friday prayer, instead of the usual one call, is a reprehensible innovation.

God has religiously sanctioned the call to prayer (*adhan*) as an indication of the time of prayer and a reminder to attend. The call to commence the prayer (*iqama*) has been religiously sanctioned to stimulate people to perform the prayer. One call to prayer is sanctioned for each obligatory prayer. The call to prayer entered the Shari'ah after the emigration to Medina during the first year of the Islamic calendar, as firmly established by the *hadith* about the visions of 'Abdallah ibn al-Zubayr and 'Umar ibn Khattab.[372]

During the eras of the Messenger of God [s], Abu Bakr and 'Umar, the Friday prayer was like any other prayer. Each prayer had one call to prayer (*adhan*) and one call to commence the prayer (*iqama*). During the time of 'Uthman, an increase in population required the addition of a second *adhan* to the Friday prayer. It is known that the *adhan* itself is religiously sanctioned, and nothing in the Shari'ah prohibits a second call to prayer from being added in a time when it is needed. This reasoning is similar to that of Bilal praying two supererogatory units of prayer after performing ablution, as well as our response to question number fifty-one regarding the evidentiary weight of an action not performed.

By narrating the observations of Sa'ib ibn Yazid, Al-Bukhari attests to the second call to prayer instituted by 'Uthman. Sa'ib ibn Yazid said, "The call to prayer on Friday was when the Imam sat on the pulpit. During the reign of 'Uthman when the population increased, the third call to prayer was added from *al-Zawra*."[373] Al-Bukhari called it the third call to prayer because he included the call to commence the prayer (*iqama*) in his count. 'Uthman's choice was not considered an aberration because all of the Companions of the Prophet approved of his actions. The second *adhan* was continued during the time of 'Ali ibn Abi Talib and has remained until this day. Al-Bukhari narrates the same report given above with added detail, "Al-Zuhri said, 'I heard al-Sa'ib ibn Yazid say that the call to

---

372. AL-TIRMIDHI, *Sunan al-Tirmidhi*, 1:359; AL-TAMIMI, *Sahih Ibn Hibban*, 4:572; and AL-NAYSABURI, *Sahih Ibn Khuzaymah*, 1:193.

373. AL-BUKHARI, *Sahih Bukhari*, 1:309.

prayer on Friday was one when the Imam sat on the pulpit during the time of the Prophet [s], Abu Bakr, and 'Umar. During the Caliphate of 'Uthman the people increased in number and he ordered the third call to prayer to be made from *Al-Zawra'* and this became an established affair.'"[374]

Ibn Hajar al-'Asqalani stated:

> What is apparent is that people all over have taken the action of 'Uthman as he was a Caliph whose orders were to be obeyed . . . all that is not found during his time is considered an innovation; however, there are praiseworthy innovations and there are others which are the opposite. From what has preceded, it is clear that 'Uthman acted in this way in order to indicate to people that the prayer time had started, making an analogy to the other mandatory prayers, so he included them in the Friday prayer and he kept the specific call to prayer after the Imam sits on the pulpit. This is an example of deriving a meaning from the original source that does not negate it. [375]

From the preceding discussion, we have learned that the second call to Friday prayer is a Sunnah established by 'Uthman and the Prophet [s]. The Prophet [s] said, "Whoever lives among you will find much dispute, so hold fast to my Sunnah and the Sunnah of the rightly guided caliphs after me."[376] 'Uthman is among the rightly guided caliphs, and consensus from the time of the companions until now supports the second call to prayer on Friday. Whoever denies the permissibility of the second call to prayer has denied consensus and the principles of Islam that the scholars have adopted throughout the ages. One fears horrible things for the one who denies such things.

In our mosques in Cairo we have two calls to prayer, just as in Mecca and in the mosque of the Prophet of Islam [s]. May God grant the people of Muhammad [s] harmony in following the Shari'ah. God is Most High and knows best.

---

374. Ibid.; and AL-SIJISTANI, *Sunan Abi Dawud*, 1:285.

375. AL-'ASQALANI, *Fath al-Bari*, 2:294.

376. AL-TAMIMI, *Sahih Ibn Hibban*, 1:179; and AL-HAKIM, *al-Mustadarak 'ala al-Sahihayn*, 1:174.

Question 65:

What is the ruling on reciting the Quran for the deceased, and does the reward of such a recitation reach the deceased?

The scholars are in agreement that reciting Quran at the grave of the deceased is not prohibited and the one who does it incurs no sin whatsoever. The majority of scholars from the Shafi'i, Hanafi, and Hanbali schools are of the opinion that such an action is recommended and praiseworthy. This opinion is based on the *hadith* narrated by Anas, who said, "Whoever enters the grave yards and recites the chapter of *Yasin* (Chapter 36), the plight of the deceased is lessened and they receive a reward equal to the amount of graves present."[377] In addition, it is soundly narrated on the authority of Ibn 'Umar that he advised the recitation of the *al-Fatiha* and the concluding verses of *al-Baqara* next to the grave of the recently deceased."[378]

As for the Maliki school, they are of the opinion that it is reprehensible to recite at the grave. However, Sheikh Ahmad Dardir said, "The later scholars of the Maliki school held that there is nothing wrong with reciting Quran and making invocations and having their reward go to the deceased, as the reward will reach them, God willing."[379]

The scholarly debate surrounding this issue is weak, and the stronger opinion supports graveside recitation as recommended and permitted. Some scholars have even argued that this issue should be resolved by consensus. One scholar who held this position was Ibn Qudamah al-Maqdisi, who wrote, "Some scholars have stated that if one were to recite the Quran for the deceased, or if one were to donate the reward of this recitation to them, the reward is for the one being recited to as those deceased are as if present and we are hopeful of mercy for them and us. What we have written here is the consensus of the scholars of Islam as in every time and place they gather and recite the Quran and do-

---

377. The author of *khilal* narrates this with a chain of transmission as has been mentioned by Ibn Qudmah AL-MAQDASI, *al-Mughni*, 2:225, as well as the author of AL-MUBARAKFURI, *Tuhfat al-Ahwudhi* 3:275.

378. Ibid.

379. AL-'ADAWI, *Sharh al-Saghir*, 1:423 with Dasuqi's gloss.

nate the reward to their deceased without any criticism."[380] Sheikh 'Uthmani also documented consensus on this issue: "The scholars of Islam have reached the consensus that asking for forgiveness, performing supplication and charity, making pilgrimage, and emancipating slaves benefit the deceased and the reward of such actions reach them. The recitation of Quran at the grave is also recommended."[381]

Based on the opinion that the deceased may receive the reward of people performing the pilgrimage for them, the scholars have opined through analogy that the reward of Quranic recitation reaches the deceased. The pilgrimage consists of prayer, and prayer consists of Quranic recitation, and whatever reaches in full reaches in parts as well. Therefore, the reward of the Quranic recitation reaches the deceased by the permission of God, especially if the one reciting asks God for it.

According to the preceding evidence, the vast majority of scholars are of the opinion that reciting Quran for the deceased is permissible. As for the reward of such a recitation reaching the deceased, the majority of scholars maintain that the reward does reach them. The Shafi'i scholars say that the reward of deeds such as supplication reaches the deceased, even when the one reciting says, "O God make the reward of what I have recited to so-and-so," instead of stating one's intention to donate the actual deed. The disagreements in this issue are slight and it is not appropriate to engage in dispute over such an issue. God is Most High and knows best.

---

380. Ibn Qudmah AL-MAQDASI, *al-Mughni*, 2:225.
381. 'UTHMANI, *Rahmah*, 157 Mu'assasat al-Risalah, 72.

Question 66:

What is the ruling on shaking hands with one another after prayer?

In and of itself, shaking hands is unanimously considered a recommended act. Al-Nawawi stated, "It is a Sunnah upon meeting
another."[382] Ibn Battal said, "The majority of scholars consider
shaking hands to be a good act."[383] Scholars of various schools
recommend shaking hands between men. They base their recommendation on the *hadith* narrated by K'ab ibn Malik, "I entered
the mosque and the Messenger of God [s] was present. Talha ibn
Ubayd Allah got up and quickly approached me, taking me by the
hand and congratulating me."[384] When Qatadah asked Anas, "Was
handshaking found amongst the companions of the Messenger of
God?" He replied, "Yes."[385] Furthermore, it was narrated by 'Ata'
ibn Abi Muslim 'Abdallah al-Khurasani that the Messenger of God
[s] said, "Shake hands with one another and hatred will vanish,
exchange gifts and you will love one another and rancor will be
known no more."[386]

As for handshaking after prayer, none of the scholars have
deemed it impermissible. According to their opinions it is a recommended act, and a praiseworthy or neutrally permissible innovation. Imam al-Nawawi decisively ruled upon handshakes with his
statement: "If you shake hands with someone you did not greet
before prayer it is a praiseworthy innovation, if you greeted them
before prayer then it is a neutrally permissible innovation."[387]

Al-Haskafi said, "Al-Timirtashi, in accordance with *al-Durr, al-
Kanz, al-Wiqayah, al-Niqayah, al-Mujma, al-Multaqi*, and other works,
ruled that shaking hands is permissible in all circumstances, even
after afternoon prayer. By using the word innovation, they mean
a praiseworthy innovation, as mentioned by al-Nawawi in his

382. AL-'ASQALANI, *Fath al-Bari*, 11:55.

383. Ibid., 11:55; and AL-MUBARAKFURI, *Tuhfat al-Ahwudhi*, 7:426.

384. IBN HANBAL, *Musnad Imam Ahmad*, 3:458; AL-BUKHARI, *Sahih
Bukhari*, 4:1607; and AL-NAYSABURI, *Sahih Muslim*, 4:2126.

385. AL-BUKHARI, *Sahih Bukhari*, 5:2311; and AL-TAMIMI, *Sahih Ibn Hibban*, 2:245.

386. ANIS, *al-Muwatta'*, 2:908; and Yusuf ibn Muhammad IBN 'ABD
AL-BARR, *al-Tamhid*. Morocco: Wizarat al-Awqaf, 21:12.

387. AL-NAWAWI, *al-Majmu'*, 3:469-70.

Adhkar.[388] After mentioning the jurists of the Hanafi school who say handshaking is praiseworthy in all circumstances, Ibn 'Abdin commented, "This ruling is in accordance with what the commentator mentioned in regards to the school's texts, and he has used the generality of the reports regarding the religious sanctioning of handshaking as textual proof."[389]

Other scholars say that handshaking after prayer is praiseworthy in all circumstances. Al-Tabari based his opinion on the *hadith* narrated by al-Bukhari and Ahmad recounting the words of Abu Juhayfa, "The Messenger of God [s] came out in midday to the city square, where he made ablution, and then prayed the noon prayer in two cycles and the afternoon prayer in two units. In front of him there was a spear before which the women would pass. The people rose and went to him to take his hand, wiping their faces with it. So I took his hand and placed it on my face and it was colder than ice, and more radiant than musk."[390] According to Al-Tabari, when their actions are coupled with good intentions, people seek solace in the shaking of hands after prayer, especially the afternoon and sunset prayers.

Al-'Izz ibn 'Abd al-Salam, who divided innovation into five categories: mandatory, prohibited, reprehensible, recommended, and neutrally permissible, said, "An example of a neutrally permissible innovation is the shaking of hands after morning and afternoon prayers."[391]

In the words of Al-Nawawi, "Regarding the common practice of handshaking after morning and afternoon prayers, Sheikh 'Abd al-Salam called it a neutrally permissible innovation that cannot be described with any reprehensibility or recommendation. What he has stated is fine, the preferred opinion is that if one shakes hands with one known to him before meeting for prayer, it is neutrally permissible, but if one shakes hands with one whom he was not acquainted with before prayer, it is recommended, since shaking hands upon meeting is a Sunnah by consensus, due to the authentic hadiths narrated on this subject."[392]

From the above body of evidence it is clear that critics of shak-

388. AL-HASKAFI, *al-Durr al-*Mukhtar, 6:380.
389. IBN 'ABIDIN, *Rad al-Muhtar 'ala al-Dur al-Muhtar*, 6:381.
390. AL-BUKHARI, *Sahih Bukhari*, 3:1304.
391. AL-SALAM, *Quwa'id al-Ahkam fi Masalih al-Anam*, 2:205.
392. AL-NAWAWI, *al-Majmu'*, 3:469-70.

ing hands before or after prayer, either have no knowledge of the texts we have mentioned, or are not on the path of knowledge to begin with. God is Most High and knows best.

Question 67:

What is the ruling on reciting the takbirs during 'Eid prayers? What if one recites the longer versions instead of those narrated by the *hadith* including the prayers for the Prophet [s] at the end?

Reciting the *takbirs* during Eid prayers is recommended. In God's words, *You should magnify God for having guided you, and that perhaps you may be thankful* [2:185]. This verse commands the recitation of *takbirs* in general. No report from the Sunnah curtails this general command by making Muslims responsible to recite a specific necessary litany or making other practices a reprehensible innovation. The litany of, *"God is great, God is great, there is no deity but God, God is great, God is great, and to God belongs all praise,"* is mentioned by many of the companions and their followers. Al-Bayhaqi narrated this same litany on the authority of Ibn 'Abbas and 'Ikrima with the addition: *". . . God is great, God is great and majestic, and God is great, for He has guided us."*[393]

For these reasons Imam al-Shafi'i said, "The Imam should begin by saying *'God is great, God is great, God is great'* until he says it three times, and if he increases in number this is good. Adding *'God is [absolutely] great, many thanks to God, praise be to God [night and day], God is great, we do not worship any other than God; we have worshiped Him sincerely even if the disbelievers hate it, there is no deity but God, He is true to his promise, He gave victory to His servant, and He destroyed the Confederates alone, there is no deity but God and God is great,'* is also good, and I like any added glorification and mention of God."[394] Jalal al-Din al-Mahalli is of the same opinion in his commentary on imam al-Nawawi's *Minhaj*.[395]

The Egyptian litany used over the centuries concluded with prayers for the Prophet [s]. According to Imam al-Shafi'i, this litany is good and religiously sanctioned as a form of glorifying God. The best way to glorify and mention God is to include the mention of His Messenger [s]. We also know that bestowing prayers and salutations upon the Messenger of God [s] opens the door for God's

393. AL-BAYHAQI, *Sunan al-Bayhaqi al-Sughra*, 1:404; and AL-BAYHAQI, *al-Sunan al-Kubra*, 3:315.

394. AL-SHAFI'I, *al-Umm*, 1:276.

395. AL-MAHALLI, *Sharh Minhaj al-Talibin*, 1:358. This is found on the margins of the gloss of Qalyubi and Umayra.

acceptance of prayers, as actions related to the exalted Prophet [s] are always accepted, even if from a hypocrite, as is mentioned in the books of the scholars.

Whoever says that these different litanies are reprehensible is himself closer to reprehensible innovations. Such persons constrict what has been expanded by God and the Prophet [s], restricting a general command without proof. What is good enough for our pious ancestors who saw value in these litanies and accepted them is good enough for us. Criticizing these litanies is absolutely incorrect and we would do best to ignore these statements. God is Most High and knows best.

Question 68:

What is the ruling on placing prayer niches (*mihrabs*) in mosques. Is the *mihrab* a prohibited innovation?

The mosque of the Messenger of God [s] did not have a prayer niche (*mihrab*) during his time or during the time of the rightly guided caliphs after him. The first to create a prayer niche was 'Umar ibn 'Abd al-Aziz. He ordered al-Walid ibn 'Abd al-Malik, then governor of Medina, to make one during the rebuilding of the Prophet's mosque after it's destruction. This destruction possibly took place in the year 91 AH. Other reports mention that it occurred in the year 88 AH and its restructuring was completed in the year 91 AH.

The jurists have disagreed regarding prayer niches in mosques. The Shafi'is consider it reprehensible, while the majority of the jurists consider it permissible and recommended, as we can deduce from the writings of the Hanafis and Malikis. Additionally, the Hanbalis unequivocally considered it beneficial. Ibn Muflih from the Hanbalis has quoted Ibn Tamim as saying, "It is recommended to build mosques, and it is recommended to place niches in the mosques and in homes. Ibn 'Aqil has stated, 'Prayer niches should be placed in mosques so the ignorant one can know the proper direction of prayer.'"[396]

Based on the above statements of the scholars, placing prayer niches in mosques is recommended, as it benefits Muslims. God is Most High and knows best.

---

396. Ibn Muflih AL-MAQDASI, *al-Adab al-Shar'iyyah*, 3:405.

Question 69:

Should women perform the night prayers of Ramadan (*tarawih*) and the rest of the prayers in the mosque or at home?

A woman should pray *tarawih* wherever she prefers. If she wants to pray at home, then she may. If she wants to go the mosque to be with her sisters and brothers for strength and support in worshiping God then she may. The location is not the point, as a woman should pray where she finds her heart in humility towards God. In Imam al-Shafi'i's opinion, praying *tarawih* in the mosque or at home is equally rewarding for both men and women.

Accordingly, a woman cannot be prevented from going to pray in the mosque, to attend a lesson, to pray *tarawih*, or to recite the Quran. This is what our Prophet [s] taught us when he said to men, "Do not keep the bondswomen of God [i.e., female Muslims] from the houses of God."[397] As for the statement of the Prophet's [s] addressing women, "Your prayer at home is better,"[398] it is based on the fact that it is better for a woman to be concealed. Women are permitted to go out to buy things, for their leisure, or other needs. There is therefore nothing wrong with women going to the mosque, and men are not allowed to dissuade them. God is Most High and knows best.

---

397. IBN HANBAL, *Musnad Imam Ahmad*, 2:16; AL-BUKHARI, *Sahih Bukhari*, 1:305; and AL-NAYSABURI, *Sahih Muslim*, 1:327.

398. IBN HANBAL, *Musnad Imam Ahmad*, 3:371.

Question 70:

What is the ruling on reading from the written Quranic text (*mushaf*) during prayer?

Aishah used to have a bondsman named Dhakwan who would lead her in prayer by reading the Quranic text aloud. [399] The jurists of both the Shafi'i and Hanbali schools accept recitation from the Quranic text by an Imam during prayer. The Shafi'i jurists went so far as to say that prayer is not invalidated even if one reads texts other than the Quran. This issue has been discussed by imam al-Nawawi:

> If one reads the Quran directly from the text of the Quran, then the prayer is not invalidated, regardless of whether one has the Quran memorized or not; reading aloud is incumbent on the one who has not memorized the *al-Fatiha*. Even, if one flips the pages during prayer the prayer is not invalidated. Gazing at something written other than the Quran and reciting it to oneself, also does not invalidate a prayer, even if done for an extended period of time; however, such an act is reprehensible. Such was the position of Imam al-Shafi'i in his book *al-Imla'*, and the companions of the school have followed it.[400]

The Hanbali jurist al-Rahibani said:

> The one in prayer may read directly from the text and gaze at it . . . Ahmad has said that there is nothing wrong with leading people in prayer by reading from the text. When asked if this includes the obligatory prayers, he responded that he had not heard anything to the contrary. Al-Zuhri was asked about a man who led people in the night prayer during Ramadan by reading from the Quranic text, and he responded that the best among them used to read from the Quranic text.[401]

The Malikis saw reading from the texts as reprehensible in both obligatory and supererogatory prayers. The Hanafi jurists disputed the issue; Imam Abu Hanifa held that reading invalidates the

---

399. This story is mentioned in AL-BUKHARI, *Sahih Bukhari*, 1:245; see also AL-KUFI, *Musannaf ibn Abi Shaybah*, 2:123; and AL-BAYHAQI, *al-Sunan al-Kubra*, 2:253.

400. AL-NAWAWI, *al-Majmu'*, 4:27.

401. Al-RAHYABANI, *Uli al-Nuha*, 1:483-484.

prayer, and the two Companions, along with the Maliki jurists, considered it reprehensible.

In accordance with the majority of the scholars, we rule that reading from the Quranic text in prayer is permissible and does not incur sin. God is Most High and knows best.

FATWAS RELATED TO ZAKAT

Question 71:

Is it permissible to give out the end-of-Ramadan alms (*Zakat al-Fitr*) in hard currency?

According to a group of reliable jurists, it is permissible to give out one's end-of-Ramadan alms in hard currency. The successors to the Companions, such as al Hasan al-Basri and Abu Ishaq al-Sabi'i, thought similarly. Al-Basri said, "There is nothing wrong with giving out silver currency for your end-of-Ramadan alms."[402] Zuhayr, said, "I saw people giving out their end-of-Ramadan alms in silver currency in value equal to that of foods."[403] 'Umar ibn 'Abd al-'Aziz designated the end-of-Ramadan alm as "half a *sa*'[404] for each person, or its worth in silver currency (*dirhams*)."[405] Al-Thawri, Abu Hanifa, and Abu Yusuf hold the same opinion.

The Hanafi school adopted the above position and its scholars issue all *fatwas* regarding *zakat* issues in accordance.[406] Al-Nasir and al-Mu'ayyad Biallah of the Zaydi school also support this opinion,[407] as do Ishaq ibn Rahuwayh and Abu Thawr. However, the latter two scholars held that it should only be applied in circumstances of necessity.

In the Maliki school, Ibn Habib, Asbagh, Ibn Abi Hazim, Ibn Dinar, and Ibn Wahb condoned the practice of giving alms in hard currency, both for the *zakat* at the end of Ramadan (*fitr*) and the general *zakat*. Ibn Qasim and Ashhab, however, differed slightly: they believed the use of hard currency permissible in charity but found it inappropriate to the charity of the fast's conclusion as well as the expiation of oaths.

In light of the above evidence, we gather that a good portion

---

402. AL-KUFI, *Musannaf ibn Abi Shaybah*, 3:174.

403. Ibid., 2:398.

404. A measure of weight. [Trans.]

405. AL-SAN'ANI, *Musannad 'Abd al-Razzaq*, 3:316.

406. AL-KASANI, *Bada'i' al-Sana'i'*, 2:970-79; and AL-SARAKHSI, *al-Mabsut*, 3:113-114.

407. Ahmad ibn Yahya b. al-Murtada AL-MURTADA, *al-Bahr al-Sukhar al-Jami' li-Madhab 'Ulama' al-Ansar*. Dar al-Kitab al-Islami, 3:302-3.

of the imams, Successors, and jurists held the opinion that paying one's end-of-Ramadan alms in cash is permissible. If they maintained this position even in medieval times when the barter system (especially trading foodstuffs) prevailed, then the opinion allowing the end-of-Ramadan alms to be paid in cash is even more appropriate to our current era in which the barter system has been widely replaced by currency based transactions. We could venture to suggest that if the jurists opposing this view back then were alive today, they most likely would change their opinion to permit cash *zakat* at the end of Ramadan. In addition, paying *zakat* in cash is clearly better for the recipient in that they can buy whatever they need on that particular day. For example, someone could be more in need of clothing than certain foodstuffs at the time of the donation.

The end-of-Ramadan alms (*zakat al-fitr*) are religiously sanctioned to benefit the poor on this special day which all Muslims celebrate. The notable scholar Ahmad ibn Siddiq al-Ghumari wrote a treatise on this issue called *Tahqiq al-Amal fi Ikhraj Zakat al-Fitr bi al-Mal* in which he gave preference to the Hanafi opinion using thirty-two textual proofs. Likewise, we prefer the Hanafi opinion permitting one to give out his or her *zakat al-fitr* as cash because hard currency is the most appropriate form of alms in our time. And God is Most High and knows best.

Question 72:

Is it incumbent that one pays *zakat* on his or her money even if this money is allocated to purchase something necessary?

Several conditions determine the nature of one's obligation to pay *zakat* on money. First, the property must belong exclusively to that individual. He or she must control it completely, it must be open to growth, and it must be in excess of the individual's needs. In addition, the required period of time must have elapsed since its acquisition. The money must be of the appropriate value (worth equal to or more than eighty-five grams of gold), and the person must be free of anything preventing his or her payment of *zakat*, such as debt.

Two of these conditions concern us most: one is the money's potential to grow in value, and the other is the money being in excess of the owner's needs. These two conditions have been illustrated well by the jurists of the Hanafi school, such as Kasani. He stated:

> The condition that the money be subject to growth stems from the definition of *zakat*, which is growth, or something that cannot be achieved except from money subject to growth. We do not mean actual growth, as this is not possible, rather we mean that the money can accrue value through investment and trade . . . if you would like, you could say that one of the conditions is that the money be in excess of one's needs, since only then can one realize the meaning of surplus wealth and pleasure, which is living in luxury, and by paying *zakat* on this surplus one fulfils the goal of purifying one's self. One cannot forgo money required for basic needs, which is not considered material pleasure since material pleasure does not come from one's basic needs, or those needs necessary for the continuation of life and one's physical upkeep. Such a person should be thankful for the blessing of their physical upkeep. By paying *zakat* on money required to meet basic needs one does not fulfill the command of purifying one's soul which the Prophet [s] commanded: "Pay *zakat* on your money to purify your souls." Being in need is an internal affair that one cannot pinpoint, we need proof to identify surplus. We define surplus money

as that which is ready for growth or is available for trade, this being the position of the majority of scholars.[408]

Based on the above passages, *zakat* is only required on money that is in excess of one's basic needs and thus goes unspent, collecting interest and remaining available for investment. The ability to invest is itself a sign that one's wealth surpasses his or her basic needs. No *zakat* is paid on money required by Muslims to purchase necessary items. God is Most High and knows best.

408. AL-KASANI, *Bada'i' al-Sana'i'*, 2:11.

Question 73:

Can you give a poor person a sum of money that would make that poor person wealthy, or should poor people receive only that which satisfies their basic needs?

Islam seeks to eradicate poverty, illiteracy, corruption, and other negative traits that harm Muslim society. The ummah is the society guided by God's final religion which follows His Chosen Prophet [s]. It is better that the *zakat* given to a poor person enriches him since this leads to the eradication of that individual's poverty and in turn allows that person to participate in the charitable endeavors of their brothers by paying *zakat* the following year. It is permissible to give a poor person *zakat* that will sustain him for an average lifespan, specifically sixty years. Other scholars, such as al-Ramli and al-Shafi'i, say it is permissible to give him that which will sustain him for up to a hundred years. Al-Nawawi said, "The adherents of our school from Iraq, as well as many from Khurasan said, "They are given that which will elevate them from need to wealth, which is 'enough to have enough continuously,' as stated by al-Shafi'i." [409]

This is confirmed by what al-Nawawi excerpted in *al-Minhaj* and its commentary by Jalal al-Din al-Mahalli. Al-Mahalli said, "(I said: The more correct position is expressly stated and is the position of the majority) is that he gives (enough for an average lifespan so he can buy real estate from which to benefit) and be wealthy enough to not require *zakat* (and God knows best). And those who gain their sustenance through a craft are given that with which they can purchase the required tools, (I said, 'Their value, even if it is a lot.') Those who make their living by trade are given that with which they can purchase what can be traded or whose profits can sustain them for an average lifespan." [410]

The Shafi'is defined an average lifespan as sixty years, and that if a person were to be poor past that age they would take enough yearly *zakat* to sustain them for one year at a time. The fatwas of al-Ramli deal specifically with this issue:

Question: Concerning the saying, 'A pauper is given enough to

---

409. AL-NAWAWI, *al-Majmu'*, 6:175.

410. AL-MAHALLI, *Sharh Minhaj al-Talibin*, 3:200 in the edition with the super-commentary of Qalyubi and 'Umayrah in the margins.

sustain him for an average lifespan,' what is the definition of an average lifespan, and what is the amount that is given if that age is passed? Answer: The definition of an average lifespan is sixty years, and that if that is surpassed, the pauper is given enough to sustain him for one year, and if that year passes, he is given enough for another year. Another answer of my father is that the limit of an average lifespan is the age that the individual is reasonably expected not to surpass, which, in the correct opinion, cannot be defined by a standard age. It has also been defined as being seventy years, eighty years, ninety years, or even one hundred years, and if he lives beyond those years he is given enough to sustain him for one year, and if he lives beyond that year he is given enough to sustain him for one year, and so on and so forth.[411]

Ibn Taymiyyah also adopted this position, as related by al-Mardawi who said, "Sheikh Taqi al-Din said, 'It is permitted to take one sum of money that would make him wealthy even if it is a lot.'"[412]

Based on the preceding quotes from the Shafi'i school and others, our opinion maintains that it is permissible to give a pauper *zakat* that would make him rich and remove him from what is considered to be poverty. It is even permissible to give him enough to sustain himself for the average lifespan. And God is Most High and knows best.

411. Ahmad ibn Ahmad AL-RAMLI, *Fatawa al-Ramli*. al-Maktabah al-Is-lamiyyah, 3:137.
412. Ibid., 3:137.

Question 74:

Is it permissible to forgive the debt of a poor person as a form of *zakat*?

Al-Shafi'i deemed this permissible in one of his rulings, as did Ash-hab from the Maliki school and Ibn Hazm from the Zahiri school, as well as al-Hasan al-Basri and 'Ata. Their reasoning states that because it is permissible to give an individual in debt enough *zakat* to pay a debt, directly forgiving a debt should be permissible as well. If the creditor pays his *zakat* to his debtor, and the debtor returns it to his creditor, or if the debtor were to borrow money to pay his debt to his creditor, who then returned it to him considering it *zakat*, then the majority of scholars and one opinion of the Maliki school consider it permissible. Any of the above arrangements would qualify as *zakat* as long as it was not a trick to escape paying *zakat* by making business agreements with those undeserving of charity or with the intention of enriching oneself. If the arrangement is a trick designed to escape paying *zakat*, then it is not permitted according to the Malikis and the Hanbalis, but it is permissible according to the Shafi'is. The Shafi'is accept this type of transaction so long as it is executed as a business agreement and does not involve conditions.

According to Ibn Hazm al-Zahiri, "If someone is owed money in the form of wheat, barley, gold, silver, or cattle, by one deserving of charity (*ahl al-sadaqat*), and gives him charity in the form of the debt upon him, and intends it to be his *zakat*, then it is counted as such. Similarly, if he were to give the right to collect on a debt to one deserving of charity intending it to be *zakat*, it would count as such. The evidence for this is that he is commanded to give the mandatory alms (*al-sadaqah al-wajibah*), and to give alms from his mandatory *zakat* to those who are deserving (*ahl al-sadaqat*). If forgiving a debt is considered charity (*sadaqah*) then it counts as *zakat*. According to Abu Sa'id al-Khudri there was a man during the time of the Prophet [s] who purchased fruit afflicted with loss (*thimar*). The Messenger of God [s] said, 'Give him charity.'[413] 'Ata ibn Abi Rabah and others also held this position."[414]

Based on the above passages, we find nothing that prevents

---

413. AL-NAYSABURI, *Sahih Muslim*, 3:1191.
414. IBN HAZM, *al-Mahala bi-l Athar*, 4:222.

the forgiving of a debt from qualifying as *zakat*, although it is better to otherwise relieve the debt in order to avoid embroiling oneself in the differences of scholarly opinion. It would be preferred for the individual to forgive the debt out of a sense of charity other than *zakat*, or to give the debtor the money and then immediately take it from him, even if it is the same money, in order to prevent the tricks that some people commit, especially when it comes to transactions between businessmen. And God is Most High and knows best.

FATWAS RELATED TO FASTING

Question 75:

Is it permissible to study and learn about astronomy? Can one rely on astronomical calculations to ascertain the beginning of Ramadan?

Islam does not oppose knowledge and learning, nor does it stand in their way. Islam encourages study and contemplation of the universe, and the formulation of scientific theories that benefit humanity. The Quran says, *Say: Behold what is in the heavens and the earth! But revelations and warnings avail not folk who will not believe* [10:101]. It says, *Say [O Muhammad]: Travel in the land and see how He originated creation, then God brings forth the later growth. Lo! God is Able to do all things* [29:20].

Astronomy is one of the fields whose study and knowledge are explicitly encouraged in the Quran. We must investigate cosmic phenomena in order to gain knowledge of their inner secrets. This is found in the following verse: *And We appoint the night and the day two portents. Then We make dark the portent of the night, and We make the portent of the day sight-giving, that you may seek bounty from your Lord, and that you may know the computation of the years, and the reckoning; and everything We have expounded upon clearly* [17:12]. Other verses also lend support: *And the sun runs unto a resting-place for it. That is the measuring of the Mighty, the Wise. And for the moon We have appointed mansions for her until she returns like an old shrivelled palm-leaf. It is not for the sun to overtake the moon, nor does the night outstrip the day. They each float in an orbit* [36:38-40].

Muslims encountered astronomy early in the history of Islam and gained proficiency in all of its equations, putting science to work in the service of their religion. They calculated the time of dawn, sunrise, noon, afternoon, sunset, and nightfall so that the *muezzin* (person who performs the call to prayer) could consult a sheet inscribed with the correct times according to astronomical calculations. Muslims could then cease to rely upon the imprecise technique of placing a stick in the ground and measuring its shadow, although a person may still resort to this method if he or she does not have a watch or is unfamiliar with the local times of prayer. The guidance provided by the Shari'ah is both easy and readily available to all people because Islam is a universal religion. Ascertaining the times of prayer and fasting by way of astronomical calculations does not oppose the prophetic methodology. Surprisingly we find no difference of opinion concerning prayer, while there is great difference of opinion concerning fasting, even though prayer is more important.

Concerning fasting in Ramadan, the beginnings of all the Arab months including Ramadan are determined by the physical sighting of the new moon. The Quran says, *And whosoever of you sights [the new moon], let him fast the month* [2:185]. And the Prophet [s] said, "Begin your fast according to the sighting of it [the waxing crescent-new moon] and end your fast according to the sighting of it [the waning crescent]."[415]

There is no doubt that the appearance of the waxing crescent is an established physical phenomenon, and there is no argument concerning its visibility to the naked eye. There is no religious opposition to calculating the time of its arrival with scientific methods known to specialists. Both Muslims and non-Muslims have access to these means, as the new moon is a common scientific fact according to the consensus of astronomers.

Al-Subki was asked about someone who sighted the new moon despite its purported invisibility according to astronomical calculations. Al-Subki responded with a long and involved answer, the relevant part of which is the following:

> This is another manifestation: when the calculations state that it is not possible to sight the new crescent, a conclusion arrived at through an exact science when it is very close to the sun. In this case you cannot allow for the physical sighting of the new crescent since it is impossible. If one or more people, whose information is open to being belied or incorrect, inform us of it [i.e., that they sighted the new crescent], the position taken is to understand their information as a fabrication or a misapprehension. If two people were to testify to its sighting, their testimonies would not be accepted since the calculations are exact and the testimony and perceptions are inexact, and what is uncertain does not disclaim what is certain, let alone take pre-

---

415. IBN HANBAL, *Musnad Imam Ahmad*, 1:221; AL-BUKHARI, *Sahih Bukhari*, 2:674; and AL-NAYSABURI, *Sahih Muslim*, 2:762.

cedence over it. In these cases, the condition of the declaration [i.e., of the sighting of the crescent] is that what is being borne witness to is physically, rationally, and legally impossible. If the evidence of the calculations indicates the certain impossibility [of sighting the new crescent] it is legally impossible to accept it due to the impossibility of that which is being sighted, since the law does not advance impossibilities.[416]

For the reason stated above, we maintain that it is better to act in accordance with astronomical calculations because they represent empirical and exact knowledge which gives us certainty. Sighting with the naked eye is an imprecise method because barriers can impede visibility. Thus we should give precedence to astronomical calculations when there is a discrepancy between calculations and physical sighting.[417] And God is Most High and knows best.

---

416. Taqi al-Din AL-SUBKI, *Fatawa al-Subki*. Dar al-Ma'arif, 1:209.

417. i.e., Calculations are to be relied upon in rejecting claims that the moon has been sighted at times when they show that to be impossible. They are not to be relied upon for establishing the beginnings of the months independently of physical sightings. [Trans.]

Question 76:

Is it permissible to fast based on the sighting of the new crescent moon in a country other than one's current location?

Residents of a given country should not begin or end their fasts based on a foreign crescent sighting. This inconsistency divides the Muslim community and sows discord. Furthermore, Islamic law establishes that the decisions of persons charged with the affairs of the Muslim community should dispel any disagreement between people. Accordingly, if a fatwa states that the new crescent of Ramadan, or of any other month for that matter, has been sighted in a given country, then it is incumbent upon the Muslims in that country to adhere to the fatwa. It is not permissible for them to disregard it.

This position traces its origin to a narration according to Kurayb that Umm al-Fadl ibn al-Harith sent him to Mu'awiyah in the Sham and he recounted his experience, "When I arrived in the Sham I tended my affairs and Ramadan began while I was there. I saw the new crescent on a Friday. Then I arrived in Medina at the end of the month. 'Abdallah ibn 'Abbas questioned me about the new crescent. 'When did you sight the new crescent?' He asked. 'We saw it Friday night,' I told him. 'Did you see it?' He asked. 'Yes,' I said, 'The people sighted it and fasted, and Mu'awiyah fasted.' 'But we saw it here on Saturday night,' he said, 'And we will continue to fast until we complete thirty days or see the new crescent.' 'Are you not satisfied with the sighting and fasting of Mu'awiyah?' I asked. 'No,' he said, 'This is what the Messenger of God [s] commanded us to do.'"[418] The *hadith* clearly indicates that each country should follow its own sighting, and according to this position we give fatwas. And God is Most High and knows best.

---

418. IBN HANBAL, *Musnad Imam Ahmad*, 1:306; AL-NAYSABURI, *Sahih Muslim*, 2:765; AL-SIJISTANI, *Sunan Abi Dawud*, 2:299; AL-TIRMIDHI, *Sunan al-Tirmidhi*, 3:76; and the phrasing is from Muslim.

Question 77:

What if someone began his fast in his homeland and then traveled to another country, or vice versa, and his second location started fasting before or after his first location by one day? What is the ruling on this situation?

According to Sheikh al-Ramli, Imam al-Nawawi said:

Whoever has journeyed from a region in which the new crescent has not been sighted "to the region of the crescent sighting, he breaks his fast with the latter," for certain, according to what has been mentioned whether the person has fasted twenty-eight days, meaning that Ramadan is missing a day and he has 'Eid on the twenty-ninth day of his fast, or he has fasted twenty-nine days so Ramadan is complete, "he makes up a day" if he has fasted only twenty-eight days, since the lunar month cannot be such; however, if he fasted twenty-nine days then there is no expiation needed, since the lunar month could be such.[419]

For this reason, it is best for a traveler to follow the moon sighting of his or her destination. If the number of days he has fasted is less than twenty-nine, then he should fast an extra day after breaking his fast with the 'Eid celebration. If, however, he has already fasted thirty days or more, and the country he visits is still fasting, then he should withhold from eating, drinking, and the like, but not with the intention of fasting, as the lunar month never exceeds thirty days and is never less than twenty-nine days. The purpose of continuing his fast is simply to avoid bothering his fellow Muslims and to prevent social unrest among people who are ignorant of religious legal rulings. And God is Most High and knows best.

---

419. AL-RAMLI, *Nihayat al-Muhtaj Sharh al-Minhaj*, 3:156.

Question 78:

Does God accept the fasting of those who do not pray?

One should never leave the habit of prayer, as God and the Prophet [s] have both made clear. The Prophet [s] stated, "The covenant that is between us and them is prayer. Whoever has left the practice of prayer has committed disbelief."[420] One does not want to fall within God's description, *Then is it only a part of the Book that you believe in, and do you reject the rest? But what is the reward for those among you who behave like this except for disgrace in this life* [2:85].

As for whether or not one's fasting is accepted, the scholars refrain from discussion and leave this issue to God. We hope that God accepts the fast of all those who fast, even if the one who prays has a better chance of his or her fast being accepted than the one who does not pray.

He who neglects prayer may still perform a sound fast because prayer is not a condition of performing a legally recognized fast. However, by not praying one exposes oneself to grave danger; the Prophet [s] used the word 'disbeliever' to describe such a person who has abandoned the main support of his faith. Discontinuing prayer is a major sin, and it is not permissible for Muslims to do this. Whoever amongst the Muslims has deserted their prayers must return to God with sincere repentance, and God is Most High and knows best.

---

420. IBN HANBAL, *Musnad Imam Ahmad*, 5:346; AL-TIRMIDHI, *Sunan al-Tirmidhi*, 5:13; AL-NASA'I, *Sunan al-Nasa'i (al-Mujtaba)*, 1:231; and AL-HAKIM, *al-Mustadarak 'ala al-Sahihayn*, 1:48.

Question 79:

What is the reward for feeding a fasting person, and does this person have to be poor?

The Prophet [s] said:

> Those who feed a fasting person receive forgiveness for their sins, and their necks have been saved from the hellfire, and they have the same reward as the fasting person without diminishing from the fasting person's reward. The companions said, "Not all of us find that with which to feed a fasting person," and he responded, "God gives this reward to whomever provides breakfast for the fasting person, be it a sip of milk, a date, or a drink of water."[421]

This *hadith* highlights the reward of feeding a fasting person and the rank the giver attains with God. This report does not stipulate that the fasting person be poor, as the text refers to all those who fast without exception. God possesses enormous bounty. Even though the deed is small, even he who feeds a fasting person with the most insignificant amount of food receives a reward, as stated by the *hadith*. God is Most High and knows best.

---

421. IBN HANBAL, *Musnad Imam Ahmad*, 4:114; AL-TIRMIDHI, *Sunan al-Tirmihi*, 3:171; 'Abdullah ibn 'Abd al-Rahman AL-DARAMI, *Musnad al-Darami*, 2:14; AL-TAMIMI, *Sahih Ibn Hibban*, 8:216; and AL-NAYSABUR, *Sahih Ibn Khuzaymah*, 3:191.

Question 80:

Is it permissible for women to make up missed days of the Ramadan fast during the six days of Shawwal and also achieve the reward for the six days of Shawwal?

According to many of the jurists, it is permissible to couple supererogatory fasting days with obligatory days of fasting. However, it is not permissible to couple the intention to perform a mandatory fast with the intention to perform a supererogatory fast. As evidence we cite Imam al-Ramli's commentary on Imam al-Nawawi's *Minhaj*:

> It is stated in the commentary of *al-Muhadhab* that if one prays more than two cycles of prayer [in praying the Sunnah two cycles for greeting a mosque] with one salutation, it is permissible as all of the cycles of prayer are the prayer of greeting the mosque as they contain the two cycles, 'this can be achieved by either an obligatory prayer or another supererogatory prayer,' whether one has made an intention for this or not, as what is sought is a prayer before sitting, and this is achieved with what has been mentioned. The intention for the greeting prayer does not invalidate this prayer, as it is a Sunnah of a non-specified nature, contrary to the intention of the obligatory prayer alongside the intention for a supererogatory prayer, which is not valid."[422]

As for the specific question posed above, the jurists of the Shafi'i school are of the opinion that whoever makes up missed days of Ramadan during the six days of Shawwal has fulfilled his or her religious obligation as well as gained the reward for the six extra days of fast during Shawwal. However, one should not intend to fast the six days of Shawwal, but should intend only to make up what one missed of the Ramadan fast. Since these make-up days will fall during the six days of Shawwal, one achieves the reward of the Sunnah fast as well. Indeed, the generosity of God is vast. This opinion is based on the *hadith* of the Prophet [s] which states, "Whoever fasts Ramadan and follows it with six days from the

---

422. AL-MAHALLI, *Sharh Minhaj al-Talibin*, 1:273.

month of Shawwal, it is as if they have fasted the entire year."[423] He did not mention that these six days require specific intention; rather, he talked about Ramadan being followed in general by six days from Shawwal. These six days can be achieved by intending a Sunnah fast or by intending to make up days missed during Ramadan.

A fatwa issued by Imam al-Ramli supports this position: "The person making up missed days from Ramadan in Shawwal, even if he has intended other than the fast of Shawwal, has also gained the reward for the six days of Shawwal. This issue has been mentioned by many of the later jurists."[424]

Based on the provided evidence, it is permissible for a woman to make up her missed days of Ramadan during Shawwal, while simultaneously receiving the reward for fasting the six days of Shawwal. Through judicial analogy (qiyas), this ruling is based on the permissibility of entering a mosque and praying two cycles of prayer intended as the obligatory prayers, or Sunnah prayers, while achieving the reward for performing the prayer of the greeting of the mosque. And God is Most High and knows best.

---

423. AL-SIJISTANI, *Sunan Abi Dawud*, 2:324; AL-QIZWINI, *Sunan Ibn Majah*, 1:547; and AL-TAMIMI, *Sahih Ibn Hibban*, 8:396.
424. AL-RAMLI, *Fatawa al-Ramli*, 2:66.

FATWAS RELATED TO HAJJ

Question 81:

What is the ruling on the following situation: one stands on 'Arafah during Hajj and then discovers that the day is not actually 'Arafah?

Al-Bayhaqi narrated the words of the Prophet [s], "The day of 'Arafah is the day when people are recognized."[425] The Prophet [s] also said, "Fasting is done the day everyone fasts, the fast is broken on the day everyone breaks fast, and the day of sacrifice is when everyone sacrifices."[426] If pilgrims should stand on 'Arafah on the 10th day of Dhu al-Hijja and later realize their mistake, they should not undergo the extreme hardship to return. This is what has been mentioned by many jurists of the Hanafi, Maliki, and Hanbali schools which is juxtaposed to the soundest position of the Shafi'i school

Likewise, should pilgrims stand on 'Arafah on the 8th, and, becoming aware of their mistake, make timely corrections, then they do not need to repeat their actions, according to Ahmad. However, the rest of the jurists rule that they are to repeat them. If they are aware of their mistake and unable to correct it, then the Hanafi school holds that their Hajj is valid, contrary to Shafi'i and Maliki jurists.

According to Al-Kasani from the Hanafi school, ". . . if people are confused about the sighting of the new crescent of Dhu al-Hijja, and they stand on 'Arafah after completing thirty days of Dhu al-Q'ida, and they were later told that the new crescent was sighted on such-and-such date, and the day they stood on 'Arafah was really the day of sacrifice, then their standing on 'Arafah is correct, and the Hajj is complete based on analogical preference (istihsan)."[427]

---

425. AL-BAYHAQI, *Kubra*, 5:176; and AL-DARAQUTNI, *Sunan al-Daraqutni*, 2:223.

426. AL-TIRMIDHI, *Sunan al-Tirmidhi*, 3:80; AL-DARAQUTNI, *Sunan al-Daraqutni*, 2:164.

427. AL-KASANI, *Bada'i ' al-Sina'i'*, 2:126-27, *istihsan* means that legal issue takes a different ruling due to another outside proof text.

In Imam al-Nawawi's opinion, "If they [the pilgrims] miss the date by two days, such that they stood on 'Arafah on the 7th or 11th, their Hajj is indisputably invalid, due to their negligence. If they differ by one day, and they stood on the 10th day of Dhu al-Hijja, their standing is valid, and their Hajj is complete without need for repetition."[428]

Imam Ibn Qudamah al-Maqdisi wrote, "If people make a mistake in keeping track of the days and they stand on 'Arafah incorrectly, validity is determined by the narrations of al-Daraqutni on the authority of 'Abd al-'Aziz ibn 'Abdallah b. Khalid b. Asid, "The day of 'Arafah is the day people are recognized." If some of the pilgrims are correct and others are incorrect regarding the day of standing, those mistaken do not count, and they are not excused in this matter."[429]

From the above evidences, we consider the opinion of the Hanbali jurists best in that it eases the Muslim practice by not distinguishing between errors made before or after the day of 'Arafah. In the best case, one mistakenly goes to 'Arafah early and is able to correct his or her mistake and leave the dispute to the jurists. God is Most High and knows best.

428. AL-NAWAWI, al-Majmu', 8:281-82.
429. Ibn Qudmah AL-MAQDASI, al-Mughni, 3:281-82.

Question 82:

Does a wife require her husband's permission to travel for the Hajj?

Mutual understanding, agreement, love, and mercy should be the foundations of a Muslim household. The husband should always be pleased with his wife, and the wife should always be pleased with her husband. This is the ideal balance we wish all Muslim households would strive to attain.

Women are required to be legally responsible just like men. The Prophet [s] said, "Obedience to a created being cannot involve disobedience to the Creator."[430] Neglecting to perform the Hajj is neglecting one of the pillars of Islam. It is not permissible for a husband to forbid his wife from going on Hajj; it is even considered sinful for him to do so. If he does forbid her, then she should not obey him, and by going on Hajj she would not be committing a sin.

To begin with, a woman does not need her husband's permission to worship her Lord. If she wishes to fast in Ramadan, or if she wants to pray, make Hajj, or pay *zakat*, she can do so without her husband's permission. The husband is not the overseer of his wife's relationship with God.

Even if she wanted to make the lesser pilgrimage, which is mandatory according to the Shafi'is and the Hanbalis, her husband's refusal could not prevent her. However, there should be mutual understanding and agreement in order to avoid hardship, strife, and conflict in marital life.

Ibn Qudamah thought similarly: "In summary, if a women gets into the pilgrim garb (*ihram*) for an obligatory major pilgrimage or the lesser pilgrimage, such as the Hajj or *'Umrah* of Islam, or one based on an oath, then her husband cannot prevent her from carrying it out, and he cannot insist that she remove her pilgrim garb. This is the opinion of most of the people of knowledge, including Ahmad, al-Nakha'i, Ishaq, the people of reason, and al-Shafi'i in the more correct of his two opinions."[431]

The husband's discontent and his refusal to permit the pilgrimage cannot affect his wife's Hajj. He cannot impose his will on

---

430. AL-KUFI, *Musannaf ibn Abi Shaybah*, 6:545.
431. Ibn Qudmah AL-MAQDASI, *al-Mughni*, 3:282.

her in this respect. But, as we mentioned, it is better for their lives to be based on mutual contentment and agreement. God is Most High and knows best.

Question 83:

We often see students and disciples of spiritual guides kissing the hands of their teachers and spiritual guides. Is this permissible?

The ways that people honor their superiors and guides differ according to the cultural norms of a given people. For example, in the Arabian Peninsula people kiss their fathers on the nose as a way of honoring them, and people also kiss the heads of their scholars. The original ruling on these practices is that they are permissible as long as Muslims do not practice prohibited forms of affection.

As for kissing the hands of scholars, this is a permissible sign of respect for a scrupulous scholar, a just ruler, one's parents, one's teacher, and anyone else who is worthy of honor. Ibn 'Umar, who was in one of the Prophet's [s] military detachments, related a story in which he [s] said, ". . . we came to the Prophet [s] and kissed his hand."[432]

The schools of jurisprudence have come to a consensus that kissing the hand of a righteous scholar is not prohibited. They have even gone so far as to say that the practice is both permitted and encouraged.

The Hanafis explicitly stated that it is permissible to kiss the hand of a righteous scholar in order to seek blessings and honor him. Al-Hasfaki al-Hanafi said, "[There is nothing wrong with kissing the hand of] a man who is [a scholar] and one who is scrupulous as a means of seeking blessings. (Taken from *Durr*). The author narrated from *al-Jami'* that there is nothing wrong with kissing the hand of a religious ruler [a just ruler]."[433]

Likewise, Ibn Nujaym said, "There is nothing wrong with kissing the hand of a scholar and a just ruler based on the narration according to Sufyan who said, "Kissing the scholar's and the just ruler's hand is Sunnah."[434]

Concerning kissing hands, al-Zayla'i mentioned the following, "When it is out of obedience and honoring someone, then it is per-

---

432. AL-SIJISTANI, *Sunan Abi Dawud*, 3:46, 4:356; AL-BAYHAQI, *Kubra*, 7:101; AL-BAYHAQI, *Shu'ab al-Iman*, 6:476; AL-KUFI, *Musannaf ibn Abi Shaybah*, 6:541; and BUKHARI, *al-Adab al-Mufrad*, 1:338.

433. AL-HASKAFI, *al-Durr al-Mukhtar*, 6:382 with the *hashiyah* of Ibn 'Abdin on it.

434. IBN NUJAYM, *al-Bahr al-Ra'iq*, 8:221.

missible. Al-Sarakhsi and some of the later scholars gave license for kissing the hand of a scholar or someone who is pious as a means of seeking blessings. Abu Bakr kissed the Prophet [s] between his eyes after he passed and Sufyan al-Thawri said, "Kissing the hand of a scholar or a just ruler is Sunnah," and 'Abdallah ibn al-Mubarak kissed his head while standing."[435]

Muhammad al-Babarti al-Hanafi said, "There is nothing wrong with kissing when it is out of obedience or to honor someone if they are wearing a shirt or a cloak [i.e., a garment symbolic of scholarship]. According to Sufyan, kissing a scholar's hand is Sunnah, but license is not given for kissing other people's hands."[436]

In the Maliki school, Imam Malik disliked the practice, though the later Maliki scholars agreed with the majority that it is permissible. Their interpretation of Imam Malik's ruling concluded that he based his opinion on situations involving arrogance. Al-Abhuri said,

> Malik disliked it [kissing of hands] if it was linked with aggrandizement and arrogance. According to Al-Nafrawi, "An example of arrogance is the bedouin who kissed the Prophet's [s] hand and demanded, 'Show me a sign,' So the Prophet [s] said, 'Go to that tree and tell it, 'The Prophet calls you.' The tree swayed right and left and came towards the Prophet [s] saying, 'Peace be upon you, Messenger of God.' The Prophet [s] told the bedouin, 'Tell it to return,' and it returned as it had been. The bedouin kissed the Prophet's [s] hands and feet and became a Muslim." And there are other stories such as this one.

If Malik's denial of what is narrated concerning the kissing of hands is based on authenticity, Malik is a proof, for he is the Imam of *hadith*. But if his denial derives from the perspective of jurisprudence, then his denial must be based on precedence. People act in accordance with the permissibility of kissing the hand of someone towards whom it is appropriate to obey and be humble towards. The Companions kissed the hand of the Prophet [s], the Prophet [s] kissed the hand of Fatimah, and the Companions kissed the hands of each other. The apparent meaning of his words is that (it is per-

---

435. AL-ZAYLA'I, *Tabyin al-Haqa'iq Sharh Kanz al-Daqa'iq*, 3:25.

436. Muhammad ibn Muhammad b. Mahmud AL-BABARTI, *al-'Inayah Sharh al-Hidaya*. Dar al-Fikr, 10:52.

missible) even if it is the hand of a scholar, old person, ruler, father, someone present, or someone returning from travel, that is the apparent position of the school.[437]

The Shafi'is explicitly stated that kissing the hand of a pious scholar is favorable, as are all kinds of honor given to scholars or other honorable persons. Al-Nawawi said, "The preferred position is that it is favorable to honor someone entering a room by standing if they have a rank based on knowledge, righteousness, honor, or authority with integrity, or if they have a sanctity through sainthood. Standing is a form of honor and not of ostentation or aggrandizement. The community has acted accordingly, both early on and in later years. . . . It is favorable to kiss the hand of a righteous man, an ascetic, or a scholar and the like from among the community of spiritual people. Kissing someone's hand because of their monetary wealth, their command of the world, their power, and the rank that they hold with people of the world and the like, is extremely disliked. Al-Mutawalli said it is not permissible, indicating that it is prohibited. The same goes for the kissing of the head or feet of such persons."[438]

Similarly Sheikh al-Islam Zakariyyah al-Ansari mentioned that, "It is favorable to kiss the hand of a living person due to their righteousness in religious matters like asceticism, knowledge, and honor as the Companions did with the Prophet [s], as is related by Abu Dawud and others with authentic chains of transmission. Kissing someone's hand is disliked when it is due to their wealth or their power or rank among people of the world."[439]

Ibn Qasim al-'Ibadi said, "It is Sunnah to kiss the hand of a scholar, a righteous man, a member of the Prophet's line, and an ascetic like the Companions did with the Prophet [s]. It is disliked when it is for rich or worldly-powerful people. It is also favorable to stand for people of rank to honor them, without ostentation or aggrandizement, i.e., pridefulness."[440]

The Hanbalis explicitly permit kissing the hand of a scholar or a ruler. In the words of the Hanbali scholar, Ibn Muflih, "It is permissible to kiss the hand of a scholar, a generous person because of

437. AL-NAFRAWI, *al-Fawakih al-Dawani*, 2:326.

438. AL-NAWAWI, *al-Majmu'*, 4:476-77.

439. AL-ANSARI, *Asna al-Matalib*, 3:114.

440. Ibn Wasim AL-'UBADI, *Hashiyah 'ala Gharar al-Bahiyah*. al-Matba'a al-Mamaniyyah, 4:100.

their generous support, and a ruler because of his authority."[441]

Al-Safarini said, "He said in *Manaqib Ashab al-Hadith*, 'The student should have great humility for the scholar and humble himself before him.' He also said, 'An aspect of humility is kissing his hand.' Sufyan ibn 'Uyaynah and al-Fudayl ibn 'Ayad, one of them kissed the hand and the other the foot of al-Husayn ibn 'Ali al-J'ufi. Imam Abu al-Ma'ali said in his commentary on the *Hidayah*, 'Kissing the hand of a scholar, a generous person because of his support, and a ruler because of his authority is permitted.' As for kissing people's hands because of their wealth it is narrated that, 'Those who humiliate themselves before a rich person because of his wealth lose two-thirds of their religion.'"[442]

From the preceding passages, kissing the hands of scholars and those of higher spiritual rank than us is clearly favorable, and there is no cause to decry the practice. Verily those who decry it are nothing more than stubborn souls that reject that which goes against their pride. God is Most High and knows best.

---

441. Ibn Muflih AL-MAQDASI, *al-Adab al-Shar'iyyah*, 2:260.
442. AL-SAFARINI, *Ghida al-Albab*, 1:334.

FATWAS RELATED TO SUFISM

Question 84:

Is Sayyidna al-Husayn's head really at his shrine in Cairo?

This inquiry regarding the burial of Sayyidina al-Husayn's head in Cairo is a historical question, not a legal question. Affirming or denying the head's presence in the shrine does not constitute a matter of belief or faith. If someone were to insist that the pyramids are not in Egypt and instead in some other country, would he or she be a disbeliever? Certainly not; they would simply be ignorant of the truth.

The historians and authors of biographies agree that the body of al-Husayn is buried in Karbala. As for his head, it was carried around until it was placed in 'Asqalan, a Palestinian port on the Mediterranean near ports of Egypt and Jerusalem. The presence of al-Husayn's head in 'Asqalan and its transfer to Egypt is supported by a great number of historians including Ibn Maysir, al-Qalqashandi, 'Ali ibn Abi Bakr, who is known as al-Sayih al-Harawi, Ibn Iyas, Sibt al-Jawzi, and Hafiz al-Sakhawi.

The historian al-Maqrizi says, "The head of Sayyidna al-Husayn was transported to Cairo from 'Asqalan on Sunday the eighth of Jumada al-Akhir 548 AH. (August 31st 1153 CE). The person who brought the head from 'Asqalan was Prince Sayf al-Mamlaka Tamim Waliha. It was brought to the palace on Tuesday the tenth of Jumada al-Akhir (September 2nd 1153 CE)." He added, "The head was brought forth by al-Ustadh hidden in a cloak. He brought it to al-Kafuri, from whence it was carried through the tunnel to the palace of al-Zumurrud, and it was then buried in the dome of al-Daylam near Bab Dahliz." Al-Maqrizi goes on to say, "Tala'i' built a mosque for the head outside of Bab Zawaylah on the side of al-Darb al-Ahmar and it is known as the mosque of *al-Salih Tala'i'*. They washed the head in the mosque on wooden boards, and it is said that they are still in the mosque."[443]

Archaeologists confirm this. 'Atiyat al-Shatwi, who was the artifacts inspector and who oversaw the renovation of the dome a few years ago said, "Documents in the possession of the Bureau of

---

443. AL-MAQRIZI, *Tarikh al-Maqrizi*. Dar Sadir, 2:171.

Artifacts confirm that the head of al-Husayn was transported to Cairo from 'Asqalan, as is stated by al-Maqrizi, on Sunday the eighth of Jumada al-Akhir 548 AH (August 31st 1153 CE), and the person who brought the head from 'Asqalan was Prince Sayf al-Mamlaka Tamim Waliha. It was brought to the palace on Tuesday the tenth of Jumada al-Akhir (September 2nd 1153 CE)."

Researchers at the British Library in London acquired a copy of a manuscript from *Tarikh Amad* by Ibn al-Awraq who died in 572 AH. The manuscript was written in 560 AH, and it is catalogued under the number 5803 East. The author established with certainty that the head of al-Husayn was brought to Cairo from 'Asqalan in 549 AH, during the lifetime of the author himself, who participated with the people of Egypt in greeting the noble head.

Al-Shabrawi, the late Sheikh of al-Azhar, wrote a book entitled *al-Ithaf* in which he definitively establishes that the head is in its well-known resting place in Cairo. He mentions a great number of other scholars who came to the same conclusion: Imam al-Mundhiri, Hafiz Ibn Dahiyyah, Hafiz Najm al-Din al-Ghayti, Imam Majd al-Din ibn 'Uthman, Imam Muhammad ibn Bashir, Qadi Muhyi al-Din ibn 'Abd al-Dhahir, Qadi 'Abd al-Rahim, 'Abdallah al-Rifa'i al-Makhzumi, Ibn al-Nahwi, Sheikh al-Qurashi, Sheikh al-Shiblinji, Sheikh Hasan al-'Adawi, Sheikh al-Sha'rani, Sheikh al-Manawi, Sheikh al-Ajhuri, Abu al-Mawahib al-Tunsi, and others.

Sheikh Muhammad Zaki al-Din Ibrahim composed a treatise on this subject called *Ra's al-Imam al-Husayn bi Mashhadihi bi'l-Qahirah Tahqiqan Mu'akkadan Hasiman*, a work full of evidence and proofs that satisfy the heart.

From this presentation of facts, one's heart is put at ease by the historical evidence regarding the head of Imam al-Husayn honoring Cairo the Protected. And all praise is due to God, Lord of the Worlds. God is Most High and knows best.

Question 85:

Do some of the righteous experience marvels (*karamat*) during their lives? Can these marvels continue even after those individuals have left the life of this world and passed over into the intermediary life after death (*barzakh*)?

A marvel is something that breaks the accustomed norms of the universe. A marvel is not necessarily accompanied or followed by a claim to prophethood. God makes these marvels apparent on the hands of a select group of His servants who outwardly manifest righteousness, adhere to the religious law, diligently follow His Prophet [s], have correct belief, and work to do good, whether they are known for it or not.

The scholars placed conditions to close the door in the face of those who would make false claims so that the issue of marvels would not lead to people leaving Islam. They closed the door of false claims by making it a condition that one adhere to the religious law and follow the Prophet [s], for one who adheres to religious law does not make false claims to the miraculous. They closed the door to leaving Islam by making it a condition that marvels are not accompanied by a claim to prophethood. Believing in the marvels of the saints is one of the creeds of Sunni Muslims. Imam al-Tahawi said, "We believe in the marvels that occur and are authenticated by the narrations of those who are trustworthy."[444]

Denying the marvels of the saints constitutes a denial of Islam, and believing in them is one of the bases of the Muslim creed. The one behind the marvels of the saints (*karamat*) is also responsible for the miracles of the Prophets (*al-mu'jizat*). The responsibility for miracles belongs to God alone, but He has made them manifest through the hands of adherents to His law.

Speaking of the marvels of the saints, Imam al-Jalal al-Mahalli said, ". . . they are the knowers of God, a state made possible for those constant in their acts of obedience, who refrain from committing acts of disobedience, and who refuse to allow themselves to be preoccupied by worldly pleasures and desires. This indicates that they [their marvels] are possible and occur. Examples are the river flowing because of 'Umar's letter, or his seeing his army in

---

444. Ibn Abi 'Izz al-Hanafi AL-'IZZ, *Sharh al-'Aqidah al-Tahawiyah*. al-Maktabah al-Islami, 494.

Nahawand while he was standing on the pulpit in Medina, yet being able to alert the leader of the army, 'O Sariya, the mountain, the mountain!' 'Umar was warning him of the enemy hiding behind the mountain, and Sariya was able to hear his words in spite of the distance. Also Khalid drank poison without being harmed by it, as well as other occurrences to the Companions and others. Al-Qushayri said, 'This [marvel] includes the likes of a child being born without a father,' and the transformation of an inanimate object into an animate one. There is, however, disagreement between the significance of the miracles of a prophet and the marvels of a saint. Most of the Mu'tazilites did not even allow for abnormal occurrences from the saints, and neither did Abu Ishaq al-Isfarayini who said, 'Everything that could be considered a miracle for a prophet cannot be a marvel for a saint. The extent of their marvels being acceptable is confined to their prayers being answered, their unexpected discoveries of water in the desert, and similar things that do not stray far from normalcy.'"[445]

Ibn Taymiyyah says, "The Prophet [s] made it clear that the heart has an aspect (shu'bah) of hypocrisy and an aspect of faith. A hypocritical heart bears both saintliness and enmity [towards God]. This is why marvels are only performed at the hands of some of them—those possessing the aspect of their faith in God and piety—and from them come the marvels of the saints."[446]

The scholars also mention that one of the marvels is the ability to perceive things that are hidden (al-ghaybiyat). Concerning this, Ibn 'Abdin says, "The books of theology mention that one of the marvels of the saints is perceiving things that are hidden. Such volumes respond to the Mu'tazilites, who cite Quranic verses[447] as evidence for a feat not being possible. The intended meaning is that hidden things are made apparent without an intermediary, and the messenger is intended to mean an angel. His unseen is made directly apparent to angels, and to others through His intermediaries. The Prophet [s] and the saints are made aware of

---

445. Jalal al-Din AL-MAHALLI, *Sharh al-Jalal al-Mahalli li-Jam' al-Jawami' bi hamishihi Hashiyat al-Banani.* Dar al-Fikr, 2:481.

446. IBN TAYMIYYAH, *al-Fatawa al-Fiqhiyya al-Kubra*, 1:194.

447. These verses are found in the Quran, "(He is) the Knower of the Unseen, and He revealeth unto none His secret, Save unto every messenger whom He hath chosen, and then He maketh a guard to go before him and a guard behind him" (72:26-27).

the hidden through the intermediary of an angel or another. We thoroughly covered this topic in our treatise *Drawing the Indian Sword in Defense of Our Master Khalid al-Naqshibandi*, so go back to it, for therein are rare pieces of beneficial knowledge. And God Most High knows best."[448]

There is no evidence to indicate that confirmed marvels of the saints end with the completion of their lives on earth. Rather, there is evidence to the contrary. It is affirmed that God protected the body of 'Asim ibn Thabit after his death. God covered 'Asim with a kind of canopy that protected him so no one could cut through any part of it."[449] This is an explicit example of a marvel that God provided for a saint after his death.

A passage relating to Al-Bayjirmi's teachings sheds further light on the issue: "It was asked in a lesson that if a dead person were to miraculously recite a verse of prostration, would the person who heard it then prostrate or not? He [Al-Bayjirmi] said, '. . . the marvels of the saints do not come to an end with their death. There is therefore nothing to prevent a dead person from reciting a beautiful recitation and taking pleasure in it. In such a case it is allowable for the person who hears it to prostrate, even though the dead person is not legally responsible; similarly one should prostrate if the dead person is a discerning youth. The dead person is not like one who is ignorant, and should not be treated as an inanimate object and the like."[450]

Belief in the marvels of the saints is widely embraced by the Muslim community, and is considered by theologians to be one of the foundations of faith. Denying marvels may be considered un-Islamic, and could result in one's leaving the faith. Marvels have been affirmed for the saints after their death by authentic traditions, as death occurs to the body, not the spirit. The marvels of the saints cannot be denied during their lives nor after their deaths. And God is Most High and knows best.

448. Muhammad Amin ibn 'Umar IBN 'ABIDIN, *Rad al-Muhtar 'ala al-Durr al-Mukhtar*. Dar al-Kutub al-'Ilmiyyah, 3:29.

449. AL-BUKHARI, *Sahih Bukhari*, 3:1108; AL-TAMIMI, *Sahih Ibn Hibban*, 15:512; AL-HAKIM, *al-Mustadarak 'ala al-Sahihayn*, 3:464; and AL-KUFI, *Musannaf ibn Abi Shaybah*, 7:97.

450. Sulayman ibn Muhammad AL-BAYJIRMI, AL-SHARBINI, and ABU SHUJA', *Tuhfat al-Habib 'ala Sharh al-Khatib*. Dar al-Fikr, 1:433.

Question 86:

What is the value of visions in Islam?

The Shari'ah is a system that governs and manages all things perceived and processed by sensory experience. This is why Islamic
law contains legal rulings on all aspects of life, including industry,
trade, medicine, and social issues. The Shari'ah's rulings are not
limited, therefore, to acts of worship and articles of faith, as some
assume. Its laws also address other aspects of human life, such as
sleep and its prescribed preparations: making ablution, mentioning the name of God, and sleeping on the right side. Those things
that occur during sleep, such as dreams, glad tidings, and night-
mares, are collectively classified by the Shari'ah under the term
"visions." Thus Islam has not left anything, no matter how small,
without guidance; says the Quran, *We have neglected nothing in the
Book* [6:38].

The scholars have sought to elucidate the meaning of "sleep,"
which is that state in which people have visions. Ibn Amir al-Hajj
said, "Sleep is a state that occurs to the intellect and necessitates
the incapacity of a person to perceive sensory things, to conduct
voluntary actions, and to use the intellect."[451] This is the meaning
of sleep; the meaning of visions is as follows.

LINGUISTIC MEANING

Visions, specifically night visions, are those images that are seen
by a person while asleep.

LEGAL IMPLICATIONS

Al-Mazari said, "God creates beliefs in the heart of the sleeping
person just as He creates [them] in a wakeful person, and He does
as He wills; He is not halted by sleep nor by wakeful states. When
He creates these beliefs, it is as if He has made them knowledge of
other things, which He will create at another time, or have been
created. So if He creates a state of flying in the heart of a person,
the most that is in it is that he believed something that is contrary
to reality, so this belief would be knowledge of another, and all if
from the creation of God.

---

451. Muhammad ibn Muhammad b. Muhammad al-Hasafi IBN AMIR
AL-HAJJ, *al-Taqrir wa al-Tahbir*. Dar al-Kutub al-'Ilmiyyah, 2:177.

VISIONS ACCORDING TO THE SUFIS

Some of the great Sufis said, "Visions are of the rulings pertaining to the realm of delineated semblances called the imaginal realm. They may be the effect of the heavenly intellects and the rational souls that perceive universal and particular meanings, in which case images that are appropriate to those meanings appear. And visions may be the effect of the lower faculty of imagination that only perceives particular meanings, in which case images that are appropriate to those appear. This could be due to an imbalance in the mind or through the self seeking to produce a certain image through this faculty of imagination, such as one who intensely imagines the form of his absent beloved so that their image appears in his imagination and he perceived it. Visions are the first beginnings revelation."[452]

Muhyi al-Din ibn al-'Arabi, said, "Know that the beginning of revelation is a true vision; it is not the confusion of dreams, but it does not occur except in the sleeping state. Aishah relates that, "The revelation first began for the Messenger of God [s] with true visions. There was not a vision that he had but it came clear as the break of morning."[453] Revelation begins through visions instead of through the physical senses because meanings of the intellect are nearer to the imagination than to the senses. Physicality is the lower aspect, while meaning is the higher, subtle aspect, and imagination lies between the two. Since revelation is meaning, the beginning of revelation is the descent of unfettered intellectual meanings, in defined physical forms, to the imaginal realm during either sleeping or wakeful states. This is a perception of something physical in the realm of physicality. If the meaning is to descend to the physical, it must pass through the imaginal realm before arriving at physicality. It is one of the essential characteristics of the imagination that it forms everything that occurs as a physical form.

If this Divine revelation appears in sleep then it is called a vision. If it appears in a wakeful state then it is called imagination, meaning it was made manifest to the person through the imagination. This is why revelation began with imagination. Then the

452. ALI GOMAA, *Mada Hujiyat al-Ruya 'ind al-Usuliyin*, 15-16.

453. AL-BUKHARI, *Sahih Bukhari*, 1:4; and AL-NAYSABURI, *Sahih Muslim*, 1:140.

imagination was transferred to an angel in the manifest world. The angel would appear to him as a man, or as a person who was physically perceptible. It may be that only the person for whom the revelation is intended perceives the angel, or those who are with him may perceive it as well, then the words of his Lord would be addressed to his hearing. This is revelation. Sometimes the revelation would descend on the heart of the Prophet [s] and he would be taken by the immense weight of it. This is what is called a spiritual state (*hal*). Human nature is not fit for this, which is why it is difficult, and it creates an imbalance in a person until the revelation is completed, then they relax and convey what was said to them."[454]

Visions are therefore not only for the prophets; they come to all Muslims, and the veracity of them increases the closer we come to the last day. The Messenger of God [s] said, "As the day draws near, a believer's vision will rarely be false. The ones who have the truest visions are those who have the truest speech. The vision of a believer is one of forty-six parts of prophecy. Visions are threefold: the true vision is a glad tiding from God, a vision from the grief produced by Satan, and a vision that occurs to people from their own selves. If one of you sees a vision that they dislike, let them arise, pray, and not speak of it to anyone."[455]

Through this discussion we have clarified the reality of visions, their importance and their relationship to the Shari'ah. God is Most High and knows best.

---

454. Muhyi al-Din IBN 'ARABI, *al-Futhat al-Makiyyah*. Dar al-Kutub al-'Arabiyya al-Kubra, 2:375-76.

455. AL-NAYSABURI, *Sahih Muslim*, 4:1773.

Question 87:

What is the ruling on a Muslim entering into a Sufi order? Why does Sufism have multiple orders? If Sufism is asceticism, invocation, and good behavior, then why can Muslims not suffice themselves with the Quran and the Sunnah as a means for knowing the manners of dealing with the soul?

Sufism is a system of spiritual growth and the acquisition of good character. It leads Muslims to the level of excellence (*ihsan*) that the Messenger of God [s] described as, "To worship God as if you see Him, for if you do not see Him, He surely sees you."[456] Therefore, Sufism is a program of growth concerned with purifying the soul of all the diseases that prevent one from reaching God, and it seeks to rectify the crookedness of the human soul as it relates to God, to others, and to one's self. The Sufi order (*tariqa*) is the school that takes care of this self-purification and rectification, and the Sufi Sheikh is the master who provides the necessary training for the seeker.

The human soul naturally acquires diseases such as arrogance, haughtiness, narcissism, delusion, selfishness, stinginess, anger, ostentation, the desire to commit sinful acts and error, gratifying one's thirst for revenge, dislike, resentment, deceit, and greed. God related the words of Joseph, *I do not blame myself. Lo! The [human] soul enjoins unto evil, save he upon whom my Lord has mercy. Lo! My Lord is Forgiving, Merciful* [12:53]. For this reason our ancestors were cognizant of the importance of a spiritual discipline that could rid the self of its diseases, be in harmony with society, and ultimately be successful in leading a person to God.

Sufi orders must have certain characteristics. First, they must have a strict adherence to the Quran and Sunnah, since Sufism is the methodology of the Quran and Sunnah. Anything that is against either the Quran or the Sunnah is not, and cannot, be a part of Sufism, rather it is rejected by Sufism. Second, the teachings of Sufism are not to be considered as separate from Shari'ah knowledge; rather, they are its essence.

Sufism has three main principles that are drawn from the Quran and Sunnah. The first is concern with the human self, ob-

---

456. IBN HANBAL, *Musnad Imam Ahmad*, 1:27; AL-BUKHARI, *Sahih Bukhari*, 1:27; and AL-NAYSABURI, *Sahih Muslim*, 1:37.

serving it with diligence, and purifying it from all that is foul: *And a soul and Him who perfected it. And inspired it [with conscience of] what is wrong for it and [what is] right for it. He is indeed successful who causes it to grow. And he is indeed a failure who stunts it* [91:7-10]. The second principle is to make much mention and remembrance of God; the Quran commands, *O you who believe! Remember God with much remembrance* [33:41], and the Messenger of God [s] said, "Let your tongue remain moist with the remembrance of God."[457] The final principle is to renounce the world, to be detached from it, and to desire the hereafter: *Naught is the life of the world save a pastime and a sport. Far better is the abode of the Hereafter for those who keep their duty [to God]. Have you then no sense?* [6:32].

As for the sheikh, he transmits and provides litanies to his disciples and guides them through the process of removing diseases from the heart. His role is to find the most suitable program for each of his disciples (*murids*), as did the Prophet [s] when he would advise people on what would draw them near to God based on their different dispositions. For example, a man came to the Messenger of God [s] and said, "Tell me of that which will keep me away from the wrath of God," and he said, "Do not become angry."[458] Another person came and requested, "Give me something to cling to," and he replied, "Let your tongue remain moist with the remembrance of God."[459] There were those amongst the Companions who increased their night prayer, others who read the Quran often, others who often participated in jihad, others who performed constant remembrance of God, and still others who regularly gave charity.

This does not mean neglecting acts of worship. Rather, a traveler on the path to God increases in some acts of worship in order to help him reach his goal. It is for this reason that there are many doors to Paradise, but there is still only one Paradise. The Prophet [s] said, "For every people of a certain righteous act there is a door

---

457. IBN HANBAL, *Musnad Imam Ahmad*, 4:188; AL-TIRMIDHI, *Sunan al-Tirmidhi*, 5:548; AL-TAMIMI, *Sahih Ibn Hibban*, 2:1246; and AL-HAKIM, *al-Mustadarak 'ala al-Sahihayn*, 1:672.

458. AL-BUKHARI, *Sahih Bukhari*, 5:2267; and AL-TIRMIDHI, *Sunan al-Tirmidhi*, 4:371.

459. IBN HANBAL, *Musnad Imam Ahmad*, 4:188; AL-TIRMIDHI, *Sunan al-Tirmidhi*, 5:548; AL-TAMIMI, *Sahih Ibn Hibban*, 2:1246; and AL-HAKIM, *al-Mustadarak 'ala al-Sahihayn*, 1:672.

from the many doors of Paradise that call those people, and for those who fast there is a special door that is called *Rayyan*."[460] For this reason Sufi orders have different methods of spiritual discipline depending on the specific spiritual guide and disciple.

Thus we have clarified the nature of true Sufism and the real path to God. We have explained that a true spiritual guide is one who adheres to the Qur'an and Sunnah. We have also learned the reasoning behind the various orders, which may adopt differing practices but in fact participate in one reality.

We should also mention that this above description does not apply to many of today's proponents of the Sufi way. There are those who distort the realities of the path. Some who claim to practice Sufism have no religiosity and no piety, such as those who dance lewdly at different occasions and those who act entranced, but are nothing but mere pretenders. This is not Sufism, and we should not formulate our opinion of Sufism based on such deviation. Those amongst the scholars who understand and practice Sufism should come together and explain these issues further to help the general public distinguish truth from falsehood.

The last matter of this discussion concerns taking one's spiritual methodology directly from the Quran and Sunnah. This idea seems logical, but in reality it can bring destruction. We have not learned prayer and its conditions by reading the Quran and Sunnah. Rather, we learned prayer from a science called *fiqh* (jurisprudence) that was developed by the jurists. From the Quran and Sunnah jurists derived the rulings that constitute the corpus of Islamic law. However, they used many tools codified by the science of juristic methodology (*'ilm usul al-fiqh*). What would we say if someone claimed that we should learn jurisprudence and the rulings of the religion directly from the Quran and Sunnah. There is not a single scholar who learned jurisprudence directly from the Quran and the Sunnah. Furthermore, there are matters not mentioned in the Quran and Sunnah and for which we need to be taught directly by a teacher such as the science of Quranic recitation (*tajwid*). The rules for how to recite the Quran must be taken from the scholars of that discipline who have established them. Similarly, Sufism is

460. IBN HANBAL, *Musnad Imam Ahmad*, 2:449; AL-BUKHARI, *Sahih Bukhari*, 2:671; AL-NAYSABURI, *Sahih Muslim*, 2:808; and the wording is Ahmad's.

a science that has been set down by the scholars since the time of al-Junayd in the 4th Islamic century up to this day. As time went on and social conditions worsened, and morals were lost, some of the Sufi orders became lost and adhered to practices that contradict the Quran and Sunnah. Despite this, God will continue to protect and preserve Sufism and its followers: *God defends those who are true. God loves not each treacherous ingrate* [22:38].

We have addressed the different parts of the question in the above discussion, and we ask God to give us insight into His religion, for He is Most High and knows best.

Question 88:

Do the deceased hear the salutations of the living or not?

Death is not the final and total annihilation of a human being, nor is it the end of one's God-given existence. Death is one of the most difficult phases in a human being's total existence, as it is the time when the soul departs from the body to live in another realm. Thus we may understand death as the actualization of the soul leaving the body. Al-Ghazali stated, "The meaning of the soul leaving the body is that the soul no longer governs the body as the body has left the soul's control."[461]

Abu Hurayrah narrates that the Prophet [s] said, "Whenever one of you passes by a grave of his believing brother that he used to know in this life and sends salutations to him, the deceased knows him and responds to the salutation."[462] After mentioning this *hadith*, al-Munawi comments, "Hafiz al-'Iraqi says, 'Cognition and responding to a salutation are results of life and a returning of the soul to the body, and there is nothing wrong with the soul being able to return partially to the body. Some of the great scholars have said that the clinging of the soul to the body is the same as intoxicating love and perpetual love in that if the soul leaves the body the intoxicating love does not immediately leave, so the soul remains clinging to the body. It is for this reason that it is impermissible to desecrate bones and trample upon graves.'"[463]

It is also authentically reported that the Prophet [s] ordered the slain enemies from the battle of Badr to be cast into a well, and he went to them and called them out one by one and asked, "Have you found what your Lord has promised you to be true? For I have found what my Lord has promised me to be true." 'Umar said to him, "O Messenger of God, why do you speak to a people that have turned into corpses?" The Prophet [s] said to him, "By the One who has sent me with the truth, you cannot hear me more clearly than

461. AL-GHAZALI, *Ihya' 'Uluma al-Din*, 4:493.

462. Abu Bakr al-Khatib AL-BAGHDADI. *Tarikh Baghdad*. Dar al-Kutub al-'Ilmiyyah, 6:137; Muhammad ibn Ahmad b. Jami' AL-SAYDAWI, *Mu'jam al-Shuyukh*. Mu'assisah al-Risalah, 1985, 1:351; and AL-MANAWI, *Fayd al-Qadir*, 5:487.

463. Ibid., 5:487.

they can, except that they cannot respond."[464]

These textual proofs show that the deceased perceive those who visit them and are pleased with the visits. For this reason the Prophet [s] ordered us to send salutations to the dead when he taught the companions to say upon passing by a graveyard, "Peace be upon you the people of the dwelling of the believers and those who have submitted to God, and May God give mercy to those who passed first and those who will come to pass, and we will, by the will of God, join you."[465]Imam al-Nawawi stated, "It is good for one visiting a grave to draw near to the deceased the same distance they would draw near to them if they were visiting them while alive."[466] Upon mentioning the *hadith* that directs us to send salutations to the deceased while visiting their graves, he said, "These are words addressed to them and words addressed are only offered to one who hears."

Ibn 'Abd Al-Barr narrated that the Prophet [s] said, "Whenever one of you passes by a grave of his believing brother that he used to know in this life and sends salutations to him, the deceased always knows him and responds to the salutation." The Sunnah narrates the Prophet's [s] words, "Increase prayers and salutations for me during Fridays, and on the eves of Friday, as your sending prayers and salutations to me is sent to me." The Companions said, "O messenger of God, how is it that our sending prayers and salutations to you is sent to you and you will have passed?" He replied, "God has made it forbidden for the earth to consume the bodies of the Prophets." The Sunnah also narrates that the Prophet [s] said, "God has tasked an angel to stand by my grave and pass to me my nation's prayers and salutations upon me." These reports and others similar in content make it clear that the deceased hear the living but not necessarily all the time; rather, this occurrence may be limited to certain conditions, just as the living can sometimes hear speech directed to them and at other times they cannot. This hearing of the deceased is by way of perception; there is no particular

464. IBN HANBAL, *Musnad Imam Ahmad*, 2131; AL-TAMIMI, *Sahih Ibn Hibban*, 15:562; and AL-HAKIM, *al-Mustadarak 'ala al-Sahihayn*, 3:241.

465. IBN HANBAL, *Musnad Imam Ahmad*, 5:670; AL-NAYSABURI, *Sahih Muslim*, 2:670; AL-NASA'I, *Sunan al-Nasa'i (al-Mujtaba)*, 4:92; AL-QIZWINI, *Sunan Ibn Majah*, 1:494; and AL-TAMIMI, *Sahih Ibn Hibban*, 16:46.

466. AL-NAWAWI, *al-Majmu'*, 5:282.

recompense that results from it."[467]

Ibn Qayyim said, "The Messenger of God [s] has legislated upon his nation that if they send salutations to the people of the graves, then they should do so in a way similar to the salutations of the living by saying, 'Peace be upon you dwellers of the believers.' This speech is for those who hear and perceive, and were it not, then this speech would be like speech to inanimate objects. The pious ancestors are in agreement and the reports narrated from them have reached the level of corroborative continuity (*tawatur*) that the deceased hear the salutations of the living and are pleased by visitation."[468]

As we have clarified that the deceased hear and are pleased by the actions of those who visit them, so it should also be understood that death is not the cessation of existence because the soul is continually attached to the body by a special relationship, even after death. We ask God to ensure that the deceased among those who have rights over us are pleased by our visitation to them. May the peace of God be upon them, and God is Most High and knows best.

467. IBN TAYMIYYAH, *al-Fatawa al-Fiqhiyya al-Kubra*, 3:60-61.
468. Muhammad ibn Abi Bakr al-Zar'i b. Qayyim AL-JAWZIYYAH, *al-Ruh*. Maktabat al-Nasr, p. 5.

Question 89:

Is it true that al-Khidr, who was with the Prophet Moses, is still alive? Is he an angel or a human?

It is not beyond the limits of either the intellect or divine revelation for al-Khidr, or any other of God's creation, to be continually alive. Muslims should not pass judgment on anything uncommon before examining what the Shari'ah has to say regarding the issue.

God is capable of prolonging anyone's life, as He has prolonged Satan's life. He did so not as a miracle for Satan or to give him a special attribute, but rather to serve a specific purpose in His ultimate plan. Likewise, God can prolong the life of a saintly person such as al-Khidr in order to attribute a miracle to him, or for another purpose we might not be aware of.

Al-Khidr was mentioned specifically by the pious ancestors and they acknowledged that he remains alive. Imam Muslim mentions in his *Sahih* the *hadith* of the man who will be killed by the antichrist, as well as Abu Ishaq's commentary upon it. Imam Muslim writes that the Prophet [s] said, "If this man is to be killed and then brought back to life, will you be in doubt?" The Companions responded in the negative and the Prophet [s] said, "He will kill him and bring him back to life and will say, 'By God I have never been more alive before you than this,' so he will try to kill the man again and he will be unable to." Abu Ishaq said that the man referred to was al-Khidr.[469]

Anas also reported that, during the death of the Prophet [s], "A large handsome man with a red beard walked over them and cried. He then turned to the companions of the Prophet and said that in God is solace from every calamity and compensation for every loss, so to God turn in repentance and in Him desire; and may you be granted respite from tribulation. Then he left. Some of the Companions asked one another if they knew who the man was. Abu Bakr and 'Ali said, 'Yes, he is the brother of the Prophet [s], al-Khidr upon him be peace.'"[470]

Anas also said:

I went out with the Prophet [s] one night carrying water for

---

469. AL-NAYSABURI, *Sahih Muslim*, 4:2256 and he did not challenge this statement.
470. AL-HAKIM, *al-Mustadarak 'ala al-Sahihayn*, 3:58.

him for purification when he heard someone call out and he
said to me, "Quiet!" The caller said, "O God, give me aid with
that which will save me from that which I fear." The Prophet
[s] said, "He should say something else." It is as if the man said
what the Prophet [s] wanted. The caller continued, "And give
me the longing of the pious for that which they long." and the
Prophet said, "Go Anas, leave the purification water and go to
the caller and ask him to make supplication for the Prophet
that He aids him with that which He has commissioned him,
and ask him to make supplications for the community and that
they take that which has been given to them by the Prophet
with truth." The caller then said to me, "Who has sent you?" I
did not want to inform him without taking the permission of
the Prophet [s] so I said to him, "With God's mercy on you, why
do you need to know?" He said, "Will you not inform me who
sent you?" I went to the Prophet [S] and informed him what
the caller had said. He told me, "Tell him you are the messenger of the Prophet [s]." The caller responded after I informed
him, "Greetings to the Messenger of God and to his messenger.
He was more worthy to have had me come to him. Send him
greetings of peace from me and say to him that al-Khidr sends
greetings of peace and he says to you that God has favored you
over all the Prophets as He has favored and honored the month
of Ramadan over all other months, and He has favored your
community over all others as He has favored the day of Friday
over all other days." As I got near to the caller I heard him say,
"O God make me from amongst this nation that has received
mercy, is guided, and receives forgiveness."[471]

Anas also reported that the Prophet [s] said, "Al-Khidr is in the seas,
and Elijah is on land, and the two of them gather each night at the
dam built by Dhu'l-Qarnayn as a barrier between the people and
Gog and Maggog. They also both make pilgrimage or they gather
each year to drink from Zamzam enough to last them the following
year." Anas added, "A third of the well is now gone."[472]

The reliable jurists have also transmitted commentaries re-

---

471. This has been narrated by AL-TABARANI, *al-Mu'jam al-Awsat*,
3:255.

472. AL-HARITH IBN USAMAH and HAYTHAMI, *Musnad al-Harith bi
Zawa'id al-Haythami*, 2:866.

garding al-Khidr. Imam al-Nawawi said, "As for the story of al-Khidr visiting the Prophet [s] after his death, it has been narrated by Imam al-Shafi'i in his *Umm* with a weak chain of transmission; however, he did not mention the name of al-Khidr and rather said the Companions heard someone say such and such. The name of al-Khidr was not mentioned by Imam al-Shafi'i, but rather by some of our fellow jurists who have their own proofs for adding al-Khidr's name. The correct opinion (regarding al-Khidr) is that he is alive, and this is the opinion of most of the scholars."[473]

Imam al-Ramli was asked about al-Khidr and Elijah, peace be upon them, and he answered:

> As for al-Khidr, the correct opinion states that he is a prophet, not a saint, which is the opinion of the majority of the scholars because al-Khidr said in the Quran, *And I did not do it on my own accord* [18:82], and God's statement, *We bestowed on Him Our mercy* [18:65], which means revelation and prophecy, not sainthood. This is the case despite the fact that some scholars claimed he was not a prophet. The correct opinion maintains that he is alive. Ibn Salah stated, "The majority of scholars have agreed that he is alive, even the commoners believe in this," and Imam al-Nawawi stated, "The majority of scholars say that he is alive and living amongst us; this is agreed upon between the Sufis and the pious people as they mention true stories of seeing him in visions, meeting him in waking states, taking knowledge from him, asking him questions, hearing his answers, and his presence at holy locations too many to enumerate." Therefore, according to the correct opinion he is a human, not an angel, and his location as well as the location of Elijah is in the land of the Arabs.[474]

The above quote clearly states that al-Khidr is a human, is living amongst us, and is able to meet with people in miraculous encounters. This should not, however, open the door to unfounded claims regarding al-Khidr. There is also dispute concerning his prophethood; the sounder opinion, as stated by Imam al-Ramli, is that he is indeed a prophet. God is Most High and knows best.

---

473. AL-NAWAWI, *al-Majmu'*, 5:275-76.
474. AL-RAMLI, *Fatawa al-Ramli*, 4:225.

FATWAS RELATED TO CUSTOMS

Question 90:

What is the Islamic ruling on women covering their faces, such as by wearing the *niqab*?

Two distinctions must be made before answering this question. The head covering (*hijab*) is what Muslim women wear to cover their hair. The face veil, or *niqab*, is a specific type of covering worn by some.

The vast majority of jurists have ruled that a woman's entire body, excluding only the hands and the face, should be kept private from all men not related to her. The face and the hands are exempt because women need to interact with men when buying selling, and conducting other public activities. Abu Hanifa ruled that even a woman's feet may be exposed; God prohibited women from exposing only adornment which is not naturally manifest, and Abu Hanifa considered the feet as part of one's naturally manifest beauty. Imam Ahmad argued that the entire body of a woman is to be covered, even her nails, as it is all considered nakedness. He is reported to have said that if the wife of one's host is present at a meal, then it is not permissible to share this meal with them because the woman's hands will become exposed while eating. Al-Qadi of the Hanbali school said that it is impermissible for a man to gaze at any part of a woman not related to him except her face and hands.

The majority of jurists have referenced the verse, *And to display of their adornment only that which is apparent* [24:31], as proof for their position. Kohl is the adornment of the eye, and rings are the adornment of the hands. Ibn Kathir quoted al-'Amash's commentary, "On the authority of Sa'id ibn Jubayr, Ibn 'Abbas said, 'And to display of their adornment only that which is apparent means her hands, including rings, and her face. This has been narrated by Ibn 'Umar, 'Ata, 'Ikrima, Sa 'id ibn Jubayr, Abu Sha'tha', Dahhak, Ibrahim al-Nakh'i, and others.'"[475]

As for the Sunnah's content on this matter, the *hadith* narrated by Aishah recounts, "Asma bint Abi Bakr entered upon the Prophet

---

475. IBN KATHIR, *Tafsir al-Quran al-'Azim*, 3:284.

[s] and she had on a light garment, so the Prophet [s] turned away from her and said, 'Asma, when a women comes of age, it is not proper for her to display anything except this and this,' and he pointed to his face and hands."[476] Another source of evidence is the *hadith* in which the Prophet [s] reminded women to give charity out of fear of Hell fire. The text of the *hadith* says, "A woman amongst the most pious of them who had dark brown cheeks asked, 'Why O Messenger of God?'"[477] The narrator of this *hadith*, Jabir, alludes to the fact that he saw this woman with her face exposed. Some claim that the verse, *O Prophet! Tell your wives and your daughters and the women of the believers to draw their cloaks close round them. That will be better, so that they may be recognized and not annoyed. God is ever Forgiving, Merciful* [33:59] abrogates the *hijab* with the commandment to wear *niqab*, but there is no clear indication this verse refers to covering the face.

Al-Marghinani from the Hanafi school stated, "The nakedness of a free woman is her entire body except her face and hands as is inferred from the statement of the Prophet [s], 'Woman is a nakedness concealed,' and he excluded the face and the hands due to the extreme hardship in covering them. This statement includes the feet as nakedness, but there is another opinion in the Hanafi school that says the feet are not nakedness, and this is the sounder opinion."[478]

Ibn Khalaf al-Baji from the Maliki school stated, "The entire body of a woman is nakedness, except her feet and hands."[479] He has stated elsewhere, "A woman eats with her husband and male guests or with her brother. This means that a man's glance at a women's face or hands is permissible as these manifest themselves

---

476. AL-SIJISTANI, *Sunan Abi Dawud*, 4:62 who commented that this *hadith* is *mursal* and Khaled ibn Dareek did not meet Aisha; AL-BAYHAQI, *Kubra*, 2:226; and AL-BAYHAQI, *Shu'ab al-Iman*, 6:125.

477. IBN HANBAL, *Musnad Imam Ahmad*, 3:318, AL-NAYSABURI, *Sahih Muslim*, 2:606; AL-SIJISTANI, *Sunan Abi Dawud*, 4:338; AL-NASA'I, *Sunan al-Nasa'i (al-Mujtaba)*, 3:186; AL-NAYSABURI, *Sahih Ibn Khuzaymah*, 2:357; and AL-DARAMI, *Sunan al-Darami*, 1:458.

478. AL-MIRGHIANI, *al-Hidayah ma' al-Binayah*, 1:258, 295, text printed with its commentary entitled *Fath al-Qadir*.

479. Sulayman ibn Khalad AL-BAJI, *al-Muntaqa Sharh al-Muwatta'*. Dar al-Kitab al-Islami, 4:105.

during eating."[480] Ibn Hajar al-Haythami of the Shafi'i school has quoted Qadi 'Iyad as saying that a woman does not have to cover her face in accordance with scholarly agreement. "Qadi 'Iyad states that a woman walking in the streets is not obliged to cover her face as it is a recommended act (not obligatory), and men passing by are to lower their gaze in accordance with the Quranic verse."[481]

Clothes and manners of dress are deeply related to the customs and traditions of a given people. In a country like Egypt where it is not common for a woman to cover her face, and where doing so causes familial problems, it is more appropriate to follow the majority opinion. As for other countries where the Hanbali opinion is more in line with local custom, it is permissible for a woman to follow this opinion and cover her face not as a sign of religiosity, but rather because it is in line with their customs and traditions.

Accordingly, we consider the majority opinion, which permits women to expose their faces and hands while covering the rest of their bodies, to be most correct. We also hold the opinion that, if covering the face becomes a symbol of division within the Muslim community, or of religiosity and worshipfulness, then it would cease to be recommended (*mandub*) or permissible (*mubah*) and it would become a reprehensible innovation (*bid'a*), especially if it is used for things which God has not ordained for us. God is Most High and knows best.

---

480. Ibid., 7:252.

481. HAYTHAMI and AL-NAWAWI, *Tuhfat al-Muhtaj Sharh al-Minhaj*, 7:193.

Question 91:

What is the ruling on trailing one's garment on the ground?

Trailing one's garment, meaning letting it go past the ankles and touch the floor, used to be a sign of haughtiness and arrogance. These attributes are major sins and amongst the worst diseases of the heart. They destroy one's spiritual life and progress to the point that some of the pious Muslims have stated, "A sin that causes abasement and causes one to feel broken is better than a good deed that causes one to be haughty and arrogant."

The Prophet [s] related the act of keeping one's trousers or garment long to arrogance in his *hadith* which says, "Whoever drags their garment out of arrogance, God will not look at them on the Day of Resurrection." Abu Bakr said, "A part of my garment sags, should I consider this what you have mentioned?" The Prophet [s] said, "You are not amongst those who do this out of arrogance."[482]

Therefore, letting one's garment reach past the ankles and drag on the floor is not prohibited in and of itself. Its impermissibility instead derives from the fact that it was a sign of arrogance, especially during the time of the Prophet [s]. Scholars have thus agreed that any form of arrogance is prohibited, whether related to clothes or not. However, rulings have differed on the trailing of a garment, distinguishing between those who do it out of arrogance and those who do not. Others have stated that it is always a reprehensible act as it imitates those who do so out of arrogance.

Sheikh al-Buhuti has stated, "If someone trails his garment out of necessity, such as to cover an ailment of the feet, then that is permissible as long as it is done without arrogance. Ahmad has stated in a narration that trailing one's garment and dragging it in prayer is fine as long as there is no arrogance."[483] Al-Shawkani has stated:

> The apparent restriction of "out of arrogance," at first glance, is an indication that trailing the garment without arrogance is not a part of this threat. Ibn 'Abd al-Barr has stated, "Keep-

482. AL-BUKHARI, *Sahih Bukhari*, 3:1340; and AL-NAYSABURI, *Sahih Muslim*, 3:1650.
483. AL-BUHITI, *Kashf al-Qina'*, 1:276.

ing the garment long without arrogance does not fall into the mentioned threat, except that the act is still not without blame." Al-Nawawi has stated, "[keeping the garment long] is a reprehensible act, and there is a statement of Imam al-Shafi'i as quoted by al-Buwiti in his compendium on the statements of Imam al-Shafi'i: 'It is not permissible to trail one's garment in the prayer or elsewhere out of arrogance. However, doing so elsewhere, i.e., outside of prayer, is a less serious transgression based on the statement of the Prophet [s] to Abu Bakr.'"[484]

Trailing the garment without haughtiness and arrogance is permissible, as stated by the school of Imam Ahmad ibn Hanbal. Arrogance is the focus of prohibitions regardless of occurring by trailing one's garments. Additionally, the custom of people has changed, and today it is not one of the habits of the arrogant to keep their clothes long, and trailing one's garment today cannot be an act that imitates the actions of the arrogant and the haughty. God is Most High and knows best.

Question 92:

What is the correct ruling on letting one's beard grow long?

The command to let the beard grow came from various hadiths such as, "Distinguish yourself from the disbelievers, let your beards grow and shorten your moustaches."[485] The jurists have disputed the nature of the command in this *hadith*, arguing whether it should be considered an obligatory act, or a recommended act. The majority of jurists rule that it is obligatory, except for jurists of the Shafi'i school who decreed it as recommended. The Shafi'i jurists have dealt with this issue extensively. Zakariyyah al-Ansari stated, "It is reprehensible (*yukrah*) to pluck out one's facial hair when it first grows, it being preferable for it to grow and look attractive."[486] Imam al-Ramli commented on Ansari's sentence as follows: "His statement, 'It is reprehensible to pluck out . . .' refers to the beard, and shaving it is similar. Therefore al-Halimi's statement in his *Minhaj* that it is impermissible for anyone to shave their beard or eyebrows is weak."[487] In the words of Imam Ibn Hajar al-Haythami, "Concerning the beard there are actions which are considered reprehensible, such as plucking and shaving it, and likewise for the eyebrows."[488] Imam Ibn Qasim al-'Ibadi confirms this ruling in his gloss on *Tuhfat al-Muhtaj* where he writes, "Our teachers have stated that shaving the beard is reprehensible."[489] The noble scholar al-Bajirmi stated in his gloss on al-Khatib's commentary that, "Shaving the beard is a reprehensible act even for a man, but it is not prohibited."[490] The reason he stated "even for a man," is not to distinguish between men and women, but to distinguish men from minor boys. This distinction was necessary because the original discussion revolved around the ruling that it was reprehensible for

---

485. AL-BUKHARI, *Sahih Bukhari*, 5:2209; and AL-NAYSABURI, *Sahih Muslim*, 1:222.

486. AL-ANSARI, *Asna al-Matalib*, 1:551.

487. AL-RAMLI and AL-ANSARI, *Hashiyat 'ala Asna al-Matalib*, 1:551.

488. HAYTHAMI and AL-NAWAWI, *Tuhfat al-Muhtaj Sharh al-Minhaj*, 9:375-76.

489. Ibn Qasim AL-'UBADI, *Hashiya Tuhfa al-Muhtaj Sharh al-Minhaj*. Dar Ihya' al-Turath al-'Arabi, 9:375-76.

490. AL-BAYJIRMI, AL-SHARBINI, and AL-ASFAHANI, *Tuhfat al-Habib 'ala Sharh al-Khatib*, 4:346.

young boys to shave their first growth of facial hair, so he commented that it being the first growth was not a delimiting restriction, but that it is reprehensible for grown men to do so as well.

Rulings on the reprehensibility of shaving one's beard are not limited to the Shafi'i school. Qadi 'Iyad from the Maliki school was in accord with this opinion, as evidenced by his statement: "It is reprehensible to shave the beard, pluck it, or burn it."[491]

The jurists who argue that keeping the beard is mandatory derive a different meaning from the aforementioned *hadith*. They are of the opinion that shaving the beard is a negative act, because it deviated from the preferred appearance of a man during their times, which gave him a certain status. Imam al-Ramli stated in his discussion of reformative punishment (*t'azir*) ". . . it should not include shaving a man's beard, as shaving was a form of deformation through which his children would also be shamed."[492]

In legal matters, if a command draws its basis from custom, the command changes from obligation to recommendation. This transformation is attested by the many instances where jurists have written hadiths with clear commands, in which their commands were understood to be recommended acts, not obligatory ones. One such *hadith* being: "Change your grey hairs so you do not imitate your enemies among the polytheists, and the best thing to use to change your gray hairs is henna and *katam*."[493] As the decision to change or alter one's grey hair or not is not considered by society to be a negative act, the jurists understood the command to be a recommendation and not an obligation. Muslim jurists have often dealt accordingly with such issues. Jurists used to consider anyone who wore Western clothing as departing from Islam. However, as this practice became widespread and commonplace among Muslims, jurists changed their opinions.

Therefore, the ruling concerning the beard during the time of the pious ancestors, when both Muslims and non-Muslims used to keep their beards, is disputed. The majority of jurists said it was mandatory to keep the beard and therefore prohibited shaving it, and the Shafi'i jurists said that shaving the beard is reprehensible,

491. Quoted in al-Hafidh al-'Iraqi in his book AL-'IRAQI, *Tarh al-Tathrib*, 2:83; it has also been quoted in AL-SHAWKANI, *Nayl al-Awtar*, 1:143.

492. AL-RAMLI, and AL-ANSARI, *Hashiyat 'ala Asna al-Matalib*, 4:162.

493. AL-BUKHARI, *Sahih Bukhari*, 5:2209; and AL-NAYSABURI, *Sahih Muslim*, 1:222.

as keeping it is only a Sunnah practice. Today, now that customs have changed, we must adhere to the Shafi'i opinion which states that shaving the beard is a reprehensible act and keeping it is a Sunnah act that entails praise and reward, as long as one keeps his beard well-groomed and presentable. God is Most High and knows best.

Question 93:

What is the ruling on singing?

Singing is defined as prolonging one's voice to create specific sounds using different pitches. If performed without musical instruments, and the lyrics are within the confines of the Shari'ah, then there is nothing wrong with it. It is better that the words praise God and His Messenger [s], promote courage and love of the homeland, or relate to other similar topics. If the words are of a different nature, but still within the confines of the Shari'ah, then that subject of song is also permitted.

In certain instances, such as celebratory occasions, singing is customary among Muslims. It serves to encourage joy and move hearts on occasions such as the days of 'Eid, weddings, homecomings, receptions honoring marriage or newborns, and during birth. Such permissibility has come to us from numerous sources from across history.

Aishah narrated that she attended a wedding of the Ansar and the Prophet [s] said, "O Aishah! Do they not have some form of amusement? The Ansar surely like amusement."[494] Ibn 'Abbas said that Aishah paired up a relative of hers with a man of the Ansar. The Prophet [s] asked her, "Did you give the young lady a gift?" She replied, "Yes." He asked, "Did you send someone with her to sing?" She replied, "No." He said, "The Ansar are a people of romance, so send someone with them to recite, '*we have come to you, we have come to you, so greetings to you and greetings to us.*'"[495]

Aishah said that Abu Bakr came to her during the days of 'Eid al-Adha when there were two young slave girls with her singing and banging on drums, and the Messenger of God [s] was concealed by his garment. Abu Bakr reprimanded them, and the Messenger of God [s] revealed himself and said, "Leave them Abu Bakr, these are days of festivity."[496] Aishah also said, "I used to have a slave girl and I married her off one day. On the day of her wedding the Mes-

---

494. AL-BUKHARI, *Sahih Bukhari*, 5:1980.

495. AL-QIZWINI, *Sunan Ibn Majah*, 1:612; IBN HANBAL, *Musnad Imam Ahmad*, 3:391; AL-NASA'I, *Sunan al-Nasa'i (al-Mujtaba)*, 3:332; and AL-TABA-RANI, *al-Mu'jam al-Awsat*, 3:315.

496. AL-BUKHARI, *Sahih Bukhari*, 1:335; AL-NAYSABURI, *Sahih Muslim*, 2:608; AL-TAMIMI, *Sahih Ibn Hibban*, 13:177; AL-BAYHAQI, *al-Sunan al-Kubra*, 7:92.

senger of God [s] came in and he did not hear any singing or forms of playful enjoyment so he said, 'O Aishah, did you sing for her or not?' Then the Messenger of God [s] said, 'The tribe of the Ansar love singing.'"[497]

Further evidence comes from 'Amir ibn S'ad who reported: "I was with Thabit ibn Wadi'a and Qurtha ibn K'ab in a wedding that had singing, and hearing the sound I asked them, 'Do you hear that?' They replied, 'License has been given for singing during weddings.'"[498]

Umm Salamah received a slave girl who belonged to Hassan ibn Thabit on the day of 'Eid al-Fitr, who came to sing her poetry with a drum. Umm Salamah chastised her for this and the Messenger of God [s] rebuked her, saying, "Leave her Umm Salamah as every people have a day of festivity, and this is our day of festivity."[499]

Rabay' ibn M'iwadh b. 'Afra' narrates, "One day the Messenger of God [s] came to me the morning after my wedding night and sat on a mat as you [Khalid ibn Dhakwan] are sitting now. Some slave girls started to beat one of their drums, lamenting those of my forefathers who were killed on the day of Badr, one of them sang, 'And amongst us is a prophet who knows what tomorrow will bring,' and the Messenger of God [s] stopped them and said, 'Omit this line and say what you were saying.'"[500]

Another account from Aishah clarifies the permissibility of singing: "The Messenger of God [s] was sitting and we heard a clamor. The Messenger of God stood and saw an Ethiopian girl dancing along with young children around her. He said, 'O Aishah, come and see.' I went and placed my chin on his shoulder and I watched what was in view between his head and shoulder, and he

497. AL-TAMIMI, *Sahih Ibn Hibban*, 13:185.

498. AL-HAKIM, *al-Mustadrak 'ala al-Sahihayn*, 2:201 and Hakim said it is rigorously authenticated on the conditions of Bukhari and Muslim; AL-KUFI, *Musannaf ibn Abi Shaybah*, 3:496. The wording of singing is in the narration of Abu Shaybah, and the narration of Hakim only mentions wedding.

499. AL-TABARANI, *al-Mu'jam al-Kabir*, 23:264; AL-HAYTHAMI, *Majma' al-Zawa'id*, 2:206 who said that the chain includes Waza' ibn Nafi' who is matruk.

500. AL-BUKHARI, *Sahih Bukhari*, 4:1496; AL-SIJISTANI, *Sunan Abi Dawud*, 4:281; AL-TIRMIDHI, *Sunan al-Tirmidhi*, 3:399; and AL-QIZWINI, *Sunan Ibn Majah*, 1:611, and the wording is Abi Dawud's.

said, 'Have you had enough?' I kept saying no to him so I could know my real rank with him. Then 'Umar came and the people started to scatter from the Ethiopian. The Messenger of God [s] said, 'Indeed I observe the devils among the Jinn and people fleeing from 'Umar.' And then I left."[501]

From the traditions narrated by the companions is one by Zayd ibn Aslam who, on the authority of his father, narrates: "Umar heard a women singing and he said 'singing is from the provisions of the traveler.'"[502]

Some have ruled that singing is prohibited even if without instruments; however, they have no supporting proofs. Qadi Abu Bakr ibn al-'Arabi has stated in his book *al-Ahkam*, "Nothing concerning its prohibition (i.e., singing) is authentic." The same is stated by Imam al-Ghazali and Ibn al-Nahwi in his *'Umda*. Ibn Tahir said, "Not one single letter of them [the arguments for the prohibition of singing] is correct." And Ibn Hazm stated, "Everything related to this [prohibition of singing] is falsehood and fabrication."[503]

There is nothing negative in singing as it is one of the beautiful things of life pleasing to one's self, one's intellect, and one's natural primordial state (*fitra*). Singing is an enjoyment of sound since it pleases one's hearing, just as food is the enjoyment of one's taste, and one's eye and vision enjoy any beautiful sight. Islam is a religion of beauty and comfort, and Islam makes the enjoyment of nice and beautiful things permissible as a mercy from God towards this nation and people. God Most High says: "They ask you (Muhammad) what is made lawful for them. Say: (all) good things are made lawful for you" [5:4]. And God has not permitted anyone to prohibit those pleasant and beautiful things that He alone has given as provision to us, no matter how pure one's intention is in doing this. Declaring things prohibited or permissible are from the authority of God alone: *Say: have you considered what provision God has sent down for you, how you have made of it lawful and unlawful? Has God permitted you, or do you invent a lie concerning God?* [10:59].

If we contemplate the issue of singing, we can suppose that enjoyment from singing and listening to song is a natural trait of humans. For example, young babies are always comforted by the

---

501. AL-NASA'I, *Sunan al-Nasa'i (al-Mujtaba)*, 5:309.

502. AL-BAYHAQI, *al-Sunan al-Kubra*, 5:68.

503. IBN HAZM, *al-Mahala bi-l-Athar*, 9:60.

singing of their mothers, which is why mothers and wet nurses throughout history have always sung to their children. One even finds that singing comforts animals, as Imam al-Ghazali wrote:

> Whoever is not moved when hearing singing, is lacking and leaning away from the middle way, he is away from spirituality, possessing an increase in hardness which forms a barrier between him and beauty, the birds, and the rest of the animals. The camel, even with its simple nature, is affected when one sings to it, making it tolerate a heavy load and a long distance since its attention is taken by the singing. A drive is created inside the camel that intoxicates and entertains it. When camels hear singing, they stretch their necks and ears to listen to it, they even rush to the sound causing their load to sway back and forth.[504]

The above discussion makes it clear that singing is not prohibited, except if it contains words that contradict the Shari'ah. Singing is permissible and can be recommended if it contains praise of God, His Messenger [s], Islam, and love of one's homeland. God is Most High and knows best.

---

504. AL-GHAZALI, *Ihya' 'Ulum al-Din*, 1152-53, Kitab al-Samma'.

Question 94:

What is the ruling on music?

The word "music" comes from ancient Greek, and refers to the myriad ways of producing harmonious sounds using instruments.[505] Music also concerns itself with combining these sounds in a harmonic way; therefore it studies the complementarity of sounds. Harmonies can be achieved both through musical instruments and human voices.

The issue of listening to music is an issue concerning which there is a difference in scholarly opinion. It is not one of the tenets of faith or something that is necessarily known of the religion, and Muslims should not denounce one another and declare one another heretics because of such issues. One can only rebuke others concerning issues that are agreed upon, not issues that have differing opinions. Since there are reputable jurists who have ruled that listening to music is permissible, it is impermissible to sow dissent in the community because of these issues. This is particularly the case since there are no definitive textual proofs in the Shari'ah that are authentic and explicitly forbid music, otherwise there would not have been a difference of scholarly opinion to begin with.

Among the scholars who have ruled that music is permissible, Imam al-Ghazali stated:

Amusement and entertainment help one in seriousness and serious matters. Only the Prophets, peace be upon them, can patiently bear pure seriousness and bitter reality. Therefore, amusement and entertainment are cures of the heart from exhaustion, so accordingly it must be permissible, however one should not engage in it with excess, just as one cannot take medicine in excess. With this intention [i.e., relaxation and aid in seriousness and serious matters] amusement and entertainment become acts of drawing near to God. This is for the person in whom listening to music does not stir a praiseworthy trait whose movement is sought. Rather such people only seek enjoyment and relaxation, so such acts are praiseworthy in that they allow one to reach the goals mentioned previously.

---

505. *The Oxford Dictionary of English Etymology*, 598-99, subject matter music.

This does indicate that one is below the height of perfection in spirituality, since the perfect person is one who does not need to calm his soul with anything other than God. The good deeds of the righteous, however, are the misdeeds of those closest to God. Whoever has mastered the science of the cures of the heart and the ways in which to soften it and lead it to the Truth, knows with certainty that bringing it ease through these sorts of things is an indispensible medicine.[506]

Imam al-Ghazali also said, "If the musical instrument is one of the signs of drunkards, such as the pipe, strings, or drums used by drinkers, these three kinds are impermissible. Every other kind of instrument remains permissible, such as frame drums, even with jingles, drums, striking drums with sticks, and other instruments."

Other scholars saw in music and listening to music moral lessons and direction for those who understand and whose souls are uplifted. Among them was Qadi 'Iyad al-Shibli who, when asked about listening to music replied, "Its [music's] apparent nature is seductive and tempting, while esoterically it is full of lessons, and whoever understands the allusion is permitted to listen to the lesson."[507]

Similar statements can be found attributed to the sultan of the scholars al-'Izz ibn 'Abd al-Salam who said, "The path of rectifying hearts is through external causes. It can be done with the Quran, and those are the best of the people of audition. It can also be done through exhortation and reminders, as well as through songs and odes. And it can be done through singing accompanied by instruments concerning which there is a difference of opinion, such as reed flutes. If the person who listens to such instruments considers them to be permissible, then they are doing good by listening to that which produces goodly states, while having abandoned scrupulousness by listening to that concerning the permissibility of which there is a difference of opinion."[508]

In his commentary on the Quran al-Jami li Ahkam al-Quran, al-Qurtubi mentioned al-Qushayri's observation that drums were

---

506. Ibn Muflih AL-MAQDASI, Kitab al-Furu', 5:236-7.

507. Quoted in Muhammad ibn Yusuf AL-'ABDARI, al-Taj wa-l-Iklil. Dar al-Fikr, 2:362.

508. Ibid., 2:362.

played in the presence of the Prophet [s] on the day he entered
Medina. This disturbed Abu Bakr. The Prophet [s] said, "Leave
them Abu Bakr, so that the Jews can see that our religion is expansive." They were playing drums and saying, "We are the daughters
of al-Najjar, and we love that Muhammad is a neighbor." Al-Qurtubi
then said, "It is said that the drum (*al-tabl*) used in weddings is like
the frame drum (*al-duff*). Similarly, the other instruments used to
spread word of weddings are permissible, as long as the lyrics are
good and contain nothing indecent."[509]

In the section "What has Been Related Concerning Musical
Instruments" in *Nayl al-Awtar*, al-Shawkani examines the arguments for and against the permissibility of listening to music. He
specifically discusses the *hadith* in which the Prophet [s] said, "Every form of amusement in which the believer engages is nought
(*batil*), except for three: a man being playful with his wife, a man's
disciplining and training his horse, and archery."[510] Al-Shawkani
then quotes Imam al-Ghazali's commentary on this *hadith*, "The
Prophet's [s] statement 'is nought' does not necessitate its impermissibility, rather it indicates its lack of benefit." Al-Shawkani
then adds, "This is indeed a sound statement, since anything that
has no direct benefit is from the category of neutrally permissible
things."[511] Al-Shawkani offers other proofs to the same effect, such
as the woman who vowed to play the tambourine if the Prophet
[s] returned from a certain battle safely. Upon his return, he allowed her to carry out her vow without any form of castigation.
This allowance indicates that the woman's actions were not an act
of disobedience.

Ibn Hazm related the words of the Prophet [s]: "All actions are
based on intentions and every person is judged by what he or she
intended." Thus whoever listens to singing, or engages in any other act, as an act of disobedience towards God, does evil, and whoever listens to singing intending the relaxation of one's soul to aid
one's obedience towards God and to help perform righteous acts,
then he is engaging in an obedient and correct act and is rewarded.
Whoever intends neither disobedience nor obedience, and listens

509. AL-QURTUBI, *Tafsir al-Qurtubi*, 14:54.

510. IBN HANBAL, *Musnad Imam Ahmad*, 4:144; AL-TIRMIDHI, *Sunan al-Tirmidhi*, 4:174; AL-QIZWINI, *Sunan Ibn Majah*, 2:940.

511. AL-SHAWKANI, *Nayl al-Awtar*, 8:118.

to music simply as amusement, is pardoned, as would be a person walking in his garden strolling, or someone sitting on their doorstep relaxing."[512]

In summary, we can say that the issue of singing, both with and without instruments, has caused scholarly dispute throughout the ages. Scholars have agreed that any sort of singing or music that causes disobedience or aids in disobedience is impermissible. Since singing is comprised of words, the good are permitted, and the bad are forbidden. Scholars also agree on the permissibility of singing a cappella, especially in times of happiness, such as weddings, homecomings, and days of 'Eid, as long as certain conditions are met, such as women not singing in front of non-related males. Scholars disagree on whether musical instruments are permitted to accompany singing.

Based on the above discussion, singing, whether with or without musical instruments, is permissible on the condition that it does not incite disobedience or lewdness, and that it does not contain any themes contrary to the Shari'ah. Excesses of music and singing that push the boundaries of permissibility may be considered reprehensible acts and are potentially impermissible. God is Most High and knows best.

---

512. IBN HAZM, al-Mahala bi-l-Athar, 7:567.

Question 95:

What is the ruling on smoking?

Smoking is the intake of the tobacco plant by burning it and inhaling its smoke. Tobacco (*al-tibgh*) is a foreign word that entered the Arabic language without being changed, as has been confirmed by the Arabic Language Council. Tobacco is a member of the nightshade family used for smoking, snuff, and chew. It also includes a variety grown for decoration. American in its origins, tobacco was unknown to the Arabs of old. It made its appearance in the late tenth/early eleventh century AH. The English first brought it to the lands of the Ottoman Empire, and someone claiming he was a physician brought it to North Africa. From there it spread to Egypt, Arabia, India, and most Muslim countries.

The ruling on smoking focuses on the harm it causes. If smoking causes harm that is prohibited by the Shari'ah, then it is forbidden due to that harm; otherwise, it is disliked or permitted. Uncertainty over the harm of smoking caused differences of opinion among past scholars. Medicine continually makes new discoveries, and contemporary medicine has arrived at the conclusion that smoking is extremely harmful to one's health, and that tobacco is generally a debilitating substance.

According to 'Ubada ibn al-Samit, the Prophet [s] once proclaimed: "[There should be] no harm and no reciprocating harm."[513] General and particular legal axioms were based on this, such as, "Harm is to be removed," and "Repelling harm takes precedence over promoting benefit." According to Umm Salama, "The Prophet [s] forbade every intoxicant and substance that causes listlessness."[514]

The Shari'ah forbids extensive harm, and medical experts have ascertained that smoking causes extensive harm to people's health. Furthermore, the Shari'ah forbids every substance causing listlessness, including tobacco and all plants that, when smoked, numb people's nerves. The Shari'ah also forbids wasting money, defined as spending on that which has no benefit or causes harm.

---

513. IBN HANBAL, *Musnad Imam Ahmad*, 5:326; AL-QIZWINI, *Sunan Ibn Majah*, 2:784; AL-BAYHAQI, *Kubra*, 6:156.

514. IBN HANBAL, *Musnad Imam Ahmad*, 6:309; AL-SIJISTANI, *Sunan Abi Dawud*, 3:329; AL-BAYHAQI, *Kubra*, 8:296.

In the words of the Prophet [s]: "God dislikes for you to gossip, waste money, and question excessively."[515] We believe that smoking is a bad habit, forbidden by our religion, and we ask God to alleviate those afflicted with addiction. And God is Most High and knows best.

---

515. IBN HANBAL, *Musnad Imam Ahmad*, 2:327; AL-BUKHARI, *Sahih Bukhari*, 2:537; AL-NAYSABURI, *Sahih Muslim*, 3:1340.

Question 96:

What is the ruling on celebrating Mother's Day?

Human beings are edifices of the Lord (*bunyan al-rabb*) whom God has honored for their Adamic nature. God created Adam with His hands, and breathed His Spirit into him. He commanded the angels to prostrate to Adam and He expelled Iblis from His mercy because he was too proud to obey. Respect for humankind is an angelic quality upon which Islamic civilization has been built. Disrespect, degradation, and contempt for humankind are satanic tendencies that have shaken the foundations of civilizations. According to the Quran, *God struck at the foundations of their building, and then the roof fell down upon them from above them, and the doom came on them whence they knew not* [16:26]; *Whoso chooses Satan for a patron instead of God is verily a loser and his loss is manifest* [4:119]; and *Will you choose him and his seed for your protecting friends instead of Me, when they are an enemy unto you? Calamitous is the exchange for evil-doers* [18:50].

Islam advocates honoring all humans simply for their humanity, regardless of their race or color, but at the same time Islam bestows additional honors upon certain individuals who fulfill specific roles based on their particular God-given attributes. Parents are especially honored because God has made them the means of one's existence. He associates being thankful to one's parents with being thankful to Him: *And We have enjoined upon man concerning his parents—His mother bears him in weakness upon weakness, and his weaning is in two years—Give thanks unto Me and unto your parents. Unto Me is the journeying* [31:14]. His command to be good to our parents is second only to His command to worship Him, *Your Lord has decreed, that you worship none save Him, and [that you show] kindness to parents* [17:23]. God made parenthood the apparent cause of creation, thus parents are honored as the universe's greatest manifestation of God's ability to create, thereby communicating an honor upon honor.

The Prophet [s] designated mothers as those most deserving of good company, and placed them even above fathers in this respect. Abu Hurayrah said, "A man came to the Messenger of God [s] and asked, 'Whom among people is the most deserving of my goodly companionship?' He replied, 'Your mother.' The man asked, 'Then whom?' He replied, 'Your mother.' The man asked, 'Then whom?' He replied, 'Your mother.' The man asked, 'Then whom?' He replied, 'Then your father.'"[516]

The Shari'ah affirms that the relationship between mother and child is natural and organic. A child's kinship to his or her mother is not contingent upon being the product of wedlock; she is the mother regardless of her marital status, whereas the child's father is only established by the legal means of wedlock. Some expressions of honoring one's mother include celebrating her, obeying her, and treating her well. Nothing in the Shari'ah forbids there being an occasion on which children express their reverence for their mothers. This is an organizational matter to which there is no impediment. Celebrating Mother's Day does not present an issue of innovation, contrary to many people's accusations.

The Prophet [s] rejected innovations that do not derive from the Shari'ah: "Whoever introduces something in this matter of ours which is not from it is rejected."[517] This statement means that an innovation within the confines of that which is already part of the Shari'ah is accepted and not rejected. The Prophet [s] approved of the Arabs' celebrations of their national remembrances and national victories, during which they would sing about the glorious deeds of their tribes and the days of their victories. According to Aishah, the Prophet [s] came upon her when she was in the company of two slave-girls singing of the day of *Bu'ath*.[518] It is related in the Sunnah that the Prophet [s] visited the grave of his mother Aminah in the company of 2,000 soldiers in armor, and he was not seen more tearful than on that day.[519]

Motherhood is a very elevated concept for Muslims, and their linguistic tradition clearly bears witness to this. The Arabic word for mother (*umm*), shares its root with the words for origin, home, leader, and one who serves the community by being in charge of food and service. This last meaning is related by Imam al-Shafi'i, who is one of the people of the language.[520] Ibn Durayd said, "Ev-

---

516. IBN HANBAL, *Musnad Imam Ahmad*, 2:327; AL-BUKHARI, *Sahih Bukhari*, 5:2227; and AL-NAYSABURI, *Sahih Muslim*, 4:1974.

517. IBN HANBAL, *Musnad Imam Ahmad*, 6:240; AL-BUKHARI, *Sahih Bukhari*, 2:959; and AL-NAYSABURI, *Sahih Muslim*, 3:1343.

518. AL-BUKHARI, *Sahih Bukhari*, 1:324; AL-NAYSABURI, *Sahih Muslim*, 2:607.

519. AL-HAKIM, *al-Mustadarak 'ala al-Sahihayn*, 2:661.

520. i.e., his opinions have evidentiary value in the field of Arabic linguistics. [Trans.]

erything to which other things that followed it are joined is called 'mother' by the Arabs. Mecca is called 'Mother of Cities' (*umm al-qura*) because it is at the center of the earth, it is the direction which people face in prayer, and it is the most honored city in the world."

Since language is the vessel of thought, the semantic value of the word *umm* binds Muslims to that honored person whom God caused to be the origin of creation for human beings, with whom He provided them a home, who raised them and inspired their ways of thought, and whose service and caretaking God has made well-loved. Mothers are the receptacles of care and mercy, with whom their children seek shelter and refuge.

If this concept is clear in the original linguistic meaning of *umm* and its derivatives, then Muslims' cultural heritage makes it even clearer. In the expression "keeping up with uterine kin," the anatomical particularity of mothers symbolizes familial connections, which are the building blocks of society. This usage stems from the fact that no one is more entitled to this association than mothers, through whom the meaning of life continues, families are established, and mercy is manifest. This concept is fully realized when considered alongside the singular religious concept that the Chosen Prophet [s] and beloved describes, "The womb is attached to the Throne. It says, 'Whoever establishes a connection with me, God connects to them, and whoever breaks a connection with me, God breaks away from them.'"[521] The divine utterance (*hadith qudsi*) narrates, "God says, 'I am God, and I am the All Merciful (*al-Rahman*). I created the womb (*al-rahim*) and derived [it's name] from My name. Whoever connects to it, I connect to them, and whoever severs ties with it I cut them off.'"[522]

In spite of the differences between Islamic culture and the cultures that have developed these occasions for celebration such as Mother's Day, there is no legal religious prohibition to our celebrating these foreign holidays. Taking part in them spreads the values of treating one's parents well in an age increasingly char-

521. IBN HANBAL, *Musnad Imam Ahmad*, 2:163; AL-NAYSABURI, *Sahih Muslim*, 4:1981; AL-TAMIMI, *Sahih Ibn Hibban*, 2:188.

522. IBN HANBAL, *Musnad Imam Ahmad*, 1:191; AL-SIJISTANI, *Sunan Abi Dawud*, 2:133; AL-TIRMIDHI, *Sunan al-Tirmidhi*, 4:315; AL-TAMIMI, *Sahih Ibn Hibban*, 2:187; AL-HAKIM, *al-Mustadarak 'ala al-Sahihayn*, 4:174; and here the phrasing is from al-Tirmidhi.

acterized by disobedience. The Prophet [s], our role model, used to love and praise virtues in everyone, even if they were adherents of another religion. When the prisoners from Tayy were brought before him, the daughter of Hatim al-Ta'i was among them. "O Muhammad," she said to the Prophet [s], "Do not take malicious joy [in my capture] and rub it in the face of the Arab clans. I am the daughter of my people's leader. My father used to protect cherished goods (*yahmi al-dhimar*), release captives, satiate the hungry, clothe the naked, entertain guests, offer food, spread peace, and he never turned away someone in need. I am the daughter of Hatim al-Ta'i." The Prophet [s] said, "O girl, these are truly the characteristics of a believer; if your father had been a Muslim we would have beseeched mercy on his behalf (*tarahhamna 'alayhi*). Let her go, for her father loved virtue, and God loves virtue." Abu Burdah ibn Niyar stood and said, "O Messenger of God, does God love virtue?" The Prophet [s] said, "By He in Whose Hand is my soul, none shall enter paradise except through virtue."[523] The Prophet [s] also said, "In the home of 'Abd Allah ibn Jad'an I witnessed virtues that are more dear to me than to own prized camels. If I had been called to it in Islam I would have agreed to it also."[524]

Based on the evidence provided, celebrating Mother's Day is permissible according to the legal tradition, and there is nothing to prevent it or be a cause for its prohibition. Expressing joy on occasions of victory and during other celebrations is also permissible. Innovation is rejected only when it contradicts the legal tradition. Activities deriving from the legal tradition are never rejected, and there is no sin involved in partaking in them. God is Most High and knows best.

---

523. AL-BAYHAQI, *Dala'il al-Nubuwwah*, 5:341; IBN KATHIR, *al-Bidayah wa al-Nihayah*, 7:299. Ibn Kathir said, "This *hadith* has a sound meaning and a very singular chain whose origin is very rare."
524. AL-BAYHAQI, *Kubra*, 6:367.

Question 97:

What is the ruling on keeping a dog in the house?

The majority of jurists have agreed that it is not permissible to keep a dog except out of need (*hajah*), such as for hunting, guarding, and other beneficial activities that the law does not prohibit. The Malikis said that keeping a dog for purposes other than agriculture, herding, or hunting is disliked,[525] but some of them ruled that it is permissible, not disliked.

The majority opinion on this matter derives from the saying of the Prophet [s], "The reward of a person who keeps a dog for reasons other than herding, hunting, or agriculture is decreased every day by a *qirat*."[526] According to Ibn 'Umar, the Prophet [s] said, "The reward of a person who keeps a dog for reasons other than hunting or herding is decreased every day by two *qirats*."[527] It is permissible to train puppies that are expected to learn for this purpose.

Imam al-Nawawi said, "Al-Shafi'i and his companions said, 'It is permissible to keep a dog for hunting, agriculture, or herding without disagreement based on what is mentioned by the author [Imam al-Shirazi]. The author mentions two positions and their evidence concerning keeping them to protect homes and neighborhoods, and the most correct view is permissibility, as is stated in *al-Mukhtasir*."[528] Sheikh 'Illaysh, one of the great scholars of the Malikis, said, "It is permissible to keep dogs for all beneficial purposes, and to ward off harm, even if it is not in the wilderness where thieves are feared.'"[529]

Based on this evidence, it is permissible to keep dogs for beneficial purposes or out of need, and it is impermissible otherwise. God is Most High and knows best.

---

525. As opposed to being forbidden. [Trans.]

526. IBN HANBAL, *Musnad Imam Ahmad*, 2:55; AL-NAYSABURI, *Sahih Muslim*, 3:1202; AL-SIJISTANI, *Sunan Abi Dawud*, 3:108; and AL-TIRMIDHI, *Sunan al-Tirmidhi*, 3;79.

527. IBN HANBAL, *Musnad Imam Ahmad*, 2:8; AL-BUKHARI, *Sahih Bukhari*, 5:20882; AL-NASA'I, *Sunan al-Nasa'i (al-Mujtaba)*, 7:188; AL-TAMIMI, *Sahih Ibn Hibban*, 12:466.

528. AL-NAWAWI, *al-Majmu'*, 9:279.

529. Muhammad ibn Ahmad b. Muhammad 'ILISH, *Minah al-Jalil Sharh Mukhtasar al-Khalil*, Dar al-Fikr, 4:453.

Question 98:

What is the ruling on Muslims possessing mobile phones with digital video cameras? What is the ruling on selling tight and revealing clothes to women? What is the ruling on selling television sets and satellite dishes?

There is no doubt that mobile phones, revealing clothing, television sets, and satellite dishes all belong to the realm of objects. Legal rulings do not deal with objects in and of themselves; they address the objects' usage. Mobile phones, for example, have many beneficial usages, and they constitute the most noticeable leap forward in the field of communications. There is nothing wrong with increasing the capabilities of these devices by adding video cameras and the like. People can use a video camera for both permissible and impermissible activities, regardless of whether it is attached to a mobile phone or stands alone, and regardless of its size. The nature of the use is the most important concern because mobile phones, or more precisely, video cameras, have multiple uses: they can be used to spread indecency by revealing what should be kept private, or they can be used to serve Islam and spread beneficial knowledge. They can also be used for things that are merely neutrally permissible.

Clothing and televisions have a similar range of uses. Women who buy revealing clothing may wear it in front of their husbands and still cover themselves in front of strangers, or they may wear the revealing garments in front of strangers, thereby committing a sin. Televisions and satellite dishes can be used for cultural and educational purposes, or for that which is forbidden.

Islamic law has established that an action is permissible so long as its impermissibility is not specified. After enumerating things whose impermissibility was not specified, such as horned rams (al-kabsh al-natuh), fighting cocks (al-dik al-muqatil), and pigeons, al-Zayla'i said that it is not impermissible to possess these things "because their essences are not reprehensible, but the reprehensibility is in [some of their] uses."[530]

Based on the evidence provided, it is permissible to sell and trade in anything that has more than one use; because the owner bears the responsibility of its usage. If one uses something in a

---

530. AL-ZAYLA'I, Tabyin al-Haqa'iq Sharh Kanz al-Daqa'iq, 3:296-97.

permissible manner, then it is permissible, and if one uses it in an impermissible manner, then it is impermissible and that person incurs sin. God is Most High and knows best.

Question 99:

Does Islamic law allow women to take medicines that seek to dictate the sex of their children?

There is great controversy surrounding the choice of some couples attempting to dictate the gender of their children through certain medical means. First of all, one must know that this practice does not fall within the category of that which God forbade in the Quran when He related Satan's words, *And surely I will command them and they will change God's creation* [4:119], because this verse refers to deforming God's creation as a means to draw closer to other than God. Nor does the practice contradict the verse, *God knows that which every female bears and that which the wombs absorb and that which they grow* [13:8], because God knows both the inwardly hidden and the outwardly manifest aspects of things. He knows if a child will be born living or stillborn, and if it lives He knows whether it will be happy or miserable.

Thus interfering with the natural operations of genetic inheritance and guiding them in accordance with human will in order to achieve certain desired ends, such as preventing possible pregnancy, facilitating pregnancies that are otherwise not possible, and controlling the characteristics or gender of a fetus, does not contest God's will, as some people think. These kinds of actions are in the realm of God's legal will of do's and don'ts. Accordingly, the beneficial aspects of these actions are in accordance with the legal will, while the corruptive aspects go against the legal will. Nothing occurs in God's creation except that which He wills. The Quran says, *He is the Omnipotent over His slaves, and He is the Wise, the Knower* [6:18].

Based on the explanation provided, it is permissible to choose the gender of a fetus by timing conception, by treating the fluids distilled by the woman's reproductive organ, by taking certain herbal remedies, or by other means. It is permissible for the husband and wife to use these tools so long as they do not harm their health or that of the fetus, and only after consulting with a medical specialist. However, it is better and safer not to interfere with these matters in order to purify the soul, affirm one's pleasure with God and His decree, and to surrender to Him. Surrendering to God's decree affords one pleasure both in this world and the hereafter. God is Most High and knows best.

Question 100:

What is the ruling on sitting for mourning and reciting
Quran over the dead in an assembly of mourners?

Al-Ta'ziyah (expressing condolences) refers in the literal sense to
one being afflicted and having patience. This is the meaning used
by jurists. Al-Nawawi said, "It is the order to have patience, to bear
it for the promise of reward, cautioning against sin, and praying
for forgiveness for the deceased and for the one who is dealing
with the loss."[531]

The jurists agree that it is favorable to offer condolences to
one struck by calamity. They base their unanimous opinion on the
Prophet's [s] saying, "Whoever offers condolences to one afflicted
has a reward similar to theirs,"[532] as well as his saying, "There is
not a believer who offers condolences to his brother in affliction
but that God clothes him in the finery of generosity on the Day of
Resurrection."[533]

The jurists have differed in their opinions concerning the family of the deceased sitting in one place to receive mourners. Some
jurists have deemed this practice disliked because it reminds people of their sorrow and incites fresh sorrow. Others have deemed
it permissible. One of the imams of the Maliki school, Sheikh Muhammad ibn Muhammad known as al-Hattab, said, ". . . Sanad said,
'It is permissible for a man to sit for mourning.' Aishah said, 'When
Zayd ibn Harithah, J'afar ibn Abi Talib, and 'Abdallah ibn Rawahah
were killed, the Prophet [s] sat in the mosque and sadness was apparent on his face.'"[534]

The hadith of Aishah referenced by Al-Hattab has been similarly employed by some other scholars as evidence for the permissibility of sitting in mourning, whether in a mosque or in another
place.

The Hanafi scholar Ibn 'Abdin said, "(His saying, 'By sitting for

531. Related in AL-MAHALLI, Sharh Minhaj al-Talibin, 1:401.

532. AL-TIRMIDHI, Sunan al-Tirmidhi, 3:385; AL-QIZWINI, Sunan Ibn Majah, 1:511.

533. Ibid.

534. AL-HATTAB, Muwahib al-Jalil fi Sharh al-Khalil, 2:230. The report from
Aishah is found in AL-SIJISTANI, Sunan ABi Dawud, 3:192 and AL-HAKIM,
al-Mustadarak 'ala al-Sahihayn, 3:237; the later includes the phrase "crying
for them" and the words "in the mosque."

it') meaning in receiving condolences. The use of 'there is no harm' here is fine because it is in opposition to what is more appropriate as has been stated in *Sharh al-Munya*. In *Al-Ahkam 'an Khizanah al-Fatawa* it says, 'There is a license for men to sit for three days due to an affliction, but women should not sit at all.' Then it said, 'But in *al-Zahiriyyah* it says 'There is no harm for the deceased family [to do so] in their home or in the mosque while people come and pay their respects to them.'"[535]

Based on the preceding evidence, it is our opinion that there is nothing wrong with sitting in mourning while listening to Quranic recitation, whether at home or in a mosque. This practice is permissible on the condition that the participants do not promote grief, annoy the neighbors with the volume of recitation, or obstruct public thoroughfares with their tents erected to receive those delivering their condolences. The offenses mentioned are impermissible because they infringe upon the rights of others. So long as these offenses are avoided, the public mourning tradition is permissible. God is Most High and knows best.

---

535. IBN 'ABIDIN, *Rad al-Muhtar 'ala al-Dur al*-Mukhtar, 2:241.

Conclusion

In conclusion we pray that God accepts our good works, unites the hearts of Muslims, removes animosity from between them, and decrees for them that which He loves and gives Him pleasure.

I have examined many of the writings of authors whose opinions differ from those offered here, and I have found that all of them answer something besides the actual question or give supposition the place of certainty, thereby letting the scale drop from their hands and disregarding priorities. In any case, these issues have forced themselves upon the minds of Muslims. We have addressed differences of opinion so that our readership may understand the evidence of those who hold these positions. We hope that differences in opinion on continually divisive issues come to be understood as acceptable, and as a mercy from God, and not as oppositional differences, which are a punishment rather than a mercy. Praise be to God, Lord of the Worlds.